REVELATION

Things your Pastor Forgot to Tell You

MARTIN MIRANDA

Comments by Martín Miranda

bibletruth4today@gmail.com

Order this book online at www.trafford.com
or email orders@trafford.com

Most Trafford titles are also available at major online book retailers.

Print information available on the last page.

ISBN: 978-1-4907-7478-7 (sc)
ISBN: 978-1-4907-7477-0 (e)

Trafford rev. 07/07/2016

North America & international
toll-free: 1 888 232 4444 (USA & Canada)
fax: 812 355 4082

Contents

INTRODUCTION

"It is impossible for anyone to begin to learn what he thinks he already knows" ~ Epictetus

For the first time reader of the book of Revelation, the book would probably not even make any sense at all. It is full of beasts, thunders, strange creatures around the throne, plagues, angels with cups and many other things that are not common in other kinds of literature. Even for those that read the Bible regularly, the book presents many challenges in its interpretation. However, the book promises a blessing for those that study it. Those that persevere in understanding it will discover that the book's main theme is not the beast or its mark, but Christ and His love for humanity. The book shows how tenderly the Divine shepherd- also portrayed as a lamb of all possible symbols- has been guiding His children all along through history and will continue to do so until evil is eradicated from the universe.

One interesting peculiarity of the book of Revelation is that in it, all the other books of the Bible are summarized. It contains both direct and indirect references to the books of the Old and New Testaments. This is particularly evident in chapter 18. It has also been said that Revelation is a commentary of Daniel chapters two and seven to twelve. One thing that I find interesting is to compare the contrasts between the books of Genesis and Revelation. This table shows how God has been working to undo all the damage caused by the entrance of sin into this world:

Genesis	Revelation
The world is created	The world will be re-created
The entrance of sin	The end of sin and sinners
The paradise lost (Eden)	Paradise recovered-new heaven and earth
A world marred by sin	All things made new
Pain and suffering announced to the first couple	God will wipe away all tears- end of suffering

Humans would die	Humans saved by the blood of Jesus will be granted eternal life
Cain built a city for himself	God built a city for His children
Sinners destroyed by water	Sinners destroyed by fire
Sinners expelled from the newly created garden	Former sinners welcomed to the new creation
The blood of the first martyr claims revenge	God does justice to His martyrs
Adam and Eve were united	Christ and his bride, the church get united
Man becomes "naked"	Man gets dressed
Man forbidden to eat fruit of tree of life	Man gets to eat fruit of tree of life
Man loses authority on this world	Man gets authority restored (2:26)
There was day and night	There will be no more night
God came to **visit** Adam and Eve	God will **dwell** with His people!!!

It is evident that the circumstances of man after the plan of redemption is completed will be superior to how it was before sin entered this world.

In order to better comprehend the book of Revelation we must understand that most of it is based on the prophecies given to Daniel. The prophecies of both books are to be studied together. Both books contain the same symbols and deal with the same issues. There are three main ways to interpret the prophecies of Daniel and Revelation. The first one is the preterist, which teaches that the prophecies are already fulfilled. The proponents of this teaching identify the little horn of Daniel as Antiochus Epiphanes. The problem with that belief is that Antiochus does not match all the points indicated by Daniel. The passage clearly says, among other things that the little horn will raise up after the reign of the Greek kings. Antiochus was in the middle, not at the end. Besides, there was nothing great about him aside from the fact that he sacrificed a pig on the altar of the sanctuary. Then we have the futurist interpretation, which proposes that the fulfillment of the prophecies is far away in the future. Ezekiel 12:27, 28 indicates that God does not like that interpretation: *"Son of man, behold, they of the house of Israel say, The vision that he seeth is for many days to come, and he prophesieth of the times that are far off. Therefore say unto them, Thus saith the Lord GOD; There shall none of my words be prolonged any more, but the word which I have spoken shall be done, saith the Lord GOD."* The futuristic view makes people relax giving them the false sense that they have plenty of time to repent. What if you die of a massive heart attack or a car accident tonight? Many years ago, D.L. Moody was preaching in Chicago. He thought about asking his audience to surrender their lives to Christ as Savior and Lord and accept His forgiveness, but decided to postpone the call for the following Sunday. He later regretted that decision because a fire killed most of the city dwellers that same night. Your salvation is the most important decision in your life- take it seriously.

After analyzing the three approaches years ago, I concluded that the correct interpretation is the third one –the historicist -in which things happen in God's time, like when Jesus was born (Galatians 4:4) and when He was crucified and confirmed the covenant (Daniel 9:26,27).

To the casual reader of the Bible, it could seem like the prophetic visions are given to satisfy human curiosity with the future, like appears to be the case with the dream of Nebuchadnezzar in Daniel chapter two. However, the hand of God was, in that occasion and in all other prophecies, giving his people a beacon that would shine for the coming centuries. He did not want any of us to be taken by surprise and thus, unprepared. What would the intent of the book of Revelation be? I believe there are a few reasons for God giving us that book:

- To show Jesus' tender care and love for His people- Jesus is the center of the book of Revelation- not the beast or its mark.
- To strengthen and encourage those persecuted for their faith over the centuries.
- To unmask the evil power that would pretend to be the true church of Christ.
- To let us know in advance what would happen so we could be prepared- like to oppose the union of church and state shown in Revelation 13 and to reject the coming mark of the beast.

- To let God's children know that even in the worst of situations, God is aware of the circumstances and will give them victory. In the midst of the worst chaos in this world, we can look at everything that goes on and still have hope.
- To help us teach the whole world about God's love and His three angels' messages so the souls will come out of Babylon and be ready for Jesus' return in glory to take us home.
- To show that evil will not have the final word. God and His people will triumph and evil will be destroyed forever to give way to a kingdom of perfect harmony and happiness, where illness, pain, death and all kinds of suffering and injustice will be excluded forever. We are often tempted to ask questions such as "How long?" and "Why is this happening? Revelation runs the curtain to show us what is going on in the background and not only provides many of those answers, but also that God is in control and evil will be defeated.
- To mercifully give the wicked the opportunity to repent and be saved – three angels messages are given, the call to leave Babylon and to come to the true fold.
- To let the end-time believers know that very soon they will go home with their precious Savior and be in His presence forever. Revelation shows that we are living in the last part of the transitional period between the kingdom of grace and the kingdom of glory. Though this wonderful book we are given a taste of what is to come, creating anticipation and desire for what is better.

One more thing:

"If any man will do his will, he shall know of the doctrine, whether it be of God, or whether I speak of myself....Judge not according to the appearance, but judge righteous judgment" (John 7:17,24). Please read this book prayerfully, asking God to illuminate your mind, and being willing to follow the truth wherever it leads you. Take notes and compare with your Bible (Acts 17:11).

REVELATION 1

He saw the voice

[1]*The Revelation of Jesus Christ, which God gave unto him, to shew unto his servants things which must shortly come to pass; and he sent and signified it by his angel unto his servant John:*

There is order in heaven as expressed by Paul in 1 Corinthians 14:40: *"Let all things be done decently and in order."* God established a chain of command to reveal the important truths of Revelation. This chart will help us understand the chain presented here:

God ⟶ Jesus ⟶ Angel ⟶ John ⟶ Us

We can see here that all heaven is involved in the plan of salvation. It is also evident that God does not send angels to proclaim the message to the masses, but He gives us a role to play in reaching sinners for His kingdom. The angel talked to John but it was the prophet who was to tell the heavenly message to his readers- not the angel. God gives us the ministry of reconciliation. If angels are sent, sinners could argue that they do not know what is like to be enslaved to sin. If a former drug addict goes to his peers and tells them that Jesus gave him power to overcome the addiction, they can believe because he was in their shoes and now is victorious.

The Revelation of Jesus Christ - It is true that the book of Revelation speaks about beasts, and conflicts and all kinds of scary things, but that is not the focus of the book. Its intent is to have us focus on Jesus. The Revelation is about Jesus and His undying love for His children. It is, to say so, a love story that will culminate in the marriage of the Lamb to His beloved wife and then all will live in a kingdom with no tears, suffering or death. Here on this earth, human marriages sooner or later go through one- or even many- stages of "martyrimony," since marriage is not easy at all. Marriage is neither for the weak nor for the quitter. Revelation is the only book that can guarantee that the bride and Groom will live happily ever after.

In this book, we find different facets of the work of Jesus for His people and we also find Him as the judge of the wicked that dare to oppress His children. In chapter four, we see Him as a lamb, inspiring trust to those that need the assurance of being accepted by God, and at the same time, we see Him as a lion, always vigilant and ready to attack and protect. For the repentant sinner He is a savior (lamb); for the impenitent, He is his worst fear come true (lion), for Jesus will protect His children like the apple of His eye.

The book shows Jesus as a victorious conqueror but at the same time as a compassionate Savior that even invites His enemies to repent so they could also enjoy the reward of the saved. We will see in the letters to the seven churches of Asia how tenderly He invites them to change what is not good and to reinforce what is positive. We can see in the Revelation that it presents a picture of God that is very different from the common human concept of a deity that is only looking for defects and sins in order to zap the sinner. As a Father with a wise and tender heart, He recognizes the efforts of His children "to bring home good grades." Although salvation is never achieved through good works, there is the expectancy of fruit- a byproduct of our relationship with Him. And not only does He keep a good record of what you do for Him, it is also evident in this book that He also notices your struggles, challenges and tears- which He promises to wipe out like a loving parent when approached by a hurting child.

The book of Revelation should be read with confidence because every chapter is full of promises. Every promise should reinforce our trust that God will make it a reality. Twice He said: *"these words are true and faithful"* (Revelation 21:5 and 22:6). Take heart because those promises are yours too. He loves you with a love that no human being is capable of demonstrating and very soon, He will return to take you home with Him.

2Who bare record of the word of God, and of the testimony of Jesus Christ, and of all things that he saw.

God opened the windows of heaven to give John the Revelation of Jesus Christ so we could be blessed by reading it.

[3]*Blessed is he that readeth, and they that hear the words of this prophecy, and keep those things which are written therein: for the time is at hand.*

The blessing is triple and includes those that read, hear (understand) and keep what is written in the book. It is not enough to read the word; we must apply it to our lives and make it permeate everything we do. It is very important to read the Bible with reverence because it is not a common book; it is the Word of God. We need to remember then that the Bible is not to be place at the level of a newspaper, novel or magazine. It was inspired by the Holy Spirit and we must pray before we read it for wisdom to comprehend the will of God. This was understood by the Jewish people returning from captivity. Twice the book of Nehemiah says that they stood for six hours (Nehemiah 8:3; 9:3) to listen attentively to the reading of the book of the law (the writings of Moses). *"So they read in the book in the law of God distinctly, and gave the sense, and caused them to understand the reading"* (Nehemiah 8:8). James wrote: *"Wherefore, my beloved brethren, let every man be swift to hear"* (James 1:19) and added: *"But be ye doers of the word, and not hearers only, deceiving your own selves"* (James 1:22). Paul, writing to the Romans, explained that *"faith cometh by hearing, and hearing by the word of God"* (Romans 10:17). Reading or listening to the Word of God produces faith in our hearts. However, that faith is not passive. Rather, it is described as a *"faith which worketh by love"* (Galatians 5:6).

This verse presents the first of seven blessings in the book of Revelation. These are the other six:

***"Blessed** are the dead which die in the Lord from henceforth."* Revelation 14:13

***"Blessed** is he that watcheth, and keepeth his garments, lest he walk naked, and they see his shame."* Revelation16:15

***"Blessed** are they which are called unto the marriage supper of the Lamb."* Revelation 19:9

***"Blessed** and holy is he that hath part in the first resurrection: on such the second death hath no power, but they shall be priests of God* *and of Christ, and shall reign with him a thousand years."* Revelation 20:6 ***"blessed** is he that keepeth the sayings of the prophecy of this book."* Revelation 22:7

***"Blessed** are they that do his commandments, that they may have right to the tree of life, and may enter in through the gates into the city."* Revelation 22:14

When we read and keep what is written in this book we are enabled by God to enjoy the other six blessings too.

In John's times, there were no presses to make copies of the inspired writings. Since all Scriptures' copies were made by hand, usually only one person had a copy from which he read while the rest of the congregation listened.

Many people, in their ignorance, do not read the book of Revelation because they believe it to be a closed book, impossible to understand. But, why God would inspire a book of which we could not receive any benefit? Even the word "revelation" should inspire the readers to study the messages in it contained. Revelation means "to open a curtain", like in a theater. The word implies God's intent to make known, to make public, to expose important truths, rather than concealing, hiding or keeping them a secret. This verse indicates that God wants us to read this book and that He has a blessing for those that do it. However, head knowledge is not sufficient because the verse also calls for us to keep those things written in this book. The word keep is translated from the Greek τηρέω (tēreō), which means "to guard (from loss or injury, properly by keeping the eye upon)" (Strong's Concordance G5083).

"...The time is at hand" Habakkuk 2:3 reads: *"For the vision is yet for an appointed time, but at the end it shall speak, and not lie: though it tarry, wait for it; because it will surely come, it will not tarry."* Many people get discouraged because evil things and tragedies seem to continue in this world and they do not see the end of evil coming any time soon. The promises of God are sure and He will make all the pieces of the prophetic puzzle come together. Evil will not triumph; God and His children will.

"Therefore to him that knoweth to do good, and doeth it not, to him it is sin" James 4:17. To ignore the book of Revelation would be sinful, because God expects us to study it and work according to its message. But, do we need to buy dozens of books and spend thousands of dollars on a college degree in theology in order to understand the message from the book? Let us read Isaiah's opinion on how to study the Scriptures: *"For precept must be upon precept, precept upon precept; line upon line, line upon line; here a little, and there a little"* (Isaiah 28:10). The *New Living Translation* renders the text like this: *"He tells us everything over and over—one line at a time, one line at a time, a little here, and a little there!"* The best way to understand the Bible is to <u>allow it to explain itself</u> by comparing an obscure verse with others that deal with the same subject. The book of Revelation is highly symbolic. To determine the meaning of those symbols, we must look them up in other parts of the Bible and allow the Holy Spirit to explain them to us. For example, when we reach chapter 13, we will see two beasts. Where did we see visions of beasts before? In the book of Daniel, chapters seven and eight, the nations are represented with beasts. See Daniel 7:23; 8:20 and 21.

Daniel chapter 12:10 also indicates that only some individuals will be capable of understanding the prophecies, while Paul wrote: *"When we tell you these things, we do not use words that come from human wisdom. Instead, we speak words given to us by the Spirit, using the Spirit's words to explain spiritual truths. But people who aren't spiritual can't receive these truths from God's Spirit. It all sounds foolish to them and they can't understand it, for <u>only those who are spiritual can understand what the Spirit means</u>"* (1 Corinthians 2:13,14- *New Living Translation*).

[4]John to the <u>seven</u> churches which are in Asia: Grace be unto you, and peace, from him which is, and which was, and which is to come; and from the seven Spirits which are before his throne;

We will discuss the seven spirits in chapter three, verse one. The number seven is used 54 times in the book of Revelation. It is the number for completeness, totality and perfection. So, if John mentions seven churches, it means just that there is not going to be an eighth. What do the seven churches represent? Although these were churches in communities existing in Johns' times, they represent the Christian church in its different historic stages until the end. They are described in chapters two and three.

Notice that these letters were addressed to churches, not to individuals, neither to any ethnic group in particular, like the Jews. *"I Jesus have sent mine angel to testify unto you these things in the churches ..."* (Revelation 22:16). It was written for the Christian believers. Why churches? Because God created us as social beings and we must be interdependent. No man is to be an island. Belonging to a church gives the individual a feeling of community and bond. He has a family that shares his hopes and extends the hand to lift him up when he is fallen down. The Greek word for church is *ekklesia* and means "the called-out (ones)." It is used to refer to a group of persons that are organized together and meet for a common purpose, in this case, to worship and fellowship. It can be correctly translated as "assembly" or "congregation." In all the New Testament, we find indications that the believers gathered to worship and did not stay home to do it. Two coals burn longer when they are together than when they are separated. God designed that we seek each other's company for encouragement and knowledge sharing. I worry when someone (an able body, not a shut-in or hospitalized person) tells me that he/she worships at home because he/she does not need to go to church. It would be beneficial for us if we all heed Paul's counsel: *"Not forsaking the assembling of ourselves together, as the manner of some is; but exhorting one another: and so much the more, as ye see the day approaching"* (Hebrews 10:25). Others yet offer another reason not to go to church: they say that it is full of hypocrites. Matthew 23:14,15 indicates that Jesus identified that as a main problem in the congregations of His days. Regardless of this terrible condition, He went to worship every Sabbath: *"And he came to Nazareth, where he had been brought up: and, as his custom was, he went into the synagogue on the Sabbath day, and stood up for to read"* (Luke 4:16). Jesus is our example (1 Peter 2:21). If Jesus considered that worshipping overshadowed the presence of the hypocrites and went to church every week in spite of them, who am I to do otherwise? Besides the spiritual and social benefits of church gathering, studies indicate that churchgoers live longer and when they go to the hospital, they need fewer days to recuperate and go home. Why, being in my right mind, would I reject all those benefits?

"from him which is, and which was, and which is to come" This verse should have been translated *"from him which is, and which was, and which is to be."* It refers to God the Father but since it was not translated correctly, it makes people think that it refers to Jesus. The Father and the Holy Spirit are presented in verse four and Jesus in verse five. What do the Scriptures have to say about the Father, Son and the Holy Spirit?

Before we study this subject, we have to mention: 1) that the nature of God cannot be understood 100%. We are finite fallen beings with a very limited intellect. And 2) the fact that there are some terms in theology that are not found in the Bible, even though the teachings are recognized by most of the Christians. Such is the case with the term omnipresent, which means present in all places simultaneously. The idea is implied in different ways, like for example in Psalm 139:7-15 *"Where can I go from your Spirit?...If I go up to the heavens, you are there..."*

Omniscience is another term that we accept as biblical, even when the word is not found in the Scriptures. In the same Psalm, verse 16, we find: *"your eyes saw my unformed body, all the days for me were written in your book before one of them came to be."* Verse 4 says: *"Before a word is on my tongue you know it completely, O Lord."* The word omniscience indicates that God knows everything that happens everywhere, even before it happens.

The word Trinity refers to the divine family, Father, Son and Holy Ghost. In order to properly analyze the idea behind the term, we have to study what the Bible so clearly says about them. The first verse of the Bible reads: *"In the beginning God created the heaven and the earth."* The word translated as "God" comes from the Hebrew Elohim (אלהים), which is plural. The same word is used in Genesis 1:26: *"And God said, Let us make man in our image, after our likeness: and let them have dominion over the fish of the sea, and over the fowl of the air, and over the cattle, and over all the earth, and over every creeping thing that creepeth upon the earth."* Notice also the use of the pronouns "us" and "our," indicating plurality. The same truth is shown in these other often-quoted passages:

"And the LORD God said, Behold, the man is become as one of us...." Genesis 3:22

"Go to, let us go down, and there confound their language, that they may not understand one another's speech." Genesis 11:7

"Also I heard the voice of the Lord, saying, Whom shall I send, and who will go for us? Then said I, Here am I; send me." Isaiah 6:8

As I do not think that the divinity of the Father is questionable, it will not be necessary to talk about Him for now, so we will start by analyzing the following table and later we will read what the Bible says about the Son and the Holy Spirit.

ATTRIBUTE	FATHER	SON	HOLY SPIRIT
He is the Truth	Deut. 32:4, Psalm 31:5	John 14:6	1 John 5:6; John 15:26
He is eternal	Psalm 90:2	Micah 5:2	Hebrews 9:14
He is Holy	John 17:11	Acts 4:30	Ephesians 4:30
He is the Creator	Genesis 1:1	John 1:3	Job 33:4
He is God	John 6:27	1 John 5:20	Acts 5:3,4

The Son

He is the author of life (Acts 3:15) - this word indicates originality, like the word inventor. Nobody else created life before Jesus came up with the idea. If Jesus was created by the Father as some people teach, He could never be called the author; He would be but an imitator. He would be a duplicator, a plagiarist; one that copies what others did before. John 1:3 says that "All things were made by him; and without him was not any thing made that was made." If Jesus had been created, John could not have written those words, especially because the words "all" and "nothing" are absolute and "all" is inclusive. Some quote John 14:28 ("the Father is greater than I am") as a proof that Jesus was an inferior god that was created. The Father was greater than Jesus only during His incarnation because Jesus took the form of a servant and suffered the limitations of the human race. As such, he got hungry, tired and thirsty. After His ascension to heaven, all power was restore to Him (Matthew 28:18). According to Romans 1:4, Jesus was not a son, but was "declared" Son. So being a Son would not be pointing to the relationship between an ancestor and a descendant, but that of assignment or appointment. The role of Son came with his work of redemption.

The following verses will help those that either believe that the Father, Jesus and the Holy Spirit are three manifestations of only one person and those that believe that Jesus was created:

He is the resurrection and life (John 11:25)

He is the creator (John 1:1-3; Hebrews 1:1,2)

He is worshipped (Matthew 28:9) - only God can be worshipped without incurring in sin (Revelation 19:10)

Has no origin, since He is eternal (Micah 5:2; Isaiah 9:2)

He is God (Titus 2:13; 1 John 5:20)

He speaks about the Father (John 14:6) - He would not make too much sense if He was talking about another person when was referring to Himself. He is not the Father. They are two different Beings.

He speaks about the Holy Spirit (John 14:16,17), and when He does it, He refers to Him as a person, not like referring to a force.

The Father himself calls Jesus God (Hebrews 1:6,8)- not "a God"

The three of them are mentioned in occasion of Jesus' baptism as three different Beings (Matthew 3:16,17). The fact that Jesus refers so many times in all four gospels to both the Father and the Holy Spirit should be enough to prove that they are not the same person posing as three as some people propose.

When in John 10:30 He says that He and His Father are one, He did not mean they were one and the same person. In Greek, one is neuter, which means "one thing", not "one person." Both are divine - of one same nature, not an identical person.

When Jesus prayed to the Father (John 17), He was not praying to himself, because that would not make too much sense. He was praying to another Person, and that Person answered to Him (John 12:27,28) in a previous event (John 11:41).

The Holy Spirit

He is not a force or power. Jesus was anointed *"with the Holy Ghost and with power"* (Acts 10:38)

He was present at the time of creation - (Genesis 1:2).

The following text shows that the Holy Spirit has a personality:

He convicts the world using the Word - (John 16:8-11)

He speaks - (Acts 8:29; Revelation 2:7,11,17 & 29)

He commands people to go places - (Acts 10:19,20)

He chooses and calls people for special projects - (Acts 13:2,4)

He gives his opinion - (Acts 15:28)

He teaches - (John 14:26)

He helps us remember - (John 14:26)

He hears, guides to the truth and knows the future - (John 16:13)

He is called the counselor (the Greek term refers to a person who helps someone in trouble with the Law) - (John 14:16)

He is not a thing like energy, but has characteristics of a person.

People can sin against Him - (Mark 3:29)

People can make Him sad - (Ephesians 4:30; 1 Thessalonians 5:19)

He is called God, and pretending to fool him cost two people their lives - (Acts 5:3,4,9)

In that passage, Peter asked Sapphira why she and her husband had tempted the Holy Spirit. The Greek word for tempt used here is πειράζω (pêirazõ) = prove, tempt, and comes from the base πέραν (péran) = to pierce through, so when we tempt the Holy Spirit, it is like when the soldiers pierced Jesus' side.

Notice how, in the record of the last words of King David, he equated the Holy Spirit with God: *"The Spirit of the LORD spake by me...The God of Israel said, the Rock of Israel spake to me..."* (2 Samuel 23:2,3).

It is interesting to note that in the letters to the seven churches in the book of Revelation, chapters two and three, the Holy Spirit not only speaks, but also makes promises. One of them is found in Revelation 2:7: *"To him that overcometh will I give to eat of the tree of life, which is in the midst of the paradise of God"* Could a force or energy (as some call the Holy Spirit) make such a promise reserved only to God Himself? Only a divine Being could make such an offer.

Titus 3:5 reads: *"Not by works of righteousness which we have done, but according to his mercy he saved us, by the washing of regeneration, and renewing of the Holy Ghost;"* Verse six is translated in the International Standard Version (ISV) as: *"And poured <u>him</u> out upon us, too, Through Jesus Christ our Savior true"*, making Him a person. Both the immediate context and the Greek allow this translation.

It is very important to remember that we cannot understand everything about God, because if we did, He would be inferior to our thoughts, a human idea, and a man's creation. God would like us to remember that there are some mysteries that our minds will never understand (Deut. 29:29).

Several sincere people are confused with the term Trinity, believing that if they accept it, they will be like the pagans. Polytheism had the concept of specialist deities. A god for everything in life, each one limited in powers and often conceived as enemies, fighting each other, like in the Greek mythology. In Bible times there were gods for fertility, war, crops, etc., but in the case of the Father, Son and the Holy Spirit, they can be called a family with unlimited power, the same nature, the same purposes, acting in total harmony. Philippians 2:6 says that Jesus was of the same <u>nature</u> or form (μορφή = morphē- pronounced morfay) of the Father:

"Who [Jesus], *being in the same nature of God, did not considered equality with God something to be grasped."*

When in Deut. 6:4 says that *"our God is one"*, it uses the word אחד 'echâd (pronounced ekh-awd'). The word is translated as: united, one, altogether, together. This word appears also in Genesis 2:24 to describe the total union that God intended for the recently created holy couple: *"Therefore shall a man leave his father and his mother, and shall cleave unto his wife: and they shall be one flesh."* The first couple was not one body, but their spiritual, intellectual and emotional union was expected. They were also one in nature and lived in complete harmony before they sinned. In marriage, 1 + 1 =1. So if a created man and his wife can be one, why can't the Father, Jesus and the Holy Spirit be one also, since the Hebrew word allows and implies a plural unity? Notice how the word is used in Judges 20:1: *"Then all the children of Israel went out, and the congregation was gathered together as one* [אחד 'echâd] *man..."* (Judges 20:1). If 400,000 men can be one, why can't God Almighty, All Wise, be one too? Why do we limit God to our feeble imagination incapable of grasping the concepts that are natural to the Eternal? Why do we pretend to define or even understand the nature of God? It is as if we are trying to put God in a test tube or dissect Him under a microscope in order to define His nature. We will never be capable of understanding the divine nature.

Paul writes referring to the Trinity (Gal. 4:4-6; 2 Cor. 13:14; Rom. 1: 1-4). When Jesus sent his disciples to baptize people, He told them to do it *"in the name"* of the Father and of the Son and of the Holy Spirit" (Matthew 28:19), which would be a nonsense if it were only one divine being.

We are not polytheist if we just accept by faith what the Bible teaches about the Divinity without attempting to get into the secrets of God (Deut. 29:29). Let us be humble and pray, so God will illuminate our minds and learn how to have the correct relationship with the three persons of the one Lord God our Creator. Conclusion: *1+1+1=1.*

[5]*And from Jesus Christ, who is the faithful witness, and the first begotten of the dead, and the prince of the kings of the earth. Unto him that loved us, and washed us from our sins in his own blood,*

Jesus Christ the faithful witness- how comforting that Jesus' word is trustworthy! The first begotten from the dead refers not to Him as the first person resurrected (because there were others, starting with Moses), but to His preeminence. The Greek word is πρωτοτόκος (pro-tot-ok'-os). In Revelation 1:11 appears the word πρῶτος (pro'-tos), translated as "first" but meaning "foremost (in time, place, order or importance)"- Strong's Concordance. Jesus is the principal of those resurrected. See also Acts 26:23.

The phrase *"him that loved us,"* should string the cords of praise in our hearts. To make it more amazing, He saved us <u>at the cost</u> of His blood (Greek text- see next paragraph). Just think for a moment. Let us imagine that we are in a city dump looking among the trashed items discarded there. What do we see? The majority of us would never go to such a place to find something valuable. It is said that centuries ago Michelangelo was walking outside the city of Florence when he spotted a piece of marble that another artist had ruined and discarded. The story says that he was inspired when he saw it and feverishly work on it to transform it into a work of art. Some witnesses reported that he said: "I saw the angel in the marble and chiseled until I could set it free." Jesus also sees possibilities when He looks at us. He does not see the darkness of our past or the rebellion and misery of the present time. All He looks at is the possibilities, the potential: what you can become if you trust in Him and let Him be your Savior. His blood is sufficient to wash us from our sins and give us a second chance. There is no past record that He cannot cleanse, nor do big skeletons in the closet that He cannot make disappear. There is no sin that He cannot forgive, as long as it is confessed and abandoned.

"washed us from our sins in his own blood" – Literal: *washed us from our sins <u>at the cost</u> of His blood.* The word wash in Greek is λούω (louō) and indicates <u>to bathe the whole person</u>, not a part of the body. Through the blood of Christ, we are not partially, but totally cleansed. How was Jesus' death different from the death of any other hero, such as a soldier that jumps on a grenade to save his comrades? Even though that sacrifice is commendable and Jesus Himself said that it is the ultimate proof of love from one friend for another (John 15:13), it is an act that lasts only a few seconds. Jesus' agony started the night before at Gethsemane when in terrible anguish of His soul He fell on his face and pleaded to the

Father: *"...O my Father, if it be possible, let this cup pass from me: nevertheless not as I will, but as thou wilt."* (Matthew 26:39). Since before the foundation of the world it had been decided that if man sinned, Jesus would provide a way to restore humanity. *"Then said I, Lo, I come (in the volume of the book it is written of me,) to do thy will, O God"* (Hebrews 10:7). He was the *"Lamb slain from the foundation of the world"* (Rev 13:8). More than once, He could have backed out of the deal to save humanity, but looking into the future, He saw you and me perishing in our sins and decided that He would allow Himself to be crucified to pay the penalty for our sins. He came to the garden with His disciples and with great distress, begged them to pray. *"...My soul is exceeding sorrowful, even unto death: tarry ye here, and watch with me"* (Matthew 26:38). His human nature longed for sympathy in that dark hour. The sins of all mankind where being placed on him and the agony He went through is described by the physician Luke: *"And being in an agony he prayed more earnestly: and his sweat was as it were great drops of blood falling down to the ground"* (Luke 22:44). The enormous weight of our sins was crushing Him. A hero usually has a fraction of a second to decide if he is going to take the risk and many times, he thinks he could come out with the victim, both alive and well. In the case of Jesus, He was embattled for hours before the cross and could have easily said "enough; they asked for it, let them have it their way." However, in His infinite love, Jesus kept enduring incredible agony and abuse at the hands of the soldiers, the priests and the rabble, both verbally and physically. The rejection and taunting were intended to play on His emotions to discourage Him from saving humanity.

The multitude that just a few days before sang hosannas and wanted to make Him king, now asked for His crucifixion. Even probably, many of those that He healed were now demanding His blood. His disciples had abandoned Him. Still, He continued because He loved you and me more than He loved Himself. That is how much you are worth: the life of the very own Son of God. *"All we like sheep have gone astray; we have turned every one to his own way; and the LORD hath laid on him the iniquity of us all"* (Isaiah 53:6). When Jesus became your substitute, your sins were placed on him and the punishment that you deserved was suffered by Him, the innocent One. *"But he was wounded for our transgressions, he was bruised for our iniquities: the chastisement of our peace was upon him; and with his stripes we are healed"* (Isaiah 53:5). He was made sin for us (2 Corinthians 5:21), which means that at the cross He was considered as if He were the only sinner on earth. Hanging on the cross between a holy God and the rebellious race, He became a bridge to unite our family with the Father. Remember that regardless of your sinful life, there is no sin that He would not forgive if you confess it to Him. He loves you and not only showed it by dying for you but also in His daily blessings. Please never take for granted the enormous sacrifice that Jesus did to save you. He took your punishment because He wanted to spend eternity with you.

Jesus Christ was *"despised and rejected of men; a man of sorrows, and acquainted with grief: and we hid as it were our faces from him; he was despised, and we esteemed him not. Surely he hath borne our griefs, and carried our sorrows: yet we did esteem him stricken, smitten of God, and afflicted"* (Isaiah 53:3,4). How afflicted was He? *"As many were astonied at thee; his visage was so marred more than any man, and his form more than the sons of men"* (Isaiah 52:14). The *Contemporary English Version* translates that verse like this: *"Many were horrified at what happened to him. But everyone who saw him was even more horrified because he suffered until he no longer looked human."* Just as if He had been a criminal, Jesus was subjected to all kinds of abuse and humiliation. *"I let them beat my back and pull out my beard. I didn't turn aside when they insulted me and spit in my face"* (Isaiah 50:6 *Contemporary English Version*). A parallel passage reads: *"The plowers plowed upon my back: they made long their furrows" (Psalm 129:3).* Strong soldiers were brought to whip Jesus' back, causing deep cuts in His skin. The instrument used (flagrum romanum) had about six pieces of lead and some sharp bones. The lead caused the leather strings to fall heavy and crush the skin and the bones cut on the pull, leaving the person gushing blood. He was punished by the soldiers in three occasions. The Jews limited the whippings to 39 lashes because 40 was considered an abuse. In total, He was hit with the whip 117 times. Multiplying that amount by 6 for the lead gives 702 blows and adding at least 3 impacts with the sharp bones per whip we have 1053 hits. There was probably not even one inch of intact flesh on His back; just raw flesh. Just imagine all the wounds that He endured and all the blood that He had already lost when He was ordered to carry the heavy cross on His open wounds.

For us as human beings, it is difficult to remain calmed and quiet when false things are said about us, when our character is maligned and our motives misunderstood. Jesus, however, endured patiently, knowing that if He failed His rescue mission, our only chance for salvation would be spoiled forever. *"He was painfully abused, but he did not complain. He was silent like a lamb being led to the butcher, as quiet as a sheep having its wool cut off"* (Isaiah 53:7 *CEV*). There were many violations of the criminal code in that trial of Jesus. Yet, he did not rebuke Pilate, Herod, or the hardened soldiers. *"He was condemned to death without a fair trial. Who could have imagined what would happen to him? His life was taken away because of the sinful things my people had done"* (Isaiah 53:8 *CEV*). It was for your sins and mine that Jesus suffered such abuse and humiliations. However, when we reach the heavenly mansion, some will notice His wounds (the only memory of sin). *"And one shall say unto him, What are these wounds in thine hands? Then he shall answer, Those with which I was wounded in the house of my friends"* (Zechariah 13:6). What love! Only Jesus can call His killers "friends" and forgive them as He pleaded while hanging between heaven and earth on the cross: *"Father, forgive them; for they know not what they do"* (Luke 23:34).

Do not postpone your decision for Christ. *"To wit, that God was in Christ, reconciling the world unto himself, not imputing their trespasses unto them; and hath committed unto us the word of reconciliation. Now then we are ambassadors for Christ, as though God did beseech you by us: we pray you in Christ's stead, be ye reconciled to God"* (2 Corinthians 5:19,20). *"We then, as workers together with him, beseech you also that ye receive not the grace of God in vain. (For he saith, I have heard thee in a time accepted, and in the day of salvation have I succoured thee: behold, now is the accepted time; behold, now is the day of salvation.)"* (2 Corinthians 6:1,2).

6 *And hath made us kings and priests unto God and his Father; to him be glory and dominion for ever and ever. Amen.*

What an honor! From sinful fallen and rebellious human beings we are promoted to kings and priests! If I ever heard a story about a pauper becoming a prince, this one betters it by far. To even consider that God can take a criminal like Samuel Woodrow

Tannyhill* or a slave trader like John Newton and change him into a saint and treat him with the utmost dignity, is unthinkable by human standards. I am so glad that God is the one in charge and not me. No wonder John wrote *"to him be glory and dominion for ever and ever. Amen."*

[7]Behold, he cometh with clouds; and every eye shall see him, and <u>they also which pierced him</u>: and all kindreds of the earth shall wail because of him. Even so, Amen.

When Jesus was about to be crucified, He told the high priest: *"...Thou hast said: nevertheless I say unto you, Hereafter shall ye see the Son of man sitting on the right hand of power, and coming in the clouds of heaven"* (Matthew 26:64). In that prophecy, Jesus indicated that those participating in that mockery of a trial would see Him coming back in glory. They will be resurrected and get free front row seats so *"they shall look upon me whom they have pierced"* (Zechariah 12:10). Terrible will be that day, not only for those directly involved in the crucifixion, but also for everybody that rejects the calls to repentance. But, how could anyone, in his right mind reject Him who loves us so much? What could be so valuable on this temporary world, destined to be burned to ashes, that is worth more than Jesus and life eternal? Neither fleeting pleasure, nor worldly glory, or fame or riches could be better than what Jesus has prepared for you and me. *"But as Scripture says: "No eye has seen, no ear has heard, and <u>no mind has imagined the things that God has prepared for those who love him</u>"* (1 Corinthians 2:9). Beauty, strength and health fade soon but when Jesus returns for us, we will have eternal life and youth to enjoy forever. Why would you prefer to have one cent worth of worldly things when you can have limitless wealth? Chapter 21 shows that the city will have streets paved with gold, while here we have asphalt or at the most concrete that eventually crumbles. That should give you an idea of how the riches here will pale in comparison to the heavenly ones. Of the first creation, it is said that it was good. However, the second time around things will be even better. If you are impressed by earthly beauty of any kind, you have no idea how beautiful things will be in the new world. It is impressive what the book of Job says about the second set of daughters that God gave him. *"There were no other women in the whole world as beautiful as Job's daughters"* (Job 42:15 *Good News Bible*). We will even be more honored than the angels that never fell because God will establish His throne here among us.

[8]I am Alpha and Omega, the beginning and the ending, saith the Lord, which is, and which was, and which is to come, the Almighty.

The words alpha and omega refer to the first and the last letters respectively of the Greek alphabet. This relates to the Verb in John chapter one. The Father does not speak in the book of Revelation; only Jesus does and here He claims to be *the Almighty.*

[9]I John, who also am your brother, and companion in tribulation, and in the kingdom and patience of Jesus Christ, was in the isle that is called Patmos, for the word of God, and for the testimony of Jesus Christ.

Brother- from the Greek ἀδελφός (adelphos). This word comes from δελφύς (delphus) which means womb. In other words, it is as if we were given birth by the same mother since we shared the same womb. We become relatives, like real flesh brothers and sisters. When we come to Christ, we are no longer Americans or Iranians or Russians. Race, sex or social status are no longer a motive for separation. We are one people and love one another like loving siblings are supposed to do.

Companion- meaning co-participant. John was one like us. If we have suffered for the cause of Christ, he also suffered. He is going to be handsomely rewarded when Jesus returns. The best part is that we all will enjoy the reward with John too.

At the end of the first century, the Romans thought that Christians were simply a Jewish sect, since it originated in Judea, used the same Scriptures and because they also kept the Sabbath. They blamed the Christians for the burning of Rome in 64 AD as their mentally ill emperor Nero made them believe. Christians were persecuted and John, the only surviving disciple, was no exception. Legend has it that emperor Domitian tried to kill John by immersing him in a big cauldron of boiling oil. The servant of God enjoyed it as if he were at a spa. Ordering to remove the unharmed prophet, he thought that since he could not silence John, the worst punishment would be to send him to a rocky, barren island-prison called Patmos. There he would be silenced – he thought- because he would not have an audience, being condemned to work in the island's quarry. Little did the emperor know that what he intended as a punishment, was going to be used by God to bless all the generations of Christians until the very end of the world. Those that exiled John became instruments in the hands of God to bless millions. The Roman government also helped in other ways to facilitate the spread of the gospel. With their paved roads, one common official language, the Pax Romana and a stable government, the doors were wide open for sharing the good news to a perishing world. From John's experience we can learn that it does not matter what the devil throws at you; God can change even a tragedy into a blessing. If you are going through tribulation, do not despair; God's help is on its way and He will never abandon you.

When you feel like throwing in the towel, remember Joni Eareckson Tada**.** One day in 1967, she went swimming with her sister, both teenagers. Unfortunately, she had a diving accident that left her a quadriplegic. Understandably, the first few months she was deeply depressed, even suicidal. She even turned against God, but little by little, she decided to trust Him instead. Although she had been a talented artist before the tragic accident, she trained herself to draw and paint holding a paintbrush with her teeth. With the understanding that the grace of God is sufficient and that He can use anyone that trust Him, she has written 30 books and recorded many songs praising God. She is an advocate for the disabled, a wife and a mother. Daily she is an inspiration not only for thousands with physical limitations, but also for us, able bodies. When you have a problem, God makes it His problem if you trust in Him as the captain of your life.

[10]I was in the Spirit on the Lord's day, and heard behind me a great voice, as of a trumpet,

The Lord's Day is the Sabbath, the seventh day of the week. I am glad God showed it to me many years ago, while reading the Bible on my own. God gave that day at the beginning of the creation (Genesis 2:1-3) when there were no Jews or any other nationality whatsoever. Jesus emphasized that when He declared that the *"Sabbath was made for man, not man for the Sabbath"* Mark

2:27. In order to dissipate any remaining doubt, the next verse nails the point clearly: *"So the Son of Man is Lord even of the Sabbath."* The Sabbath is sacred time that belongs to God. Together with the tithe, it was to be considered the Lord's property and no one had the right to use it as he willed. If withholding the tithe is considered stealing from God (Malachi 3:8-10), then using the Sabbath for our own purposes is considered sinful because that time does not belong to us. *"If thou turn away thy foot from the Sabbath, from doing thy pleasure on my holy day; and call the Sabbath a delight, the holy of the LORD, honourable; and shalt honour him, not doing thine own ways, nor finding thine own pleasure, nor speaking thine own words: Then shalt thou delight thyself in the LORD; and I will cause thee to ride upon the high places of the earth, and feed thee with the heritage of Jacob thy father: for the mouth of the LORD hath spoken it"* (Isaiah 58:13,14). If there is a doubt as to who was supposed to keep the Sabbath, it is dispelled when reading Isaiah 56:4-7 where foreigners (non-Jewish people) were encouraged to keep the same Sabbath holy. *"For thus saith the LORD unto the eunuchs that keep my Sabbaths, and choose the things that please me, and take hold of my covenant; Even unto them will I give in mine house and within my walls a place and a name better than of sons and of daughters: I will give them an everlasting name, that shall not be cut off. Also the sons of the stranger, that join themselves to the LORD, to serve him, and to love the name of the LORD, to be his servants, every one that keepeth the Sabbath from polluting it, and taketh hold of my covenant; Even them will I bring to my holy mountain, and make them joyful in my house of prayer: their burnt offerings and their sacrifices shall be accepted upon mine altar; for mine house shall be called an house of prayer for all people."* The Sabbath was not only to be a special time to being humanitarian with fellow citizens and foreigners, but also to practice mercy even with the animals, as we can see in Exodus 23:12: *"Six days thou shalt do thy work, and on the seventh day thou shalt rest: that thine ox and thine ass may rest, and the son of thy handmaid, and the stranger, may be refreshed."* Thus the Sabbath was destined to be a blessing for all creation and was not a Jewish institution, for God rested it at the beginning when there were no nationalities yet.

Many argue that the Sabbath was temporary and that it ended on the cross. This is an erroneous idea based on the false premise that the Sabbath- Saturday was only for the Jews. If any part of the

Ten Commandments was meant to be temporary, then it would render Psalm 119:152 untrue: *"Concerning thy testimonies, I have known of old that thou hast founded them for ever."* Jesus never changed the sanctity of the Sabbath to transfer it to **Sun**day, whose observance is based only on pagan tradition. See additional information in comment to chapter two.

[11]Saying, I am Alpha and Omega, the first and the last: and, What thou seest, write in a book, and send it unto the seven churches which are in Asia; unto Ephesus, and unto Smyrna, and unto Pergamos, and unto Thyatira, and unto Sardis, and unto Philadelphia, and unto Laodicea.

Here we see a common practice in the book of Revelation: repetition. Again, it is mentioned that Jesus is the Alpha and Omega. With the words *the first and the last* He identifies Himself with the Jehovah of the Old Testament. He is claiming both, divinity and eternity. This verse refers to a quote from Isaiah 44:6. *"Thus saith the LORD the King of Israel, and his redeemer the LORD of hosts; I am the first, and I am the last; and beside me there is no God."* The following table will help us to see the concept more clearly.

He used to be called Jehovah

The following verses show how the same attributes are applied to Jehovah and to Jesus in the same way, some of them emphasizing that there is only one Being with such a characteristic.

Jehovah	Jesus
"I, even I, am the Lord [Jehovah] and beside me there is no savior." Is. 43:11	"Salvation is found in no one else, for there is no other name under heaven given to men by which we must be saved." Acts 4:12
"Extol him who rides upon the heavens by his name JAH..." Psalm 68:4	"There before me was a white horse, whose rider is called Faithful and True..." Rev. 19:11
"The Lord [Jehovah] is my shepherd." Psalm 23:1; Is.40:10,11	"I am the good shepherd." John 10:11

"For the Lord shall judge his people..." Deut. 32:36	"The Father judges no man, but has committed all judgment unto the Son." John 5:22
"I the Lord, the first, and with the last, I am he." Is. 41:4	"I am the first and the last." Rev. 1:17; 2:8
"For I am God,...The Holy One." Hosea 11:9	"The words of him who is holy." Rev. 3:7
"Who should not fear you, O King of the nations?" Jeremiah 10:7	Jesus is "King of kings and Lord of lords" Rev. 19:16
"I the Lord [Jehovah] search the heart and examine the mind." Jeremiah 17:10	"I am he who searches hearts and minds" Rev. 2:23
For your Maker is your husband; the Lord of host is his name." Is. 54:5	"I promised you to one husband, to Christ." 2 Cor. 11:2
"The sun will no more be your light by day, nor will be the brightness of moon shine on you, for the Lord will be your everlasting light, and your God will be your glory." Is. 60:19	"The city does not need the sun or the moon to shine on it, for the glory of God gives it light, and the Lamb is its lamp." Rev. 21:23
"He is the Rock...A faithful God.." Deut.32:4	"...That rock was Christ." 1 Cor. 10:4
"The Lord Almighty is the King of glory." Psalm 24:10	"...They would not have crucified the Lord of glory." 1 Cor. 2:8
"Men will flee to caves in the rocks and to holes in the ground from dread of the Lord and the splendor of his majesty when he rises to shake the earth." Is. 2:19	When Jesus comes, the wicked men will hide in the caves and between rocks for fear of Jesus. Rev 6:15-17
"...Before me every knee will bow; by me every tongue will swear." Is. 45:23	"That at the name of Jesus every knee should bow,...and every tongue confess that Jesus is Lord..." Phil 2:10,11
"I have trodden down the winepress alone." Is 63:3	"He treads the winepress of the wrath of God Almighty" Rev 19:15
"See, the Sovereign Lord comes with power, and his arm rules for him, see his reward is with him, and his recompense accompanies him." Hosea 5:14	"Behold, I am coming soon! My reward is with me, and I will give to everyone according to what he has done." Rev 22:12

"For I will be like...a great lion to Judah." Hosea 5:14	"See the Lion of the tribe of Judah." Rev 5:5b
"The Lord my God will come and all the holy ones with him." Zech. 14:5b	"May he strengthen your hearts so that you will be blameless and holy in the presence of our God and Father when our Lord Jesus comes with all his holy ones." 1 Thes. 3:13
"I am God Almighty." Genesis 17:1	"The Lamb...had seven horns." Rev 5:6. The number seven means all, total, absolute, and a horn is a symbol of power. Therefore, this means that the Lamb is Almighty.
The prophet Isaiah was shown a vision of Jehovah. Isaiah 6:1,10	John applies that vision to Jesus-John 12: 40,41

Now He is called Jesus

Jehovah was the name given to Jesus in the Old Testament. The Father rarely spoke in the Scriptures. God spoke through the prophets and, in many instances in the Old Testament, it was Jesus pre-incarnated who spoke. Jesus is the spokesperson for the Divinity according to Hebrews 1:1, 2. This is why the first chapter of John calls him the Word. Consider these two parallel passages from Jeremiah regarding the Messiah and how He would be called:

"Behold, the days come, saith the LORD, that I will raise unto David a righteous Branch, and a King shall reign and prosper, and shall execute judgment and justice in the earth. In his days Judah shall be saved, and Israel shall dwell safely: and this is his name whereby he shall be called, THE LORD OUR RIGHTEOUSNESS" (Jeremiah 23:5, 6).

"Behold, the days come, saith the LORD, that I will perform that good thing which I have promised unto the house of Israel and to the house of Judah. In those days, and at that time, will I cause the Branch of righteousness to grow up unto David; and he shall execute judgment and righteousness in the land In those days shall Judah be saved, and Jerusalem shall dwell safely: and this is the name wherewith she shall be called, The LORD our righteousness" (Jeremiah 33:14-16).

The Hebrew world used for Lord in both passages is יהוה (Yod, He, Waw and He), which is found in some Bible versions rendered as Jehovah (y^ehôvâh). These four letters are known as the tetragrammaton (Greek term for a four-letter word). Since the Hebrew words are read right to left, the four letters transliterated into English are: YHWH (pronounced Yahweh). The vowels were added lately because the Hebrew alphabet (known as Alephbet for its first two letters, aleph and bet) only consisted of consonants (22 in total). A careful analysis of the Hebrew indicates that the pronunciation of the tetragrammaton cannot be Jehovah, as this was a misinterpretation. The name Yahweh is most likely the correct pronunciation or the closest, being that the Hebrew people took extreme measures to ensure that no gentile ever attempted to pronounce the sacred name. However, in reality no one can be 100% sure of the correct pronunciation of the Sacred name, since there were no vowels and the pronunciation of the consonants may have changed over the centuries. One thing I know for sure: if we approach Him with a humble and grateful heart, He will listen to our prayers and He will be understanding of our incapability to pronounce His name correctly, which is to be expected with so many languages and dialects in the world.

What thou seest, write in a book, and send it unto the seven churches which are in Asia -John had been exiled to Patmos because of his faith. That island was used as a quarry and was 80 miles from Ephesus. Sending a messenger from Patmos to Ephesus and around to the church in Laodicea, the messenger would have travel in a circle to return to Patmos with a good report from his trip. That is also how the Word of God is. *"So shall my word be that goeth forth out of my mouth: it shall not return unto me void, but it shall accomplish that which I please, and it shall prosper in the thing whereto I sent it"* Isaiah 55:11.

12*And I turned to <u>see the voice</u> that spake with me. And being turned, I saw seven golden candlesticks*

"See the voice." Doesn't that sound awkward? To see a sound? We **<u>hear</u>** a sound. We do not **<u>see</u>** a sound. John uses this phrase to prepare us for another occurrence of the phrase in chapter seven when he describes the 144,000. Please keep that in mind.

[13]And in the midst of the seven candlesticks one like unto the Son of man, clothed with a garment down to the foot, and girt about the paps with a golden girdle.

Seven is a representative number. The seven candlesticks are defined as the churches of the cities above mentioned (see verse 11 and then 20). Why the candlesticks? Because Jesus said that we are the light of the world (Matthew 5:14-16). His light shines through us.

[14]His head and his hairs were white like wool, as white as snow; and his eyes were as a flame of fire; [15]And his feet like unto fine brass, as if they burned in a furnace; and his voice as the sound of many waters.

These three preceding verses are similar to Daniel 10:5 & 6.

Daniel 10	Revelation 1	Symbol
a certain man	*one like unto the Son of man*	Jesus the Son of man (Gospel of Luke)
clothed in linen	*clothed with a garment down to the foot*	Priestly clothes. Linen represents righteousness- Revelation 19:8
loins were girded with fine gold	*girt about the paps with a golden girdle*	"**righteousness** shall be the girdle of his loins, **and faithfulness** the girdle of his reins." Isaiah 11:5
his eyes as lamps of fire	*his eyes were as a flame of fire*	Eyes that can see the darkest secrets. Jeremiah 16:17
his feet like in colour to polished brass	*his feet like unto fine brass, as if they burned in a furnace*	Jesus was going to identify Himself with those that were going to be burned at the stake for their faith. He wanted them to know that He was going to be there with them. His presence sustained them. That is why those martyrs died singing.

the voice of his words like the voice of a multitude	*his voice as the sound of many waters*	"...I heard the noise of their wings, like the noise of great waters, as the voice of the Almighty..." Ezekiel 1:24

like wool, as white as snow -There is a verse with the same words in the Old Testament: *"Come now, and let us reason together, saith the LORD: though your sins be as scarlet, they shall be as white as snow; though they be red like crimson, they shall be as wool"* (Isaiah 1:18). Our forgiveness of sin is so complete that we are seeing by God at the same level of purity and holiness than Jesus- like if we had never sinned!

16And he had in his right hand seven stars: and out of his mouth went a sharp two edged sword: and his countenance was as the sun shineth in his strength.

Seven stars- In the book of Daniel chapter 12 it is written that those that teach righteousness to many will shine like the stars. Verse 20 of this first chapter of Revelation indicates that the stars are a symbol of the angels of the seven churches. We know that God sends human beings to reach human beings. The word angel means messenger. Those seven angels were the preachers of the seven churches. There are presented as being in His hand as an indication of His constant protection. Jesus said about those that hear His voice: *"And I give unto them eternal life; and they shall never perish, neither shall any man pluck them out of my hand"* (John 10:28). In addition, the image represents caring love: *"See, I have engraved you on the palms of my hands; your walls are ever before me"* (Isaiah 49:16 *New International Version -NIV*).

"two edged sword" Paul also mentioned this symbol for the word of God in Hebrews 4:12: *"For the word of God is quick, and powerful, and sharper than any two edged sword, piercing even to the dividing asunder of soul and spirit, and of the joints and marrow, and is a discerner of the thoughts and intents of the heart."* Jesus declared "He that rejecteth me, and receiveth not my words, hath one that judgeth him: the word that I have spoken, the same shall judge him in the last day" (John 12:48). Depending on your choice, one edge

of the sword can carve the sin out of your life, or the other can cut you off from the book of life in the judgment.

There is another mention of Jesus shining as the sun in Matthew 17:2: *"And was transfigured before them: and his face did shine as the sun, and his raiment was white as the light."* He appeared as He will be seen when He comes in His glory.

17And when I saw him, I fell at his feet as dead. And he laid his right hand upon me, saying unto me, Fear not; <u>I am the first and the last</u>:

John had the same reaction as Daniel. We cannot contemplate the holiness of God without feeling the misery, nakedness and sinfulness of our human nature. With Isaiah, we will say *"Then said I, Woe is me! for I am undone; because I am a man of unclean lips, and I dwell in the midst of a people of unclean lips: for mine eyes have seen the King, the LORD of hosts"* (Isaiah 1:5).

18I am he that liveth, and was dead; and, behold, I am alive for evermore, Amen; and have the keys of hell and of death. Jesus is presented as God in verse 17 and as a man in verse 18.

John believed that Christ destroyed the chains of the tomb. He knew that Christ had resurrected. He also knew that Jesus was alive and that in the same way that death could not hold Christ, it would not be able to keep prisoners those that believe in Him. With Job, he could say: *"And after my skin is destroyed, this I know, That in my flesh I shall see God"* (Job 19:26 NKJV). *"But your dead will live; their bodies will rise. You who dwell in the dust, wake up and shout for joy. Your dew is like the dew of the morning; the earth will give birth to her dead"* (Isaiah 26:19).

Now, how do you and I, two thousand years after the fact, can have the assurance that Jesus' death and resurrection are not a fairy tale? First, let us examine the facts surrounding his death:

- Jesus was crucified, not only according to his disciples but also on the account of secular writers of that time.
- No one ever survived being crucified.
- The Roman soldiers stayed with the victim until they were sure the condemned did die.

- The excruciating torment of the cross made it very difficult to breathe and this was after Jesus was beaten 3 times and not allowed to eat or rest all night. From the medical standpoint, it would have been impossible for Him to survive, especially after being pierced on an upward angle with a spear that would have penetrated one of His lungs first and then the heart. The position in which Jesus was crucified made His system accumulate water, which was suffocating Him and eventually would have caused a massive heart attack.
- The reaction of the disciples after the crucifixion- they went on hiding and the Scriptures say that they were "assembled for fear of the Jews" (John 20:19). If Jesus were alive, they would have been rejoicing, planning their future together. Instead, they were heart-broken, sadness-stricken, cowering in the corners for fear to be next.

How about the resurrection? Do we have reliable evidence that it indeed happen? What would the disciples have to gain with making up a story about Him being resurrected? In first place, were they a bunch of masochists, seeking thrill through being rejected, persecuted, tortured and killed? No, they were not. They were sane people that worry about what they were leaving behind (the cost of discipleship) to follow Christ. "Then answered Peter and said unto him, Behold, we have forsaken all, and followed thee; what shall we have therefore?" (Matthew 19:27). In other words, they were worrying about the benefits and bonuses of the job. They did not bargain for persecution, perils and death. If Jesus did not resurrect, why would they lie about it risking so much? How much time would pass before one of them broke under pressure and confessed the scheme? All the disciples were not only persecuted but also incarcerated and eleven (counting Paul) of them were killed. John was the only one that escaped death (miraculously) and died close to 100 years old, but not without suffering his share of troubles and persecution.

The eleven men that had been in hiding for all that tragic weekend lost all fear after the resurrection and became emboldened and fearless missionaries to the end of the world. By the way, I have never seen an atheist going to the end of the world to do what David Livingston did, much less with the spirit of self-sacrifice that he showed. Neither have I heard of an alcoholic becoming sober after reading Marx. There must be something special in that book that changes lives for the better. For all I know, after Marx read the book of Darwin, went on to write his own (The Communist Manifesto) and the world changed for the worst. The Bible is not only a book that can change lives for the better, but also improve circumstances. If that book has such power, I am sure it also tells the truth about the resurrection of Christ.

Could it have been a case of mass hallucinations as some naively claim? It would be something like this: "Do you see what I see?" "I do..." "Me too." "I see it too." If more that one person is seeing something, then it is not a hallucination, since these experiences vary from person to person and cannot be canned to ensure everyone will see the same thing. First Corinthians 15:6 tells us that over 500 people saw Jesus resurrected. Only a person unwilling to recognize the truth for the sake of pride would concoct such a bizarre argument of "mass hallucinations."

The account of the contemporary writers does not contradict the resurrection. Pilate and Herod could have attempted to deny it but they did not. The Sanhedrin only offered an initial bribe to the soldiers so they would lie about the resurrection, but nowhere does it say that they persisted in doing so. Had any point of the Gospels account on the resurrection be false, the Jewish society would not have rested until the scammers would be exposed, tried and even executed. The fact that the Gospels identify the tomb's owner as a Jewish Sanhedrin member named Joseph of Arimathea, is a solid evidence that Jesus died and was buried and now that tomb is empty. Had the claim that one of the Sanhedrin members owned the grave where Jesus' body had been kept being false, and that the body of Christ disappeared from it, that body of authority would not have wasted any time to disprove the claims. The submission of the name of Joseph in written form was an intentional proof that went undenied because it could not be. If anyone wanted to have the story verified, all they had to do was to go to Joseph's property and see the track indicating the moving of the rock that covered the entrance to the tomb and the broken Roman seal that was placed on it. If the evidence did not back up the claim, it would have been impossible to keep preaching the resurrection. The absolute Sanhedrin's silence is an evidence on the side of the resurrection. Furthermore, would anyone dare to steal the body from the Roman guard- the best-trained army in the world? Not a chance! The Sanhedrin wanted the soldiers to tell everyone that Jesus' body had been stolen while they slept. The penalty for them losing the body for falling asleep would have been instant execution. Did the Sanhedrin hide the body? Less likely. Besides, if they did hide it, why didn't they produce it when Peter was preaching and brought 3,000 and 5,000 people to believe in the resurrection? See Acts 4:2,4. How about in the subsequent festivities that brought worshippers from all the corners of the planet? They could have mummified the body of Jesus to present it in those holidays and very soon, no one would dare to say that He was resurrected.

Would the disciples dare to steal the body from the fierce and fearless Roman guards, well armed with sharp swords and spears and rigorously trained for battle? I feel like laughing at this one. The disciples were in hiding for fear of the arm-less Jews (John 20:19). If they were cowardly hiding from the Jews, how could they find valor to confront armed soldiers that would not think twice of cutting them up in half? Obviously, those who teach that the resurrection never happened not only have a great imagination but also poor reasoning and defective use of logic.

How about if a look-alike (an impostor) took the place of Jesus to deceive the disciples? This is very unlikely since the disciples had spent three and a half years in daily contact with Jesus and would have recognized him by either his mannerisms, his voice or any physical difference on the face or body built. This was also very difficult to copy (and painful) because the disciples saw the wounds in Jesus' hands and side. Thomas even touched them, so we cannot claim that it was stage makeup.

Some people even claim that Jesus just fainted on the cross and later taken somewhere to recover. Really? Were the Roman soldiers that dumb that could not know the difference between a dead person and one that just fainted? The Bible portrays one of the ways they assured themselves that the prisoners were dead: they broke their legs to make it impossible to breathe. Once the legs were broken, the condemned asphyxiated. However, when they came to break Jesus' legs, they found that He was already dead.

Just to make sure that He was, a soldier pierced Him with his spear in His heart. If He was fainted, it lasted only until that spear went through His side. To confirm His death, the Bible tells us that out came blood and water (John 19:34). The water was a product of the congestive heart failure that Jesus developed while on the cross. There was no way that His death and resurrections were faked.

[19]Write the things which thou hast seen, and the things which are, and the things which shall be hereafter;

John was encouraged to write everything shown him, except the vision of chapter 10. We see here how God inspired His Prophets. He showed them visions and allowed His servants to write in their own words what they saw.

[20]The mystery of the seven stars which thou sawest in my right hand, and the seven golden candlesticks. The seven stars are the angels of the seven churches: and the seven candlesticks which thou sawest are the seven churches.

The preceding verse was explained above.

*For more information on how God changed Sam Tannyhill, read the book *Three Hours to Live*. Here is the information on the book from the publisher (Pacific Press) website:

"His troubled childhood brought him into contact with the wrong crowd, and his brushes with the law became bolder and more frequent. Then, in 1955, a botched robbery attempt in Fremont, Ohio, cost a waitress her life, and Sam was convicted of first-degree murder and sentenced to die in the electric chair. But before the chair ended his earthly life, Jesus Christ gave Sam Tannyhill a new one. Told through the eyewitness account of Faith For Today founder William Fagal, Three Hours to Live is the classic true story of how God's grace transformed the life of a condemned criminal. The story of Sam Tannyhill has just as much power to move hearts today as it did when it was first published in 1967. Though his voice has long been stilled, the miraculous change in Sam's life will be a powerful witness to draw men and women to the Savior for years to come."

REVELATION 2

The letters to the seven churches- part I

The letters to the seven churches were addressed to real churches in the times of John. Each one had characteristics that described their historic, social and spiritual condition at the time the letter was written, but also each church description represents a specific period in the history of the church all the way to the end of the world. They constitute a timeline that accurately paints the spiritual relationship that prevailed at different times in history. The meaning of each church's name has a spiritual message too. These are the churches presented in chapter two:

Church	Meaning	Dates	Problem	Promise to those that overcome
Ephesus	Desirable	31-100 AD	Lost first love	Tree of life
Smyrna	Sweet fragrance	100-313 AD	None	Crown of life, escape 2nd death
Pergamos	Exaltation	313-538 AD	Tolerance of idolatry and immorality	Hidden manna, white stone, new name
Thyatira	Sweet savor of sacrifice	538-1517	Tolerance of idolatry and immorality	Power over the nations

[1]Unto the angel of the church of Ephesus write; These things saith he that holdeth the seven stars in his right hand, who walketh in the midst of the seven golden candlesticks;

We indicated in chapter one that the angel of the church was the preacher in charge of that congregation, since the word angel means messenger, and God gave us- not the angels- the ministry of reconciliation. The name Ephesus signifies desirable. This represents the church from the year 31 AD When Jesus died) to 100 AD (when John the Revelator died). Jesus is presented here again (as a reminder) as holding the church leaders in his right hand and walking among the churches. Jesus shows Himself as holding the preachers of the churches in His powerful right hand. As long as they are faithful to Him, He will keep them. John 10:28

says: *"And I give unto them eternal life; and they shall never perish, neither shall any man pluck them out of my hand."* His protection and companionship are constant. Let us rejoice because He is close to us: *"...though he be not far from every one of us"* (Acts 17:27).

"in the midst of the seven golden candlesticks"- The candlesticks were located in the holy department of the sanctuary. Here Jesus is presented as our High Priest in the heavenly sanctuary.

[2]I know thy works, and thy labour, and thy patience, and how thou canst not bear them which are evil: and thou hast tried them which say they are apostles, and are not, and hast found them liars:

"I know" is a common phrase in the messages to all the churches. God is omniscient and He knows everything about us. The Scriptures show that He knows how many hairs are in our head and all the secrets in our hearts. *"Shall not God search this out? for he knoweth the secrets of the heart"* (Psalm 44:21). *"Fear them not therefore: for there is nothing covered, that shall not be revealed; and hid, that shall not be known."* (Matthew 10:26). We could live a life that amazes others, but God knows the motives of our hearts. The day of judgment will reveal all the secrets of the hearts. First Chronicles 28:9 says, in the words of David to Solomon: *"...for the LORD searcheth all hearts, and understandeth all the imaginations of the thoughts."* We need to strive to allow Jesus to live His life through us as Paul wrote: *"I am crucified with Christ: nevertheless I live; yet not I, but <u>Christ liveth in me</u>: and the life which I now live in the flesh I live by the faith of the Son of God, who loved me, and gave himself for me"* (Galatians 2:20).

How well does God know us? He even knows our address and what activities we do: *"And the Lord said unto him, Arise, and go into the street which is called Straight, and enquire in the house of Judas for one called Saul, of Tarsus: for, behold, he prayeth"* (Acts 9:11).

Jesus is aware of everything that goes on in a church, as this passage indicates. He knows if there is jealousy, competition, discrimination, tyranny, oligarchy or hypocrisy. In the time He was on this earth, there were many of those in His church but he still went (Luke 4:16). Regardless of how bad the situation is in your church, do not stop going and keep loving each one of them even if they have been hurtful. Keep on praying for those members and ask God for a revival and reformation, specifically, that they begin with you. Go to the church to be a blessing to others and you will be blessed.

He also knows the pain of our hearts. He was there when Agar thought that she and her son would die of thirst and provided them water (Genesis 21:14-19). One of my favorite verses is Psalm 56:8: *"Thou tellest my wanderings: put thou my tears into thy bottle: are they not in thy book?"* There is no wrong done to us, no heartache that He would not know about. God sympathizes with our situations. I imagine this was what inspired Paul to write: *"Rejoice with them that do rejoice, and weep with them that weep"* (Romans 12:15). Isaiah had a similar thought: *"In all their affliction he was afflicted, and the angel of his presence saved them: in his love and in his pity he redeemed them; and he bare them, and carried them all the days of old"* (Isaiah 63:9). Do you have a heavy burden? Jesus can remove it from your shoulders (Matthew 11:28). Are you tired, overwhelmed, of fighting your problems or temptations? He can carry you and give you peace (John 14:27). He knows if you lost your job or your home, if you are going through a divorce, or if a loved one just died. It does not escape His knowledge if your dear children are alcohol or drug users. Regardless of the circumstances you are going through, He offers you His loving embrace. You can be assured that He feels your pain and can give you His comforting love.

"hast tried them which say they are apostles, and are not, and hast found them liars" Satan had always infiltrated the church with his spies since the beginning of church history. That is why 1 John 4:1 tells us to test the spirits: *"Dear friends, do not believe every spirit, but test the spirits to see whether they are from God, because many false prophets have gone out into the world"* (1 John 4:1). Paul added: *"Prove all things; hold fast that which is good"* (1 Thessalonians 5:21). It is our responsibility to compare everything that we hear or read with the Scriptures regardless of who said it or wrote it, be it a friend, relative or even our pastor or a famous evangelist. When Paul went to Berea, the believers did not take his word at face value until they could verify his teachings with the Scriptures. *"These were more noble than those in Thessalonica, in that they received the word with all readiness of mind, and searched the scriptures daily, whether*

those things were so" (Acts 17:11). Can you imagine questioning Paul? Yet they did so and Paul commended them for doing it. Therefore, I, a lot less than Paul, expect that you compare what I wrote here with the Scriptures. I feel sad when I see Christians going to church without a Bible and when the truth is presented to them, they reply saying: "Let me ask my pastor," instead of "let me pray and check my Bible."

[3]And hast borne, and hast patience, and for my name's sake hast laboured, and hast not fainted.

"And hast borne"- or "have endured hardships" (NIV). As mentioned above, He knows all our challenges. He also knows all of our victories and acts of bravery and faithfulness. This world might never recognize our good deeds done in the love of Christ, but they are written in the book on heaven: *"Then they that feared the LORD spake often one to another: and the LORD hearkened, and heard it, and a book of remembrance was written before him for them that feared the LORD, and that thought upon his name."* (Mal 3:16)

[4]Nevertheless I have somewhat against thee, because thou hast left thy first love.

One of the most beautiful things that can happen to us is to fall in love. That person suddenly becomes the center of our existence. Everything we do revolve around that person. When we see a beautiful sunset or we contemplate any other marvel of nature, we wish to have that special someone there to see it too. When we first get to know Jesus and we find that He is all-desirable, we want to spend time with Him and we tell people about Him. *"Like an apple tree among the trees of the forest is my lover among the young men. <u>I delight to sit in his shade</u>, and his fruit is sweet to my taste"* (Song of Solomon 2:3 NIV). But how sad is when we lose that love. Like with our earthly relationships, we separate and eventually we could even divorce our Lord. To stop loving Jesus means that a person just goes through the church rituals but there is no heart connection. Everything becomes a mere formalism. *"These people come near to me with their mouth and honor me with their lips, but their hearts are far from me"* (Isaiah 29:13 NIV).That fall is not sudden. It is gradual. Along the way, God gives us warnings to help us to return. Sometimes we get those warnings through dreams. At times, it is through friends. Unfortunately, we often perceive those warnings as intrusions and we think that the other person is being judgmental.

[5]Remember therefore from whence thou art fallen, and repent, and do the first works; or else I will come unto thee quickly, and will remove thy candlestick out of his place, except thou repent.

"Remember therefore from whence thou art fallen, and repent, and do the first works." There are three words in imperative: remember, repent, and do the first works. Although there is an order to return to our roots in our relationship with Jesus, to the time when we fell in love with Him, there is no lack of divine mercy mixed with the requirement. It is not a harsh authoritative order dictated by a tyrant, but rather, the love of our tender savior permeates in these words. They are more of an invitation to restore the lost relationship. Jesus always offers His mercy to those that are errant. The divine shepherd always looks for ways to restore the lost sheep to the fold. The call to repent is not to say a simple childish "I am sorry," because it requires a recognition of wrongdoing, a change of attitude and of direction. It is doing an about-face and turning our backs on sin of thoughts and behavior. Notice that the verse mentions the word repent twice, while do appears only once. This is because we cannot do the works of God, if repentance has not been experienced.

Are you cold in your relationship with God? He longs to take you back. He misses you and tenderly bids you to return to Him and be saved. He is willing to forgive all our sins. *"If thou return to the Almighty, thou shalt be built up..."* (Job 22:23). *"It may be that the house of Judah will hear all the evil which I purpose to do unto them; that they may return every man from his evil way; that I may forgive their iniquity and their sin"* (Jeremiah 36:3). *"Have I any pleasure at all that the wicked should die? Saith the Lord GOD: and not that he should return from his ways, and live?"* (Ezekiel 18:23). Jesus always offers His mercy to those that are errant. The divine shepherd always looks for ways to restore the lost sheep to the fold.

"...do the first works". The church of this period was not lacking works. When Paul wrote to the Colossians, he wrote that the gospel had been *"preached to every creature which is under heaven"* (Colossians 1:23). The missionary zeal of the primitive church lead

them to every corner of the planet to preach Jesus to the lost. It is believed that the gospel was even preached in China and that some of the old Chinese characters present the salvation message. The problem of this church was the motivation for those works. Love was supposed to provide the drive: *"For Christ's love compels us, because we are convinced that one died for all, and therefore all died"* (2 Corinthians 5:14). At the end of the first century, they have lost their first love. They now were formalists. They did things because they were supposed to do them and not because they wanted from the bottom of their hearts to do them. What motivates you, wife and mother to serve your family? What motivates you, husband to provide for your family? What makes you son or daughter to obey and help your parents? If the incentive is duty, or you see it as an obligation, that is not love. Love is about giving without expecting any benefit. We all know John 3:16: "For God so loved the world that He gave...."

"And do the first works" Even though we are not saved by works, they are considered an undeniable proof of what is in the heart. *"For by grace are ye saved through faith; and that not of yourselves: it is the gift of God: Not of works, lest any man should boast. For we are his workmanship, created in Christ Jesus unto good works, which God hath before ordained that we should walk in them."* Ephesians 2:8-10.

6But this thou hast, that thou hatest the deeds of the Nicolaitanes, which I also hate.

Who were the Nicolaitanes? They taught that the law of God has been abolished and no longer binding. This was one of the first attempts to do away with the seventh-day Sabbath. They also claimed that the clergy were superior to the laity and should rule over them. This teaching set the base for the Catholic priesthood rulership. The Bible teaches that we all are a nation of royal priests (1 Peter 2:9). They also taught that what they did with their bodies did no affect their salvation, so they practiced immorality.

7He that hath an ear, let him hear what the Spirit saith unto the churches; To him that overcometh will I give to eat of the tree of life, which is in the midst of the paradise of God.

All the messages to the seven churches end with the phrase *"He that hath an ear, let him hear what the Spirit saith unto the churches"* and all receive a promise for those that overcome. This invitation is given to all the seven churches. His voice is shown in the Scriptures as guiding His people and tenderly inviting us to repent. *"Therefore say to the house of Israel, 'This is what the Sovereign LORD says: Repent! Turn from your idols and renounce all your detestable practices!' "*(Ezekiel 14:6). *"Say to them, 'As surely as I live, declares the Sovereign LORD, I take no pleasure in the death of the wicked, but rather that they turn from their ways and live. Turn! Turn from your evil ways! Why will you die, O house of Israel?'"* (Ezekiel 33:11).*"For he is our God; and we are the people of his pasture, and the sheep of his hand. Today, if ye will hear his voice, harden not your heart, as in the provocation, and as in the day of temptation in the wilderness"* (Psalm 95:7,8). Regardless of the condition of the church in some periods, God still had people faithful to Him, just like in times of the prophet Elijah. When the servant of God thought that he was the only believer left, God told him that He had 7,000 that had remained faithful in the midst of a great time of apostasy. God does not only asks us to be perfect (Matthew 5:48), but also gives us the wisdom and strength to overcome the natural inclinations to sin. He does not have to add any promises or incentives, but He is generous and wants to give us more than forgiveness. He also wants to be close to us and He will bring us to live in His presence *"in the midst of the paradise of God."* I am looking forward to eating the fruit of that tree, regardless of what flavor or shape. I am sure that it will taste better that my favorite fruits, such as mango and passion fruit. The fact that I am invited to be there with Jesus is more than enough encouragement to be faithful.

"To him that overcometh" The Greek is in the present active tense, which indicates a continuous and deliberate action. In other words, "continue to overcome daily." This in itself is a promise, for God does not make requirements without providing assistance for us to get the victory. There is in this verb the element of purpose. We cannot obtain the victory as spectators. We must want the victory and allow our Commander to lead us to obtain it. We must- as Christ told His disciples- carry our crosses daily.

8And unto the angel of the church in Smyrna write; These things saith the first and the last, which was dead, and is alive;

Smyrna is an ancient Greek word that means sweet smelling and it is related to myrrh. Just as myrrh was used in the formulation of incense, the Christians of this period were going to be sacrificed for their faith. Myrrh is one of the bitterest spices but also produces a great aroma when it is crushed. In the same manner, the tests that we go through in our lives are all bitter but at the end produce a sweet smell that glorifies God. When we share the knowledge of God with others, it is like if we perfume their lives. *"But thanks be to God, who always leads us in triumphal procession in Christ and through us spreads everywhere the fragrance of the knowledge of him. For we are to God the aroma of Christ among those who are being saved and those who are perishing."* (2 Corinthians 2:14,15 NIV).

Smyrna was located 35 miles north of Ephesus. It is believed that the city grew to about 100,000 in the first century AD. This church corresponds to the period of 100 AD to 313 AD and the period is known as the age of the martyrs. The state persecuted Christians and they were killed for refusing to recant their beliefs. The Roman government arrested, judged, condemned and executed the followers of Jesus but that made the church grow. For those that would be killed, Jesus reminded them that He had been dead but was alive again. His resurrection was the guarantee of theirs.

"the first and the last" -Jesus identifies Himself with a divine title from the Old Testament because at that time in the history of the church Arius was claiming that Jesus was created.

[9]I know thy works, and tribulation, and poverty, (but thou art rich) and I know the blasphemy of them which say they are Jews, and are not, but are the synagogue of Satan.

The word *tribulation* implies being under a crushing weight, while the word *poverty* describes total indigence. The persecuted church was needy (Paul had organized a collection for the saints), but they were reminded that they were laying treasures in heaven. Jesus had made a wonderful promise to His disciples: *"And everyone who has left houses or brothers or sisters or father or mother or children or fields for my sake will receive a* ***hundred*** *times as much and will inherit eternal life."* (Matthew 19:29). Paul contrasted what Jesus was before His incarnation with what we are going to received from Him: *"For you know the grace of our Lord Jesus Christ, that though he was rich, yet for your sakes he became poor, so that you through his poverty might become rich."* (2 Corinthians 8:9). James 2:5 indicates that God has chosen the poor of this world to be rich in faith and to inherit the kingdom promised to those that love Him. The Bible tells us that the streets of the New Jerusalem will be made of pure gold (Revelation 21:21), so if that is the material that we are to walk on, just imagine the enormous riches to be enjoyed there.

"them which say they are Jews, and are not" When Satan cannot destroy the church through persecution, he tries to destroy it from the inside with heresy. Paul wrote that Satan's *"mysterious power is already at work, but someone is holding him back. And the wicked one won't appear until that someone is out of the way."* (2 Thessalonians 2:7). All throughout history, many had joined the church to act as spies for the government. Such was the case in those early times, which forced the church to go underground. It was also a common practice in the middle ages when the established church wanted to destroy those that sustained the message of righteousness by faith. Such has also been the case in recent times in Russia, China and Cuba. The false church also has infiltrated the Protestant churches with her spies. In some cases, there were men and women that concocted strange ideas or told lies that resulted in divisions, confusion and ruined reputations. Fortunately, God can transform each of these challenges into blessings and miraculously the church always grows.

Who was the one holding Satan's earthly partner back? Many have argued about the identity of that character with some believing that it refers to the Holy Spirit, others Paul, or John. However, Tertullian, a Christian apologist from the second century wrote accurately: "He who now hinders, must hinder until he be taken out of the way. What obstacle is there but the Roman State? The falling away of which, by being scattered into ten kingdoms, shall introduce antichrist" (Tertullian, *On the Resurrection, chapter 24*).

The word Jews here is figurative. Paul wrote that it is not a Jew the one according to the flesh, but according to the spirit (Romans 2:28,29). In other passages like Romans 9:6, 7; Galatians 3:28,29;

1 Cor. 12:13 and Colossians 3:11, Paul indicated that there is no distinction between Jew and Gentile. We are now one. We are sons of Abraham and we constitute spiritual Israel. John the Baptist told the multitudes in Israel by the Jordan river and the Roman soldiers there present to: *"Bring forth therefore fruits worthy of repentance, and begin not to say within yourselves, We have Abraham to our father: for I say unto you, that God is able of these stones to raise up children unto Abraham. And now also the axe is laid unto the root of the trees: every tree therefore which bringeth not forth good fruit is hewn down, and cast into the fire"* (Luke 3:8,9). The nation of Israel rejected God's plan of salvation. God would eventually give the torch to other people who became spiritual children of Abraham. We need to remember this for our study on Revelation chapters 7 and 14.

10 Fear none of those things which thou shalt suffer: behold, the devil shall cast some of you into prison, that ye may be tried; and ye shall have tribulation ten days: be thou faithful unto death, and I will give thee a crown of life.

Fear, be it of disease, unemployment, poverty, relationship problems, or any other kind, is one of the biggest walls that we can build between an all-powerful God and us. *"But now, this is what the LORD says—he who created you, O Jacob, he who formed you, O Israel: "**Fear not**, for I have redeemed you; I have summoned you by name; you are mine."* (Isaiah 43:1 NIV).

"When John said that some will be thrown into prison he knew that Roman imprisonment was frequently a prelude to execution. He encouraged the believers to be faithful even unto death. In this persecution, John's own apprentice, Polycarp, was martyred here in 155 A.D. An example of John's warning and exhortation, he refused to blaspheme the Lord's name and was subsequently burned alive." http://www.bibleplaces.com/smyrna.htm

When we fear only God, it shows. There is a story that comes to my mind regarding one of the experiences that brought conversion to John Wesley, the founder of the Methodist Church. "Wesley returned to England depressed and beaten. It was at this point that he turned to the Moravians. Wesley had encountered the Moravians three years earlier on his voyage to Georgia. At one point in the voyage a storm came up and broke the mast off the ship. While the English aboard all panicked the Moravians calmly sang hymns and prayed. This experience led Wesley to believe that the Moravians possessed an inner strength which he lacked." http://www.answers.com/topic/john-wesley. That strength was the absolute trust in the power of God to save those that He loves. It is also the assurance that if we lose our lives here doing His will, He will raise us up again with immortal bodies to live in a perfect world.

"ye shall have tribulation ten days" -A day in prophecy is equivalent to a year (Numbers 14:34; Ezekiel 4:6). The ten days tribulation happened under Emperor Diocletian from 303-313 AD. His edict ordered the destruction of Christian scriptures and churches, prohibited Christian assemblies, and eliminated various legal rights from the Christians that refused to renounce Christ. Life was not easy for them as it is not for us today. Jesus never promised a trouble-free life. He is not the one constantly producing difficulties, but He promises to be with us. Our attitude must be of complete surrender to His will and wisdom and He will see us through any tribulation. *"We are like clay jars in which this treasure is stored. <u>The real power comes from God</u> and not from us. We often suffer, but we are never crushed. Even when we do not know what to do, we never give up. <u>In times of trouble, God is with us</u>, and when we are knocked down, we get up again. We face death every day because of Jesus. Our bodies show what his death was like, so that his life can also be seen in us"* (2 Corinthians 4:7-10 *Contemporary English Version*). The *1965 Bible in Basic English* translates verse 9 as follows: *"We are cruelly attacked, but not without hope; we are made low, but we are not without help."*

Crown- from the Greek *stephanos*. It was the crown given in the Olympic Games and to public servants as a recognition for having done a good job. Paul, in agreement with John, wrote: *"Now there is laid up for me the crown of righteousness, which the Lord, the righteous Judge, shall give me at that Day; and not to me only, but also to all those who love His appearing"* (2 Timothy 4:8 *Modern King James Version*). And James reemphasized the promised: *"How blessed is the man who endures temptation! When he has passed the test, he will receive the victor's crown of life that God has promised to those who keep on loving him"* (James 1:12 International Standard

Version). We must persevere because the promises of God will never fail.

"Affliction, persecution, sickness, etc., may be regarded as, in a certain sense, temptations to sin; that is, the question comes before us whether we will adhere to the religion on account of which we are persecuted, or apostatize from it, and escape these sufferings; whether in sickness and losses we will be patient and submissive to that God who lays his hand upon us, or revolt and murmur. In each and every case, whether by affliction, or by direct allurements to do wrong, the question comes before the mind whether we have religion enough to keep us, or whether we will yield to murmuring, to rebellion, and to sin. In these respects, in a general sense, all forms of trial may be regarded as temptation. Yet in the following verse (James1:13) the apostle would guard this from abuse. So far as the form of trial involved an allurement or inducement to sin, he says that no man should regard it as from God. That cannot be his design. The trial is what he aims at, not the sin. In the verse before us he says, that whatever may be the form of the trial, a Christian should rejoice in it, for it will furnish an evidence that he is a child of God" (*Albert Barnes' Notes on the Bible*).

The trials that we suffer here will be of short, insignificant duration compared to the vastness of eternity. *"For I reckon that the sufferings of <u>this present time</u> are not worthy to be compared with the glory which shall be revealed in us"* (Romans 8:18). *"For our light affliction, which is but <u>for a moment</u>, worketh for us a far more exceeding and eternal weight of glory"* (2 Corinthians 4:17). While I write this, I am going through trials myself, but I am resting on the faithful promises of God and have decided to trust Him regardless of what lays ahead. He has been with me in the past and I am certain that He will intervene on my behalf again and open new doors for me. After all, who is born in this world and is exempt from suffering in one way or the other? We all suffer disease, separation, loss and many more forms of hardships. Regardless of what afflicts us we count on a merciful God to intervene on our behalf and either change things around or to give us His grace to withstand the most challenging situations. *"And the God of peace will be crushing Satan under your feet <u>before long</u>. The grace of our Lord Jesus Christ be with you"* (Romans 16:20, *1965 BBE*).

[11]He that hath an ear, let him hear what the Spirit saith unto the churches; He that overcometh shall not be hurt of the second death.

The second death is eternal separation from the Father; it is the death that Jesus suffered on the cross on our behalf. Those that accept Jesus as Savior and Lord will be spared from it. *"Blessed and holy are those who have part in the first resurrection. The second death has no power over them"* (Revelation 20:6 NIV). The Bible also mentions being cast into the *"fiery lake of burning sulfur"* (Revelation 21:8) as the second death.

[12]And to the angel of the church in Pergamos write; These things saith he which hath the sharp sword with two edges;

Pergamos means exaltation. This was the time when Sunday was exalted as a day of rest and the bishop of Rome as the head of Christianity. Constantine's "Edict of Milan" (313 AD) marked the end of the ten-year persecution initiated by Diocletian. The emperor "converted" to Christianity and made it the state religion, thus exalting it. The sword mentioned here is the penetrating Word of God. The sword of the state now was sovereign but Jesus wanted to remind everyone listening that His sword was the final authority. *"For the word of God is quick, and powerful, and sharper than any two-edged sword, piercing even to the dividing asunder of soul and spirit, and of the joints and marrow, and is a discerner of the thoughts and intents of the heart"* (Hebrews 4:12).

[13]I know thy works, and where thou dwellest, even where Satan's seat is: and thou holdest fast my name, and hast not denied my faith, even in those days wherein Antipas was my faithful martyr, who was slain among you, where Satan dwelleth.

Antipas- "It is supposed that Antipas was not an individual, but a class of men who opposed the power of the bishops, or popes, in that day, being a combination of two words, 'Anti,' *opposed*, and 'Papas,' *father*, or *pope*; and many of them suffered martyrdom at that time in Constantinople and Rome, where the bishops and popes began to exercise the power which soon after brought into subjection the kings of the earth, and trampled on the rights of the church of Christ." William Miller as quoted by Uriah Smith, *Daniel and the Revelation*, pages 373,374.

"where Satan dwelleth" -Now Satan is the ruler of the church that claims to represent Christ. It is a church thirsty of worldly power and influence that persecutes those that uphold the truth. After Babylon was conquered by the Persians, the mystery-religion priests escaped to Pergamos where they established their religion and introduced sun worship. Many elements of their religion can be seen in the rituals of the Catholic Church. They also brought the rosary, which is used in other religions, including Hindus and Catholics.

[14]But I have a few things against thee, because thou hast there them that hold the doctrine of Balaam, who taught Balac to cast a stumbling block before the children of Israel, to eat things sacrificed unto idols, and <u>to commit fornication</u>.

Now the church, being favored by the state, became secularized because the emperor introduced pagan elements into the worship. This was the time when images crept into the church. Statues of pagan deities were cleansed and renamed as Peter or Paul. This time also opened the door for the adoration of Mary as the mother of Jesus and intercessor for man, when the Scriptures only show Jesus doing that work.

"...to eat things sacrificed unto idols" This refers to when the priests offer the wafer in the altar before the statues. There is no place in the Scriptures in which God tells his church to make statues of His saints and make them part of the liturgy or to even celebrate the mass.

"...<u>to commit fornication</u>" Fornication in the book of Revelation refers to the mix of truth with error. Pagan doctrines crept into the church and influenced the worship service and the theology. This set the stage for unbiblical doctrines that developed later on in the church, such as the natural immortality of the soul (the only immortal is God)- *"Which in his times he shall shew, who is the blessed and only Potentate, the King of kings, and Lord of lords;* ***Who only hath immortality****, dwelling in the light which no man can approach unto; whom no man hath seen, nor can see: to whom be honour and power everlasting. Amen"* (1 Timothy 6:15,16). Paul wrote that *"To those who by persistence in doing good <u>seek</u> glory, honor and <u>immortality</u>, he will give eternal life"* (Romans 2:7). It is clear

to me that if we have to look for something it is because we do not have it yet. This doctrine originated with Plato the philosopher and it is not Biblical. When God created man, He breathed into his nostrils and the dust plus the breath of God became a man. Let us read Genesis 2:7: *"And the LORD God formed man of the dust of the ground, and breathed into his nostrils the breath of life; and man* ***became*** *a living soul."* If we represent this as a math equation, we would have something like this: dust + breath= soul. You remove the breath, there is no soul or life. We can compare this with a light bulb and electricity. If you combine both, you have light, when you remove the electricity, there is no light. The truth taught in Genesis is that we **become** a soul, not that we **have** a soul. John taught again and again the truth of eternal life being linked to our relationship with Jesus. Here are two examples: *"He that believeth on the Son hath everlasting life: and he that believeth not the Son shall not see life; but the wrath of God abideth on him"* (John 3:36). *"He that hath the Son hath life; and he that hath not the Son of God hath not life"* (1 John 5:12). Only God is eternal and He grants that gift only to those that belong to Him as His followers. The wicked are not eternal because they made the choice to reject the source of life. See comments on Revelation 6:9 and chapter 20.

The false church is presented in Revelation 17 as a woman *"...arrayed in purple and scarlet colour, and decked with gold and precious stones and pearls, having a golden cup in her hand full of* ***abominations*** *and filthiness of her* ***fornication****:"*

[15]So hast thou also them that hold the doctrine of the Nicolaitanes, which thing I hate.

The church of Ephesus rejected this doctrine. Now this exalted church embraced that which Jesus hated. We already mentioned that these people taught that the Ten Commandments were no longer binding. Today I was listening to a preacher on the radio saying the same thing. Preachers confuse the Scriptures of the Old Testament with the Old Covenant and tell their congregations that since the Ten Commandments were given in the Old Testament, we no longer have to observe them. I went to Detroit the other day to bring an acquaintance to the train station. I pointed to him that in an area in Woodward Avenue that spans several blocks, there is a church in just about every corner, yet it is one of the wickedest cities in the whole nation. This is because the members are taught that they do not have to keep the law. Preachers misunderstand the Bible and teach their congregations that the law is no longer required, that it was only for the Jews. We need to understand that the Ten Commandments were just one of the laws – the main one- in the Old Testament. The law nailed to the cross was not the law of God (the Ten Commandments), but the provisional law that Moses wrote in a book. That temporary law was to be abolished because it consisted in the ceremonies that pointed to the sacrifice of Jesus.

The moral law (the Ten commandments)	**The ceremonial law**
1. It is a real law (James 2:8)	1. It was a ritual law (Ephesians 2:15)
2. It was written by God on stone (Exodus 24:12; 31:18	2. It was written by Moses on a book (Deut. 31:24) Galatians 3:10 refers to this law.
3. It was placed in the arc (Exodus 40:20	3. It was placed by the ark (Deut. 31:26)
4. It was to be magnified by Jesus (Isaiah 42:21; Matthew 5:17)	4. It was abolished by Jesus (Ephesians 2:15)
5. It is immutable and eternal (Psalm 111:7,8; 119:152)	5. It was mutable (Hebrews 10:1)
6. It is perfect (Psalm 19:7)	6. It did not make anything perfect (Hebrews 10:1,3,4)
7. Is spiritual (Romans 7:14)	7. It is carnal (Hebrews 7:16)
8. Is a delight to obey it (Psalm 119:77)	8. It is a "yoke of bondage." (Gal. 5:1)
9. He who obeys it is happy (James 1:25)	9. He who obeys it is not happy (Gal. 3:10;5:1-6)
10. It is a law of freedom (James 2:11,12)	
11. It is holy, just and good (Romans 7:12)	

The purpose of this table is to prove that the law of the Ten Commandments is different from the one that required circumcision and the sacrifice of animals. This later one was abolished by Jesus (nailed to the cross) and it is known as the ceremonial law. This law included the observance of days that due to their ritual meaning were called sabbaths but did not necessarily fall on the 7th day of the week. Let us see Leviticus 23.

"Speak unto the children of Israel, saying, In the seventh month, in the first day of the month, shall ye have a sabbath, a memorial of blowing of trumpets, an holy convocation. ...27Also on the tenth day of this seventh month there shall be a day of atonement: it shall be an holy convocation unto you; and ye shall afflict your souls, and offer an offering made by fire unto the LORD. 34Speak unto the children of Israel, saying, The fifteenth day of this seventh month shall be the feast of tabernacles for seven days unto the LORD. 35On the first day shall be an holy convocation: ye shall do no servile work therein. 36Seven days ye shall offer an offering made by fire unto the LORD: on the eighth day shall be an holy convocation unto you; and ye shall offer an offering made by fire unto the LORD: it is a solemn assembly; and ye shall do no servile work therein. 39Also in the fifteenth day of the seventh month, when ye have gathered in the fruit of the land, ye shall keep a feast unto the LORD seven days: on the first day shall be a sabbath, and on the eighth day shall be a sabbath." Leviticus 23:24,27,34,35,36 & 39. Here we see that these sabbaths fell on specific days of the month and were not tied to the weekly cycle. They were to be observed on the 1st, 10th and 15th days of the seventh month.

Now notice that verse 38 clearly indicates that these sabbaths were *"Beside the Sabbaths of the LORD."* These sabbath days had a symbolic meaning that pointed to Christ's sacrifice and ministry. Since they were a symbol or shadow, they were to be expired, as Paul wrote: *"Let no man therefore judge you in meat, or in drink, or in respect of an holyday, or of the new moon, or of the sabbath days: 17Which are a shadow of things to come; but the body is of Christ"* (Colossians 2:16,17).

Besides, how could anyone in clear conscience, claim that God contradicted himself? If He was planning to abolish the law that prohibits killing, stealing and cheating, don't you think He would announce it before hand through His prophets? Rather, He announced through the gospel prophet that He would exalt it: *"The LORD is well pleased for his righteousness' sake; he will magnify the law, and make it honourable"* (Isaiah 42:21).

Some verses to consider:

Matthew 5:18,19 *"For verily I say unto you, **Till heaven and earth pass**, one jot or one tittle shall in no wise pass from the law, till all be fulfilled. Whosoever therefore shall break **one** of these least commandments, and shall teach men so, he shall be called the least in the kingdom of heaven: but whosoever shall do and teach them, the same shall be called great in the kingdom of heaven."*

Referring to the time of the end, John wrote: *"And the dragon was wroth with the woman, and went to make war with the remnant of her seed, which **keep the commandments of God**, and have the testimony of Jesus Christ"* (Revelation 12:17). Therefore, the real followers of Christ in the final days of the history of this planet will keep the commandments even against the advice of their blinded religious leaders.

Romans 3:31 *"Do we then make void the law through faith? God forbid: yea, **we establish the law**."*

Psalm 119:152 *"Concerning your testimonies [commandments], I have known of old that you have **founded them for ever**."*

Romans 7:7 *"What shall we say then? Is the law sin? God forbid. Not, I had not known sin, but by the law: for I had not known lust, except the law had said, Thou shalt not covet."*

Romans 7:22 *"**For I delight in the law of God** after the inward man."*

James 1:25 *"But whoever looks into the **perfect law of liberty**, and continues therein, he being not a forgetful hearer, but a doer of the work, this man will be blessed in his deed."*

James 2:10-12 *"For **whosoever shall keep the whole law, and yet offend in one point, he is guilty of all**. For he that said, Do not commit adultery, said also, Do not kill. Now if you commit no adultery, yet if you kill, you become a transgressor of the law. So speak you, and so do, as they that shall be **judged by the law of liberty**."*

If James calls the commandments "law of liberty" (twice), he obviously is not referring at all to the temporary ceremonial law that required sacrifices and was a burden. If I do not kill, steal, or lie I am free. If I steal, I am not free because my conscience will accuse me and will also fear to be caught. Breaking one of the Ten Commandments is what the Bible refers to as being under the law, because we are under its condemnation.

Many believe that the Ten Commandments originated at Mount Sinai, but if we carefully study the Scriptures, we will see them all over the book of Genesis. Let us consider the story of Adam and Eve:

1. God had told the first couple not to eat of certain tree because if they did, they would die. Satan approached Eve and told her that she would not die but rather achieve a higher level of knowledge not attainable in any other way. Because Eve trusted more in Satan than in God, she displaced the Creator from the first place in her heart. She substituted God. Now she had another (new) deity in her life. She had violated the first commandment of the Decalogue *("**You shall not have other gods before me**"* -Exodus 20:3). She also implied that God lied to them.
2. She coveted the **only** fruit that was prohibited to her. She passed the fence of the neighbor's yard because she decided that that other fruit had to be hers also. She just transgressed the tenth commandment *("**You shall not covet"***- Exodus 20:17).
3. The gracious curves of that stunning sculpture from nature had her enraptured. It was already in her hands. At last was hers. She broke the eighth commandment *("**You shall not steal**"*- Exodus 20:15).
4. In an indirect way, Eve caused the death of her husband. Giving him the fruit was a premeditated action. Doing so, she infringed the sixth commandment *("**You shall not kill**"*).
5. When Eve saw herself accused, she blamed the serpent (and of course, God made that animal and let it go to the garden). In the end, it was God's fault, according to both. Everybody but them! They were laying on others the responsibility that was only theirs. "**You shall not slander**," says the ninth commandment.

Adam and Eve broke five Commandments (for each one Jesus suffered five piercing wounds- our sins hurt Christ). The Bible clearly says that *"sin is not imputed when there is no law"* (Romans 5:13). We could not have said that the first couple sinned if there was no previous knowledge of the law. How else could God righteously expel them from Eden if they "did not know" how to distinguish right from wrong? Would it be fair if a child were grounded for getting a cookie from the jar if he had never been told not to touch or eat them? Regarding Eve, was that all that Eve did? John provides a little more light:

"For all that is in the world, the lust of the flesh, and the lust of the eyes, and the pride of life, is not of the Father, but is of the world" (1 John 2:16).

"The woman saw that the tree had fruit that was good to eat, nice to look at, and desirable for making someone wise..." (See Genesis 3:6).

Genesis 3:6	1 John 2:16
The woman saw that the tree had fruit that was **good to eat**	the lust of the flesh
nice to **look** at	the lust of the eyes
desirable for making someone **wise**	the pride of life

"'Your eyes shall be opened,' the enemy had said; 'ye shall be as gods, knowing good and evil.' Genesis 3:5. Their eyes were indeed opened, but how sad the opening! The knowledge of evil, the curse of sin, was all that the transgressors gained. There was nothing poisonous in the fruit itself, and the sin was not merely in yielding to appetite. It was distrust of God's goodness, disbelief of His word, and rejection of His authority, which made our first parents transgressors, and that brought into the world the knowledge of evil. It was this that opened the door to every species of falsehood and error.

"Man lost all because he chose to listen to the deceiver rather than to Him who is Truth, who alone has understanding. By the mingling of evil with good, his mind had become confused, his mental and spiritual powers benumbed. No longer could he appreciate the good that God had so freely bestowed." *Education*, page 25.

"What shall we say then? Is the law sin? God forbid. Nay, I had not known sin, but by the law: for I had not known lust, except the law had said, Thou shalt not covet" (Romans 7:7).

Those that say that the law was for the Jews and it did not exist before Sinai, forget that Joseph, when tempted, asked: *"how then can I do this great wickedness, and* ***sin*** *against God?"* (Genesis 39:9b). That sin was adultery and he knew that it was wrong. It is evident that the Law was passed from generation to generation orally. Since the human memory would grow weaker through the ages, God put the law in writing at Sinai.

Let us see the law in the book of Genesis, centuries before there was a Jewish nation:

Commandment	Passage
Thou shalt have no other gods before me	Genesis 35:2,4
Thou shalt not make unto thee any graven image	Genesis 31:19
Thou shalt not take the name of the LORD thy God in vain	Genesis 21:23,24; 24:3
Remember the Sabbath day, to keep it holy	Genesis 2:1-3
Honour thy father and thy mother	Genesis 22:9,10; 28:6-9
Thou shalt not kill	Genesis 4:8-11; 49:5,6
Thou shalt not commit adultery	Genesis 26:10; 35:22 with 49:4 (Reuben with Bilhah); 39:7-9
Thou shalt not steal	Genesis 27:35; 30:33
Thou shalt not bear false witness (do not lie)	Genesis 26:10; 12:10-19
Thou shalt not covet (do not envy)	Genesis 26:14

All of the commandments were known even by the pagans, who held in high regard those that told the truth. Some of those so-called pagans even kept the true Sabbath. Archaeologists have found evidence of Sabbath observance among people of different nations before the Exodus. The word Sabbath exists today in over 120 languages, which indicates that the day was universally known, even when other days of the week carried pagan names or were just called first, second, third day, etc. Even some indian nations in North America kept the seventh day Sabbath and also ate clean when the pilgrims came from Europe. Before the Ten Commandments were proclaimed in Sinai, the Bible indicates clearly that they knew them. Keep in mind that God would not expect obedience if there was no knowledge of what was right and wrong. Consider the following verses referring to obedience to the commandments before they were given in writing, proving that they were transmitted from generation to generation verbally- notice also that the only commandment that God was concerned with was the Sabbath keeping- the commandment at the heart of the law; the one that Satan and apostate churches fight against:

"Then said the LORD unto Moses, Behold, I will rain bread from heaven for you; and the people shall go out and gather a certain rate every day, that I may prove them, whether they will walk in my law, or no...And he said unto them, This is that which the LORD hath said, Tomorrow is the rest of the holy Sabbath unto the LORD: bake that which ye will bake to day, and seethe that ye will seethe; and that which remaineth over lay up for you to be kept until the morning." (Exodus 16:4,23). Until then, the law had been transmitted from one generation to the next in the same way that Abraham did with his family. *"For I know him, that he will command his children and his household after him, and they shall keep the way of the LORD, to do justice and judgment; that the LORD may bring upon Abraham that which he hath spoken of him"* (Genesis 18:19). In those times there was something very crucial for society that is lacking in our days: good parenting. Parents recognized their sacred duty and made sure their children knew the will of God. Our society today has deteriorated beyond hope due to the lax attitude of fathers and mothers, especially after evolution started to be taught in public schools.

The law was known before the proclamation at Sinai.

"And he said unto them, This is that which the LORD hath said, Tomorrow is the rest of the holy Sabbath unto the LORD: bake that which ye will bake to day, and seethe that ye will seethe; and that which remaineth over lay up for you to be kept until the morning" (Exodus 16:23).

"And it came to pass, that there went out some of the people on the seventh day for to gather, and they found none. And the LORD said unto Moses, How long refuse ye to keep my commandments and my laws? See, for that the LORD hath given you the Sabbath, therefore he giveth you on the sixth day the bread of two days; abide ye every man in his place, let no man go out of his place on the seventh day. So the people rested on the seventh day" (Exodus 16:27-30).

It sounds contradictory that those who say that the Ten Commandments are no longer valid still consider that killing, adultery and stealing are wrong, while they reject the only commandment that starts with the word "**Remember**." All of them are part of the Decalogue. To say that a law that was called eternal in Psalm 119:152 has a temporary section (the Sabbath part), would be equivalent to declare that a man was granted eternal life but his right hand is mortal. It is either ALL eternal or not eternal at all, since eternal and temporary exclude each other like light and darkness. I recently heard on the radio that keeping any day is acceptable. To be fair, we should apply the same relativism to the other commandments. Let us see how it would sound:

Original commandment	As changed to match the modern observance of the Sabbath commanded by God Himself but kept loosely
"Remember the Sabbath day to keep it holy"	"Any day will do. God is not that picky."
"Thou shalt not kill"	"It's OK to kill some people."
"Thou shalt not steal"	"It's OK to take stuff from others if you need to have it- like office supplies. Or cheat on taxes, or on a test."
"Thou shalt not commit adultery"	"It's OK to take any woman; after all, they are a lot more of them than men and if some guys do not take more than one, some women will never marry."
"Thou shalt not covet"	"It is OK to envy that 50 carats necklace on the rich lady. After all, it will encourage me to do better in my job, so I can have one too."

Some say that it is impossible to keep the Commandments. First, they are insulting God's intelligence because they are saying that He gave Commandments (orders) to be kept but no one can keep them. Second, it is true that we, as fallen human beings, with sinful tendencies, cannot obey the law on our own strength. Peter wrote that Jesus gave us an example to follow. How? Through His communion with His Father. He obeyed as a human depending on the Father to give Him strength, in order to teach us the secret to victory over sin. It is said that a church is like a hospital. Patients are admitted to a hospital hoping that they will come out cured after a stay for treatment. If we go to Christ as fallen, guilty sinners, Jesus will forgive us instantly, but He will tell us *"go and sin no more"* (John 8:11). Can you tell your children not to take money from your wallet if you know that it will be impossible for them to obey you? Every commandment is a promise that our Creator will help us obey. Besides, if it is impossible to keep the Commandments, why do they find it so objectionable when someone commits adultery, steals, or kills another human being? After all, it would be just part of his nature to do those things because it would be out of their possibilities to do right. If the Commandments cannot be kept, there is no reason to have prisons or courts of justice or reformatories because there is no reason either to condemn bad behavior. We would be like brute beasts. However, God implanted within us a sense of what is right, fair and just. We teach our children the behavior that we want them to observe. If they disobey us, we ground them because we expect them to learn to obey our requirements and amend their behavior. We learned by experience that we could decide to do what is right. In the same manner, we can choose to obey God and He will supply the strength to render the obedience. *"For it is God who is producing in you both the desire and the ability to do what pleases him"* (Philippians 2:13 *International Standard Version*). That obedience that He expects from us is based on a loving relationship (John 14:15), rather than one of fear. We obey Him out of love and gratitude for what He has done for us as Creator, Redeemer, friend (John 15:14) and provider of all the things that we enjoy in life. If we believe that our children can get to obey us in things like not hitting others, not lying, not using drugs and not stealing, why would it be any different to obey our heavenly Father in just ten simple commands? *"I can do all things through Christ which strengtheneth me"* (Philippians 4:13). *"God planned for us to do good things and to live as he has always wanted us to live. That's why he sent Christ to make us what we are"* (Ephesians 2:10 *CEV*). *"But, idle boaster, are you willing to be taught how it is that faith apart from obedience is worthless?"* (James 2:20

-1912 Weymouth New Testament). Yes, we are saved only by faith. However, faith is like an electric cord that only when plugged to the outlet enables the machine to do the work it was designed to do.

"There has been an awful letting-down in this country regarding the Sabbath during the last twenty-five years, and many a man has been shorn of spiritual power, like Samson, because he is not straight on this question. Can *you* say that you observe the Sabbath properly? You may be a professed Christian: are you obeying this commandment? Or do you neglect the house of God on the Sabbath day, and spend your time drinking and carousing in places of vice and crime, showing contempt for God and His law, or shopping and doing your own pleasure? Are you ready to step into the scales? Where were you last Sabbath? How did you spend it?

"I honestly believe that this commandment is just as binding to-day as it ever was. I have talked with men who have said that it has been abrogated, but they have never been able to point to any place in the Bible where God repealed it. When Christ was on earth, He did nothing to set it aside; He freed it from the traces under which the scribes and Pharisees had put it, and gave it its true place. "The Sabbath was made for man, not man for the Sabbath." It is just as practicable and as necessary for men to-day as it ever was-in fact, more than ever, because we live in such an intense age.

"The Sabbath was binding in Eden, and it has been in force ever since. This fourth commandment begins with the word "remember," showing that the Sabbath already existed when God wrote this law on the tables of stone at Sinai. How can men claim that this one commandment has been done away with when they will admit that the other nine are still binding?

"I believe that the Sabbath question to-day is a vital one for the whole country. It is the burning question of the present time. If you give up the Sabbath, the church goes; if you give up the church, the home goes; and if the home goes, the nation goes. That is the direction in which we are traveling.

"The church of God is losing its power on account of so many people giving up the Sabbath, and using it to promote selfishness." Dwight Moody, Weighed and Wanting

Regarding the ceremonial law (Ephesians 2:15), that one was temporary and is the one that Paul refers to in Galatians 3:10. This is the one he called a shadow (Colossians 2:16, 17) because it pointed towards Jesus' first advent and His sacrifice to pay the penalty of our sins. The same cannot be said of any of the Ten Commandments because neither of them is a shadow of Christ's sacrifice as it was sacrificing a lamb. Some people still believe that as Christians, we ought to observe those ceremonial days. Jesus is the body that casted those shadows. Since He is the reality, why would those shadows still be observed?

On the other hand, the Moral Law (the Ten Commandments) is eternal because it is a reflection of the character of God. See table on chapter seven. The law cannot change because God, whose character it reflects, does not change. It was the enemy of the soul who inspired his false church to attempt to change God's Commandments and teach commandments of men (Daniel 7:25).

Now, let us go back in history, specifically the time when the church and the government united (church and state never made a good marriage). In the year 321 AD, Emperor Constantine proclaimed Sunday as the day of rest. The apostate church saw in this an opportunity to attract the pagans into the fold of the church because they worshipped the sun in that day (hence it is call **<u>Sun</u>**day). Until then, Christians had been meeting on Saturday, the Sabbath (see Acts 18:4 for example), following Jesus' example (Luke 4:16). Ironically, the church would soon <u>forget</u> the only commandment that contains the word *"<u>Remember</u>."* This was Constantine edict: "Let all judges and all city people and all tradesmen rest upon the <u>venerable day of the sun</u>. But let those dwelling in the country freely and with full liberty attend to the culture of their field; since it frequently happens that no other day is so fit for the sowing of grain or the planting of vines; hence, the favorable time should not be allowed to pass, lest the provisions of heaven be lost."

<u>Sun</u>day in the New Testament

The word "Sunday" does not even appear in the Bible, being simply called the "first day of the week." It is mentioned only eight times in the New Testament. The first five of those references are found in relation to the visit to the tomb by Mary Magdalene and other women. They were not even aware of Jesus' resurrection. These are the verses in the gospels (notice that none of them commands us to keep Sunday holy or even insinuate that the disciples or Jesus Himself did, much less change the sanctity of the day to Sunday):

- *"In the end of the Sabbath, as it began to dawn toward the first day of the week, came Mary Magdalene and the other Mary to see the sepulcher"* (Matthew 28:1)
- *"And when the Sabbath was past, Mary Magdalene, and Mary the mother of James, and Salome, had bought sweet spices, that they might come and anoint him. And very early in the morning the first day of the week, they came unto the sepulchre at the rising of the sun"* (Mark 16:1,2).
- *"Now when Jesus was risen early the first day of the week, he appeared first to Mary Magdalene, out of whom he had cast seven devils"* (Mark 16:9).
- *"Now upon the first day of the week, very early in the morning, they came unto the sepulchre, bringing the spices which they had prepared, and certain others with them"* (Luke 24:1).
- *"The first day of the week cometh Mary Magdalene early, when it was yet dark, unto the sepulchre, and seeth the stone taken away from the sepulchre"* (John 20:1).
- *"Then the same day at evening, being the first day of the week, when the doors were shut where the disciples were assembled* ***<u>for fear of the Jews</u>****, came Jesus and stood in the midst, and saith unto them, Peace be unto you"* (John 20:19). Did you catch that? They were not meeting to worship but because they were afraid. They were in hiding.

In addition, notice in the previous passages that the gospel writers referred to Saturday as the Sabbath but Sunday was merely called the first day of the week. A day without a name is just a common day. If Jesus Christ never changed the day of rest, what mortal could dare to have the authority to bypass Him and make the change? Only the mystery of iniquity (2 Thessalonians 2:7; Revelation 17:5) would do such a thing as prophesied in Daniel 7:25. "We have in <u>the authoritative voice of the Church the voice of Christ Himself</u>. <u>The Church is above the Bible</u>; and <u>this transference</u>

<u>of Sabbath observance from Saturday to Sunday is proof positive of that fact</u>."

If Jesus appearing on Sunday is a proof that the day should be kept sacred, then we should also keep Monday because He appeared to them on that day too. *"And after <u>eight days</u> again his disciples were within, and Thomas with them: then came Jesus, the doors being shut, and stood in the midst, and said, Peace be unto you"* (John 20:26).

None of those meetings was meant to celebrate the resurrection because the Bible says that until they saw Him, they did not believe that Christ was raised from the dead, as was the case with all the disciples, not only Thomas. See Mark 16:14 and Luke 24:27-41. Romans 6:3-6 says that baptism is the way by which we are to celebrate or remember the resurrection.

When we read the book of Acts, the first day of the week is mentioned only once. The passage is found in Acts 20:7-12. *"Now on the first day of the week, when the disciples came together to break bread, Paul, ready to depart the next day, spoke to them and continued his message until midnight"* (verse 7). This was a farewell meeting and meal, not a regular worship service because Paul was going to be traveling. Some point to the breaking of bread as if were a communion service- far from it. The phrase is used loosely to indicate just eating. Such is the case when Paul was encouraging the sailors, soldiers and prisoners to eat after their shipwreck. *"And when he had thus spoken, he took bread, and gave thanks to God in presence of them all: and when he had <u>broken it</u>, he began to eat"* (Acts 27:35). Biblical time reckoning counted the days from sunset to sunset, so Friday at sunset was the start of the Sabbath. The Good News Bible correctly translates verse seven as follows: *"On Saturday evening we gathered together for the fellowship meal. Paul spoke to the people and kept on speaking until midnight, since he was going to leave the next day."* Verse eight reinforces that rendering by mentioning the "<u>many lamps</u>" being used. Paul spoke to them "until sunrise" (verse 11)- all night long, because he wanted to be sure that they would be prepared for the apostasy that was coming as he later did with the churches of Miletus and Ephesus (verses 27-31). Paul spent that Sunday on a long tiring journey, not worshipping, so we can disqualify this passage as a proof that Sunday is to be kept.

The last mention of the first day of the week is found in 1 Corinthians 16:1,2, where Paul requested a donation for the church in Jerusalem: *"Now concerning the collection for the saints, as I have given order to the churches of Galatia, even so do ye. On the first day of the week let each one of you lay something aside, storing up as he may prosper, that there be no collections when I come."* These three versions will shed light on the subject:

"On the first day of every week let each of you put on one side and store up at his home whatever gain has been granted to him; so that whenever I come, there may then be no collections going on." 1 Corinthians 16:2, Weymouth New Testament

"On each first day of the week, let every one of you lay aside and preserve at home, what he is able; that there may be no collections when I come." 1 Corinthians 16:2, Murdock

"After the Sabbath ends, each of you should set aside and save something from your surplus in proportion to what you have, so that no collections will have to be made when I arrive." 1 Corinthians 16:2, International Standard Version

The collection was to be done at home after the Sabbath ended. No part of this passage indicates Sunday worship. There are eight facts that must be considered from this passage:

- The collection was for the saints, not for the church. It was not a Sunday offering.
- The collection was vey likely done at the individual believer's homes, not at the church.
- Paul did not want them to worry about their budget on the Sabbath and that is why he instructed to do it on Sunday, a common day of work, suitable for a worldly activity.
- No part of the passage specifies that the offering was monetary. It could have been food as when the Israelites took goods to the temple. Or it could have been a combination of monetary aid and goods. Verse 3 insinuates that many people were going to take it to Jerusalem. *"After*

I come, I shall give letters of introduction to those you have approved, and send them to take your gift to Jerusalem" (*GNB*). If this was only money, there was no need for a group to transport it. A group would have attracted robbers' attention.

- If this was money, it was to be taken after they gave the portion to God on the previous day, on the Sabbath. In that way, they knew how much they had left after the tithe and offerings and could budget for the offering destined to the poor in Jerusalem.
- Paul kept 78 Sabbaths (a year and a half) with the Corinth church (Acts 18:1,4,11) with Jewish and Gentile worshippers. The Corinthians then, did not keep Sunday, but the seventh day Sabbath.
- The collection was to stop at Paul's arrival and commissioning of people to take it to Jerusalem. It was not going to continue once the dedicated amount for the poor got collected.
- Paul was just directing a charity drive and not establishing a Sunday worship ritual

As we were able to see, Sunday worship does not originate in the Bible but in paganism. Church leaders from various denominations have acknowledged that God only approved the 7th day as His day to meet with His people. Still others, use passages such as Colossians 2:16 (that refers to the ceremonial Sabbath) to attempt to prove that we no longer have to keep the Sabbath on the 7th day of the week. Many say that the Sabbath was for the Jews ignoring what Jesus Himself declared: *"The Sabbath was made for the good of human beings; they were not made for the Sabbath."* (Mark 2:27). The whole humankind should benefit from meeting with God on that His special day. That commandment, like the other nine, was to remain for ever. Specially that one that is the only of the ten that starts with the word *"Remember." "Remember the Sabbath day, to keep it holy. Exodus 20:9 Six days shalt thou labour, and do all thy work: But the seventh day is the Sabbath of the LORD thy God: in it thou shalt not do any work, thou, nor thy son, nor thy daughter, thy manservant, nor thy maidservant, nor thy cattle, nor thy stranger that is within thy gates: For in six days the LORD made heaven and earth, the sea, and all that in them is, and rested the seventh day: wherefore the LORD blessed the Sabbath day, and hallowed it"* (Exodus 20:8-11). No other commandment shows that God cares for human rights and complete human equality such as this one. There is even a show of mercy for animals included. Had this commandment been kept, many abuses and human and animal suffering would have been avoided.

Since Jesus never changed the worship obligations from Saturday to Sunday, and the disciples being mere human beings, did not have the authority to do such a change, we can't not deny that Christians ought to observe only the day specified by God, who never changes (Psalm 89:34). In His discourse in the mount of Olives, Jesus, looking into the future when Jerusalem would be surrounded by the Roman armies, said to the disciples: *"But pray ye that your flight be not in the winter, neither on the Sabbath day"* (Matthew 24:20). It was precisely on a Sabbath in the year 70 AD that Vespasian attacked the Jews. If the solemnity of the Sabbath were going to be transferred into Sunday, why would Jesus ask His disciples to elevate such a prayer?

Talking to the believers in Ephesus during his farewell, Paul said: *"I know that after I leave, savage wolves will come in among you and will not spare the flock. Even from your own number men will arise and <u>distort the truth</u> in order to draw away disciples after them."* (Acts 20:29,30). The apostle considered diluted truth as contaminated truth. The apostasy had been prophesied and soon will come to full bloom in order to fill the churches- and of course, the coffers.

The book of Revelation shows that Satan will not be fighting those that keep a spurious day that is kept with the excuse that it was the day when Jesus resurrected, but rather those *"which keep the commandments of God"* (Revelation 12:17). Jesus warned about pretending to serve Him and not being obedient: *"Watch out for false prophets. They come to you in sheep's clothing, but inwardly they are ferocious wolves.... "Not everyone who says to me, 'Lord, Lord,' will enter the kingdom of heaven, but only <u>he who does the will of my Father</u> who is in heaven. Many will say to me on that day, 'Lord, Lord, did we not prophesy in your name, and in your name drive out demons and perform many miracles?' Then I will tell them plainly, 'I never knew you. Away from me, you evildoers!"* (Matthew 7:15, 21-23 NIV). How do we know that He was talking about obedience here? A few verses down He mentions the man who built his house on the sand: *"But everyone who hears these words of mine and does not put them into practice is like a foolish man who built his house on sand. The rain came down, the streams rose, and the winds blew and beat against that house, and it fell with a great crash"* (Matthew 7:26,27 NIV). Those TV miracle-working evangelists know that Jesus never replaced Saturday with Sunday but since they make a living (and what an opulent living!) with their preaching and fear to lose their influence, prestige and in most cases, their income, they do not preach the truth to their listeners. Paul contrasts himself and his associates with those that *"peddle the word of God for profit"* (2 Corinthians 2:17 NIV). Jesus declared: *"If ye love me, keep my commandments"* (John 14:15). Even though we are saved by grace, we are expected to obey in the power of God, just as our children are expected to do chores around the house and to be obedient (and who calls his own children legalist for being obedient?).

Why is the Sabbath important? What message does the Sabbath has for us? When the Sabbath was mentioned in the Scriptures for the first time, it was in the context of creation. God had just finished creating everything in this world and rested, blessed and sanctified the seventh day of the week. He did not do it because He was tired- for He does not get tired. He did it because He wanted to spend time with Adam and Eve. What a God! I am sure He had many important things to do in the vast universe. However, He decided that the newly created couple was too important to Him so He wanted to have those 24 special hours with them. The Sabbath would allow Adam and Eve to get to know their creator intimately, to develop a bond. It would permit them to understand the loving character of their God who made them to His image and likeness. That would give them a sense of family, of belonging. None of the other creatures was made to His likeness. Adam was even personally and artistically crafted by the hand of God, while the animals were merely spoken into existence- not to talk down the marvels of the animal kingdom. We are special to Him. The Sabbath thus, speaks of our value before the eyes of God.

The Sabbath then became the medium through which every seven days the human race was to have a special time with their creator and grow closer in their relationship. With the entrance of sin into the world, the Sabbath became even more important because also provided man with a most needed rest after the toils of the week. The Sabbath is today an oasis where we can refresh the thirst of our souls when we come to Jesus in those 24 hours. Surely, we can come to Jesus any day of the week, but He specifically dedicated the Sabbath for us. It is our date day with our Creator and Savior. It is not the rest on itself what matters, but the presence of God what makes Sabbath special. It must be set apart and kept free of worldly worries and unnecessary burdens so we can really enjoy His presence. Doing things to help sick people is in harmony with the spirit of the Sabbath. Jesus taught this by example, healing on that special day. Another way to enjoy it is spending quality time with our friends and loved ones. Going out to contemplate nature is very refreshing in those holy hours. After entering in the rest of the Lord (Hebrews 4:3-10), we can start the new week with renewed physical strength and mental vigor. "The good effect on a nation's health and happiness produced by the return of the Sabbath, with its cessation from work, cannot be overestimated. It is needed to repair and restore the body after six days of work. It is proved that a man can do more in six days than in seven. Lord Beaconsfield. said: 'Of all divine institutions, the most divine is that which secures a day of rest for man. I hold it to be the most valuable blessing conceded to man. It is the corner-stone of all civilization, and its removal might affect even the health of the people.'...

"'Our bodies are seven-day clocks,' says Talmage, 'and they need to be wound up, and if they are not wound up they run down into the grave. No man can continuously break the Sabbath and keep his physical and mental health. Ask aged men, and they will tell you they never knew men who continuously broke the Sabbath, who did not fail in mind, body, or moral principles.' Dwight Moody, *Weighed and Wanting*

When Jesus came to this world, we are told that, *"as his custom was, he went into the synagogue on the Sabbath day"* (Luke 4:16). By example in Eden and when He became one with humanity, Jesus our Creator kept the Sabbath, not only to give us an example, but also to get closer to us. He wanted to reach out, to tell us: "I care about you," because many times, as stated before, He healed those burdened by disease in that day. In the same manner that Jesus showed His love on that day, we are also to minister to the sick and needy when required. To visit the orphans, widows, the sick and those in prisons on that day is according to the spirit of the Sabbath. *"And he said unto them, What man shall there be among you, that shall have one sheep, and if it fall into a pit on the Sabbath day, will he not lay hold on it, and lift it out? How much then is a man better than a sheep? Wherefore it is lawful to do well on the Sabbath days"* (Matthew 12:11,12).

"Many mothers have written to me at one time or another to know what to do to entertain their children on the Sabbath. The boys say, 'I do wish 'twas Night,' or, 'I do hate the Sabbath,' or, 'I do wish the Sabbath was over.' It ought to be the happiest day in the week to them, one to be looked forward to with pleasure. In order to this end, many suggestions might be followed. Make family prayers especially attractive by having the children learn some verse or story from the Bible. Give more time to your children than you can give on weekdays, reading to them and perhaps taking them to walk in the afternoon or evening. Show by your conduct that the Sabbath is a delight, and they will soon catch your spirit. Set aside some time for religious instruction, without making this a task. You can make it interesting for the children by telling Bible stories and asking them to guess the names of the characters. Have Sunday games for the younger children. Picture books, puzzle maps of Palestine, etc., can be easily obtained. ... Set aside attractive books for the Sabbath, not letting the children have these during the week. By doing this, the children can be brought to look forward to the day with eagerness and pleasure." Dwight Moody, *Weighed and Wanting*

The holy Sabbath never lost its value when Jesus died. In fact, He rested in the tomb and the Bible tells us that His followers did the same. *"And they returned, and prepared spices and ointments; and rested the Sabbath day according to the commandment"* (Luke 23:56).

Some have argued that the calendar has been changed and that we have no way to know for sure which day is the Sabbath. That argument puts a smile on my face because they certainly do not have a problem knowing which day is Sunday! The duration of the week has been always seven days, so that has not been altered. For sixteen centuries, the western world used the calendar created by Julius Caesar but its length was not accurate. In the year 1582, Pope Gregory XIII ordered a change that was implemented in October of that year. The length of the week as we know it was not changed and neither were the sequence of the days. Only the number on the days changed. According to the Julian calendar, the first Friday of that month was supposed to be Friday the 5th. Instead, it became Friday the 15th to compensate for the accumulated difference in additional minutes of the old calendar. The month of October in the new calendar was shortened by ten days. Here is how the calendar looked that year:

October 1582						
Sunday	**Monday**	**Tuesday**	**Wednesday**	**Thursday**	**Friday**	**Saturday**
	1	2	3	4	15	16
17	18	19	20	21	22	23
24	25	26	27	28	29	30
31						

As it can be clearly seen, the sequence of the days of the week remained unaltered (Thursday was followed by Friday), so the Sabbath that Jesus and the disciples kept is the same that we keep today.

Illustration: Let us say that a man has 12 children. As his birthday approaches, he sends invitations to all of them to come on Tuesday the 11th to spend the day together. He is looking forward to that day. Two of them go on that day but the other ten (the big majority) decide that one day or another makes no difference. After all, their father should not be so particular. So they show up on Wednesday the 12th instead. When they arrived, the musicians are gone, there is no food, no balloons, no ice cream, no snacks, no cake, and worst of all, their father is not there.

16Repent; or else I will come unto thee quickly, and will fight against them with the sword of my mouth.

Here again, and as always, Jesus does not want anyone to perish, but that we repent and come to Him to be cleansed and receive everlasting life. Notice that He is not talking about fighting against you, but against those that uphold error because they make you stumble. His fight so far is against your religious leader that does not want you to know and follow the truth because his boat will not be paid if you leave his flock. I do recognize that some preachers are sincere and those will open their eyes and come to the light. Soon the time will come when you will receive a special and final call by God to leave Babylon (Revelation 18:4) and you must do so without delays and without looking back like the wife of Lot did. What could be holding you up? Leave it behind. Nothing is worth losing eternal life over it. Remember Jesus' promise if you are faithful: *"And every one that hath forsaken houses, or brethren, or sisters, or father, or mother, or wife, or children, or lands, for my name's sake, shall receive an hundredfold, and shall inherit everlasting life"* (Matthew 19:29).

[17]*He that hath an ear, let him hear what the Spirit saith unto the churches; To him that overcometh will I give to eat of the hidden manna, and will give him a white stone, and in the stone a new name written, which no man knoweth saving he that receiveth it.*

"the hidden manna (bread of angels –Psalm 78:25)"- as opposed to the wafer from the mass.

"will give him a white stone" It is said that those acquitted in court trials on those days received a white stone.

"a new name" A name in Scriptures is a symbol of the character of the person (see chapter 7). When we get to heaven, we are going to reflect Christ in His perfect holiness. His character will reflect in ours.

[18]*And unto the angel of the church in Thyatira write; These things saith the Son of God, who hath his eyes like unto a flame of fire, and his feet are like fine brass;*

eyes like unto a flame of fire- Eyes that can see everything even if done in the most absolute darkness, but also are a threat of justice against those that use the flames of the inquisition to intimidate and destroy the true believers.

This church was the church of the Dark Ages when the Catholic paganism reined supreme and unchallenged and named and deposed kings. He promptly identifies Himself as the Son of God to remind the readers that He was the one in charge because the pope and priests were claiming supremacy and taking the eyes of the people off from Jesus. This was the time of the inquisition and the persecution of the church in the wilderness. Jesus identified Himself with the persecuted when shown as having His feet *"like fine brass."* This is brass when it is passed through fire just as some of the true believers were. The amazing thing is that when these Christians were being burned at the stake, they were not screaming in horror, but rather singing. Yes, they were joyful to be found worthy of suffering for their beloved Master (James 1:2-4) and He was there with them. Experiencing a daily walk with God, enabled them to have the certainty of His presence on those crucial last minutes of their lives and felt no pain while their bodies were consumed by the flames.

[19]I know thy works, and charity, and service, and faith, and thy patience, and thy works; and the last to be more than the first.

Jesus commended them for their efforts and spirit of sacrifice. Either this passage could refer to the missionaries that risked their lives sharing the truth or to the few real Christians in the convents doing charity work among the poor, like Mother Theresa did in the 20th century. Yes, not all of them were corrupt and God notices those acts of sincere self-denial, being the judge of the hearts. There have been thousands of sincere Catholics that have acted in true fear of God and shown real love for humankind. I also believe that I will see pope John Paul I in heaven and even Pius XII, since he showed signs of repentance and a willingness to follow the Bible in the last days of his reign. Some believe (me included) that these two popes were assassinated for wanting to follow the Bible and for their plans to reform the corrupted church. Pope Pius XII, after he favored Hitler in World War II, received two books from a cousin in New York. He placed those books at either side of a Bible in his study. The two books were *The Great Controversy* and *The Desire of Ages*. They inspired him to start his plans to reform the church. Unfortunately, he was found dead before he could accomplish his plans. Pope John Paul I lasted only 33 days because when he was asked about his plans, he replied that he would continue the reforms of Pius XII. Neither of them had an autopsy done, which raises suspicion of foul play, possibly poisoning as some authors have claimed.

[20]Notwithstanding I have a few things against thee, because thou sufferest that woman Jezebel, which calleth herself a prophetess, to teach and to seduce my servants to commit fornication, and to eat things sacrificed unto idols.

Jesus is talking to both churches here (Jezebel vs. my servants) as we can see it implied in verse 24. This is the same conflict originated in Eden that would include true worshoppers and false ones all the way to the very end of the world. Jezebel was the wife of King Ahab and she introduced the worship of Baal and Asherah, building temples and offering sacrifices to the idols. Fornication was used in the Bible to indicate not only blasphemies but also the union of church and state. How does a woman seduce a man? By been very sweet. We see it in the book of Proverbs: *"For the lips of an adulteress drip honey, and her speech is smoother than oil;"* (Proverbs 5:3 NIV). The services of the Catholic Church are very impressive and solemn. They exert a hypnotic effect on the worshippers- but it is copied from the pagans, down to the clothes of the priests. The problem of even giving a little attention to error has the same result as committing adultery: *"but in the end she is bitter as gall, sharp as a double-edged sword. Her feet go down to death; her steps lead straight to the grave. She gives no thought to the way of life; her paths are crooked, but she knows it not."* (Proverbs 5:4-6). Error is fatal even if it is mixed with some truth. We can never forget that a drop of cyanide is as much poison alone as when it is drank with a teaspoon of water. It can still hurt you. Just giving up a little bit for the sake of Christian unity opens the door for Satan to completely separate us from God.

That is why I consider that ecumenism (the movement to unite churches regardless of their doctrines) is not God's plan. He cannot be behind the confusion of so many beliefs. So many churches teach so many diverse ideas and yet claim to be guided by the Holy Spirit, of whom the Bible say He will guide us to ***all*** the truth (John 16:13)- not part of it. If they were really guided by the Spirit, then their doctrines would agree. The ecumenical movement is just a Romish idea to make Protestants come back to the mother church. Many church leaders are willing to ignore the enormous sacrifice that it cost the Reformers, many of whom died in the flames, to uphold the sacred truths of salvation by grace and *sola scriptura*. Compromising in any part of the truth will allow the wolf to eat the sheep. "The wide diversity of belief in the Protestant churches is regarded by many as decisive proof that no effort to secure a forced uniformity can ever be made. But there has been for years, in churches of the Protestant faith, a strong and growing sentiment in favor of a union (with the Catholic Church) based upon common points of doctrine. To secure such a union, the discussion of subjects upon which all were not agreed--however important they might be from a Bible standpoint--must necessarily be waived" –*The Great Controversy*, page 444

"to seduce my servants to commit fornication" Celibacy has been a curse to religious orders. There were in Spain, a convent and a monastery connected by a tunnel. Years ago, somebody discovered a great amount of babies' corpses in that tunnel. Since the Catholic Church condemns abortion, the fruit of the fornication of nuns and monks were suffocated at birth. In other words, abortion is evil, kill already born babies instead. The hypocrisy of that dichotomy reminds me that the Church does not allow divorce but permits to annul a marriage.

Regarding the spiritual meaning of this passage, the teachings of the Catholic Church are considered by God as fornication because her doctrines are paganism dressed as Christianity.

[21]And I gave her space to repent of her fornication; and she repented not.

Literally, *"I gave her time."* The period of this merciful opportunity lasted until 1517 when Luther wrote his famous 95 thesis against the indulgences. His thesis # 82 reads: "They ask, e.g.: Why does not the pope liberate everyone from purgatory <u>for the sake of love</u> (a most holy thing) and because of the supreme necessity of their souls? This would be morally the best of all reasons. Meanwhile he redeems innumerable souls <u>for money</u>, a most perishable thing, with which to build St. Peter's church, a very minor purpose."

Had the Catholic Church heeded the messages to reform from those that she persecuted, no Reformation would have been needed and Luther would have remained an obscure monk. Many messengers were sent to call the church to repentance but they were persecuted and slaughtered. How merciful is our God. He even called to repentance those that were so adamantly opposed to His truth and persecuted His followers. None of us deserves His grace and yet He wants all to be saved.

[22]Behold, I will cast her into a bed, and them that commit adultery with her into great tribulation, except they repent of their deeds.

God even warns the wicked so they can reconcile with Him and be saved. *"Say unto them, As I live, saith the Lord GOD, I have no pleasure in the death of the wicked; but that the wicked turn from his way and live: turn ye, turn ye from your evil ways; for why will ye die, O house of Israel?"* (Ezekiel 33:11). For 120 years, God warned the pre-flood people through Noah to repent. A beautiful proof that He does not want people to perish in spite of their past wickedness can be found in the book of Jonah. The prophet was sent to preach to the cruel enemies of his people. The reason why Jonah did not want to go to that city was because they used to attack the Israelites and even kill pregnant women. In spite of their violence and terrible crimes, God saw possibilities in them and gave them another chance. Doesn't this encourage you to turn to such a God to ask for another chance too?

[23]And I will kill her children with death; and all the churches shall know that I am he which searcheth the reins and hearts: and I will give unto every one of you according to your works.

I will kill her children with death - This is the historic period of the Inquisition. Pope Gregory IX instituted the papal institution in 1231. The use of torture to obtain the names of other "heretics" and confessions was authorized in 1252 by Innocent IV. Thousands were killed by the "holy tribunal." Millions more were killed in other campaigns like the persecutions against the believers in the mountains. Now, God talks about retribution. The time will come when the false church will be dealt with. *"Dearly beloved, avenge not yourselves, but rather give place unto wrath: for it is written, Vengeance is mine; I will repay, saith the Lord."* (Romans 12:19). Do not take matters into your own hands. Leave it on God's. Who knows if down the road of life your forgiving example will touch the heart of your enemy and he will become a fellow believer. It will help to read verses 17,18, 20 & 21 of Romans 12 because they teach us how to treat our enemies (contrary to the philosophy of the fallen church that persecuted those that did not agree with her erroneous teachings): *"Do not repay anyone evil for evil. Be careful to do what is right in the eyes of everybody. If it is possible, as far as it depends on you, live at peace with everyone."* (Romans 12:17,18 NIV). *"On the contrary: "If your enemy is hungry, feed him; if he is thirsty, give him something to drink. In doing this, you will heap burning coals on his head. Do not be overcome by evil, but overcome evil with good."* (Romans 12:20, 21 NIV). Vengeance does not satisfy. Forgiveness takes the weight off our shoulders and allows us to sleep, eat and enjoy life. This does not mean that you will let your guard down. You have to be vigilant to avoid even risking your life.

24But unto you I say, and unto the rest in Thyătira, as many as have not this doctrine, and which have not known the depths of Satan, as they speak; I will put upon you none other burden.

None other burden - God weighs the trials before they come to our lives. *"There hath no temptation taken you but such as is common to man: but God is faithful, who will not suffer you to be tempted above that ye are able; but will with the temptation also make a way to escape, that ye may be able to bear it."* (1 Corinthians 10:13). The way to escape for these believers was first the mountains in Europe and then America. We will see this in more detail in chapter 12.

25But that which ye have already hold fast till I come.

They had the precious promises of God to sustain them and no one would be able to take salvation away from them.

26And he that overcometh, and keepeth my works unto the end, to him will I give power over the nations:

These believers had been under Roman Catholic rulership and oppression. Jesus' promise was to reverse that. Observe that Jesus talks about keeping his works. Even though salvation is obtained by faith, God expects obedience from the believer. *"For we are his workmanship, created in Christ Jesus unto good works, which God hath before ordained that we should walk in them."* (Ephesians 2:8-10). Not our works with the intent of obtaining merits like the popular church taught, but works that come out spontaneously from love, not premeditated or planned. I am not meaning that planning a mission trip is wrong. I would also like to go one day. I am referring to works to gain favor before God and even to be noticed by people. The Christian also has to grow spiritually: *"For this very reason, make every effort to add to your faith goodness; and to goodness, knowledge; and to knowledge, self-control; and to self-control, perseverance; and to perseverance, godliness; and to godliness, brotherly kindness; and to brotherly kindness, love. For if you possess these qualities in increasing measure, they will keep you from being ineffective and unproductive in your knowledge of our Lord Jesus Christ."* (2 Peter 1:5-8).

27And he shall rule them with a rod of iron; as the vessels of a potter shall they be broken to shivers: even as I received of my Father.

This by no means indicates that the persecuted believers would become oppressors, but rather, that they will share an unquestionable authority with their Savior as *"joint-heirs with Christ"* (Romans 8:17) when He establishes His kingdom.

28And I will give him the morning star.

The light of a star- In contrast with the darkness of the Middle Ages.

29He that hath an ear, let him hear what the Spirit saith unto the churches.

Are we listening to the admonitions and taking heed of the promises of God?

REVELATION 3

The letters to the seven churches- part II.

These are the churches presented in chapter 3 and the period of church history that they represent:

Church	Meaning	Dates	Problem	Promise to those that overcome
Sardis	Remnant or what remains	1517-1798	Dead works	White raiment, name in book of life
Philadelphia	Brotherly love	1798-1843	Little strength	Kept from hour of trial, pillar in temple, name of God written on them
Laodicea	Judging of the people	1843-End	Lukewarm, spiritual poverty, blindness, and nakedness	Sit with Christ on His throne. Sup with Christ.

[1]*And unto the angel of the church in Sardis write; These things saith he that hath the seven Spirits of God, and the seven stars; I know thy works, that thou hast a name that thou livest, and art dead.*

Sardis means *"what remains."* It is the church of the Reformation. The Catholic Church was selling indulgences (a document that ensured forgiveness, even on sins not yet committed or on behalf of people already dead to get them out of "purgatory" sooner). A Roman Catholic monk named Martin Luther, having found himself unable to justify the practice by the Scriptures, nailed the famous 95 Theses on the doors of the Castle Church in Wittenberg, Germany, on October 31, 1517. The theses "... challenged the teachings of the Catholic Church on the nature of penance, the authority of the pope and the usefulness of indulgences. It sparked a theological debate that fueled the Reformation and subsequently resulted in the birth of Protestantism and the Lutheran, Reformed, and Anabaptist traditions within Christianity." http://www.theopedia.com/95_Theses. This act started the Reformation. Within a few weeks, the theses had been translated into the diverse languages of Europe and spread like a wild fire in a hot summer. Until that time, the church had a padlock on the consciences of the believers, keeping them in ignorance of the plan of salvation. Superstition was taught as if it were the gospel. The believers were taught to do pilgrimages and to give big offerings to obtain the favor of God. It was believed that when people died, they would go either to heaven (and for that they had to be a real saint), to hell, or to a place of transition called purgatory where the souls would be purged through suffering until they paid for all their sins and were deemed worthy of moving to heaven. In order to accelerate "the transfer of loved ones" to heaven, the church invented the indulgences. Johann Tetzel, an unscrupulous Dominican priest, was selling them in Germany using a rhyme that said something like: "the coin the coffer hitting, the soul purgatory fleeing." Tetzel was commissioned by the Archbishop of Mainz and Pope Leo X. The money collected in that fundraising campaign was used to build St. Peter's Basilica in Rome. Many people even bought indulgences to sin in advance (by buying a plenary indulgence), "claiming they no longer had to repent of their sins, since the document promised to forgive all their sins." *Ibid.*

"the seven Spirits of God" -It is not that God has seven spirits; it is the ways in which the Spirit manifests Himself in the work of salvation: *"And the spirit of the LORD shall rest upon him, the spirit of wisdom and understanding, the spirit of counsel and might, the spirit of knowledge and of the fear of the LORD"* (Isaiah 11:2).

"thou hast a name that thou livest, and art dead" This reminds me of the oldest brother in the parable of the prodigal son. *"Meanwhile, the older son was in the field. When he came near the house, he heard music and dancing. So he called one of the servants and asked him what was going on. 'Your brother has come,' he replied, 'and your father has killed the fattened calf because he has him back safe and sound.' "The older brother became angry and refused to go in. So his father went out and pleaded with him. But he answered his father, 'Look! All these years I've been slaving for you and never disobeyed your orders. Yet you never gave me even a young goat so I could celebrate with my friends. But when this son of yours who*

has squandered your property with prostitutes comes home, you kill the fattened calf for him!' "'My son,' the father said, 'you are always with me, and everything I have is yours. But we had to celebrate and be glad, because this brother of yours was dead and is alive again; he was lost and is found.'" (Luke 15:25-31 NIV). Thus, in the same way many in the church act with self-righteousness. We see in this parable one that seemed to be dead but was alive and one that seemed to be alive but was dead. How do we know our condition? Paul gives us guidance in 2 Corinthians 13:5: *"Examine ourselves, whether ye be in the faith; prove your own selves. Know ye not your own selves, how that Jesus Christ is in you, except ye be reprobates?"* The Pharisees in the times of Jesus thought about themselves to be righteous and looked down on other people. I am glad that God looks in the heart.

One of my favorite Bible passages is the parable of the Pharisee and the publican (Luke 18:10-14). Regarding those that justify themselves, Paul wrote that they had *"a form of godliness but denying its power"* (2 Timothy 3:5). Having just a form will not create a transforming relationship with Jesus. We have to allow Him to come to our lives and live His life in us. *"I am crucified with Christ: nevertheless I live; yet not I, but Christ liveth in me: and the life which I now live in the flesh I live by the faith of the Son of God, who loved me, and gave himself for me"* (Galatians 2:20).

[2]*Be watchful, and strengthen the things which remain, that are ready to die: for I have not found thy works perfect before God.*

The city of Sardis was captured twice even though its topography made its inhabitants believe that it was inexpugnable. It is believed that it was conquered because the guard fell asleep. That is why Jesus reminds them to be "watchful." In times of John, the city that at its prime was very populous, was almost dead.

I have not found thy works perfect before God- Their works were not the fruit of faith and love but of duty. Our works and the motivation behind them are not unknown to the eyes of Jesus: *"Ye shall know them by their fruits. ..."* (Matthew 7:16).

[3]Remember therefore how thou hast received and heard, and hold fast, and repent. If therefore thou shalt not watch, I will come on thee as a thief, and thou shalt not know what hour I will come upon thee.

Jesus is telling us to remember HOW we received His knowledge. Do you remember how you got to know Jesus? Sometimes we have a hard time to remember the first time we met another human being. But to forget Him? Do you remember how you felt when you found out that Jesus loves you and that He wanted to forgive your sins and take you to heaven with Him? Did you rejoice on His love for you? Did His sacrifice move the most inner cords of your heart to produce a melodious praise to Jesus for being such a great friend of sinners?

Again, Jesus emphasizes the need to be watchful and announces that He will come as a thief, completely unexpected. The only difference is that this Thief is telling us to be watchful so we cannot be taken by surprise, unlike ordinary thieves that will never give us such a hint.

[4]Thou hast a few names even in Sardis which have not defiled their garments; and they shall walk with me in white: for they are worthy.

"The Lord knoweth them that are his" (2 Timothy 2:19). The world might forget about you and even malign your character, but Jesus will never forget about you. *"Can a woman forget her sucking child, that she should not have compassion on the son of her womb? yea, they may forget, yet will I not forget thee"* (Isaiah 49:15).

They shall walk with me in white - The white garments are a symbol of the righteousness of Jesus (Revelation 19:8) that replaces your sinful character before God. Jesus takes the record of His perfect life and it is attributed to you just as if you were the one who lived without sin. When God then looks towards you, He sees the perfection of Christ and that alone grants you the right to heaven.

[5]He that overcometh, the same shall be clothed in white raiment; and I will not blot out his name out of the book of life, but I will confess his name before my Father, and before his angels. [6]He that hath an ear, let him hear what the Spirit saith unto the churches.

As Uriah Smith noted, if those faithful will not have their names blotted out of the book of life, it is implied that those that are not faithful will have their names removed. Remember that the book of life contains the names of those that ever professed to follow Jesus. We need to remain in the faith if we want our names to be kept by the Faithful Witness. That salvation can be lost, it is presented in the book of Ezekiel 33:13 *"When I shall say to the righteous, that he shall surely live; if he trust to his own righteousness, and commit iniquity, all his righteousnesses shall not be remembered; but for his iniquity that he hath committed, he shall die for it."* Paul confirmed it in his sermon to the Hebrews 10:26 *"For if we sin willfully after that we have received the knowledge of the truth, there remaineth no more sacrifice for sins."* In addition, God had told Moses: *"And the LORD said unto Moses, Whosoever hath sinned against me, him will I <u>blot out of my book</u>"* (Exodus 32:33).

I will confess his name before my Father, and before his angels" Those that overcome do so because they are not ashamed of their beloved Master. *"Whosoever therefore shall confess me before men, him will I confess also before my Father which is in heaven"* (Matthew 10:32). *"Whosoever therefore shall be ashamed of me and of my words in this adulterous and sinful generation; of him also shall the Son of man be ashamed, when he cometh in the glory of his Father with the holy angels."* (Mark 8:38). .

[7]*And to the angel of the church in Philadelphia write; These things saith he that is holy, he that is true, he that hath the key of David, he that openeth, and no man shutteth; and shutteth, and no man openeth*

Philadelphia means "brotherly love." This church corresponds with the years 1798-1843. This was the time when the modern missions were started. Great missionaries went to Africa, China and other dark areas of the world to bring the light of the gospel.

David Livingstone (1813-1873), a doctor, wanted to be missionary to China but the doors were closed due to the opium war. At that time he became acquainted with Robert Moffat, the great missionary to South Africa, and the man who said, "Oh, that I had a thousand lives and a thousand bodies, all should be devoted to preach Christ to these benighted people." Moffat encouraged

Livingstone to make Africa the field of his labors. Livingstone traveled some 30,000 miles into the heart of that continent. From 1851 to 1856, he walked across Africa from west to east. Like the prophet Jeremiah, he had a burning desire to bring the gospel message to lost men.

After spending a few years in Africa without anyone receiving news from him, it was believed that he was either lost or dead. Then, an American newspaper sent a reporter on a special mission to find him. The man chosen was Henry Stanley. He traveled through the African jungles until finally he found Livingstone serving the sick and needy while preaching the gospel. After spending four months with the dedicated doctor, Mr. Stanley wrote: "I went to Africa as prejudiced as the biggest atheist in London. But there came a long time for reflection. I saw this solitary old man there and asked myself, 'How on earth does he stay here? What is it that inspires him?' For months I found myself wondering at the old man carrying out all that was said in the Bible,...But little by little my sympathy was aroused. Seeing his piety, his gentleness, his zeal, his earnestness, I was converted by him although he had not tried to do it! It was not Livingstone's preaching which converted me. *It was Livingstone's living*!" Such was the spirit of these great missionaries. They did not have to speak. Their lives were a living gospel. We need to revive that zeal.

The following were some of the great preachers and evangelists from the period of Philadelphia. Their sacrificial missionary spirit characterized the feelings of the church of that time:

William Carey (1761-1834)	Pioneer Missionary to India
George Liele (1773-1828)	African American missionary to Jamaica
Henry Martyn (1781-1812)	India, Persia
Robert Morrison (1782-1834)	China missionary
Adoniram Judson (1788-1850)	Burma missionary
Ann Hasseltine Judson (1789-1826)	Pioneer missionary to Myanmar
Robert Moffat (1795-1883)	South Africa
Alexander Duff (1806-1878)	India
J. Hudson Taylor (1832-1905)	China
Charles Haddon Spurgeon (1834-1892)	The greatest preacher from England
D.L. Moody (1837-1899)	American evangelist

Some quotes from missionaries from the period of Philadelphia:

"If I had 1,000 lives, I'd give them all for China" -- Hudson Taylor

"To know the will of God, we need an open Bible and an open map." - William Carey

"If a commission by an earthly king is considered an honor, how can a commission by a Heavenly King be considered a sacrifice?" - David Livingstone

"Sympathy is no substitute for action." - David Livingstone

"Someone asked '*Will the heathen who have never heard the Gospel be saved?*' It is more a question with me whether we - who have the Gospel and fail to give it to those who have not - can be saved." - Charles Spurgeon.

8I know thy works: behold, I have set before thee an open door, and no man can shut it: for thou hast a little strength, and hast kept my word, and hast not denied my name.

Jesus is referring here to the door of the most holy place in the heavenly sanctuary that was about to open. This refers back to the work of judgment (cleansing of the sanctuary) described in Daniel 8:14.

In contrast with Sardis, this church was actively confessing Jesus' name before the world.

9Behold, I will make them of the synagogue of Satan, which say they are Jews, and are not, but do lie; behold, I will make them to come and worship before thy feet, and to know that I have loved thee.

Jesus wants us to remember that *"thou wast precious in my sight, thou hast been honourable, and I have loved thee"* (Isaiah 43:4). Do you know where Jesus has your name recorded? It is in the wounds of His hands. *"Behold, I have graven thee upon the palms of my hands..."* (Isaiah 49:16). When His hands were nailed to the cross taking your place and paying for your sins, your name was engraved by the nails and will remain there as a proof that your debt has been paid. That is why you are precious in His sight.

10Because thou hast kept the word of my patience, I also will keep thee from the hour of temptation, which shall come upon all the world, to try them that dwell upon the earth.

This is the hour of trial or great disappointment described in chapter 10. That chapter describes the time when many Christians around the world expected Jesus to return for His people and it did not happen. They misunderstood the prophecy of Daniel 8:14.

11Behold, I come quickly: hold that fast which thou hast, that no man take thy crown.

In the times of John, the winners of athletic competitions were rewarded with a crown of leaves. The crown offered by Jesus to His followers is an eternal crown of glory (1 Peter 5:4)- one that will never wither.

12Him that overcometh will I make a pillar in the temple of my God, and he shall go no more out: and I will write upon him the name of my God, and the name of the city of my God, which is new Jerusalem, which cometh down out of heaven from my God: and I will write upon him my new name.

Philadelphia was in an area prone to have earthquakes. There was a column in the middle of the city that remained standing quake after quake. The storms of temptation embattle God's children but in His power, we can remain standing regardless of how hard we are hit. If we fall, He will stretch His mighty hand and make us stand again. The temple is mentioned here because the work of judgment foretold by Daniel was about to begin during the next and last period of church history. "Among the Greek colonies and Churches of Asia, Philadelphia is still erect—a column in a scene of ruins,—a pleasing example that the paths of honour and safety may sometimes be the same." Trench, *Commentary on the Epistles to the Seven Churches in Asia, 188.*

13He that hath an ear, let him hear what the Spirit saith unto the churches.

The church of this time (Philadelphia) did hear what Jesus had to say. Not so with the one that followed:

[14]And unto the angel of the church of the Laodiceans write; These things saith the Amen, the faithful and true witness, the beginning of the creation of God;

Laodicea means "judging of the people" or "people of the judgment." It is not a coincidence that the meaning of the name of the church that covers the last period of church history points to the work of Jesus in the heavenly sanctuary. Later on in chapter 14, we read about three angels with an urgent message. *"He said in a loud voice, 'Fear God and give him glory, because* ***<u>the hour of his judgment has come</u>****. Worship him who made the heavens, the earth, the sea and the springs of water'"* (Revelation 14:7). God is calling our attention to the work of judgment being done by Jesus. Too bad Christian leaders do not recognize the Bible doctrine of the investigative judgment that started in the year 1844. This is the year of the fulfillment of the prophecy found in Daniel 8:14: *"And he said unto me, Unto two thousand and three hundred days; then shall the sanctuary be cleansed."* As we discussed before, a day in Bible prophecy is equivalent to a year. The prophecy was to begin when the order was given to rebuild Jerusalem. That order was given in the year 457 BC. By adding 2,300 years to 457, we reach the year 1844. During the Day of Atonement in ancient Israel, the Israelites had to afflict their souls (see Leviticus 16:29,30). Jewish scholars consider that day one of judgment. Their sins had been symbolically transferred to the sanctuary all previous year through their daily sacrifices. The Day of Atonement was the day when their sins were removed from the sanctuary, pointing to the work that Jesus was going to do in the heavenly sanctuary by removing our sins from the books (see Revelation 20:12).

"the beginning of the creation of God" Why did Jesus identifies Himself this way? Considering that the church of Laodicea represents the church after 1843, we can see that Jesus wanted to emphasize His role as Creator. The word "beginning" refers to origin, so it could be translated as "the origin of the creation of God." The gospel of John identifies Jesus as Creator (John 1:1-3). Moreover, when Peter was preaching, he called Jesus *"the author of life"* (Acts 3:15 NIV). Do you already see why Jesus called

Himself the origin of creation in His message to the last church in history? During the 19th century, Charles Darwin wrote a book that contradicted Jesus' claim: *The Origin of Species.* Our Lord is the real origin of the species. It was as if Jesus was predicting the title of the book that was to deviate so many millions of souls from the truth. Satan has always presented a contrast to everything that God has (Sabbath vs. Sunday; Spirit of Prophecy Vs. false prophet, etc.); now he presents evolution (and atheism) to try to argue against creation. Later in chapter 14, Jesus will use the three angels to emphasize His claim as Creator. *"worship him that made heaven, and earth, and the sea, and the fountains of waters"* (Revelation 14:7). We are not the product of coincidence, but of careful design.

Evolutionists teach that it took millions of years for one creature to evolve into another completely different. Let us imagine that a one-cell organism that lives in the water is going to develop into a dog. How long could that creature live without a respiratory system with lungs? How long would it take to develop a musculoskeletal system and legs so he could walk to procure his food? How did it know that it needed not only bones, but also tendons, cartilage, a nervous system, and more important, how did the creature know about walking so it could use all of the above? How was its DNA encoded to contain the necessary information to perpetuate those changes so they could be passed to the next generations? Without that, the dogs would continue changing and we have never seen one animal changing into a completely different one. Regardless of the diverse breeds of canines in the world, a dog is still, well, a dog- and still behaves like one too.

DNA codes genetic information for the transmission of inherited traits and also dictates the structure and function of living things. The structure of the DNA strand has a specific design that varies from species to species. It does not just happen. Retired professor Ariel Roth, Ph.D., wrote:

"...What is the chance that in the proposed evolution of the first life, the right enzyme will form (assuming that all the necessary components [amino acids] present are already present)? Mathematical calculations indicate that it is only one chance of the number 49 followed by 190 zeros. This incredibly small chance, which borders on the impossible, gives you just one enzyme; and you need several hundred different enzymes for just one organism.

"Another study indicates that the probability of forming even the smallest microbe is only one chance out of the number 1 followed by 5,000 million zeros. To write out that number would require 6,000 books of zeros. Those books would make very boring reading." *Signs of the Times, October 2003, page 18.*

When scientists claim that our DNA is 94-98% (depending on the source) similar to the DNA of chimps, they do not admit to remove genomes- DNA components-in order to make us "related" to apes. In humans there are 3,000,000,000 base pairs containing up to 100,000 genes. "It is also important to recognize that the term the human genome is somewhat misleading, because there is no single genome sequence that defines everyone. No two humans other than identical twins share identical genomes. For the rest, although the genomes are more than 99% identical, each is unique." (Britannica Encyclopedia 2002, article *Human Genome Project: Road Map for Science and Medicine*). If humans are different from each other, why scientists insist in comparing us to animals? There are 60,000,000 differences between chimps and humans' DNA but they do not want to admit it.

Unexpected changes in one species are called mutations. In reality, they are bloopers from nature and in no case, these changes have produced a completely different species. On the contrary, when they reproduce, the offspring is not a different creature, but looks like the grandparents in that species. For example, when was the last time that you saw a fly laying an egg and a bird, puppy or kitten came out of it?

In an article published in the Journal of Experimental Biology February 9, 2012, Susanne Åkesson, an evolutionary ecologist at Lund University in Sweden and her colleagues detailed their findings regarding the stripes on zebras. The article indicates that the stripes may deter bloodsucking insects. Since zebra embryos start out with a dark skin but go on to develop white stripes before birth, the researchers wondered if their striped hides might help make zebras less attractive to pests such as horseflies. Such findings are, as the great majority of evolution-oriented "findings" just a theory because they admit not having yet performed these experiments in Africa where the zebras live. Such is the arrogance of these scientists when they present an idea and put it at the level of a law, giving to it a weight that in reality it lacks. One thing that caught my attention was their effort to try to explain why zebras evolved their stripes without considering how the body of any living being works. Every living cell is a complicated chemical factory and all the body functions are regulated by electrical impulses. The chemical reactions necessary to preserve life occur with mathematical precision. Such intricacy requires complicated equations that a cell on its own cannot produce. If a whole animal is not capable of working with complex chemical and electrical formulas, how can we expect a single cell to decide to develop (in this case) stripes and register that knowledge and complicated formulas in the DNA in order to preserve it for future generations? The sum of the individual components is always more complex than the individual parts, so the brain of an animal must be capable of greater accomplishments than those of an individual cell or groups of cells. I have yet to find a zebra capable of understanding chemistry, biology or calculus. The idea that the zebra developed (or evolved, as the article calls it) stripes, implies that at some point the zebra saw it necessary to develop the new design and somehow came up with the plan to allocate resources for the implementation of the changes. The factories at cell level had to be re-tooled to launch the changes and a series of trial and error experiments had to occur until the zebra got it right and then registered the patent details in the DNA encoding. I know that Thomas Edison and Henry Ford would have been proud of the Zebra.

And what about reproduction in general? How did the different species reproduce before sexual organs developed? How come so many thousands of creatures suddenly had a male and female version and both had what was needed to reproduce alike life (not only the sperm and the egg but also the correct amount of chromosomes in each)? I do not think that anyone could calculate the probabilities that each one of the members of the mammal kingdom would have male and female, not to mention the inclusion of the birds, fish, reptiles and even insects in the formula. How did they share the knowledge of what worked so the other beings could reproduce in like manner? I wonder what would have happened, for example, if the first cat was a female. How many years would pass before a male appear? It would have to take just a few short years, probably no more that six to make reproduction more feasible. What are the probabilities that they would meet and produce kittens? What if the female was in what is now China and the male in Argentina? There was no matchmaker's service like eharmony.com or match.com back then and much less for cats- neither was a priceline.com to help them buy the airline tickets (and who would fly the plane if none at that time existed to design it and manufacture it?). To assume that sexual reproduction just happened across all nature (thousands upon thousands of species) is a complete non-sense. Either it would have to happen with a 100% successful launch of the new design or it would have been through trial and error. The first option points to planning, decision making, design. Design has to forcibly point to a designer. The second option is the haphazard (random, hit and miss) effort, mostly fruitless, to come up with a solution that eventually- across the whole of nature- would produce success. That means that some primitive, uncultured, untrained being would brilliantly come up with the idea of the need for reproduction and successfully also come up with a solution to change infertility into fertility producing, at least at first, a perfect clone. Somehow, that reproduction was very probably asexual and would have to eventually produce a male and a female to continue the cycle of life- all within only one lifetime. We all know that infertility problems do not resolve on their own, even for us humans, being such "advanced creatures." That is why we have fertility clinics and complicated interventions to accomplish that which nature could not do on its own. What in the world would make a reasonable person believe that in one generation- failure would have require starting all over again- a cat would reproduce a fertile litter of kittens, born as babies (not adult size)? It would also be required that she would have maternal instincts to tenderly care for them, raise them up and produce milk to keep them alive until they could chase Mickey Mouse and feed themselves.

Several times, I have heard about new species being discovered in different places of the world. The thing is that they all have male and female. Is that a coincidence? I think not. Even some trees do not reproduce unless there is one of each. For example, kiwis and mulberry trees need a pair of male and female in order for fruit to appear after the blooms. Talking about tree, what came first, the roots or the leaves?

How about the eye, with all its components? How did all those parts of the eye come together to make a functional organ? How long would it take to learn how to use those eyes? Why two eyes, and not one, or even three? Again, how did the first being with eyes know about the concept of sight? Why the mammals, birds, reptiles and amphibians have eyes? Was it by word of mouth that the knowledge of how good was to have eyes spread? At what stage of the development chain did eyes appear? Some creatures such as bats and dolphins even have sonar in addition to eyes. Did those tools develop by coincidence? Let us see: rats (have eyes- two of them, symmetrical); cats (have eyes- two of them, symmetrical); dogs (have eyes- two of them, symmetrical); cows (have eyes- two of them, symmetrical); horses (have eyes- two of them, symmetrical).... We cannot say that they had some kind of internet back then to google the word "eye" –to find out how to develop, place and use them. After all, they had no eyes yet to read the computer screen and no computers were known either. Birds, mammals, reptiles, fish and amphibians, all have the same configuration of two eyes, one mouth, one nose and two ears in the head- coincidence? We can see symmetry in all creation. The left side mirrors the right side. As I type this, I am glancing at my dog and feel so grateful that he was designed and looks beautiful, not like a freak of nature, as I know he would look if he had evolved, coming out of a "soup." Talking about soups, I just made potato soup for dinner and nothing in my bowl was in order.

Why our noses have built-in air warmers? Without them, we would be constantly getting sick, even with pneumonia. Why the sense of smell? If it is just a development and nothing else, why that sense bows to great aromas such as those of food and perfume? Why make it enjoyable to smell? It would just have sufficed to enable us to distinguish rotten food from fresh one. Why our mouths have tongues to help us chew and swallow our meals? Why our tongues can taste? If we are the product of evolution, why enjoy what we eat and not just eat to survive? How did we grow our teeth- two sets with the first of them temporary and small so they fit in the mouths of the young?

Or how long until birds developed hollowed bones and feathers to enable them to fly? How many generations of birds froze to death before they learned how to migrate? *"Even storks know when it is time to return; doves, swallows, and thrushes know when it is time to migrate...."* (Jeremiah 8:7). How did the first pair that migrated transmit the knowledge of routes to the new chicks? Was there a conversation like this after the first successful trip?:

Papa bird: "Mama bird, did you take note of all the landmarks that we flew over and the position of the stars in heaven as we agree before our trip?

Mama bird: "Yes, papa bird. I did and I drew it in two maps- one for landmarks so they know where to stop for a meal, and another for the stars so they can fly at night. When we have our chicks, I will show them the maps and help them memorize them. They will know every 'McCornfield' and every 'Bulgur King' location- we need to work on site loyalty. We have to make hard efforts to invent the biological GPS and pass it in the DNA to our future chicks so it will be standard factory equipment. I also took note of the air currents to save some energy, although your belly is telling me that you need to burn a few more calories my dear. Loose the worm remote Virgil!"

How did they manage to have the chicks at the appropriate time and not at any time of the year- like in the middle of winter? After all, they had no Franklin planners or the Farmers' Almanac back then. How did they know how far to travel, how long to stay and the way back? Although at times the routes vary, they end up in the same areas year after year- and to think that it took humans such a long time to develop an electronic GPS. If we are the highest expression of the evolutionary process, why don't we develop an internal GPS and sonar too- to supply the lack of night vision?

How many birds could live a normal life waiting for a heart and other components of the cardiovascular system to develop so it would pump and circulate oxygen-transporting blood? Could they live more than just a few days without a liver or kidneys to purify their blood? Without kidneys to filter our blood, our bodies would quickly fill with toxins and we would soon die. How did the pre-bird creature know that it needed those organs and how to produce them? At the least, we would have to give some credit to that primitive creature for being so smart in executing such complicated and harmonious design. It seems that those primitive creatures had a higher IQ than some of today's scientists. I lost a friend because the organs started to shut down. You see, it requires a lot of faith to accept the fallacy of evolution because it teaches that the things that we know about the living creatures and in human beings developed over a long period of time. How can a being survive without vital organs? We even forget about the largest of them all: the skin that protects us and at the same time is permeable and breathable so we can obtain oxygen through it. Not only animals across all fauna, but also fruits and vegetables count with skin protection. How could an intelligent person, such as a scientist with a doctorate degree allows himself or herself to be fooled into believing that all life on earth is pure and simple coincidence? Just look at yourself in the mirror and see if you can say, after a careful and conscientious examination of the details on your face and body, "I am an accident." *"You turn things upside down! Is the potter no better than his clay? Can something that has been made say about its maker, 'He didn't make me'? Can a piece of pottery say about the potter, 'He doesn't understand'?"* (Isaiah 29:16 *God's Word*).

All the proposed trial and error of the evolutionary theories point more to the error side than to success and accuracy in the development of functional systems of true survival. The point would not be the survival of the fittest, but rather survival in itself, because there is no way that all the necessary elements to accomplish the successful simultaneous development of all the organs would be in place without an intelligence to guide such colossal feat. I chose the word colossal because it must be taken into consideration the design elements involved in the development of new organs, down to the kind of cells that would perform the function, then, the chemicals needed to accomplish it, the voltage (in the case of the heart specially), how the organ would interact with the others, the blood demands, the arrangement of the blood vessels, the disposal of waste, the method of repair when damage occurs and last but not less crucial, how to make sure that the DNA would include the necessary information at the time of reproduction. Otherwise, it would be back to the drawing board again and again while more beings continue dying until all the elements work right as expected. But, could I afford to use the word expected when all these processes were supposed to happen randomly?

I once had 126 carburetor components on a table. I left them there for a few hours while I slept for the night. None of them came together on their own. You can be sure that I was disappointed. I had to assemble them so the final product would do what I needed it to do: in combination with the precisely timed spark and measured intake of air, produce an explosion that would move the pistons, which would turn the crankshaft, which would transfer the rotational movement to the transmission, which ultimately would turn the tires so my vehicle would ride. I put only one part backwards and that caused problems. The car was drivable but hesitant. It was only after that only part was placed correctly that the car roared hungry for the road ahead. I am glad that all my components were designed properly and assembled correctly at the factory *"I praise you because I am fearfully and wonderfully made; your works are wonderful, I know that full well"* (Psalm 139:14). If those carburetor parts that had once worked together before I took them apart did not come back together on their own, how can we expect that parts that were never associated and that are structurally and functionally diverse will join and cooperate with each other as one on their own? Stomach connected to intestines? Gallbladder and pancreas to the duodenum? Bones to flesh? Eyes-to brain nerve-to brain? Hairs to skin? Veins and arteries to heart, lungs and tissues? Wow! All the things that I learned from a carburetor! Of course, I recognize that my sarcasm had surface by using an inanimate object but I consider that fits the purpose of the illustration of how our human body could not have evolve by a coincidental chain of events. It is not my intent to offend anyone but to awaken the reasoning power of the human brain to the reality of a plan behind everything that exists on this planet and the whole universe.

Let us suppose that in reality a cell from a "soup" in the ocean was able to create all those organs, continually evolving into a superior form of life. According to evolution, today's cells are more complicated, and after so many generations of progressive evolution (aka, experience), they could be even more capable of producing a complicated life form and do it faster- but it is not happening. I remember watching a neighbor cutting off a hen's head. I saw the head falling to the ground. It bled out but it did not develop a new body. Neither did the body grow a new head. All a body is capable of doing is heal a wound as long as the correct conditions are present such as, yes, keeping the head. If a simple cell supposedly was capable of evolving into a more complex form of life, why then, a whole set of cells with a brain (from the chicken) could not recreate a body and then evolve into some superior being? My neighbor would have been so scared that he would never have dared to kill another chicken for fear of revenge while he slept. Even if the head could artificially be kept alive, it could not recreate the body (like a star fish can) without external help or manipulation. If a simple creature like a starfish can reproduce from a body part, a more complex animal like a chicken that can raise a family, distinguish sounds and colors and can find its way back home, could also recreate its body. Somewhere "evolution" seemed to have failed the poor chicken and work only for the less complex starfish, and although if reproduces, the product is still a starfish and does not evolve into any superior or more complex being- like a shark. Now I have a question, what came first in mammals, birds, reptiles and fish, the head or the body?

Can you imagine having your eyes at the bottom of your feet (Visine stock would be more valuable), or just above your belly button (clothes would be more complicated to make)? They are on our face so we can look effortlessly. If we evolved, what would have guaranteed that the eyes would not appear in the middle of our backs? It certainly would not make it easy for us to walk unless we had also been fit with a mirror to see where we go. It would feel like driving a car in reverse all the time. If the first eyes appeared on the back of the tights, how many attempts to place them in the right place would it take? They would have to be moved upwards by every generation and then to the front, both at the same time and to the same location next to each other on opposite sides of the face, connected to the brain and protected by the eyelids and eyebrows. And we should not forget the eye sockets in which they sit and the two sets of muscles to move them and to focus, and the system to keep them lubricated. Is all that a coincidence? Which was the first creature that accomplished all that? For all those details to be achieved across all the fauna worldwide, across the oceans and across species, it had to be an implanted code in the DNA. It has yet to be found how to communicate it or share the knowledge to the other beings so they too could have two functioning eyes in the correct place- the head, and a way to keep the achievement stable in the DNA so it would not be lost and all descendants would have like eyes too.

How that early cell developed four legs for mammals and two for humans? Can you imagine having the incredible intellectual capabilities such as we human beings have and live in the body of a chicken? Could we have developed the marvelous architectural beauties, the sculptures and paintings that impress and captivate us today? How could Beethoven have composed his famous and inspiring music using chicken wings? How could the other chickens play that music? I mean, could they play the violin and the other instruments (and they have to make the instruments first)? Can you imagine a chicken surgeon? I am glad that the correct combination of brain-body exists. It is not an accident that we are how we are! The first living creature had to have a brain, knowledge or instinct of the need to find food, an opening to get the food (mouth), the ability to ingest that food and digest it. There are digestive enzymes in the saliva, which chemically breaks down carbohydrates into simpler compounds. The tongue moves the food around to mix it properly with the saliva and to surrender it to the crushing molars to break the food down. Then there are muscles to facilitate swallowing. Further down, the stomach, pancreas and liver produce digestive fluids and mix them up with the food. From there the food goes to the small intestine. The function of the small intestine is to break down food and to remove proteins, carbohydrates, fats, vitamins, and minerals. Additionally, the "creature" had to have a way to dispose of the waste so it had to, at the least, guess that it had the need for a large intestine. In there, water and inorganic salts are reabsorbed. For a great description of how the digestive process works and an idea of how complex it is, see this website:

http://www.lab.anhb.uwa.edu.au/mb140/CorePages/GIT/git.htm#topiclargeintestine

How long could a being go without having a stomach and intestines? I once had a dear friend, an elderly lady, who had her stomach removed due to cancer. The doctor said that a person could not survive long without a stomach. I had the sad honor of officiating her funeral just a few months later. Although modern medicine can help a person survive longer without a stomach, he or she will likely be obese due to the function of that organ to start the digestion of proteins and carbohydrates. The whole process of digestion requires a delicate balance of different PH's according to the phase of digestion and also the type of food ingested. The digestion is affected by temperature of the food and amount of water in it. If the food is too cold, the stomach raises its temperature. It there is too much liquid so as to dilute the gastric juices, the stomach must dispose of the excess of liquid to then continue a proper digestion-that is why we must not drink with our meals. Drinking water <u>between</u> meals is the best practice. How is all that operation coordinated? If the stomach just appeared, it will probably do only one function: squeeze the food and expel it to the next department down the road until it "learn" to do better and become more efficient. After all, the body needed return on investment. The digestive process follows an orderly and complicated procedure, and only when the food is ready for the next department is then released.

How is the stomach protected against the effect of its own enzymes and acids (it can even dissolve zinc)? First, there is a gastric mucus layer, a glycoprotein that forms a protective coating over the lining epithelium of the stomach cavity. This is the first defense mechanism the stomach has against being digested by its own enzymes, and its production is due to the secretion of bicarbonate (alkaline) into the surface layer from behind the mucosa. This action is initiated by the prostaglandins; hormone-like substances derived from dietary lipids that fuel the migration of cells to the surface of the mucosa for repair and replacement of the mucosal lining (the stomach lining actually renews itself so fast that there is not enough time for the acid to eat through it). Another element in the protection of the stomach walls from digestive juices is a membrane that, by being rich in lipoproteins, is resistant to attack by acid. The whole process of digestion, from varying the PH, to releasing the different chemicals needed just in time for every step in the process, works as finely tuned as the best orchestra in the world.

I wrote only on the stomach, but the process of digesting the food continues in the intestines and involves other organs such as the pancreas and the liver, which at the precise time release their chemicals necessary to break down the food. Even blood circulation is altered during this process. How could all of this complication be the product of coincidence at a time when science did not exist to help supply the need (through human engineering sciences, biochemistry, counseling or consultation) for all those enzymes, acids, etc. needed for the proper assimilation of foods? Those first organisms were obviously on their own- and do not forget that this was across the board. The whole fauna on the planet was on the same predicament, all trying to develop a functional digestive system. What way of communication did they use to share the progress and knowledge of what worked and what did not?

That first inhabitant of this planet had to have also the ability to efficiently use oxygen and water. How did the sources of nourishment like fruits, grains, vegetables and nuts appear with all the necessary nutrients to sustain life? How about mammary glands to feed the babies? Breast milk is different for every species because it must supply the nutritional needs of the specific baby. The first milk, called colostrum, also provides the baby with antibodies because the new creature's immune system has not developed yet. It develops on the eighth day- that is why God instructed to circumcise males when they were eight days old. In addition, milk contains growth factors proper to that species. On a different note, milk from cows can cause diabetes type 1 in infants because it contains specific antibodies for the calf that the human baby's immune system sees as invaders. The baby's defenses will produce antibodies to destroy the foreign particles but this will cause a problem because it will also attack the pancreas cells because they are very similar. This does not happen when the baby ingests his human mother's milk. Now, that milk goes through chemical changes as the baby grows to meet the changes in the baby's body. For example, the milk that the mother makes for a newborn has a different formulation than the milk produced for a one year old toddler or a two year old infant. All this happens even if the mother never took a chemistry class or just hated chemistry. She does not even have to know what elements to put in the milk. It just happens automatically. Doctor William Sears, an advocate for breast-feeding, wrote: "Each species of mammal makes a unique kind of milk, which meets all the nutritional requirements of its offspring at the beginning of life. Each species' milk has specific qualities that insure the survival of the young in a particular environment. This principle is known as the biological specificity of milk. Mother seals, for example, make high-fat milk because baby seals need lots of body fat to survive in cold water. Since brain development is crucial to the survival of humans, human milk provides nutrients for rapid brain growth." http://www.askdrsears.com/topics/feeding-eating/breastfeeding/why-breast-is-best/nutrient-nutrient-why-breast-best

Was all of this a coincidence? How would the breast know how old is the child in order to adjust the calcium, iron, phosphorus and other nutrients in the milk? How about the amount and proportions of protein and enzymes needed for the development of the baby of any species? Was all this coincidence? How many millennia would have taken for the human breast to properly tool its factory so the baby would develop into a toddler, then an infant and finally a child that will then feed himself in order to grow into an adult and continue the cycle? If we evolved, why human females do not have three or four pair of breast like animals do? What prompted the first pregnant female of every mammal species to start producing milk so their offspring would survive? How long did it take to get it right? How many attempts? Edison failed 2,000 times with the light bulb- and he had a brain and knew chemistry and math. There is no brain in any breast and it never went to school to learn the manufacturing process and to become certified in milk production. What female could afford to fail 2,000 times (= 2,000 dead babies!)? Wouldn't her species disappear before reaching the eureka moment? Then there is the issue of the dispensing of the product. How would it happen? How much needed to be produced? Which formula to use at every specific stage of the development of the offspring- because the milk composition must change as the baby grows? There are too many inconsistencies with the theory of evolution and the big bang theory. Well, I do believe somewhat in that last one. God spoke and bang!!! -life appeared on this planet: *"By the word of the LORD were the heavens made; and all the host of them by the breath of his mouth....For he spake, and it was done; he commanded, and it stood fast"* (Psalm 33:6,9). He is a God of order that created not only life on this planet but also established natural laws to keep the order in creation. The tissues that compose our organs are so different from each other, like heart, liver and brain cells, and yet, they work in a symbiotic way. Like Paul wrote in my favorite biology book: [14]*For the body is not one member, but many.* [15]*If the foot shall say, Because I am not the hand, I am not of the body; is it therefore not of the body?* [16]*And if the ear shall say, Because I am not the eye, I am not of the body; is it therefore not of the body?* [17]*If the whole body were an eye, where were the hearing? If the whole were hearing, where were the smelling?* [18]*But now hath God set the members every one of them in the body, as it hath pleased him.* [19]*And if they were all one member, where were the body?"* (1 Corinthians 12:14-19). The complexity of our organs, regardless of their cells diversity and how they work harmoniously, are an undeniable indication of design. We know that the cells from the liver are different from the cells of the stomach, and yet, they work in concert to produce the digestion process. The configuration of each organ is so precise, that arranged differently, it would simply not work- just imagine having your kidneys where the heart is now, connected to the lungs (they will always fill with fluid). The ability of the individual organs to work with other organs points to a predetermined purpose.

There is a supreme intelligence behind our existence in this world and all that allows for life to be sustainable in this planet. We are not the product of an accident or the evolution from lesser forms of life. To exist as a creature with limited capabilities or organs is an impossibility that goes beyond reason. No life can be sustainable while the creature is only half done (very likely for generations) because the species will likely disappear with the first of its type without even a feasible way to reproduce after its own kind. If a Christian believes in evolution, I could say that my mother was more powerful than the god he/she worships because it took her only nine months to make me and not a million years of evolving. The Bible says that we were created at the image of God. We are the crown of creation. All other creatures were spoken into existence. We, in contrast, were expressively and personally created by the artistic hand of God. To be both a Christian and to believe in evolution is incompatible because it will imply that God Himself is evolving since we were made after His own perfect image.

We need to make sure that we do not accept fallacies just to be agreeable with the world. We do not have to be politically correct but we must take a stand for what is true even if it is not popular or if no person with good credentials backs up what we believe.

Just because an eminent scientist says something, it does not mean that I have to accept it. *"You adulterous people, don't you know that friendship with the world is hatred toward God? Anyone who chooses to be a friend of the world becomes an enemy of God"* (James 4:4). At the same time that evolutionists discredit themselves fabricating evidence, there are serious scientists observing the complexity of nature and concluding that none of this can ever be the product of a coincidence (what is called evolution). Evolution is just a lame attempt to deny the rights of God over His creatures. If they only could understand that the claims from God are only for their own benefit just as a loving, responsible and caring father would do for his children. As if David were looking into the future contemplating the debate on the origin of life on this planet and the consequent denial of God, he wrote in solemn words: *"...The fool hath said in his heart, There is no God"* (Psalm 53:1). I am sure there were tears of sadness on David's eyes when he wrote those words.

How about the conscience -that inner little voice that tells us when we do wrong? Only humans have it. It was placed in our beings as a mechanism to keep us in the right path, to have a benevolent behavior, conductive to live in harmony and to treat others how we expect to be treated. The conscience can be awakened by the Spirit of God to bring conviction and repentance. Repentance will ideally bring us to confess our sins to God and work hard to amend our behavior.

And what about the fossil record? The evident rapid burial of animals in different parts of the world indicates that rapid sedimentation, such as it would occur in a flood, happened universally even in high altitudes and places where those species are not found today. For example, scientists have found over 1,500 specimens of well-preserved, fossilized baleen whales at four localities in the Pisco Formation in western Peru. Something amazing about this find is that their connected vertebrae is for the most part intact (about 72%). In some cases, the baleen plates (located in the upper jaw and used to filter seafood from the water) are preserved, even within the mouth. Baleen is made of the protein keratin, which decays in a matter of hours. This indicates that the whales were buried quickly, probably in just a few hours. These whales were not found in a lake or the bottom of the sea but in a dry desert over 20 km from the Pacific Ocean. In the same area, now above sea level, was also discovered the fossil of sperm whale with teeth that measure up to 36 centimeters long. This fossil is almost complete. How did these whales ended up in a desert, so far from the sea, and in the case of the baleen whales, buried so fast? Only a universal cataclysm such as the Biblical flood could explain this phenomenon. What about the shells found in sedimentary rocks atop mountains, hundreds of miles away from the sea?

Now, to conclude this section, I must mention the notion of beauty. The concept of beauty is a property related to human beings and although it varies from culture to culture, and it has through the ages, it produces the same reaction in the brain of humans. Although some cultures deform the body in the pursue of their concept of beauty, it is nevertheless inspiring to them. Ironically, beauty makes things to be desirable and estimated as more valuable than things that can be of better quality and functionality. Beholding beauty stirs feelings of joy and many times of peace. Enjoying the handiwork of nature can become an inspiring and wonderful medicine for people afflicted with depression.

As I mentioned above, only humans can appreciate beauty. I have been blessed with a very smart dog that understands hand and voice commands in English, some in Spanish and even mute lip gestures. He can distinguish between doors according to the word that I use. However, I have never seen him appreciating an amazing sunrise or sunset, much less the abundant flowers that grace my house from spring to fall. I have tried several times to have him pay attention to the flowers but he has not been impressed (by the way, what came first, the flowers or the bees?). I cannot deny that I was disappointed after all the time spent planting and cultivating them, but I have to understand that there are differences between humans and animals, which are limited in the role that they play in this creation. Only humans, created at the image of the Creator, are capable of processing the concept of beauty. Beauty not only refers to what we visualize like stunning landscapes, a sunset or sunrise, a male peacock displaying his plumage, a majestic wild or Arabian horse, the smile of a baby, a starry night, or the concepts of symmetry and proportion, but also things that appeal to other senses such as aromas or music. We also find pleasure on objects soft to the touch such as silk or velvet. On occasions, we can be attracted to things that appeal to more than one sense, such as food. We eat for pleasure while animals eat by instinct (although they can taste too). How could evolution produce such a perfect set of useful qualities that contribute to our enjoyment of life? What cells "board meeting" occurred to decide what was needed and how to design it if there was no knowledge, let us say, of what a smell was? And how about the different tastes like salty, bitter, sweet or sour? Those first humans had very smart tongues that developed those taste buds.

Humans posses an innate attraction to beauty that inspires artistic creativity. Thus, men are capable of creating their own masterpieces in the many arts that delight humankind. Although not everyone can appreciate a painting or classical music, everyone has the capability to enjoy or even create other things that provides him/her with sensorial pleasure.

However, the concept of beauty in relation to human beings can be biased towards what society dictates at one time or another. Usually cover girl models and movie stars become the standard for our perception of beauty- and even that varies by the decade. The Bible teaches that *"beauty is vain"* (Proverbs 31:30) because it fades to give place to wrinkles, age spots and grey hair/baldness. Many times, those people that we admire for their outward beauty are full of selfishness, envy, pride and hate. There were, in times of Jesus, some people that prided themselves on the way they dressed. What was Jesus' opinion on them? *"Woe unto you, scribes and Pharisees, hypocrites! for ye are like unto whited sepulchres, which indeed appear beautiful outward, but are within full of dead men's bones, and of all uncleanness"* (Matthew 23:27). Paul asked: *"Do ye look on things after the outward appearance?..."* (2 Corinthians 10:7). Peter, always outspoken, contributed this gem to the subject regarding the custom of wearing jewelry to make the person more "attractive": *"Whose adorning let it not be that outward adorning of plaiting the hair, and of wearing of gold, or of putting on of apparel; But let it be the hidden man of the heart, in that which is not corruptible, even the ornament of a meek and quiet spirit, which is in the sight of God of great price"* (1Peter 3:3,4).

In the eyes of God, the abstract concept of beauty is the one that really matters and He put in us the capability to appreciate it.

Employers usually request that their prospect employees be honest and exhibit good behavior. The character of the person is what really matters. Only human beings come to this world equipped with a moral code in their brains. Only we are bothered when we lie, disobey our parents, kill, steal or do anything that we know it is wrong even if everyone around us is doing it. Animals do not care about telling the truth, not stealing, not killing or disobeying their parents. Even in atheist societies there are rules based on the inner concepts of heart beauty implanted by God. They condemn crime because there is something inside their brains that tells them that killing the neighbor or stealing from the factory where they work is wrong. Even though those societies oppress their citizens, who have no rights, and are far from the ideal form of government, their leaders still abide by some kind of moral code imbedded –like it or not- by the Creator. Is this just an accident? No, but it is a proof of intentional design. The function of that little voice is to start training us for life in heaven where all the inhabitants will live in harmony motivated by love.

But, why it is important to believe in creation? Simple: we have the knowledge of a God that cares enough to make us with His own hands, to give us eternal life, to give us hope every day and provide all of our needs. Atheists do not have hope. They live the present life without the joy of expecting a better (in reality perfect) world. In this, they equal themselves with the lesser creatures that do not have the promise of eternal life. They live and die and that is it. Christians, on the other hand, know that just as the sun rises up every morning, they too will resurrect and enjoy life eternal with the Creator, who will move His throne here, to this planet, to be close to them.

[15]I know thy works, that thou art neither cold nor hot: I would thou wert cold or hot.

The Greek word means cold to the point of freezing and the word hot means hot to the point of boiling. Jesus said: *"but whoever drinks the water I give him will never thirst. Indeed, the water I give him will become in him a spring of water welling up to eternal life"* (John 4:14 NIV). If we are frozen, the waters of salvation will not flow to refresh anyone.

16So then because thou art lukewarm, and neither cold nor hot, I will spue thee out of my mouth.

Laodiceans were very familiar with this phrase because their only source of water came from a thermal source 10 kilometers in Hierapolis (means *sacred city*). The hot waters of the Pamukkale springs were used as a spa since the 2nd century B.C. People came to soothe their ailing bodies there. By the time the water arrived to Laodicea, it was lukewarm. Cold water refreshes; lukewarm produces nausea. Cold water is a symbol of good news from a far away land (heaven). *"As cold waters to a thirsty soul, so is good news from a far country"* (Proverbs 25:25). Hot water is a good medicine to clean our gut in the morning, producing a bowel movement while warm water produces nausea. What defines a warm Christian? It is one who is satisfied with the *status quo* of his spiritual growth. He withdraws from the daily spiritual battle that will demand being a committed Christian. He feels a strong attraction to sin and even entertains sinful thoughts but does not necessarily execute the actions for fear of being caught *in fraganti*. "The message to the church of the Laodiceans applies especially to the people of God today. It is a message to professing Christians who have become so much like the world that no difference can be seen." *Review and Herald, August 20, 1903*. It is a church that only keeps the appearance of godliness but without its power. The lukewarm Christian is an instrument in the hands of the enemy of the souls. He is neither a good Christian, nor a good wordling. We must strive to get rid of the sheep custome and stop pretending to be something that we are not for we are just deceiving ourselves and are a stumbling block to others. As long as we are happy being lukewarm Christians, we close the doors of the kingdom to ourselves, and we are also closing the doors to those that want to get in.

We often employ our time doing things that dishonor God and disqualify us for the kingdom of heaven. If we completely surrender to God and allow Him to change us, then we can have hope of salvation. We can not be satisfied to be almost saved, for this is the same as being completely lost. We must ask God to open our eyes to our own spiritual condition. We have to see how hateful sin is to God that required such a terrible sacrifice. Let us look at Calvary and behold how much cost God to work our salvation when He placed our sins on the innocent Savior. This message of Laodicea is for us as individuals. We must apply it to ourselves and not point to the condition of others. When we point to the sin in the lives of others, we are just doing our best to hide the sin in our own lives. It is time that we wake up and see that it is us who are lukewarm, that it is us who crucify Jesus again with our actions. If we turn to Him, He will forgive us and transform us into His likeness and use us as instruments, no longer in the service of self and the enemy, but to bring life, to love the lost and to help propare them for the new perfect world that Jesus has prepared for those that love Him.

[17]*Because thou sayest, I am rich, and increased with goods, and have need of nothing; and knowest not that thou art wretched, and miserable, and poor, and blind, and naked:*

Laodiceans had become very rich due to an eye salve that was in high demand in many countries. However, even though they possessed a good medicine for the physical eyes, they were spiritually blind. At one time, the city was destroyed and the Roman government offered help to rebuild it. The inhabitants refused the offer saying "we have need of nothing." Self- sufficiency casts Jesus out of our hearts. We need to remember that without Him we can do nothing against evil (John 15:5). We need to be alarmed if we find ourselves being content with our spiritual condition. Amos 6:1 says, *"Woe to them that are at ease in Zion."* When we are content, we do not feel the desire to grow closer to Jesus. *"More of Jesus"* should be a constant melody ringing in our souls.

[18]*I counsel thee to buy of me gold tried in the fire, that thou mayest be rich; and white raiment, that thou mayest be clothed, and that the shame of thy nakedness do not appear; and anoint thine eyes with eyesalve, that thou mayest see.*

"Buy of me"- The purchase price has been paid by Jesus. *"Ho, every one that thirsteth, come ye to the waters, and he that hath no money; come ye, buy, and eat; yea, come, buy wine and milk <u>without money and without price</u>"* (Isaiah 55:1). We obtain goods from the heavenly merchant by faith.

Gold- represents love and faith

*"Hearken, my beloved brethren, Hath not God chosen the poor of this world **rich in faith**, and heirs of the kingdom which he hath promised to them that love him?"* (James 2:5). *"That the trial of your faith, being much more precious than of gold that perisheth, though it be tried with fire, might be found unto praise and honour and glory at the appearing of Jesus Christ"* (1 Peter 1:7).

White raiment- represents righteousness. Revelation 19:7,8; Isaiah 61:10 says: *"I will greatly rejoice in the LORD, my soul shall be joyful in my God; for he hath clothed me with the garments of salvation, he hath covered me with the robe of righteousness, as a bridegroom decketh himself with ornaments, and as a bride adorneth herself with her jewels."*

"the shame of thy nakedness" In these last days God is going to undo what happened in Eden when the first couple sinned. At that time, He covered humankind's nakedness but now it will be exposed. In the parable of the wedding, Jesus mentioned that a man was cast out because he did not wear the clothes prepared beforehand for the guests (Matthew 22:11-13). Why do we stubbornly refuse to remain covered by the robe of righteousness of Jesus when it is provided for us free of charge?

eyesalve- is the ability to distinguish good from evil through the Ten Commandments and the Word of God: *"Open thou mine eyes, that I may behold wondrous things out of thy law... Thy word is a lamp unto my feet, and a light unto my path"* (Psalm 119:18, 105). What is interesting is that the inhabitants of the historical Laodicea were known by their eye salve and yet, they were blind. This reminds me of the parable of the lost coin, which represents those that are lost but neither do they know that are lost, nor do they know the way to be saved.

19As many as I love, I rebuke and chasten: be zealous therefore, and repent.

God does not want any of us to perish but that we all have eternal life. As a caring father, He corrects us when we err. *"And if they be bound in fetters, and be holden in cords of affliction; Then he sheweth them their work, and their transgressions that they have exceeded. He openeth also their ear to discipline, and commandeth that they return from iniquity. If they obey and serve him, they shall spend their days in prosperity, and their years in pleasures"* (Job 36:8-11).

[20]*Behold, I stand at the door, and knock: if any man hear my voice, and open the door, I will come in to him, and will sup with him, and he with me.*

Knock- Jesus does not burst into anyone's life. He does not force Himself inside any heart. He will come to our lives only if invited.

at the door – In the parable of the ten virgins, the five foolish did not prepare properly, so they had to leave to procure oil- a symbol of the Holy Spirit. While they were out, the Bridegroom came and shut the door (Matthew 25:1-13). They returned and begged to be let in but it was to no avail. According to this parable, up to half of those who profess to be Christians will be lost because they procrastinate and are not preparing to come to meet their God. Amos 4:12 (*The Message*) reads: *"...Time's up, O Israel! Prepare to meet your God!"* It is time for us to wake up. *"Wherefore he saith, Awake thou that sleepest, and arise from the dead, and Christ shall give thee light"* (Ephesians 5:14). *"And that, knowing the time, that now it is high time to awake out of sleep: for now is our salvation nearer than when we believed. The night is far spent, the day is at hand: let us therefore cast off the works of darkness, and let us put on the armour of light"* (Romans 13:11,12). Long time ago an artist painted Jesus knocking at a door. A friend went to see the painting and pointed to what he thought was an error of omission: the door had no knob, to which the artist replied that the door represents the heart and can only be opened from the inside. Jesus does not force His way into your heart. You must open the door and invite Him in.

"sup with him-" This is referring to the meal that we will have in heaven with Jesus. *"Blessed are they which are called unto the marriage supper of the Lamb"* (Revelation 19:9; Matthew 26:29). I once was invited to the wedding of the daughter of a politician. Even though I had the honor to sit at the dining table with famous personalities, they were still human. They were no better or superior than any of their "common" companions at the table. Our great Lord Jesus is preparing a great feast and we will count with

His presence in that joyful event. All of us will be equal at that table. The price paid for our salvation has made us one. I am planning to be at that supper. How about you? What is holding you up?

[21]To him that overcometh will I grant to sit with me in my throne, even as I also overcame, and am set down with my Father in his throne.

To no other church in history was given this marvelous promise. Do you have an idea what it means for us, sinners, once rebellious against God, alienated by our sinful natures, rebels without a reason, to have the honor of sitting on God's throne with Him? *"He withdraws not His eyes from the righteous, but they are like kings on the throne; yes, He causes them to sit forever, and they are very high"* (Job 36:7 *Modern King James*).

[22]He that hath an ear, let him hear what the Spirit saith unto the churches.

Are we ready to listen faithfully and consistently?

REVELATION 4

The 24 elders in the book of Revelation

[1]*After this I looked, and, behold, a door was opened* ***in*** *heaven: and the first voice which I heard was as it were of a trumpet talking with me; which said, Come up hither, and I will shew thee things which must be hereafter.*

John is called to witness things **in** the heavenly sanctuary right after he was given the message to the church of the judgment time.

Come up hither- So far John had been focused on the history of the church on earth. Now he must take a look at what is going on in heaven on our behalf, where Jesus is our High Priest in the sanctuary that no man made, but God Himself.

[2]*And immediately I was in the spirit: and, behold, a throne was set in heaven, and one sat on the throne.*

The throne is found in the most holy place in the sanctuary. John, like Daniel, knows that there was One sitting on the throne but could not see, much less describe His appearance.

[3]*And he that sat was to look upon like a jasper and a sardine stone: and there was a rainbow round about the throne, in sight like unto an emerald.*

The jasper here is described by author and nature philosopher Pliny as a translucent but very brilliant stone. It would be bright like a diamond. John could not see who was on the throne because of the splendor but was allowed to see some of His majesty. It is said that the sardine stone (bright red) was found in Sardis, which gave it its name. John is trying to convey more the brightness than the colors.

Some elements of the visions of Daniel are seeing in this vision of John that also covers chapter five.

Daniel 7	Revelation 4
1-There was a throne for God the Father and other thrones	1-There was a throne for the Father and 24 thrones
2-The throne was like flame of fire (red)	2-There was a red color coming from the throne (sardine stone)
3-*"thousand thousands ministered unto him, and ten thousand times ten thousand stood before him"* (Daniel 7:10)	3-*"I heard the voice of many angels round about the throne and the beasts and the elders: and the number of them was ten thousand times ten thousand, and thousands of thousands"* (Revelation 5:11)

"there was a rainbow round about the throne, in sight like unto an emerald."- The rainbow was first seen by Noah and his family. Notice that this rainbow is round- not an arch as normally we see them. We have three elements to consider here:

- A rainbow- a symbol of the divine promise (Genesis 9:13-16). We know that He keeps His word.
- Round- The circle is a symbol of eternity.
- The color is green- a symbol of hope and life (see Psalm 1), is a mix of blue (which represents righteousness or justice) and the yellow from the healing mercy like the light of the sun *"But unto you that fear my name shall the Sun of righteousness arise with **healing** in his wings"* (Malachi 4:2). *"Administer true **justice**; show **mercy** and compassion to one another"* (Zechariah 7:9 NIV).

By combining the above elements, we have the eternal assurance of righteousness and mercy.

Both Daniel and John saw a throne. This is not the throne of glory. It is the throne of grace (Hebrews 4:16). In their fallen condition, human beings *"come short of the glory of God"* (Romans 3:23) but not of His grace. We are the offenders but God loves us so much that He was the one that took the initiative to bring peace. His hand is stretched out to offer His salvation (Isaiah 65:2) to each one of us. Why does it take so many calls from God to makes us react to His love? Ancient Israel rejected His offer. He is lovingly and patiently calling us today. *"Today, if you hear His voice, do not harden your hearts"* (Hebrews 4:7). He is extending the white flag of peace to all of us. There is still time to accept the offer of reconciliation offered by God.

However, one day the Savior will finish His priestly duties and will no longer occupy the throne of grace but the throne of glory. Very soon He will stop His intercession on our behalf and *"how shall we escape if we neglect so a great salvation?"* (Hebrews 2:3). Let us make our paths straight and follow Jesus faithfully all the way.

4And round about the throne were four and twenty seats: and upon the seats I saw four and twenty elders sitting, clothed in white raiment; and they had on their heads crowns of gold.

Who were the 24 elders? By being shown as clothed in white raiment, a symbol of righteousness, and having crowns of victory (στέφανος- stef'-an-os), the elders are portrayed as redeemed humans. In the Gospel of Matthew 27:52, 53, it says that after Jesus died, *"the graves were opened; and many bodies of the saints which slept arose and came out of the graves after his resurrection, and went into the holy city, and appeared unto many."* This had been prophesized in Hosea 6:2, it says: *"After two days will he revive us: in the third day he will raise us up, and we shall live in his sight."* Why were those saints resurrected? In Ephesians 4:8 we read: *"Wherefore he saith, When he ascended up on high, he led captivity captive, and gave gifts unto men."* The Greek in that verse means: "those that had been captives," They were the first fruits (Leviticus 23:16,17) indicating that when Jesus ascended to heaven, He brought those saints with Him as representing those that He will raise up at His second coming. The book *The Desire of Ages*, page 786, paragraphs two and three reads: "those who came forth from the grave at Christ's resurrection were raised to everlasting life. They ascended with Him as trophies of His victory over death and the grave. These, said Christ, are no longer the captives of Satan; I have redeemed them. I have brought them from the grave as the first fruits of My power, to be with Me where I am, nevermore to see death or experience sorrow. These went into the city, and appeared unto many, declaring, Christ has risen from the dead, and we be risen with Him. Thus was immortalized the sacred truth of the resurrection. The risen saints bore witness to the truth of the words, 'Thy dead men shall live, together with My dead body shall they arise.' Their resurrection was an illustration of the fulfillment of the prophecy, 'Awake and sing, ye that dwell in dust: for thy dew is as the dew of herbs, and the earth shall cast out the dead.' Isaiah 26:19"

"Christ came to earth as God in the guise of humanity. He ascended to heaven as the King of saints. His ascension was worthy of His exalted character. He went as one mighty in battle, a conqueror, leading captivity captive. He was attended by the heavenly host, amid shouts and acclamations of praise and celestial song. . . ."

Psalm 24:7-10 is a description of when Jesus ascended to heaven: *"Lift up your heads,* ***O ye gates****; and* ***be ye lift up****, ye everlasting doors; and the King of glory shall come in. [8]Who is this King of glory? The LORD strong and mighty, the LORD mighty in battle. [9]Lift up your heads, O ye gates; even lift them up, ye everlasting doors; and the King of glory shall come in. [10]Who is this King of glory? The LORD of hosts, he is the King of glory. Selah."* But Jesus did not ascend alone. This is what Isaiah 26:2 refers to when he wrote: *"****Open ye the gates****, that the righteous nation which keepeth the truth may enter in."* Both passages refer to the same victorious entrance into the heavenly city. Other than presenting then to the Father as the first fruits, there was another purpose to bring the resurrected saints to heaven. When David organized the service of the sanctuary, he established 24 priestly orders to assist the high priest (1Chronicles 24:4-sixteen chiefs plus eight chiefs). The gospel of Luke indicates that Zechariah, the father of John the Baptist was officiating in his turn. *"In the time of Herod king of Judea there was a priest named Zechariah, who belonged to the priestly* ***division*** *of Abijah; his wife Elizabeth was also a descendant of Aaron. Once when Zechariah's* ***division*** *was on duty and he was serving as priest before God, he was chosen by lot, according to the custom of the priesthood, to go into the temple of the Lord and burn incense"* (Luke 1:5, 8, 9 *NIV*). We see in Revelation 5:8 that the 24 elders were offering incense in the heavenly sanctuary. That was a priestly duty. These resurrected saints became the 24 elders.

"crowns of gold" The word translated as crowns is the Greek word *stephanoi*, which is an emblem of victory. Through the power of Christ, they are victors over sin and death.

[5]And out of the throne proceeded lightnings and thunderings and voices: and there were seven lamps of fire burning before the throne, which are the seven Spirits of God.

When Moses received the Ten Commandments, there was a similar manifestation of nature (Exodus 19:16). Moses eventually placed the tables of the law in the Ark of the Covenant, which is a representation of the throne of God and the foundation of His government. *"Righteousness and justice are the foundation of your throne; love and faithfulness go before you"* (Psalm 89:14 NIV).

"seven lamps of fire burning" –The Holy Spirit was represented as tongues of fire coming over the disciples on the day of Pentecost. Fire purifies. When the He comes in our hearts as the representative of Jesus, He produces sanctification, likeness to God. For an explanation of the 7 Spirits, see comment on chapter 3:1. These lamps are not the seven candlesticks from chapter 1, since those represented the churches. These lamps were before the throne (represent the Holy Spirit), indicating that John was looking inside the holy place in the sanctuary. Remember that in verse one he was shown a door opened in heaven- not into heaven.

[6]And before the throne there was a sea of glass like unto crystal: and in the midst of the throne, and round about the throne, were four beasts full of eyes before and behind.

"Sea of glass like unto crystal" – the word crystal can also be translated as ice. I see this as an indication of the transparency of the government of God. Very soon, the mortal beings will see the heavenly books open and all will witness the righteous judgments of our creator. If a soul is lost, it will not be due to lack of God's efforts to save him. See 1 Cor. 6:2 & Revelation 20:4 & 12. Please do not shut you ears to the voice of mercy.

"four beasts" The Greek work is *zoa*, which is better translated as living creatures. They resemble the ones described by the prophet Ezekiel, which he calls cherubim. See Ezekiel 1:5-26 & 10:20-22. Although "full of eyes" can be understood as a symbol of intelligence, I prefer to interpret this as a symbol of vigilance as we can see in Zechariah 4:10. In chapter five, the Lamb has seven eyes and it says that those are the seven Spirits of God "sent forth

into all the earth." This brings to memory Psalm 139 where some elements of the omniscience of God the Spirit are presented. Here are some of the verses:

> [1] *"O LORD, you have searched me*
> *and you know me.*
>
> [2] *You know when I sit and when I rise;*
> *you perceive my thoughts from afar.*
>
> [3] *You discern my going out and my lying down;*
> *you are familiar with all my ways.*
>
> [4] *Before a word is on my tongue*
> *you know it completely, O LORD.*
>
> [7] *Where can I go from your Spirit?*
> *Where can I flee from your presence?*
>
> [8] *If I go up to the heavens, you are there;*
> *if I make my bed in the depths,* [a] *you are there.*
>
> [9] *If I rise on the wings of the dawn,*
> *if I settle on the far side of the sea,*
>
> [10] *even there your hand will guide me,*
> *your right hand will hold me fast.*
>
> [11] *If I say, "Surely the darkness will hide me*
> *and the light become night around me,"*
>
> [12] *even the darkness will not be dark to you;*
> *the night will shine like the day,*
> *for darkness is as light to you."* NIV

[7]*And the first beast was like a lion, and the second beast like a calf, and the third beast had a face as a man, and the fourth beast was like a flying eagle.*

The four beasts have been linked with the four gospels. "Commentators for centuries have linked these symbols with the four aspects of our Saviour as emphasized particularly in the four Gospels. Matthew writes on the kingly side of our Lord, emphasizing the King and His kingdom. This is well symbolized by the Lion, the majestic king of beasts. Mark deals largely with the Saviour as the servant of man, the ox symbolizing service. Luke, the physician, reveals His human aspect as the Son of man, Hence the face of a man. John emphasizes His deity-Christ the Eternal Word-who created all things. This phase of our Lord is symbolized by the flying eagle." Roy Alan Anderson, *Unfolding the Revelation*, page 51. The number four represents the world. The reason why there are four gospels is because the glorious message of salvation is meant to reach every soul in the four corners of the world.

It is also noteworthy that when the tribes of Israel camped around the tabernacle in the desert, they did it according to their banners- Numbers chapter two. The festivals held in the sanctuary portrayed the story of redemption all the way until the establishment of the kingdom of heaven. The banners (according to Jewish scholars) of the north, south, east and west tribes coincided with the symbols mentioned by John. Someone also noted that the four gospels show Jesus work from a different angle and coincides with the four creatures' description.

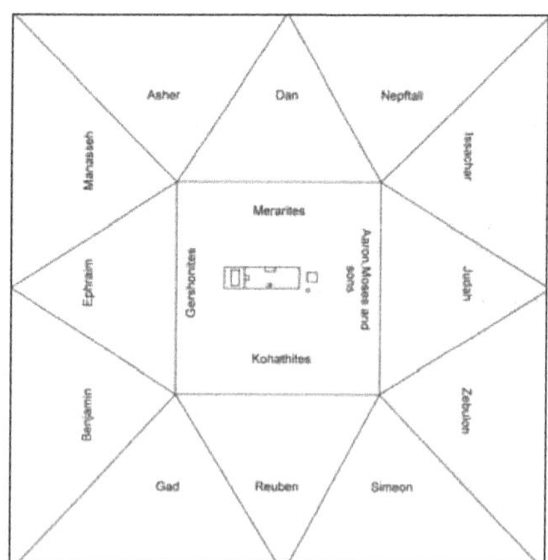

The tribes of Israel were encamping, forming a square, around the tabernacle like the New Jerusalem from Revelation. The four leading tribes where positioned forming a cross. These tribes' flags had the same symbols that represent the four creatures of Revelation 4:7 (man, eagle, ox and lion). Those tribes were in the middle on each side. The tribe of Judah was in front of the entrance to the tabernacle (He is called "the door") on the east because from there would come Jesus, a descendant of Judah. Their banners were as follows:

Judah - East (Lion)- represents the kingship of Jesus, as in the gospel of Matthew

Ephraim - West (Ox)- represents Jesus as our sacrifice and as servant as in the gospel of Mark

Reuben - South (Man)- represents the incarnation of Jesus as in the gospel of Luke

Dan - North- the main cardinal point (Eagle)- represents the divinity of Jesus as in the book of John

In Numbers two, Moses indicated that the tribes faced the tabernacle. Each second tribe mentioned was at the right side of the middle one.

All the tribe's tents were at a great distance from the tabernacle complex with the tabernacle (tent) in the middle. The tabernacle was divided into the holy place and the most holy place. In the former were the candlestick (Jesus the light), the table of showbread (Jesus the bread of life), and the altar of incense (the merits of Jesus that wrap our prayers to make them pleasant before God). In the latter, was the ark with glory (shekinah) representing the divine presence.

Face of creature	Corresponding tribe banner around the sanctuary	Gospel
Lion	Judah –To the east, from where Jesus, the Lion of the tribe of Judah, will return-symbolizing Strength, Kingship, Divinity	Matthew
Ox	Ephraim- to the west-symbolizing Humility, Service, Sacrifice	Mark
Man	Reuben- to the south-symbolizing Intelligence, Wisdom, Incarnation	Luke
Eagle	Dan- to the north symbolizing the Divinity. God's throne is said to be in the north (Isaiah 14:13)	John

The tabernacle, where the ark representing the throne of God was found, was in the middle of those banners (as in the heart), just as these creatures surrounded the throne in heaven. These are the meanings of the tribes' names:

Judah- praise

Ephraim- fruitful

Reuben- behold the son

Dan- vindication

If we combine those names, we could have a phrase like this: *"Praise abundantly beholding the Son being vindicated."* The book of Revelation presents judgment scenes where eventually God's character will be vindicated before the universe from the accusations of Satan. Since Satan is the "accuser of our brothers" (Revelation 12:10), we too will be vindicated in the judgment because we are covered with the righteousness of Jesus. Zechariah 3:1-4 reads:

"Then he showed me Joshua the high priest standing before the angel of the LORD, and Satan standing at his right side to accuse him. The LORD said to Satan, 'The LORD rebuke you, Satan! The LORD, who has chosen Jerusalem, rebuke you! Is not this man a burning stick snatched from the fire?' Now Joshua was dressed in filthy clothes as he stood before the angel. The angel said to those who were standing before him, 'Take off his filthy clothes.' Then he said to Joshua, "See, I have taken away your sin, and I will put rich garments on you" (NIV). Joshua (Hebrew equivalent to Jesus) is representing the human race. As a priest, he was a sin bearer just as Jesus carried our sins, which eventually will be placed back on Satan as the instigator as we saw in Leviticus 16.

Since the Bible does not explain who the four creatures are (probably seraphims- Isaiah 6:2), we can only interpret what their work indicates. They undoubtedly <u>reflect the work of the Divinity in the plan of salvation</u>.

[8]And the four beasts had each of them six wings about him; and they were full of eyes within: and they rest not day and night, saying, Holy, holy, holy, LORD God Almighty, which was, and is, and is to come.

"full of eyes" – The eyes are a symbol of intelligence and vigilance. In this case, that God sees everything. *"For who hath despised the*

day of small things? for they shall rejoice, and shall see the plummet in the hand of Zerubbabel with those seven; they are the eyes of the LORD, which run to and fro through the whole earth" (Zechariah 4:10). *"The eyes of the LORD are in every place, beholding the evil and the good"* (Proverbs 15:3). How different our behavior would be if we were conscious that God sees everything that we do!

"which was, and is, and is to come" Here, like in chapter 1:4, refers to the Father. The *Worldwide English Translation* renders it more correctly this way: *"He always has lived. He lives now. And he always will live."*

9And when those beasts give glory and honour and thanks to him that sat on the throne, who liveth for ever and ever,

Our lives will be a lot better if we stop complaining and start to praise God for all His blessings.

10The four and twenty elders fall down before him that sat on the throne, and worship him that liveth for ever and ever, and cast their crowns before the throne, saying,

Every aspect of the plan of salvation has been taken care of by God. As He provided in the past, so He will take care of our needs in the future. We have uncountable reasons to praise God.

crowns- Greek στέφανος (stephanos)- a wreath, a prize in the public games. They have achieved the victory through the blood of Christ and the power given to them by the Holy Spirit. According to 1 Corinthians 9;25 these were people temperate in all things. James adds that those that receive this crown are those that endure temptation. This is the same word used in Matthew 27:29 for the crown of thorns made for Jesus. The fact that the 24 elders have crowns, imply that they have been human beings that once lived on this earth and obtained victory over sin, in contrast with the four creatures that are never shown with crowns.

11Thou art worthy, O Lord, to receive glory and honour and power: for thou hast created all things, and for thy pleasure they are and were created.

Here it is emphasized again, in case we have forgotten, that God is the creator. He deserves our praises. Did you ever wonder about you worth as a human being, perhaps asking yourself why are you in this world? This verse has the answer: you bring pleasure to God. It is just as when a loving parent takes his/ her child to the park and watches him/her play. Mine brought many smiles to my face. It does not matter if you screwed up your life, God still looks at you with loving eyes. *"Since thou wast precious in my sight, thou hast been honourable, and I have loved thee...."* (Isaiah 43:4).

REVELATION 5

A book that could not be read

[1]*And I saw in the right hand of him that sat on the throne a book written within and on the backside, sealed with seven seals.*

John was shown now the book on the hand of the Father. Books in his days were different from the ones we know now. Ours are bound and have pages, chapters and paragraphs. In ancient times, the books were written in rolls of leather or papyrus and did not have the divisions that our books have. Since it was difficult and expensive to acquire the material on which to write and to avoid having more than one scroll, the writers utilized both sides.

[2]*And I saw a strong angel proclaiming with a loud voice, Who is worthy to open the book, and to loose the seals thereof?*

Now the prophet hears a question regarding who was worthy of opening the book. I am sure he was thinking "not me" judging by his reaction in chapter 1.

[3]*And no man in heaven, nor in earth, neither under the earth, was able to open the book, neither to look thereon.* [4]*And I wept much, because no man was found worthy to open and to read the book, neither to look thereon.*

John here recognizes the unworthiness of the human race and with Paul, he concludes: *"What shall we conclude then? Are we any better? Not at all! We have already made the charge that Jews and Gentiles alike are all under sin. As it is written: 'There is no one righteous, not even one; there is no one who understands, no one who seeks God. All have turned away, they have together become worthless; there is no one who does good, not even one.' 'Their throats are open graves; their tongues practice deceit.' 'The poison of vipers is on their lips.' 'Their mouths are full of cursing and bitterness.' 'Their feet are swift to shed blood; ruin and misery mark their ways, and the way of peace they do not know.' 'There is no fear of God before their eyes'"* (Romans 3:9-18). There is nothing good in us that can serve as a letter of recommendation to be in the presence of God. Isaiah describes our condition this way: *"Why bother even trying to do anything with you when you just keep to your bullheaded ways? You keep beating your heads against brick walls. Everything within you protests against you. From the bottom of your feet to the top of your head, nothing's working right. Wounds and bruises and running sores—untended, unwashed, unbandaged"* (Isaiah 1:6, The Message). John wept due to the sinfulness of the human race. Ezekiel 9:4 says that the seal of God will be placed on those who *"sigh and that cry for all the abominations that be done in the midst"* of Jerusalem (the church). Do we criticize those that fall into temptation and even leave the church or we weep for them, pleading for their souls, with anguish in our hearts hoping to see them restored to the flock? Do we just "go with the flow" and ignore the Laodicean condition of the church or when we sin, does it cause us to seek a closer walk with Christ?

5 *And one of the elders saith unto me, Weep not: behold, the Lion of the tribe of Judah, the Root of David, hath prevailed to open the book, and to loose the seven seals thereof.*

Our champion has obtained the victory over Satan and that makes Him worthy of opening the book.

6 *And I beheld, and, lo, in the midst of the throne and of the four beasts, and in the midst of the elders, stood a Lamb as it had been slain, having seven horns and seven eyes, which are the seven Spirits of God sent forth into all the earth.*
7 *And he came and took the book out of the right hand of him that sat upon the throne.*

"I beheld...a lamb as it had been slain" (Revelation 5:6)- Behold the Lamb of God in the Garden of Gethsemane, *"a man of sorrows, and acquainted with grief" (Isaiah 53:3).* Behold how He agonized in the garden while the devil tempted Him to abandon His mission to save you and me from the wages of sin. Looking far beyond His pain, His eyes saw you and me condemned in our sins and trespasses, without God or hope in this world, eternally lost, in despair and in the direst of needs. He saw that we would perish if no action was taken. In His stressful agony, His sweat was bloody. He prayed to God to find another way, but there was only one: He had to stick

to the plan. That plan was designed from the foundation of this world. When man was created, a question surfaced: if man joins Satan's rebellion, what would we do? Immediately, with the heart of a father full of tender love for his little one, He offered Himself to take man's punishment for his sins, so mankind could be saved. The Creator, the author of life Himself (Acts 3:15) would take a human body, live among cruel men and take the punishment for their sins on Himself.

In Gethsemane, oppressed by the enormous weight of our sins already being placed on Him, He made the decision to climb Mount Calvary and pay what you and I owe to God. <u>What mercy, what grace, that the innocent must die so the guilty can walk away free</u>! May our hearts melt contemplating the Lamb, suspended between heaven and earth to make a bridge between God and man, bringing reconciliation. After being punished and brought from one place to another four times, he was forced to walk from Pilate's palace down La Via Dolorosa to Mount Calvary, where the worst criminals were executed. Behold Him on Calvary, being taunted by the crowds, when He saw Himself separated from the Father, being the carrier of our sins and in anguish claimed : *"My God, my God, why hast thou forsaken me?"* (Mark 15:34). The position on the cross, hanging with the arms stretched above the head and the cold air of that time of the year were producing pneumonia. His lungs were filling with fluid (which flowed out when His side was later pierced by the soldier). To pronounce every sentence was a great struggle for Him. He had to stretch up, putting pressure on his nail-wounded feet to grasp every breath of air, then tiredness and gravity pulled His body down, straining His hand wounds, to start the painful breathing process all over again. He could only pronounce one word at a time, inhale with great difficulty and speak again, so every one of His few sentences was a labor-intense effort. While his laboring breath was difficult, we must not forget that his back, wounded 117 times in three whippings by the soldiers, was rubbing against the rugged cross, causing a sharp pain with every movement up and down gasping for air, re-opening the wounds (40 lacerations with a sharp bones and lead-loaded whip were considered too many so they hit the condemned only 39 times to show mercy). *"They have plowed my back like farmers plow fields. They made long slashes like furrows"* (Psalm 129:3 God's Word). All that and a lot more that we could not even begin to grasp in our feeble minds, Jesus, the Lamb of God, endured for you and me. *"Surely he hath borne our griefs, and carried our sorrows: yet we did esteem him stricken, smitten of God, and afflicted. But he was wounded for our transgressions, he was bruised for our iniquities: the chastisement of our peace was upon him; and with his stripes we are healed. All we like sheep have gone astray; we have turned every one to his own way; and the LORD hath laid on him the iniquity of us all. He was oppressed, and he was afflicted, yet he opened not his mouth: he is brought as a lamb to the slaughter, and as a sheep before her shearers is dumb, so he openeth not his mouth" (Isaiah 53:4-7)*

Now you and I have been granted a second chance. Are we going to take Him and His sacrifice for granted and make it null for us? Let that never happen!

Having secured our salvation, the victorious Lamb is now the only one qualified to take the book (scroll) from the hand of the Father. He looks defeated as a slain lamb, but by His wounds, He obtained victory over sin and Satan and guaranteed our salvation.

8And when he had taken the book, the four beasts and four and twenty elders fell down before the Lamb, having every one of them harps, and golden vials full of odours, which are the prayers of saints.
9And they sung a new song, saying, Thou art worthy to take the book, and to open the seals thereof: for thou wast slain, and hast redeemed us to God by thy blood out of every kindred, and tongue, and people, and nation;

This is an act of worship, indicating the divinity of the Lamb. The NIV translates the passage like this: *"with your blood you purchased men for God from every tribe and language and people and nation."* This is a more original-faithful translation, specially considering that the four living creatures are included in the passage and there is no indication that they are human.

10And hast made us unto our God kings and priests: and we shall reign on the earth.

What an honor! We, sinful, rebellious, hypocrite human beings are taken from the mud and made into kings and priests! We were by nature slaves to sin but God promises that by His grace we will "reign on the earth."

[11]And I beheld, and I heard the voice of many angels round about the throne and the beasts and the elders: and the number of them was ten thousand times ten thousand, and thousands of thousands;
*[12]Saying with a loud voice, Worthy is the Lamb that was slain to receive **power**, and **riche**s, and **wisdom**, and **strength**, and **honour**, and **glory**, and **blessing**.*

The uncountable angelical host now joins in the worship with a perfect praise (seven elements). The incredible number of angels around the throne gives us an idea of the immensity of the heavenly sanctuary. No wonder Paul wrote in Hebrews 9:11 that Jesus entered into a "greater" tabernacle.

[13]And every creature which is in heaven, and on the earth, and under the earth, and such as are in the sea, and all that are in them, heard I saying, Blessing, and honour, and glory, and power, be unto him that sitteth upon the throne, and unto the Lamb for ever and ever.

Very soon all creatures will recognize the kingship of Jesus: *"So God raised him to the highest place. God made his name greater than every other name So that every knee will bow to the name of Jesus—everyone in heaven, on earth, and under the earth"* Philippians 2:10 (New Century Version). Father and Son receive the same praise. In times of John and Paul heaven, earth and under the earth represented the cosmos with God located where Isaiah 14:13 calls north. For me, the phrase "under the earth" represents the inhabitants of the unfallen worlds, those represented by the 99 sheep that were not lost.

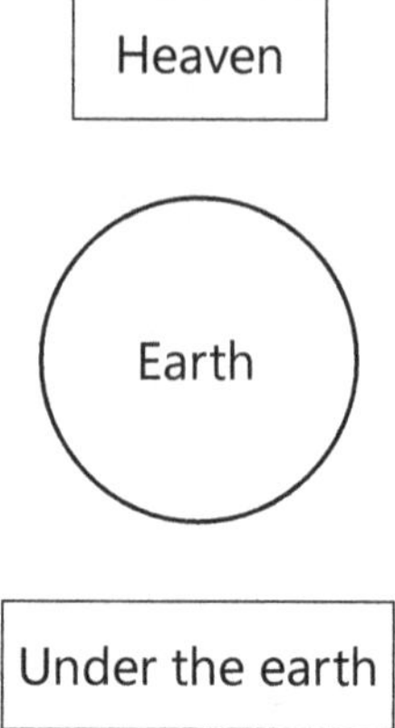

[14]*And the four beasts said, Amen. And the four and twenty elders fell down and worshipped him that liveth for ever and ever.* Now the Father is worshipped in the same way the Lamb was, again indicating their equality.

Revelation 6

Dead people talking

[1]*And I saw when the Lamb opened one of the seals, and I heard, as it were the noise of thunder, one of the four beasts saying, Come and see.*

At last, John was going to be able to find out what was written on the scroll. He was of course, invited to take a closer look. Just as the seven churches represented stages in church history, the seven seals point sequentially to periods of time but present a different angle of that history.

Here is a comparison between the first four churches and the four seals:

Church	What John saw when the seals were opened	What that indicated	Period covered
Ephesus= desirable. *"I know you are enduring patiently and are bearing up for My name's sake, and you have not fainted or become exhausted or grown weary."* Revelation 2:3 Amplified Bible	White horse – the rider went forth conquering, and to conquer.	The victorious pure church of the first century that preached the gospel *"to every creature under heaven"* (Col. 1:23). The white color is a symbol of Jesus' righteousness.	31 AD- 100 AD
Smyrna= myrrh. *"Don't be afraid of what you are about to suffer. The devil will throw some of you into prison to test you. You will suffer for ten days. But if you remain faithful even when facing death, I will give you the crown of life."* Revelation 2:10 (New Living Translation)	Red horse-power was given to him that sat thereon to take peace from the earth, and that they should kill one another: and there was given unto him a great sword	Conflict on earth- the church persecuted by the Roman empire. The red color indicates the shedding of the saints' blood by the persecutors and also the heresies being introduced by false brethren.	100AD- 313 AD

Pergamos= exaltation. *"I will give some of the hidden manna to everyone who wins the victory."* Revelation 2:17 (New Century Version)	Black horse-he that sat on him had a pair of balances in his hand.	The balances indicated a rationing, hunger- for the word of God. Rome prohibited the reading of the Scriptures and introduced paganism, tradition and superstition. However, Jesus promised to feed His followers with hidden manna. The black color is in contrast with the white of the first horse, indicating that the church of this time had disposed of Jesus' righteousness (obtained by faith) and establish its own by works.	313 AD-538 AD
Thyatira= sacrifice. *"And I will kill her children with death; and all the churches shall know that I am he which searcheth the reins and hearts: and I will give unto every one of you according to your works."* Revelation 2:23	Pale horse-And power was given unto them over the fourth part of the earth, to kill with sword, and with hunger, and with death, and with the beasts of the earth.	The rider's name was Death. This is the period of the dark ages when believers were tortured and burned at the stake. The day of reckoning is coming and God will reward those that raised their hands against God's children. It is interesting to note that while the former Imperial Rome executed criminals, the Roman church executed Bible readers.	538 AD- 1517 AD

Although the four horsemen do not represent the first four churches, they illustrate the situations or conditions that prevailed as apostasy developed. In the churches one through four and the seals one through four, we can see contrasts and similarities. Later, when the trumpets sound, the focus will shift completely to the world outside the church.

[2]And I saw, and behold a white horse: and he that sat on him had a bow; and a crown was given unto him: and he went forth conquering, and to conquer.

Each one of the first four seals is introduced by one of the living creatures. In this case, the lion called John to look. The lion, representing the kingship of Jesus, introduces a rider that came as a conqueror. Notice that the horseman had a crown, indicating victory. Commentators usually interpret this rider to be Jesus heading the church in the first century, probably because He is the rider of the white horse in chapter 19:11: *"I saw heaven standing open and there before me was a white horse, whose rider is called Faithful and True. With justice he judges and makes war."* Marvin Maxwell proposes that this rider is a concept, just as the other three are concepts. The first one represents the true Christianity, thus the color white. In contrast, the other three riders bring suffering, hunger and death. White horses seemed to be the favorites among conquerors, since Alexander, Napoleon and others chose that color for their rides.

[3]And when he had opened the second seal, I heard the second beast say, Come and see.

The ox (symbol of sacrifice) introduces the second seal.

[4]And there went out another horse that was red: and power was given to him that sat thereon to take peace from the earth, and that they should kill one another: and there was given unto him a great sword.

The time of the first horseman is now over. Now the following horsemen are cruel and show an abusive and disturbing behavior that took "peace from the earth." The second horse was red in color as a symbol of the cruel persecution under the Roman Empire. The sword mentioned is that of the state (Romans 13:4).

[5]And when he had opened the third seal, I heard the third beast say, Come and see. And I beheld, and lo a black horse; and he that sat on him had a pair of balances in his hand.

At this time, the apostate church was joined with the state. This apostasy was prophesied by Paul: *"For I know this, that after my departing shall grievous wolves enter in among you, not sparing the flock. Also of your own selves shall men arise, speaking perverse things, to draw away disciples after them"* (Acts 20:29,30). The pure church of the first century would give way to a different and strange institution.

The marriage of church and state is always a bad combination because it inevitably ends in persecution of the minorities and elimination of their rights. We saw it in times of Nebuchadnezzar when he as the head of the state made a statue and commanded worship. We find also in Revelation 13 a beast enacting a law with religious tones threatening with death those that disobey it. Many prominent religious leaders are promoting a unity of church and state here in America. Pat Robertson once ran for president to promote his religious agenda if elected. The time is coming when America will eliminate the freedom of speech. We are already seeing attempts conductive to that condition. Now if we speak, it has to be "politically correct," as to not to "offend" anyone." Right now, it is illegal in Canada and other countries to make any mention of the atrocities committed by the popular church because that would be considered bigotry and hate language. There are books such as *The Great Controversy* that are forbidden there because they contain historic accounts of those abuses. America is soon to follow. Once this is accomplished, it will be easy for the wolf to launch a surprise attack on the now carefree sheep.

The third seal was introduced by the beast that resembles a man. At this time in history, the church was being persecuted. Jesus identified himself with those millions being victimized. When Saul of Tarsus was persecuting the believers, he heard a voice from heaven asking: *"...Saul, Saul, why are you persecuting Me?"* (Acts 9:4). Jesus wanted His children to know that they were not alone and just as in human form He walked among the three faithful Hebrew youth through the fiery furnace (see Daniel 3), He would walk with them too in any trial. Although He might not be visible to them or their enemies, His presence is felt by the peace brought to them by the Holy Spirit.

[6]*And I heard a voice in the midst of the four beasts say, a measure of wheat for a penny, and three measures of barley for a penny; and see thou hurt not the oil and the wine.*

The NKJV translates penny as denarius, which was the amount of money that a worker was paid for a day of labor. Can you imagine working all day, very probably from sunrise to sunset and making just enough to buy the equivalent of two loaves of bread-only bread to feed your family (no fruits or vegetables)? Barley was mainly the food of the poor, slaves and horses. It too was going to be expensive. Bread is a symbol of the Word of God. Papal Rome started to replace the Scriptures with human thought. The teachings of Aristotle, Socrates and Plato were placed above the words of Jesus and His disciples, which caused spiritual hunger. The text is indicating the scarcity of the Word of God. The oil is a symbol of the Holy Spirit (Who inspired the Bible) and the wine is symbol of doctrines, meaning in this case, the truth. When the voice from the throne ordered not to hurt the oil and the wine, it gives us assurance that God watches over His Word to preserve it. Although there have been cases in which the Scriptures have been burned, there have been countless inspiring stories of Bibles that survived fires and floods miraculously as a testimony to both believers and unbelievers.

[7]*And when he had opened the fourth seal, I heard the voice of the fourth beast say, Come and see.*

The fourth beast is the eagle, a bird known for its keen vision. The message to the church of Thyatira says: *"These things saith the Son of God, who hath his eyes like unto a flame of fire"* (Revelation 2:18). Nothing can be hidden from His eyes. In the Old Testament the eagle was seen as a symbol of the Divinity (Deuteronomy 32:11,12) watching over His children. The symbol is also used to represent his stern judgment against transgressors: *"Set the trumpet to thy mouth. He shall come as an eagle against the house of the LORD, because they have transgressed my covenant, and trespassed against my law"* (Hosea 8:1).

[8]And I looked, and behold a pale horse: and his name that sat on him was Death, and Hell followed with him. And power was given unto them over the fourth part of the earth, to kill with sword, and with hunger, and with death, and with the beasts of the earth.

Of the four riders, this is the only with a name: "Death." Why was the horse pale? Have you ever seen a creature such as a snake after it accidentally falls in a hole and stays there for months? How is the skin? It is pale because it had not received light. The people during this time had been in the dark for a very long time, deprived from the light of the Word of God. Hell is translated from the Greek word hadēs, meaning grave. The sequence "sword, famine and plague" could be identified with wars since famine follows the results of the carnage brought by the sword and precedes the plagues, such as cholera. There were many wars initiated by the Roman Church with devastating results. Another way to understand this is by placing this sword in contrast with the sword of the Spirit (Hebrews 4:12). In this case, it would represent a false gospel, which Rome promoted by teaching other means of salvation apart from Jesus. The resulting "famine" for the Scriptures-for it was hard to find- caused diseases to the starving souls and spiritual death. The beasts could be representing those later shown in Revelation 11 and 13.

Even though Rome persecuted those that had copies of at least portions of the Bible, it kept the Scriptures in its monasteries and universities (although chained to a wall) which permitted some of the reformers, such as Martin Luther and Calvin, to know the truth of the gospel. This allowed the converted church teachers to eventually translate the Word of God into the languages of the masses, contributing to end the hunger imposed by the church of darkness.

Before we continue, let us see a comparison between the last three churches and the remaining seals:

Church	**What John saw when the seals were opened**	**What that indicated**	**Period covered**
Sardis= remnant. *"Thou hast a few names even in Sardis which have not defiled their garments; and they shall walk with me in white: for they are worthy."* Revelation 3:4.	Fifth seal – *"white robes were given unto every one"* of the souls under the altar.	The character of Christ. The white color is a symbol of Jesus' righteousness.	1517 AD- 1798 AD
Philadelphia= brotherly love. *"I come quickly: hold that fast which thou hast, that no man take thy crown"* (Revelation 3:10).	Sixth seal-*"And the... great men, and... every free man, hid themselves in the dens and in the rocks of the mountains; And said to the mountains and rocks, Fall on us, and hide us from the face of him that sitteth on the throne, and from the wrath of the Lamb: For the great day of his wrath is come; and who shall be able to stand?"* (Revelation 6:15-17).	While the wicked are fearful of the presence of the Lord soon to return, the believers are encouraged by this blessed hope.	1798-1844

Laodicea= judgment of the people or people of the judgment. *"I counsel thee to buy of me gold tried in the fire, that thou mayest be rich; and white raiment, that thou mayest be clothed, and that the shame of thy nakedness do not appear; and anoint thine eyes with eyesalve, that thou mayest see. As many as I love, I rebuke and chasten: be zealous therefore, and repent."* (Revelation 3:18,19).	Seventh seal- *"And another angel came and stood at the altar, having a golden censer; and there was given unto him much incense, that he should offer it with the prayers of all saints upon the golden altar which was before the throne"* (Revelation 8:3).	The gold is related to the character that must be developed for our preparation for heaven. It is through the time spent in prayer that such character is built. The sincere prayer of repentance will never be rejected.	1844- end

[9]And when he had opened the fifth seal, I saw under the altar the souls of them that were slain for the word of God, and for the testimony which they held:

Which altar? Obviously, it was not the altar in heaven, because they were not slain there. Who would keep all those millions of martyrs that papal Rome slaughtered trapped under an altar? Sardines would have more space in a can. It must be remembered that Revelation is a book loaded with symbols and these souls under the altar are no exception. Revelation 20:4 comes to our help, which clearly indicates that they will come to live in the future: *"I saw thrones on which were seated those who had been given authority to judge. And I saw the souls of **those who had been beheaded** because of their testimony for Jesus and because of the word of God. They had not worshiped the beast or his image and had not received his mark on their foreheads or their hands. They **came to life** and **reigned with Christ a thousand years**."* It is clear then that they come to life at the time of the judgment to reign with Christ, that they are dead, and thus, not alive and speaking right now. The altar is symbolic of the books of records in heaven.

The first time that the word soul appeared in the Bible was in Genesis 2:7: *"And the LORD God formed man of the dust of the ground, and breathed into his nostrils the breath of life; and man* ***became a*** *living* ***soul****."* Notice that man did not get a soul; he became a soul. The soul is the sum of the ingredients used by God to make a human being: dust + breath. It is like a light bulb and electricity; you disconnect the source of power and you have no light. Likewise, if you take away the breath, there is no soul. The idea that there is a soul that can live as a separate entity from the body has a pagan origin but it was adopted by the church when hordes of pagans joined the believers. Here we have to ask ourselves: "do I believe the Word of God or I believe what my family has been taught for generations?" For me, the choice was clear although not easy (suffered persecution and oppression at home and college) and I sided with God, rejecting tradition.

The word soul, both in the Old and New Testaments, refers to life, to a living flesh body and never to a non-material being. On some passages, the Hebrew and Greek words for soul are translated as *person*. Of all the times that the word soul appears in the Bible, never it is found with the words eternal or immortal next to it. The only time in the Bible where we can find a being called immortal is in 1 Timothy 6:15 & 16. There, writing about *"the King of kings, and Lord of lords,"* Paul adds that He is *"Who only hath immortality."* Thus, the only immortal being is God, not His creatures. In contrast, 1 John 3:15 indicates that *"Whosoever hateth his brother is a murderer: and ye know that no murderer hath eternal life abiding in him."* Ezekiel 18:4 and 20 indicate that *"the soul that sinneth, it shall die." "I alone am the one who comforts you. Why, then, are you afraid of mortals, who must die, of humans, who are like grass?"* (Isaiah 51:12 – *God's Word*). There is no natural, immanent immortality in any human being, except in Christ.

When Adam and Eve were expelled from the Garden of Eden, it was so they would not eat of the fruit of the tree of life and live forever. See Genesis 3:22,23. Throughout all human history, only those that believe have eternal life: *"He that hath the Son hath life;*

and he that hath not the Son of God hath not life" (1 John 5:12). Romans 2:7 says: *"To them who by patient continuance in well doing* ***seek*** *for glory and honour and* ***immortality, eternal life****."* Do I have to seek for my car if I am sitting inside it, driving it? If we have natural immortality of the soul, why would we have to seek for it? It is only through believing that mortals can obtain eternal life: *"But is now made manifest by the appearing of our Saviour Jesus Christ, who hath abolished death, and hath brought life and immortality to light through the gospel"* (2 Tim. 1:10). If He brought it, it is because we did not have it available and naturally. However, only some people will have it. The most memorized verse in the Bible in any language is John 3:16: *"For God so loved the world, that he gave his only begotten Son, that whosoever believeth in him should not perish, but have everlasting life"*. Unfortunately, it is committed to memory without digesting its meaning. This verse teaches that eternal life is conditional. The person must believe in order to have eternal life. *"Should not perish"*. The penalty for not believing is not hell, but, as Romans 6:23 says, *"the wages of sin is death."* This verse teaches clearly that we do not burn forever, but rather perish forever, just as dry is the opposite of wet and darkness is contrary to light. The everlasting life granted to the believer must be in contrast with the punishment of the wicked. If the believer gets eternal life in heaven, the antithesis of that condition is eternal death for the unbeliever. The idea of an eternal hell is contrary to the character of God and portrays Him as sadistic. The bottom line is that the evil people will die forever as an act of mercy (see comment on Revelation 14:11).

The Bible teaches clearly that the person that dies is not conscious. Let us see some of those passages:

"For the living know that they shall die: but the dead know not any thing, neither have they any more a reward; for the memory of them is forgotten. Also their love, and their hatred, and their envy, is now perished; neither have they any more a portion for ever in any thing that is done under the sun" (Ecclesiastes 9:5,6). Then Solomon adds: *"Whatsoever thy hand findeth to do, do it with thy might; for there is no work, nor device, nor knowledge, nor wisdom, in the grave, whither thou goest"* (Ecclesiastes 9:10). Notice that we go to the grave (see also Psalm 6:5 below), not to heaven or any other place. When Jesus called Lazarus from his tomb, He did not tell his beloved dead friend to come down, like if he were in heaven, but to

come forth. Besides, wouldn't it be construed as cruel and unusual punishment to bring Lazarus from the bliss of heaven back to this dark and sad world? The Bible compares death with a sleep (see John 11). The believers in the first centuries were very well aware of this for they called a place with graves a *cemetery*. This word means "dormitory." It was only after the infiltration of paganism in the church that the idea of the natural immortality of the soul became popular among Christians and Bible passages were misinterpreted to provide support for the teaching of Plato.

"*The dead praise not the LORD, neither any that go down into silence*" (Psalm 115:17). "*For in death there is no remembrance of thee: in the grave who shall give thee thanks?*" (Psalm 6:5). "*Put not your trust in princes, nor in the son of man, in whom there is no help. His breath goeth forth, he returneth to his earth; in that very day his thoughts perish*" (Psalm 146:3,4). "*What will you gain if I die, if I sink into the grave? Can my dust praise you? Can it tell of your faithfulness?*" (Psalm 30:9 New Living Translation). "*Wilt thou shew wonders to the dead? shall the dead arise and praise thee? Selah. Shall thy lovingkindness be declared in the grave? or thy faithfulness in destruction? Shall thy wonders be known in the dark? and thy righteousness in* ***the land of forgetfulness****?*" (Psalm 88:10-12). "*For the grave cannot praise thee, death cannot celebrate thee: they that go down into the pit cannot hope for thy truth*" (Isaiah 38:18). "*But man dieth, and wasteth away: yea, man giveth up the ghost, and where is he? As the waters fail from the sea, and the flood decayeth and drieth up: So man lieth down, and riseth not: till the heavens be no more, they shall not awake, nor be raised out of their sleep...His sons come to honour, and he knoweth it not; and they are brought low, but he perceiveth it not of them*" (Job 14:10-12,21). If the dead continue to live under a different form and conscious, then it would be OK to talk to them through mediums, but the Bible forbids the practice because those are spirits of demons taking the identity of our loved ones: "*...for Satan himself is transformed into an angel of light*" (2 Corinthians 11:14). I know. I once walked in the path of spiritism and was told more than once that I had been chosen to be a medium. After seeing the failed attempts to heal my eyes and some other evidences of the lack of infallibility, I decided not to pursue the development of my "talent." I do believe that something was preparing me for communion with the darkness because my eyes were opened a few times to the invisible world. Fallen angels can take any form and imitate any dead person. That is how I saw the neighbor's wife, who had just died early that morning, walking in the hallway of my house and going through the wall on her way out.

I once was called by a concerned mother to help her teenage boy of about seventeen years old, who always refused to join the body of Christ, but now was scared and wanted help. His problem was that while walking through a sugar cane plantation, he heard a noise behind and felt that he was being followed. When he looked back, there was indeed a woman on a white dress following him. The issue that disturbed him was that the woman had no legs and was hovering without touching the ground. Since the lad had rejected Christ, now Satan could play tricks on him to make him a believer and his follower. After talking to him a couple of times and praying with him, I realized that he did not want anything to do with Jesus. He just wanted to be free from the apparitions so he could have fun in the world. It was sad to see that he called on Jesus for the wrong reasons and could not be free indeed. For a few years of false pleasure, he chose to lose an eternity of real enjoyment and peace. *"Even him, whose coming is after the working of Satan with all power and signs and lying wonders, And with all deceivableness of unrighteousness in them that perish; because they received not the love of the truth, that they might be saved. And for this cause God shall send them strong delusion, that they should believe a lie"* (2 Thessalonians 2:9-11).

Those manifestations are one of the methods by which the world is being enticed to listen to doctrines of devils. *"Now the Spirit speaketh expressly, that in the latter times some shall depart from the faith, giving heed to seducing spirits, and doctrines of devils"* (I Timothy 4:1). I read about a woman who received news about her soldier son been killed in battle. Distraught, she consulted a medium who brought her son and they talked. He looked good and indicated that he was in a great place and was happy. Every Friday she made the trip to another city to see and talk to her son. One day there was a knock on the door. When she opened it, she got great news: it was her son- alive and in person. It was a case of mistaken identity. Who was she seen and speaking to in those weekly trips? Obviously, it was not her son, who had only been wounded. In my experience (I was once a follower of the occult and counseled people affected by these forces), when the name of Jesus is called, these "relatives" get lost, indicating their true origin.

It is clear, by the Biblical evidence presented above, that the saints do not go straight to heaven when they die. They are in the grave waiting for the great day when Jesus will return to take them to glory. *"If I wait, the grave is mine house: I have made my bed in the darkness"* (Job 17:13). *"For the Lord himself shall descend from heaven with a shout, with the voice of the archangel, and with the trump of God: and the dead in Christ shall rise first: Then we which are alive and remain shall be caught up together with them in the clouds, to meet the Lord in the air: and so shall we ever be with the Lord"* (1 Thessalonians 4:16,17).

Does Jesus take body-less people into heaven? The Scriptures mention three specific people taken into heaven and all seem to have been taken with their physical bodies. The first was Enoch: *"And Enoch walked with God: and he was not; for God took him"* (Genesis 5:24). *"And it came to pass, as they still went on, and talked, that, behold, there appeared a chariot of fire, and horses of fire, and parted them both asunder; and Elijah went up by a whirlwind into heaven"* (2 Kings 2:11). The prophets volunteered to search for Elijah and could not find his body. The third person was Moses. *"But when the archangel Michael, contending with the devil, was disputing about the body of Moses, he did not presume to pronounce a blasphemous judgment, but said, 'The Lord rebuke you'"* (Jude 1:9 *ESV*). Why would Jesus bother for a body if all that needed to be in heaven was a "soul"? Couldn't He wait until His second coming to retrieve it? The answer is simple: if a human being is saved, he is not separated into two parts –one dead and the other alive- when he dies. Heaven is for complete human beings; those formed with dust + breath (Genesis 2:7). There are no body-less saved people in heaven (see chapter 4). The saints are in the grave until Jesus calls them to life at His second coming (see John 5:28,29) and then all will be conscious.

Those that believe that the souls claim for revenge under the altar contradict themselves, ignoring that this is a figurative scene. They preach that heaven is a happy place. I believe that too, but how could these "souls" be happy if all they think about is revenge? How can heaven be a place of enjoyment if we harbor hate or resentment of any kind? We are told to forgive our enemies-without condition. We could never be happy or have peace if we hold a grudge. Besides, many times we are offended by other people that never meant to hurt our feelings. Are we going to wait for them to apologize in order to forgive them, especially if they are not aware that they offended us? Let go of that grudge and be happy. You will even sleep better. When Stephen was being stoned, he asked God to forgive his killers, just as Jesus did on Calvary. The real spirit of the Christian makes them to be forgiving, not revengeful. We can conclude without a doubt in our minds that this passage is figurative and that the believers rest in their tombs until Jesus returns. Revelation 22:12 tells us when the saints will enjoy their reward: *"And, behold, I come quickly; and my reward is with me, to give every man according as his work shall be."* At His return, He will resurrect His children to give them eternal life in His presence. The same goes for the wicked regarding the time of their reward, but we will discuss that in chapter 20.

My advice to you, dear friend, is that you stop believing your preacher unless you can find it in the Bible by yourself under the guidance of the Holy Spirit, because he or she might be as deceived as Saul of Tarsus was before he met Jesus.

10And they cried with a loud voice, saying, How long, O Lord, holy and true, dost thou not judge and avenge our blood on them that dwell on the earth?

"But it is urged that these souls must be conscious, for they cry to God. This argument would be of weight were there no such figure of speech as personification. But while there is, it will be proper on certain conditions to attribute life, action, and intelligence to inanimate objects. Thus the blood of Abel is said to have cried to God from the ground. (Genesis 4: 9, 10.) *"For the stone shall cry out of the wall, and the beam out of the timber shall answer it"* (Habakkuk 2:11). The hire of the laborers kept back by fraud cried, and the cry entered into the ears of the Lord of sabaoth. (James 5:4). So the souls mentioned in our text could cry, and not thereby be proved to be conscious." *Smith, Uriah, Daniel and Revelation. 433. "And to Jesus the mediator of the new covenant, and to the **blood** of sprinkling, that speaketh better things than that of **Abel"*** (Hebrews 12:24).

[11]And <u>white robes</u> were given unto every one of them; and it was said unto them, that they should rest yet for a little season, until their fellow servants also and their brethren, that should be killed as they were, should be <u>fulfilled</u>.

The fifth seal corresponds with the fifth church, Sardis (1517-1798 AD). White robes were offered to them too. The white robes were an indication that those that had been killed under a false label of heresy would be vindicated later. This is the period of the Reformation.

Some Bible versions added the word "number" to this verse but it is not found in the older Greek manuscripts. The word "fulfilled" can be also translated as completed or perfected. Jesus is waiting for His character to be completely reproduced in His people. Then He will return. This verse can be translated as follows: "... that they should rest for a little while, until their co servants and brethren, that are to be killed as them, be made complete." The verse shows that God is concerned about quality and not quantity. The divine holiness should be reflected in the lives of every professed servant of Christ before He returns to claim them as His own. Difficulties and persecution help to cleanse our characters as gold is purified by fire. Some difficulties are brought to our lives by other people-friends and foes. Other times the challenges are due to the foolishness of our own bad choices. In both cases, God can change the outcome to produce spiritual growth and character maturity.

[12]And I beheld when he had opened the sixth seal, and, lo, there was a great earthquake; and the sun became black as sackcloth of hair, and the moon became as blood; [13]And the stars of heaven fell unto the earth, even as a fig tree casteth her untimely figs, when she is shaken of a mighty wind.

This seal corresponds with the church of Philadelphia (1798-1844), although the first sign overlaps the end of the previous period in order to keep the signs together.

This passage gave a great push to the preaching of the gospel because its fulfillment convinced scores of unbelievers of the inspiration of the World of God. The Bible not only describes the manner and purpose of Christ's coming, but also presents signs by which men are to know when it is near. Jesus said: *"There shall be signs in the sun, and in the moon, and in the stars"* (Luke 21:25). *"The sun shall be darkened, and the moon shall not give her light, and the stars of heaven shall fall, and the powers that are in heaven shall be shaken. And then shall they see the Son of man coming in the clouds with great power and glory."* Mark 13:24-26.

A great earthquake- This was the earthquake of Lisbon, Portugal on November 1st, 1755. It was written that it was felt in an area of at least four million square miles covering Europe, Africa, and America. These are some of the nations that informed feeling it: Norway, Sweden, Switzerland, Germany, Holland, France, Great Britain, Ireland, and Italy. It was also felt in Greenland, in the West Indies, in the island of Madeira, Antigua and Barbados. The city of Lisbon, previous to that calamity, contained about 150,000 inhabitants. It was estimated that 90,000 persons in that city were lost on that fatal day. It was said also that a city a short distance from Morocco in Africa, of eight or ten thousand persons, together with all their cattle, were swallowed up and soon after, the earth closed again over them. See *Uriah Smith, Daniel and Revelation, pages 439 & 440.* At Cadiz the inflowing wave was said to be sixty feet high. Mountains, "...some of the largest in Portugal, were impetuously shaken, as it were, from their very foundations, and some of them opened at their summits, which were split and rent in a wonderful manner, huge masses of them being thrown down into the adjacent valleys. Flames are related to have issued from these mountains."-- Sir Charles Lyell, *Principles of Geology,* page 495." 'The shock' of the earthquake 'was instantly followed by the fall of every church and convent, almost all the large public buildings, and more than one fourth of the houses. In about two hours after the shock, fires broke out in different quarters, and raged with such violence for the space of nearly three days, that the city was completely desolated. The earthquake happened on a holyday, when the churches and convents were full of people, very few of whom escaped.'-- *Encyclopedia Americana,* article "Lisbon," note (ed. 1831)- As quoted in *The Great Controversy page 305.*

The sun became black and the moon was red- this happened May 19, 1780. Everywhere people were terrified fearing heaven's judgments.

"An eyewitness living in Massachusetts describes the event as follows: 'In the morning the sun rose clear, but was soon overcast. The clouds became lowery, and from them, black and ominous, as they soon appeared, lightning flashed, thunder rolled, and a little rain fell. Toward nine o'clock, the clouds became thinner, and assumed a brassy or coppery appearance, and earth, rocks, trees, buildings, water, and persons were changed by this strange, unearthly light. A few minutes later, a heavy black cloud spread over the entire sky except a narrow rim at the horizon, and it was as dark as it usually is at nine o'clock on a summer evening. . . .'

"Fear, anxiety, and awe gradually filled the minds of the people. Women stood at the door, looking out upon the dark landscape; men returned from their labor in the fields; the carpenter left his tools, the blacksmith his forge, the tradesman his counter. Schools were dismissed, and tremblingly the children fled homeward. Travelers put up at the nearest farmhouse. 'What is coming?' queried every lip and heart. It seemed as if a hurricane was about to dash across the land, or as if it was the day of the consummation of all things.

"Candles were used; and hearth fires shone as brightly as on a moonless evening in autumn. . . . Fowls retired to their roosts and went to sleep, cattle gathered at the pasture bars and lowed, frogs peeped, birds sang their evening songs, and bats flew about. But the human knew that night had not come. . . . *The Great Controversy, pages 306, 307*

At midnight the moon showed up red as blood.

The stars of heaven fell- November 13, 1833- these were seen in all New England and were an instrument to give credibility to the preaching of the second coming of Christ.

[14]*And the heaven departed as a scroll when it is rolled together; and every mountain and island were moved out of their places.* [15]*And the*
kings of the earth, and the great men, and the rich men, and the chief captains, and the mighty men, and every bondman, and every free man, hid themselves in the dens and in the rocks of the mountains;
[16]*And said to the mountains and rocks, Fall on us, and hide us from*

the face of him that sitteth on the throne, and from the wrath of the Lamb:

This passage describes the time of the second coming of Christ from the perspective of the wicked, who will hide from Christ when He returns as a conqueror. The majority of the people mentioned are leaders. They led people the wrong way into rebellion against God and His law, specifically against the true Sabbath. Knowing the truth, they kept it hidden from those that trusted them for guidance and inspiration. Their reasoning could be the potential lost of income or prestige or influence. Regardless of their motivation to hide the truth from the people, their decision was in reality a fight against God. This passage reminds me of Isaiah 2:18-21: *"And they shall go into the holes of the rocks, and into the caves of the earth, for fear of the LORD, and for the glory of his majesty, when he ariseth to shake terribly the earth. In that day a man shall ... go into the clefts of the rocks, and into the tops of the ragged rocks, for fear of the LORD, and for the glory of his majesty, when he ariseth to shake terribly the earth."*

Isaiah 24:19-21 adds: *"The earth is utterly broken down, the earth is clean dissolved, the earth is moved exceedingly. The earth shall reel to and fro like a drunkard, and shall be removed like a cottage; and the transgression thereof shall be heavy upon it; and it shall fall, and not rise again. And it shall come to pass in that day, that the LORD shall punish the host of the high ones that are on high, and the kings of the earth upon the earth."* Very soon the day of God's revenge will come. Are we getting ready? Are we cleansing our souls of everything that is offensive to our Holy God, so His Holy Spirit will be pleased to abide in us and prepare our hearts for heaven? *"Wherefore seeing we also are compassed about with so great a cloud of witnesses, let us lay aside every weight, and the sin which doth so easily beset us, and let us run with patience the race that is set before us, Looking unto Jesus the author and finisher of our faith; who for the joy that was set before him endured the cross, despising the shame, and is set down at the right hand of the throne of God"* (Hebrews 12:1,2).

17 *For the great day of his wrath is come; and who shall be able to stand?*

We find this question answered in chapter 7 where it shows the 144,000 as the answer. May the Lord find us all faithful in that day.

REVELATION 7

God's Mathematics; An Analysis Of The 144,000 and The Great Multitude

Chapter seven of Revelation is one of the chapters that produce great excitement among Christians. Powerful minds are being captivated by questions and thoughts about the special group that will be alive when Jesus comes again. Chapter 14 is a complement of this one and would be studied together in order to see all the facets of this group. This chapter is parenthetic between the sixth and seventh seals. It's the answer to the question asked in chapter 6:17: *"For the great day of their wrath has come, and who can stand?"*

The answer is clear: the 144,000 will stand, not for something immanent or natural in them, but because they are covered by the merits of Christ (His righteousness). Note: this chapter will be studied in a different format than the previous six because it will not follow a verse-by-verse order. However, the whole chapter will be analyzed.

The aforementioned question from Revelation 6:17 has parallels in other parts of the Bible. Let us see those passages and the answers:

Psalm 15:1-5	Psalm 24:3-5	Isaiah 33:14-17
The question: *who shall abide in thy tabernacle? Who shall dwell in thy holy hill?*	The question: *Who shall ascend into the hill of the LORD? Or who shall stand in his holy place?*	The question: *Who among us shall dwell with the devouring fire? Who among us shall dwell with everlasting burnings?*
The answer: *He that walketh uprightly, and worketh righteousness, and speaketh the truth in his heart. He that backbiteth not with his tongue, nor doeth evil to his neighbour, nor taketh up a reproach against his neighbour. In whose eyes a vile person is contemned; but he honoureth them that fear the LORD. He that sweareth to his own hurt, and changeth not. He that putteth not out his money to usury, nor taketh reward against the innocent. He that doeth these things shall never be moved.*	The answer: *He that hath clean hands, and a pure heart; who hath not lifted up his soul unto vanity, nor sworn deceitfully. He shall receive the blessing from the LORD, and righteousness from the God of his salvation.*	The answer: *He that walketh righteously, and speaketh uprightly; he that despiseth the gain of oppressions, that shaketh his hands from holding of bribes, that stoppeth his ears from hearing of blood, and shutteth his eyes from seeing evil; He shall dwell on high: his place of defense shall be the munitions of rocks: bread shall be given him; his waters shall be sure. Thine eyes shall see the king in his beauty: they shall behold the land that is very far off.*

It is evident that not everyone will qualify to be part of this elite group. The traits of character contained in those three passages combined with those listed in this chapter seven of Revelation indicate that these individuals have a unique experience with their Savior. They will have such a relationship with Jesus that it will enable them to withstand the fiercest winds of opposition in the history of the human race. It takes time to develop that relationship and God has taken the first step by extending us an invitation. The rest is up to us. *"O taste and see that the LORD is good: blessed is the man that trusteth in him"* (Psalm 34:8).

[1]And after these things I saw four angels standing on the four corners of the earth, holding the four winds of the earth, that the wind should not blow on the earth, nor on the sea, nor on any tree. [2]And I saw another angel ascending from the east, having the seal of the living God: and he cried with a loud voice to the four angels, to whom it was given to hurt the earth and the sea, [3]Saying, Hurt not the earth, neither the sea, nor the trees, till we have sealed the servants of our God in their foreheads.

In- The seal of God is not placed on the forehead but *inside* it, indicating that the most intimate parts of the human intellect and reasoning are involved.

Let us explain the symbolism mentioned above.

- Four comers of the earth = number four represents the whole word. There are four gospels because the salvation message is to go to the whole world.
- Winds = Wars, according to Isaiah 29:6, 7 & Jeremiah 51:1,2,11 & 12. Jeremiah 49:36 reads: "I'll bring the four winds from the four corners of heaven against Elam and scatter its people in every direction."
- Sea = High population areas (Revelation 17:15).
- Land = Low population areas (in contrast with the many waters of the sea).
- Trees = Symbol for world leaders (Daniel 4: 21,22).
- East = From where Jesus will come for the second time (Matthew 24:27).

This sealing activity covers all the nations. The governments of the earth will remain at least relatively stable until the winds of strive are released. The sealing will be done in big and small nations in very difficult times.

Seal = The Bible says in the New Testament that we are sealed with the Holy Spirit-more on that later. The seal is also mentioned in Ezekiel 9:4, where the prophet says that it will be *imprinted* (Hebrew- *by implication a signature- Strong's* note) on the foreheads of those who grieve and lament over all "detestable things" that people do. The word *seal* or *mark* in Ezekiel was translated from "täv," which in ancient Hebrew was just a letter in the shape of a cross. That was the mark that the Jews painted with blood on their doors before they left Egypt (Passover)- foretelling the cross. It was the mark of redemption indicating that they were protected by the shadow of the cross. These people will grieve because they will find sin hateful. They see sin as the cause of the crucifixion of their beloved Savior. They know that Jesus' death was caused by their own sins and the sins they see being committed. That will cause a deep sorrow in their hearts. They are zealous for the character of God being maligned by the behavior of those that profess to follow Him.

"*Sigh and cry*-similarly sounding verbs in Hebrew, as in [the] English Version, expressing the prolonged sound of their grief. 'Sigh' implies their inward grief ('groanings which cannot be uttered,' Romans 8:26); 'cry,' the outward expression of it. So [it was with] Lot (2 Peter 2:7, 8). Tenderness should characterize the man of God, not harsh sternness in opposing the ungodly (Psalms 119:53, 136; Jeremiah 13:17; 2 Corinthians 12:21); at the same time **zeal for the honor of God** (Psalms 69:9, 10; 1 John 5:19)." *Jamieson-Fausset-Brown Bible Commentary.* Note: Although Genesis four reads that Cain received a "mark" on his forehead, the word used is different from the one chosen by Ezekiel regarding the mark of the saints. The similarity is dual since both were a mark and both were placed on the forehead, but Cain was disobedient and rebellious while those mentioned by Ezekiel follow God's will. The marks of the end times are going to be placed on the foreheads of the wicked for following the beast and on the foreheads of the righteous because their characters resemble the character of their Savior.

Do we cry, and are we hurt, disappointed or sad when a church member turns his back on Christ or do we point fingers? Let us trade places with that tormented soul and have sympathy. *"Now we exhort you, brethren, warn them that are unruly, **comfort** the feebleminded, **support** the weak, **be patient** toward all men"* (1 Thessalonians 5:14). In 2008, I brought a very intelligent, talented and sweet lady to what could be her new church. She had been embattled at her previous church for wanting to do what was right (opposing money-squanderers, etc.). After the service, four of us (myself and three ladies) sat at a table to have lunch. One of the ladies proposed that this newcomer helped with the teen girls at an upcoming camp. She had been asked as a chaperone before a couple of times. The other church lady almost choked on her food, extended her arm full length across the table and frantically moved her pointing finger side to side saying: "No, no, no." Then, trying to cover her anti-Christian attitude, said "She can stay here and pray." One of the members from the previous church was her friend and had called her to give her a twisted version of some facts fearing that the new comer would uncover what was going on. This caused my lady friend to go away and not return to where she was hoping would be her new church where she could serve. Knowing the full story first hand, I know that my friend was an innocent victim and still suffered. Real mercy is lacking in our churches today.

This passage from Ezekiel specifically refers to the two groups in the church. This brings to memory two parables that refer to the two kinds of church members:

1. The parable of the ten virgins- I would like to think that the five prudent were always looking for ways to spend time with God in prayer, while the foolish were indifferent and lived like the world. This last group was looking for ways to entertain themselves. Sacred, ennobling church music bored them. They took no real pleasure to follow Jesus wherever He led because they wanted to be comfortable. Today we could identify the video game/iPod generation with the foolish virgins.
2. The parable of the prodigal son- One son, after wandering away and squandering his gifts from the father, returned repented and confessed his sins. The other brother was a finger pointer. A person whose favorite one word was *"you..."* and whose favorite two words were: *"you always...."* The oldest brother was constantly busy finding fault in others and wondering "what is in for me?"

The seal of God will show the difference between the sheep and the goats; those that follow the Lamb and those that follow their own path. Many today have a religion of their own choosing. They follow only what they want and discard what they do not want. This is what the people that repopulated Samaria did in ancient times: *"They feared the LORD, <u>and</u> served their own gods, after the manner of the nations whom they carried away from thence. Unto this day they do after the former manners: they fear not the LORD, neither do* *they after their statutes, or after their ordinances, or after the law and commandment which the LORD commanded the children of Jacob, whom he named Israel"* (2 Kings 17:33-34). This kind of people mixes the truth with error and celebrates pagan customs at the manner of their friends. How could they represent the truth if their friends see no difference?

"It is a great comfort to believers, that in the midst of destroyers and destructions, there is a Mediator, a great High Priest, who has an interest in heaven, and in whom saints on earth have an interest. The representation of the Divine glory from above the ark, removed to the threshold, denoted that the Lord was about to leave his mercy-seat, and to pronounce judgment on the people. The distinguishing character of this remnant that is to be saved is such as sigh and cry to God in prayer, because of the abominations in Jerusalem [church]. Those who keep pure in times of general wickedness, God will keep safe in times of general trouble and distress." *Matthew Henry's Concise Commentary*-Comment on Ezekiel 9:1-4. God has promised His blessing. It is up to us to exercise faith. *"Never worry about anything. But in every situation let God know what you need in prayers and requests while giving thanks. Then God's peace, which goes beyond anything we can imagine, will guard your thoughts and emotions through Christ Jesus"* (Philippians 4:6.7- *God's Word*).

A very sad part of the passage of Ezekiel 9 is that there is going to be a killing just like in the days of the Exodus. *"As I listened, he said to the others, "Follow him through the city and kill, without showing pity or compassion. Slaughter old men, young men and maidens, women and children, but do not touch anyone who has the mark. Begin at my sanctuary." So they began with the elders who were in front of the temple"* (Ezekiel 9:5,6). We have to wake up from our slumber so we can be sealed and thus protected from the wrath that is coming against the hypocrites. I find it less painful if Jesus burns the defects of my character and the affections that tie me to this world now and not that He burns me up in the day of reckoning. He loves me, so why would I like to disappoint Him and embrace what separates me from him? *"How shall we* ***escape****, if we neglect so great* ***salvation...?"*** (Hebrews 2:3)**.** Just imagine that you were one of the Roman soldiers in charge of crucifying Jesus. You were holding a hammer in one hand and the other hand holds the nails. How could you have found it in your heart to trespass those holy hands? That is what we do when we go against our conscience. We *"are crucifying the Son of God all over again and subjecting him to public disgrace"* (Hebrews 6:6 *NIV*). *"Therefore, since we are surrounded by such a great cloud of witnesses, <u>let us throw off everything that hinders and the sin that so easily entangles</u>, and let us run with perseverance the race marked out for us. <u>Let us fix our eyes on Jesus</u>, the author and perfecter of our faith, who <u>for the joy set before him endured the cross, scorning its shame</u>, and sat down at the right hand of the throne of God. Consider him who endured such opposition from sinful men, so that you will not grow weary and lose heart"* (Hebrews 12:1-3 *NIV*).

Isaiah 8:16 identifies the seal with the law of God: *"**seal** up the law among my disciples."* Is in the law of God that we can find the three most important characteristics of a complete seal: <u>**name**</u>, position, <u>**title**</u> or rank, and <u>**jurisdiction**</u>. We can find all of them only in the fourth commandment:

Name: Yahweh
Title: Creator
Jurisdiction: Heavens and earth.

According to Romans 4:11, **sign** and **seal** are equivalent words: *"And he received the <u>**sign**</u> of circumcision, a <u>**seal**</u> of the righteousness of the faith which he had yet being uncircumcised: that he might be the father of all them that believe, though they be not circumcised; that righteousness might be imputed unto them also."* Ezekiel 20:12 & 20 mentions the Sabbath as a **sign** between God and his people and that by the observance of that day, God sanctifies his children. In other words, by keeping the Sabbath, we participate of the divine nature and God prepares us to live in heaven. The sealing angel from Ezekiel nine collaborates in writing the law in the heart of the believers. Isaiah declares emphatically that those that so not have the law do not have light. This means that they rejected the truth and embraced the error. Their consciences get to be cauterized. *"To the law and to the testimony: if they speak not according to this word, it is because there is no light in them"* (Isaiah 8:20). Revelation 14 shows the 144,000 as <u>having the name of God on their foreheads</u>. The name is a symbol of character and the law has been identified by scholars as the reflection of the character of God. See the following table:

Attribute	God is:	The Law is:
Good	Luke 18:19; Psalm 100:5	Romans 7:12
Holy	Isaiah 5:16	Romans 7:12
Just	Deuteronomy 32:4	Romans 7:12
Does not change	James 1:17	Matthew 5:18
Truth	John 14:6; Psalm 31:5	Psalm 119:142,151
Perfect	Matthew 5:48	Psalm 19:7
Eternal	Isaiah 40:28	Psalm 119:152; 11:7,8

The attributes that we find describing the divine character describe the law also. Therefore, the 144,000 are the remnant *"which keep the commandments of God"* (Revelation 12:17), for that reason they have the character of God in their foreheads. To say that the law has been changed would imply that the character of God – who He is- could change. In Psalm 89:34 God says that He will not *"alter the thing that is gone out"* of His lips. If He changes His mind about what reflects His character, could you trust Him for your salvation? Maybe He could change His mind on that too. Jesus was very clear on the subject: *"For verily I say unto you, <u>Till heaven and earth pass</u>, one jot or one tittle shall in no wise pass from the law, till all be fulfilled"* (Matthew 5:18). I am glad that we have a trustworthy God who is consistent with His will. *"Every good gift and every perfect gift is from above, and cometh down from the Father of lights, <u>with whom is no variableness</u>, <u>neither shadow of turning</u>"* (James 1:17). *"Jesus Christ is the same yesterday, today, and forever"* (Hebrews 13:8).

Why is the seal placed in the forehead? Because the frontal lobe of the brain is where we make decisions, show determination, and it is the seat of the intelligence, the will, the conscience, moral values and also indicates a relationship of faith. Notice that, unlike the mark of the beast, the seal of God is not placed on the hand, because salvation is only obtained by faith, not by works, so nobody would boast (Ephesians 2:8-10).

The 144,000 have a mark and a name but there are differences with the mark of the beast:

God's people	**Beast's followers**
Have a seal in their foreheads-Revelation 7:3	Receive a mark in their right hand, or in their foreheads
Have their Father's name written in their foreheads-Revelation 14:1	Have the name of the beast
	Have the number of the beast (666)

Paul; wrote: *"In whom ye also trusted, after that ye heard the word of truth, the gospel of your salvation: in whom also after that ye believed, ye were sealed with that Holy Spirit of promise"* (Ephesians 1:13). *"And grieve not the Holy Spirit of God, whereby ye are sealed unto the day of redemption"* (Ephesians 4:30).We can safely conclude that the seal is primarily the Holy Spirit, and secondarily, the law, specifically the Sabbath that He writes in our hearts. *"And I will put my Spirit within you, and cause you to walk in my statutes, and ye shall keep my judgments, and do them"* (Ezekiel 36:27).

The word translated as seal in Revelation 7:3 and Ephesians 1:13 & 4:30 is σφραγίζω (read sphragizō). Strong's notes say: "to *stamp* (with a signet or private mark) for security or preservation (literally or figuratively); by implication to *keep secret*, to *attest*: - (set a, set to) seal up, stop." Therefore, the sign or seal of God will be placed on the forehead of His people to preserve them during the difficult times ahead.

"We seal what we wish to guard securely. When all things else on earth are confounded, God will secure His people from the common ruin. God gives the first charge as to their safety before He orders the punishment of the rest (Psalm 31:20; Isa 26:20, 21). So in the case of Lot and Sodom (Gen 19:22); also the Egyptian first-born were not slain till Israel had time to sprinkle the blood-mark, ensuring their safety (compare Revelation 7:3; Amos 9:9). So the early Christians had [the city of] Pella provided as a refuge for them, before the destruction of Jerusalem." *Jamieson-Fausset-Brown Bible Commentary*

Then, John heard the number of the sealed: 144,000 (this is a multiple of 12). The number 12 identifies the people of God:

12 tribes

12 judges

12 stones removed from the Jordan River, to represent Israel.

12 precious stones on the chest of the high priest. Same purpose as above.

12 apostles

12 doors in the heavenly city

12 foundations in the celestial Jerusalem

12,000 stadia - length of the city (another multiple of 12).

144 (12 x 12) cubits- this is the thickness of the wall of the Holy City.

The number is only representative of the people of God from all around the world, not a literal number, because God does not show favoritism (Acts 10:34). He will never say: "Only 144,000 will be a special group with exclusive privileges." If this number is literal then we would have to accept other parts of the description of the 144,000 as literal too and I supposed that many people would oppose to do just that. For example, Revelation 14:4 reads that these *"...have not defiled themselves with women, for they are virgins."* If this is literal, then they are males. Women do not have the right to be part of that group and only single men would qualify. That would be unconceivable because God invented marriage and He says very clearly that a man is not defiled by marriage: *"Marriage is honourable in all, and the bed undefiled"* (Hebrews 13:4).

If the number is literal, then the tattoo on the forehead must be literal too, for John wrote that they *"had his name and his Father's name written on their foreheads"* (Revelation 14:1). However, God is against tattoos (Leviticus 19:28). This passage is to be interpreted as a parable; either we take it all literally or as totally symbolic. To pick and choose capriciously is walking on sinking sand and there is no guarantee that it will stop there. We might then go to the parable of the rich and Lazarus and dissect it the same way (it is explained in chapter 20).

There are different interpretations of this subject regarding the identity of the 144,000 and the great multitude. There is a reason why so many misunderstand this chapter: they forget important principles of Bible interpretation:

- The Bible is its own interpreter. We must compare Bible passages to obtain the full body of the truth. All the symbols of Revelation are explained in other parts of the Bible and in itself. For example, water symbolizes multitudes of people and refer to populated areas (see Revelation 17:15). You cannot have a sandwich with only bread. So it is with Bible truth. There are elements in different parts of the Bible that are like building blocks. When you put them together, you see how harmoniously they fit. If you do not understand a passage, use a concordance and look up other places where the Bible touches on the subject and compare the passages.
- The Bible is the final authority, not a church leader with his "I think this means..."
- We must consider the context. In this case, we will compare verses within chapter seven and some from chapter 14 that are pertinent to this subject

Now, imagine that God has 143,999 (being short of the 144,000 by just one), and 153 children are converted with all of their hearts. Will God put their names in a bag, close His eyes and select just one from the group? What about the remaining 152 children? Don't they have the same right? Praise the Lord, because He will never do such an injustice.

The numbers in the Bible are not always literal. Regarding them, when you read the size of the Israelite army's accounts in Numbers and other books, you will notice that the numbers of people are rounded. For example, Numbers chapter one has these amounts for the soldiers of the tribes:

46,500

59,300

45,650

74,600

54,400

57,400

40,500

32,200

35,400

62,700

41,500

53,400

You can see that there was rounding either up or down and that all the numbers end in zero. Otherwise, there was some very strict birth control going on there and that would have made Moses the world's foremost expert in population control. This would require that he not only would decide how many babies would be born, but also the gender and among the males, they had to be fit to become soldiers (not crippled, deformed or mentally slow)- that would have made Moses the greatest connoisseur in gene manipulation. We all know that this would be an absurdity. There are other passages like this one from Numbers that show "flexibility" with the amounts. For example, 1 Samuel 11:8 mentions how many soldiers Israel and Judah had in times of King Saul. There were 300,000 for the former and 30,000 for the latter. 2 Samuel 24:9 shows 800,000 soldiers for Israel and 500,000 for Judah in the census. Gideon saved Israel with 300 men. The special forces in David's army were also a rounded number: *"Again, David gathered together all the chosen men of Israel, thirty thousand"* (2 Samuel 6:1). That is significant because there are called "chosen," just as it appears to be with the 144,000. In 2 Chronicles 13:3, the Israelite army had 800,000 men of which 500,000 fell in battle according to verse 17. I find it hard to believe that even the dead fall in exact numbers that happen to end in zero. In 2 Chronicles 14:8, Judah's army totaled 300,000 and those of Benjamin were 280,000. In the same chapter, verse 9, it totals the Ethiopian forces at 1,000,000. In the same book, chapter 17, verses 14-19 totals Jehoshaphat's army at 880,000. King Amaziah's army was 300,000 strong (2 Chronicles 5:5). The army in times of King Uzziah counted with 307,000 soldiers (2 Chronicles 26:13). Every time that there was a count for the soldiers, the numbers ended in zero. It is clear then, that these numbers. Moreover, the number of the sealed in Revelation is symbolic and not an exact amount of people. To believe that is like believing in predestination (the erroneous teaching that God decided, before you were born, if you were going to be saved or lost, regardless of your sins or piety during your life).

Why did the soldiers numbers and the 144,000 end in zero? God has an army prepared for the last days. The 144,000 will be considered by God as His army – His militant church- to give the final push to the preaching of the gospel.

Some people make a literal interpretation of this passage and focus their attention on the tribes of Israel, but they forget that the captivities of the people of God had erased all vestige of distinction between the different tribes because they had been intermarrying even with non-Jewish people. Some people mingled with the Israelites even when they came out of Egypt (Exodus 12:38; Numbers 11:4). Ezra 2:62 and Nehemiah 7:64 mention priests (of all people!) excluded from the priesthood because they could not find their names in the genealogies. Paul is the only person in the New Testament that could say which tribe he belonged to- probably because of his resources. There is no mention of the tribe origin of any of the other eleven disciples, evidently because they did not know, or did not have the resources to investigate, or because the records were missing or because it was irrelevant. Of Ephraim, not included in the list of Revelation 7, Isaiah 7:8 says: "*...Within sixty-five years Ephraim will be broken, So that it will not be a people (American Standard Version)*." Hosea 4:17 says: "*Ephraim is joined to idols; leave him alone!*" The same book adds: "*Ephraim will be laid* *waste on the day of reckoning. Among the tribes of Israel I proclaim what is certain...Ephraim is oppressed, trampled in judgment, intent on pursuing idols."* Hosea 5:9, 11 *NIV.* The version *The Message* translates verse 11 this way: *"Brutal Ephraim is himself brutalized—a taste of his own medicine! He was so determined to do it his own worthless way."* Asaph wrote: *"The children of Ephraim, being armed, and carrying bows, turned back in the day of battle. They kept not the covenant of God, and refused to walk in his law; And forgot his works, and his wonders that he had shewed them"* (Psalm 78:9-11). This psalm presents the steps that led them into full apostasy: neglect of duty, they stop following God's law and finally they forgot all about Him and His blessings. Let this be a warning for all of us. Even though God pleaded with them, at the end they were destroyed because they separated themselves from the source of life, their only protection. In the same way that a light bulb cannot brighten any dark area without a source of power connected to it, we cannot pretend to have life if we separate from God and have a religion of our own making as mentioned above.

In addition, several people joined Israel for different reasons like those that nationalized as Jews (Esther 8:17). When James wrote his letter to his brothers, he addressed it to the twelve scattered tribes (James 1:1). He wrote to people converted to Christianity from Judaism as well as from paganism. However, all of them are included as part of the 12 tribes. They are called scattered because they were living all around the world. Paul, a Jew, wrote that those who believe are children of Abraham. He adds: *"There is neither Jew nor Greek...for you are all one in Christ Jesus. If you belong to Christ, then* ***you are Abraham's seed****, and heirs according to the promise"* (Galatians 3:7, 28 & 29). Jesus said that even from the stones could God raise children *"unto Abraham"* (Matthew 3:9). Probably the stones mentioned here were the apparently hardened hearts of the pagan people that usually were among the audience of Jesus. The Israel of God is not anymore the Jewish people, but now it is everyone who believes. Here Paul comes to illustrate our understanding of who Israel is: *"For he is not a Jew, which is one outwardly; neither is that circumcision, which is outward in the flesh: But he is a Jew, which is one inwardly; and circumcision is that of the heart, in the spirit, and not in the letter; whose praise is not of men, but of God"* (Romans 2:28, 29). *"Not as though the word of God hath taken none effect. For they are not all Israel, which are of*

Israel: Neither, because they are the seed of Abraham, are they all children: but, In Isaac shall thy seed be called. That is, They which are the children of the flesh, these are not the children of God: but the children of the promise are counted for the seed" (Romans 9:6-8). *"For* ***there is no difference between the Jew and the Greek****: for the same Lord over all is rich unto all that call upon him"* (Romans 10:12). In addition, the nation of Israel had been filling up the cup of the patience of God and He had given them an ultimatum. They would have a limited window of opportunity to continue being God's representatives on earth. Daniel 9 teaches that God granted them 490 years (70 weeks), after which, the privilege of being the people of God would go to others more appreciative. That prophecy began in the year 457 BC and ended in the year 31 AD when they stoned Stephen (Acts 7) and the gospel then went to us, the gentiles, who can be grateful for it. For a more detailed explanation, see my other book, Daniel; *Walking Thought Fire and Sleeping Among Lions*, verses 24-27 of chapter nine.

The main authority on this subject- Jesus Himself- pronounced these words to the Jewish nation on the subject: *"Therefore say I unto you, The kingdom of God shall be* ***taken from you****, and given to a nation bringing forth the fruits thereof"* (Matthew 21:43). He also told them: *"There shall be weeping and gnashing of teeth, when ye shall see Abraham, and Isaac, and Jacob, and all the prophets, in the kingdom of God, and you yourselves thrust out. And they shall come from the east, and from the west, and from the north, and from the south, and shall sit down in the kingdom of God"* (Luke 13:28, 29). Those coming from the four cardinal points are the Gentiles that would join the church. By rejecting Christ, the nation of Israel was itself rejected as a people. Now in our days, the Christian church is the people of God- it is no longer the Jewish nation. So, if Jesus said that the kingdom of God was going to be removed from Israel, why the preachers insist that Israel is the elected nation? To sustain such a claim it is against the clear words of Jesus Himself. Are these preachers greater than Jesus Christ is? I do not think so. Believe the Bible and the Bible only as the exclusive source of unadulterated truth. So, if your preacher says that Israel is the chosen people, beware. Believe the Bible only, in spite of how godly he or she looks and how much you love him or her. Your preacher is twisting the Scriptures, either willingly or by ignorance based merely on tradition. Jesus Christ should be supreme in your affections and loyalty. Jesus, after His resurrection, asked Peter: *"...Simon, son of Jonas, lovest thou me more than these?..."* (John 21:15). Do you love Jesus more than anyone regardless of who the person is?

Now, let us talk about the meaning of the names of the 12 tribes. The clue to understand this passage in Revelation 7 is to remember that each Hebrew name had a special meaning. That is why God was specific about certain names. He named Abraham and Sarah, Isaac, Israel, Solomon, Cyrus, John the Baptist and Jesus. In Old Testament times, the names given to the children had a spiritual and sometimes prophetical meaning, expressing the attributes of character that the parents wanted to develop in their children. The meanings of the names of Revelation 7 represent the characteristics of the people of God of the time of the end.

Let us start with Israel = *one who prevails.* No one will walk on the golden streets of the New Jerusalem defeated or with bowed head, but like over comers with the forehead lifted up (Luke 21:28). To succeed in the battle with evil, we have to surrender our wills before God and allow Him to direct our lives, for He can do in us *"to will and to act"* (Philippians 2:13).

Now, the analysis of the tribes' names and their meanings for us, the last days' Church.

1) Judah = *praise.* Instead of complaining all the time, the real Christian finds always one or more reasons to give thanks and praise to the Lord *"Rejoice in the Lord always: and again I say, rejoice. Let your moderation be known unto all men. The Lord is at hand. Be careful for nothing; but in every thing by prayer and supplication* ***with thanksgiving*** *let your requests be made known unto God. And the peace of God, which passeth all understanding, shall keep your hearts and minds through Christ Jesus"* (Philippians 4:4-7), because he finds that whatever we suffer now *"is nothing compared to the glory that he will give us later"* (Romans 8:18).
2) Reuben = *behold the Son.* The Christian's life and character are changed while he contemplates the Lord. *"Look unto me, and be ye saved, all the ends of the earth: for I am God, and there is none else"* (Isaiah 45:22); *"But we all, with open face beholding as in a glass the glory of the Lord, are changed into*

the same image from glory to glory, even as by the Spirit of the Lord" (2 Corinthians 3:18) and he, having *"the ministry of reconciliation"* leads others to contemplate *"the Lamb of God, who takes away the sin of the world"* (John 1:29).

3) Gad = *good fortune.* In the sense of receiving blessings, because we have been given the opportunity to become part of the divine family. *"To redeem them that were under the law, that we might receive the adoption of sons"* (Gal. 4: 5); *"Having predestinated us unto the adoption of children by Jesus Christ to himself, according to the good pleasure of his will"* (Eph. 1:5).
4) Asher= *Eternal bliss, beatitude.* How joyful are the children of God regardless of the circumstances! They walk through *"the valley of the shadow of death"* (Psalm 23:4) with joy and peace. Paul said: *"I rejoiced in the Lord greatly"* (Philippians 4:10).
5) Naphtali= *overcomer.* To the last church of history, Jesus says: *"To him who overcomes, I will give the right to sit with me on my throne"* (Revelation 3:21). No other church period in history had been in worst spiritual condition than the one in the times that we are living now. We are content with our little knowledge of the Scriptures and we do not feel the need to grow closer to God. We have to wake up and ask to be given the Holy Spirit. A time of great trouble is approaching and we are not prepared. Probably not even one in a hundred is ready, but it is to this church (us) that Jesus makes the most wonderful promise- to have the honor of sitting with Him on his throne!
6) Manasseh = *forget.* God helps us to forget all the shameful defeats of our past life, and also the size of our problems. As Paul, the last days Christians can live *"forgetting what is behind and straining toward what is ahead..."*, pressing *"on toward the goal to win the prize..."* (Philippians 3:13). See also Job 11:13 -16.
7) Simeon = *heard.* The believer is a man or a woman of prayer. He has the assurance that if he asks for something according to the will of God, He listens (1 John 3:22; 5:14). He has a healthy relationship with his Creator, and has the faith that will be necessary for the end time -a faith able to withstand tiredness, Jesus' delay and even hunger.

8) Levi = *union*. Peter says that we are a kingdom of priests (1 Peter 2:9), and as them, we are a bond of union between God and men, The Old Testament priests were like a bridge between the sinner and God, prefiguring Christ. The Father *"gave us the ministry of reconciliation"* (2 Corinthians 5:18). The Bible teaches that the last generation of Christians will preach the gospel to all nations, and then, the end will come (Matthew 24:14).
9) Issachar = *salary*. The Christian does not serve God looking for a reward, but God offers it *"...be strong and do not give up, for your work will be rewarded"* (2 Chronicles. 15:7). Jesus offers a mansion (John 14:1-3) and eternal life to the faithful ones.
10) Zabulon = *dwelling*. The 144,000 allow the Holy Spirit to dwell in them (John 14:17). The word used in Greek for in is εν =in the most intimate part (of the heart in this case). They will received what the prophet Joel names the later rain - the full presence of the Holy Spirit of Jesus (Joel 2:23, 28 & 32). Paul wrote that we are the temple of the Holy Spirit (1 Corinthians 6:19).
11) Joseph = *augmentation, increase*. The believer is a born again creature that is growing constantly *("But speaking the truth in love, may grow up into him in all things, which is the head, even Christ"* Eph. 4:15; *"That ye might walk worthy of the Lord unto all pleasing, being fruitful in every good work, and increasing in the knowledge of God" "And not holding the Head, from which all the body by joints and bands having nourishment ministered, and knit together, increases with the increase of God."* Colossians 1:10; 2:19; *"As newborn babes, desire the sincere milk of the word, that ye may grow thereby"* 1 Peter 2:2; *"But grow in grace, and in the knowledge of our Lord and Saviour Jesus Christ. To him be glory both now and forever. Amen"* 2 Peter 3:18).
12) Benjamin = *Son of the right* (hand). This means that the 144,000 will be unconditionally of the side of God, no matter what they have to go through, because their love for Jesus is stronger than the fear for death, hunger, treason from friends and relatives, persecution (Romans 8:35-39) and the great tribulation that they will confront. What makes them different and worthy of praise? *"Then shall the King say unto them on his right hand, Come, ye blessed of*

my Father, inherit the kingdom prepared for you from the foundation of the world: for I was hungry, and ye gave me to eat; I was thirsty, and ye gave me drink; I was a stranger, and ye took me in; naked, and ye clothed me; I was sick, and ye visited me; I was in prison, and ye came unto me" (Matthew 25:34-36).

Therefore, the meaning of their names point to their characters:

*They **praise** while they **behold** the Son, considering their **good fortune** and **eternal bliss**, being **overcomers**, **forgettin**g their past sinful life, knowing that they are **heard**, and that in their **union** with Christ, they will have a **salary**. By the in**dwelling** of the Spirit, they will experience **growth** and remain faithful as the **sons of the right** (hand).*

"After this" applies to a scene that John sees after he beheld the same group, now glorified, following their suffering through the great tribulation mentioned in Daniel 12:1. But, how do we know that the 144,000 will be on earth during the great tribulation? For more than a century, sincere Christians were thinking that this group is different from the great multitude, but we read in the Bible that God did not -and never will –have special groups of people that will receive better treatment than others will. We have to remember also, that Israel is not the Jewish nation anymore, but it is the Christian Church (which is constituted by every person that believes in Jesus, both Jews and Gentiles). If we compare chapters 7 & 14 of Revelation, we can see that both groups are really one, just as the head of the statue of Daniel 2 is also the lion of Daniel 7. They are just presented from different perspectives.

Now, let us see what the Bible teaches about both groups. Please keep an open mind and let the Bible be its own interpreter, discarding all preconceived ideas that you might have learned.

The 144,OOO	The Great Multitude
1) They will be in front of the Lamb (Revelation 14:1).	1) They will be in front of the lamb (7:9)
2) They will stand in front of the throne (14:3).	2) They will stand before the throne (7:9,15)
3) They will stay together with the 4 living creatures and the 24 elders (14:3)	3) They will be together with the four living creatures and the 24 elders (7:11)
4) They follow the Lamb wherever He goes (14:4)	4) The Lamb will be their Shepherd, so they follow Him (7:17).
5) They are blameless. This indicates innocence (14:4).	5) They have washed their robes in the blood of the Lamb. This indicates innocence (7:14). Like if they have never sinned.
6) They kept themselves pure(14:4)	6) They are clothed with white robes- indicates purity (7:9). They will not have any more tendencies to sin
7) They had been redeemed from the earth (14:3,4)	7) They were from the nations of the earth (7:9) redeemed after the great tribulation (7:14)
8) They were first fruits to God (14:4)	8) They were holding palm branches in their hands (7:9), which identifies them as first fruits for God (see Leviticus 23:39,40)
9) They praise God with a loud voice (14:2)	9) They praise God with a loud voice (7:10)
10) They sing a song unique to their experience (14:3), the song of Moses and the Lamb (15:2,3), a song that refers to the great struggle that they experienced. Moses was persecuted by the army of Pharaoh, just like the beast will persecute the followers of Jesus during the time of the great tribulation. When Moses and the Israelites were set free, they sang a song of praise to God.	10) They came from the great tribulation after suffering persecution by the beast (7:14)

Just like in Daniel 2,7 and 8, in God presents the different nations of the world under different symbols, He shows the saved in the last days under two symbols: the 144,000 and the great multitude. To say that the 144,000 and the great multitude are two different groups and that the former will have special treatment over the latter, it is as conflicting with the real character of God (which is love), as it is the theory of predestination (which is based solely on a misunderstanding of the Bible). The theory of predestination teaches that God already decided beforehand who is going to be saved and who is going to be lost, regardless of their decisions. Such believe is absurd and lacks biblical foundation, not to mention that it stains the character of the Creator. He is sovereign all right, but He does not work against His just nature. All the redeemed will receive the same reward according to the parable of the workers in the vineyard (Matthew 20:1-15). Those that were hired on the eleventh hour received the same pay as those that endured the heat of the day.

"After these things I saw a large crowd from every nation, tribe, people, and language..." Hank Hanegraaff wrote this regarding the "saw" and the "heard:" "As Richard Bauckham explains, literarily, the 144,000 and the great multitude are comparable to the Lion and the Lamb. Just as John is told about a Lion and turns to see a Lamb (Revelation 5:5–6), so he is told about the 144,000 and turns to see a great multitude (Revelation 7). Thus, the 144,000 is to the great multitude what the Lion is to the Lamb, namely, the same entity seen from two different vantage points. From one vantage point the purified bride is numbered; from another, she is innumerable—a great multitude that no one can count." *The Complete Bible Answer Book*

Some propose that the 144,000 will evangelize and bring the great multitude to the truth. There is no biblical evidence to support that theory. Neither for the belief that the 144,000 will live in the city and the great multitude in the country after God establishes His kingdom among the saved. Combining what Isaiah wrote with the words of Jesus, we discover that all will have two dwellings. One will be the mansion promised by Jesus (John 14:1-3) and the other will be built by the redeemed in the countryside (Isaiah 65:21). It is that simple.

The Bible makes the same description of both groups because they are only one group. They are the believers that will be alive when Jesus comes *"to be glorified in His holy people"* (2 Thessalonians 1:10). They will have to pass through the greatest probation time that humankind ever had faced, but they know in whom they have believed. They will have the victory over the flesh, the world and the beast. The 144,000 are presented in chapter 7 as holding palm branches. "The palms signify that they have gained the victory, and the white robes that they have been clothed with the righteousness of Christ. Thank God that a fountain has been opened to wash our robes of character, and make them as white as snow" *S.D.A. Bible Commentary Vol. 7, page 970.* They already have had their triumphal arrival to the celestial city with Jesus. The Bible shows the 144,000 as the church militant as it becomes the church triumphant going through the great tribulation.

The great multitude and the 144,000 are only one group. In the eyes of the Lord, all of us are equal: neither rich, nor poor, nor white, nor black, nor Jew nor gentile. God does not even see a difference between a man and a woman, because we all are simply His children. These two groups are a description of the same group just like the visions of Daniel 2, 7 and 8 represent the same nations under different descriptions. I know that this is hard to grasp, but God shows the same things under different representations in both Daniel and Revelation. The great empires from the past are first represented as components of the statue, then as wild beasts and finally as domestic animals. In the same way, He presents the last day saints as both, the 144,000 and as the great multitude. There will only be one group going to go through the great tribulation and only one reward for all. Praise the Lord for His justice and well distributed love.

Now Let us read the last verses of the chapter:

Rev 7:15-17 *Therefore are they before the throne of God, and serve him day and night in his temple: and <u>he that sitteth on the throne shall dwell among them</u>. They shall hunger no more, neither thirst any more; neither shall the sun light on them, nor any heat. For the Lamb which is in the midst of the throne shall feed them, and shall lead them unto living fountains of waters: and God shall wipe away all tears from their eyes.*

According to Revelation 21:10, the New Jerusalem will descend from heaven (after the millennium) and it will be the dwelling of the redeemed. The biggest blessing for them is that God will come to dwell among them. Jesus' incarnation was a disguised prophecy of what God had planned. John 1:14 reads: *"And the Word was made flesh, and dwelt among us...."* The word "dwelt" is translated from the Greek σκηνόω (skay-no'-o) which means to tent or encamp, to reside. Jesus' incarnation was God pitching His tent among mankind just as He did in the old tabernacle in the desert (Exodus 25:8), prefiguring the future dwelling among us in the new earth.

They shall hunger no more, neither thirst any more - This obviously refers to the difficult times that await the faithful. The time will come when they will not be able to buy food at the stores because they will refuse to accept the mark of the beast (see chapter 13). However, God will provide them food to sustain them during the short time of trouble. To them, Isaiah says that they will be given water and bread (probably manna) and their *"refuge will be the mountain fortress"* (Isaiah 33:16). We will, at times, look for water and have to pray for it: *"When the poor and needy seek water, and there is none, and their tongue faileth for thirst, I the LORD will hear them, I the God of Israel will not forsake them. I will open rivers in high places, and fountains in the midst of the valleys: I will make the wilderness a pool of water, and the dry land springs of water"* (Isaiah 41:17,18).

Going through that time of trouble will require a special training. God prepares us little by little every day by allowing small trials to come our way, which will enable us to be stronger in preparation for the greater challenges to our faith. So it was in the case of Joseph. He was not sent to prison at once. He first suffered the ridicule and rejection of his own brothers, then he was sold as a slave and later he was accused of attempted rape. Only then was he prepared to face the challenges of being in prison. Moses had to spend forty years as a shepherd in the desert before he was ready to bring two million rebels through the desert for forty additional years.

"The season of distress and anguish before us will require a faith that can endure weariness, delay, and hunger—a faith that will not faint though severely tried. The period of probation is granted to all to prepare for that time. Jacob prevailed because he was persevering and determined. His victory is an evidence of the power of importunate prayer. All who will lay hold of God's promises, as he did, and be as earnest and persevering as he was, will succeed as he succeeded. Those who are unwilling to deny self, to agonize before God, to pray long and earnestly for His blessing, will not obtain it. Wrestling with God—how few know what it is! How few have ever had their souls drawn out after God with intensity of desire until every power is on the stretch. When waves of despair which no language can express sweep over the suppliant, how few cling with unyielding faith to the promises of God. Those who exercise but little faith now, are in the greatest danger of falling under the power of satanic delusions and the decree to compel the conscience. Even if they endure the test, they will be plunged into deeper distress and anguish in the time of trouble, because they have never made it a habit to trust in God. The lessons of faith, which they have neglected, they will be forced to learn under a terrible pressure of discouragement. We should now acquaint ourselves with God by proving His promises. Angels record every prayer that is earnest and sincere. We should rather dispense with selfish gratifications than neglect communion with God. The deepest poverty, the greatest self-denial, with His approval, is better than riches, honors, ease, and friendship without it. We must take time to pray. If we allow our minds to be absorbed by worldly interests, the Lord may give us time by removing from us our idols of gold, of houses, or of fertile lands" (*The Great Controversy*, pages 621-622).

In the hour of temptation we must turn to God as naturally as the sunflower turns to the sun because He will not leave us to fight temptation alone. *"There hath no temptation taken you but such as is common to man: but God is faithful, who will not suffer you to be tempted above that ye are able; but will with the temptation also make a way to escape, that ye may be able to bear it"* (1 Corinthians 10:13).

Neither shall the sun light on them, nor any heat- During the tribulation, the sun will heat up to seven times hotter, but it will affect the wicked only. *"Moreover the light of the moon shall be as the light of the sun, and <u>the light of the sun shall be sevenfold</u>, as the light of seven days, <u>in the day that the LORD bindeth up the breach of</u>*

his people, and healeth the stroke of their wound" (Isaiah 30:26). How could this be? If God put the earth on its orbit, He can also alter it to bring fulfillment to this prophecy. It will surely be a short period of time but it will certainly affect the whole planet causing terrible cataclysms. The intense heat will melt the ice at the poles causing a big rise on sea levels, which will bring the fulfillment of Revelation 6:14 and 16:20: *"...every mountain and island were moved out of their places."* However, God will protect His children from the extremes of the heat: *"For thou hast been a strength to the poor, a strength to the needy in his distress, a refuge from the storm, a shadow from the heat, when the blast of the terrible ones is as a storm against the wall"* (Isaiah 25:4). Later on, Isaiah adds: *"I will plant in the wilderness the cedar, the shittah tree, and the myrtle, and the oil tree; I will set in the desert the fir tree, and the pine, and the box tree together"* (Isaiah 41:19). That means that God will purposely create trees to shade His children and make the heat bearable. Christians have nothing to fear regarding the seven last plagues. Since Isaiah mentions that they will find refuge in *"the mountain fortress"*, I have no doubt that there will also be caves where they can be protected from the high temperatures.

For the Lamb which is in the midst of the throne shall feed them, and shall lead them unto living fountains of waters- What a wonderful and caring God we serve. He takes care of all our needs like a faithful shepherd. The King of the universe Himself will feed us. What an honor to serve a God that loves us so.

God shall wipe away all tears from their eyes- This chapter, which previously mentioned the great tribulation, ends now in a comforting tone to encourage those that are fearful of the future. It will do you a great deal of good if you start to write down all the marvelous ways in which God has intervened on your behalf in small and big problems. Remembering those experiences will strengthen you for the trials in the future. I remember that when our children were little, I was very sick and could not find a job for six months. There was a day when my wife told me that all we had left was rice, tomato sauce and condiments. We prayed and I went to the side of the house. There I saw a vine of some kind of peas that I had not planted but knew they were edible. It was loaded with both tender and dried peas. We ate those in different ways for days until I was able to earn some money. The following are some great promises to keep in mind:

"I have been young, and now am old; yet have I not seen the righteous forsaken, nor his seed begging bread" (Psalm 37:25).

"For the LORD will not forsake his people for his great name's sake: because it hath pleased the LORD to make you his people" (1 Samuel 12:22).

"Be strong and of a good courage, fear not, nor be afraid of them: for the LORD thy God, he it is that doth go with thee; he will not fail thee, nor forsake thee" (Deuteronomy 31:6).

"The LORD also will be a refuge for the oppressed, a refuge in times of trouble. And they that know thy name will put their trust in thee: for thou, LORD, hast not forsaken them that seek thee" (Psalm 9:9,10).

"The LORD is my light and my salvation; whom shall I fear? the LORD is the strength of my life; of whom shall I be afraid? When the wicked, even mine enemies and my foes, came upon me to eat up my flesh, they stumbled and fell. Though an host should encamp against me, my heart shall not fear: though war should rise against me, in this will I be confident... For in the time of trouble he shall hide me in his pavilion: in the secret of his tabernacle shall he hide me; he shall set me up upon a rock" (Psalm 27:1-3,5).

Isaiah also wrote about the day when God will wipe our tears: *"He will swallow up death in victory; and the Lord GOD will wipe away tears from off all faces; and the rebuke of his people shall he take away from off all the earth: for the LORD hath spoken it. And it shall be said in that day, Lo, this is our God; we have waited for him, and he will save us: this is the LORD; we have waited for him, we will be glad and rejoice in his salvation"* (Isaiah 25:8,9). No man or demon will be able to touch any of us during the time of tribulation because God will send His angels to protect us. During that time of self-examination, the wicked will suffer the seven last plagues. However, the righteous will not be affected by any of them.

When will this time of tribulation for the church occur? It will be parallel to the time of the plagues for the wicked. In the same way that He sent the Muslims in the Middle Ages to cause a distraction so the Catholic would give a break to the Protestant Sabbath keepers, God will send the plagues upon the wicked so they limit their incursions against the saints who will be praying day and night for their deliverance. That deliverance will come just as when the children of Israel were in Egypt. The Lord visited the Egyptians with judgment at midnight and all the firstborns died (Exodus 11:4,5). According to the parable of the ten virgins, it will be at midnight when the bridegroom will come (Matthew 25:6). And just like it was at midnight that Paul and Silas were praying and God produced a strong tremor that set them free, God will send the ultimate earthquake to set us free from our enemies in our darkest hour. *"In a moment shall they die, and the people shall be troubled at midnight, and pass away: and the mighty shall be taken away without hand"* (Job 34:20). Do we have anything to fear from the wicked? *"The LORD is good; <u>he protects his people in times of trouble</u>; he takes care of those who turn to him"* (Nahum 1:7 *GNB*). Never fear. In the same manner that Noah trusted God and did not fear the strong currents of water, we must also trust Him because He will never let us drown in our everyday problems or in the final test for mankind.

Be of God cheer because God truly loves and cares for you. *"Wait on the LORD: be of good courage, and he shall strengthen thine heart: wait, I say, on the LORD"* (Psalm 27:14).

REVELATION 8

The angels got quiet

[1] And when he had opened the seventh seal, there was silence in heaven about the space of half an hour.

Let us take a trip to heaven. In the middle of the Sanctuary, we find Jesus ministering before the Father. There we see the cherubim and seraphim together with thousands and thousands of angels. There is order including in the way God is praised and worshipped. The heavenly music fills every corner of the celestial dwelling of God and you feel enraptured by the melodious angelical singing. There is never silence in heaven. One song of praise ends, the next one begins. But now you notice silence. What must be going on?

The passage obviously refers to the occasion when Jesus will leave heaven to return to this earth to get you and me to the mansions He went to prepare for us. Matthew 25:31 reads that all the angels will come with Jesus, so heaven is not going to have any music or praises at that time, therefore it will be silent. *"When the Son of Man comes in His glory, and <u>all the holy angels with Him</u>, then He will sit on the throne of His glory".*

There is another possible interpretation for the silence. We often see people keeping or observing a minute of silence in honor of someone who passed away. When I was a child, if someone that we knew died, we were told not to sing or listen to music as a sign of mourning. Could it be that the merciful heart of God orders sometime of silence while He mourns the loss of so many souls that He tried to save but refused His offer of salvation?

Now, how much is half an hour in prophetic time? The Hebrew calendar had only 360 days. So, 360/24 hours in a day= 15 days. This divided by ½ hour is 7-½ days. What event could be lasting 7 days?

Our trip to heaven will last a week. Why so long? I imagine that you always dreamed with sightseeing across the universe. According to Isaiah 40:31, we will have wings to fly with the angels. When Jesus calls us up to heaven, we will be able to fly. That will give you the opportunity to see the planets, comets and stars up close and rejoice in the power, wisdom and perfection of God's creation. This will provide the chance to those that never kept the Sabbath holy to keep it on the way there. I expect to see there people such as Hus, Jerome, Luther and even Spurgeon and Moody. I hope also to see at least two popes. The scriptures also hint that there will be people saved that did not know about Christ. God knows the intentions of the heart as we can read in Romans 2:13-16: *"(For not the hearers of the law are just before God, but the doers of the law shall be justified. For when the Gentiles, which have not the law, do by nature the things contained in the law, these, having not the law, are a law unto themselves: Which shew the work of the law written in their hearts, their conscience also bearing witness, and their thoughts the mean while accusing or else excusing one another;) In the day when God shall judge the secrets of men by Jesus Christ according to my gospel."* There will be pagans in the procession to heaven that were faithful to what the Holy Spirit taught them through their consciences and nature. *"And one shall say unto him, What are these wounds between thine arms? Then he shall answer, Those with which I was wounded in the house of my **friends**"* (Zechariah 13:6 ASV). Those people will ask Jesus about His wounds through which we are healed. How He got those wounds? In the 7-day trip to heaven, they will hear about the marvelous plan of salvation and will have the opportunity to keep the Sabbath. Heaven will be empty and silent during that week but forever more will be filled with the praises of both the angelical host and the redeemed from all the ages when they arrive to the Holy City. Oh, wonder of wonders that God sent His son to be wounded for our transgressions and still calls us friends!

This verse deals with the seventh and last of the seals that we studied in Chapter 6. The sealing of the 144,000 in chapter 7 was a parenthesis.

2And I saw the seven angels which stood before God; and to them were given seven trumpets.

More literally, "the seven angels that stand (*NIV*)." This implies that they are constantly in His presence near His throne. Trumpets were used in the Bible mostly to announce war or conflicts, although they were also utilized during the time of the atonement. The seven trumpets deal with historical and political issues related to the nations that surrounded the children of God. While the seven churches and the seven seals refer to the church, the trumpets describe events against the oppressors of the true church. The first four trumpets bring judgment against Pagan Rome indicating how it fell, and the last three show the judgments against Papal Rome that will bring its final ruin.

Let us see some uses of trumpets in the Bible:

- Moses received the Ten Commandments amidst thunder, lighting and the sound of the trumpet. *"And it came to pass on the third day in the morning, that there were thunders and lightnings, and a thick cloud upon the mount, and the voice of the* ***trumpet*** *exceeding loud; so that all the people that was in the camp trembled"* (Ex:19:16). The law has been trampled for too long. It is time for it to be exalted again.
- The trumpets were also used in the Day of Atonement: *"Then shalt thou cause the* ***trumpet*** *of the jubilee to sound on the tenth day of the seventh month, in the Day of Atonement shall ye make the trumpet sound throughout all your land"* (Lev:25:9). This Day of Atonement required that people be afflicted for their sins. Now, when we rapidly approach the end of earth history, we must be pleading with God for forgiveness and the indwelling of the Holy Spirit in our hearts.
- The book of Ezekiel mentions another purpose of the trumpet: to warn people of the impending conflict: *"If when he seeth the sword come upon the land, he blows the* ***trumpet,*** *and warn the people; Then whosoever heareth the sound of the* ***trumpet,*** *and taketh not warning; if the sword come, and take him away, his blood shall be upon his own head. He heard the sound of the* ***trumpet,*** *and took not warning; his blood shall be upon him. But he that taketh warning shall deliver his soul"* (Ezekiel 33:3-5). The seven trumpets have been sounding to wake up mankind so no

one perish but have the opportunity to accept the offer of eternal life in Jesus.

- The trumpet must be used to awaken God's people: *"Cry aloud, spare not,* ***lift up thy voice like a trumpet****, and shew my people their transgression, and the house of Jacob their sins.* Joel 2:1: ***Blow ye the trumpet in Zion****, and sound an alarm in my holy mountain: let all the inhabitants of the land tremble: for the day of the LORD cometh, for it is nigh at hand"* (Isaiah 58:1). It is clear that the trumpets were blown to wake up people so they could save their lives. *"And it shall come to pass in that day, that the* ***GREAT trumpet shall be blown****, and they shall come which were ready to perish in the land of Assyria, and the outcasts in the land of Egypt, and shall worship the LORD in the holy mount at Jerusalem"* (Isaiah 27:13). We have a work to do to prepare the nations to encounter God. As the following hymn says: "Lift up the trumpet, and loud let it ring: Jesus is coming again! Cheer up, ye pilgrims, be joyful and sing: Jesus is coming again!
- The trumpet was needed to announce the approaching enemy: *"If when he seeth the sword come upon the land, he blow the trumpet, and warn the people"* (Ezekiel 33:3).

Finally, the trumpet was used to announce deliverance in the year of jubilee: *"Then shalt thou cause the trumpet of the jubilee to sound on the tenth day of the seventh month, in the Day of Atonement shall ye make the trumpet sound throughout all your land. And ye shall hallow the fiftieth year, and proclaim liberty throughout all the land unto all the inhabitants thereof: it shall be a jubilee unto you; and ye shall return every man unto his possession, and ye shall return every man unto his family"* (Leviticus 25:9–13).

Verses 3-5 are again, a parenthesis. Here the narration interrupts the presentation of the seven trumpets to present a scene of intercession in the heavenly sanctuary.

[3,4]*And another angel came and stood at the altar, having a golden censer; and there was given unto him much incense, that he should offer it with the prayers of all saints upon the golden altar which was before the throne. And the smoke of the incense, which came with the prayers of the saints, ascended up before God out of the angel's hand.*

This scene is similar to the one described in chapter five where the *"twenty-four elders fell down before the Lamb. Each one had a harp and they were holding golden bowls full of incense, which are the prayers of the saints"* (Revelation 5:8). God wants us to be encouraged by the fact that in spite of the difficult situations that we confront, our prayers are of the utmost importance to Him and are constantly flowing towards His throne wrapped in the incense of the merits of Christ. No action on our part could ever open the doors of heaven for us. Only the righteousness of Jesus applied to our lives can recommend us before a Holy God. Even those saved among the pagans will be admitted into heaven through the merits of Jesus. Every one of us is *"weighed on the scales"* (Daniel 5:27) of heaven. However, all our works are weightless for salvation. Here is the good news: Jesus' life takes the place of ours in the judgment and when the roll calls our names, Jesus answers in our stead. His life of perfect obedience replaces our faulty record and produces an eternal weight of Glory (2 Corinthians 4:17) that grants us entry into His kingdom. We must make preparation through daily surrender of our wills to God, prayer and Bible study. We must shed the weight of sin (Hebrews 12:1) so God will replace it with the weight of glory.

[5] And the angel took the censer, and filled it with fire of the altar, and cast it into the earth: and there were voices, and thunderings, and lightnings, and an earthquake.

Now the angel takes fire from the altar, which was set by God, and throws it into the earth. This is not an intercessory act. This implies judgment and that is why the action of the angel is followed by *"thunderings, and lightnings, and an earthquake."* Very soon our High Priest will become the judge of the human race and there will be no more intercession on behalf of the impenitent mankind. Although John has not been shown the trumpets, he is instructed as to what will happen at the end of their blast. That is why he was shown the censer (a symbol of intercession) being cast into the earth. It will no longer be needed. Very soon, the voice of the Spirit will cease to call you and me to repentance and confession. Very soon our High Priest will pronounce the solemn words: *"He that is righteous; let him be righteous still and he that is unjust, let him be unjust still."* (Revelation 22:11). Soon the door of salvation will be forever closed. That will be the time when the five foolish virgins

Christianity almost disappeared wherever he gained an influence; and the smoke of the pit produced nearly total darkness throughout the eastern church" (Josiah Litch- *The Three Woe Trumpets*). Locust swarms are known for their voracity. In Bible times, they ravaged the plantations consuming everything green in their path. So it was the case with the Egyptian plague. *"For they covered the face of the whole earth, so that the land was darkened; and they did eat every herb of the land, and all the fruit of the trees which the hail had left: and there remained not any green thing in the trees, or in the herbs of the field, through all the land of Egypt"* (Exodus 10:15). However, these locusts in Revelation have characteristics of scorpions, which is an indication of their symbolism. "'Was given power, as the scorpions of the earth have power.' Martinicus says, Scorpions have nippers, or pincers, with which they keep hold of what they seize, after they have wounded it with their sting....' "Like the scorpion, Mahomet stung the subjects of his proselytism, and infused the poison of his doctrines, and continued to hold them by the force of arms, until it had affected the whole man, and the subject settled down in the belief of his delusive errors. Wherever his arms triumphed, there his religion was imposed on men, whether they believed it or not.

"The successors of the prophet propagated his faith and imitated his example; and such was the rapidity of their progress, that in the space of a century, Persia, Syria, Egypt, Africa, and Spain had submitted to the victorious arms of the Arabian and Saracen conquerors.' Ruter" (Josiah Litch- *The Three Woe Trumpets*).

[4]And it was commanded them that they should not hurt the grass of the earth, neither any green thing, neither any tree; but <u>only those men which have not the seal of God in their foreheads</u>.

The symbolism is explained as follows:

- *Grass* – people (Isaiah 40:6,7; Isaiah 51:12)
- *Trees* – leaders (Daniel 4:20-22)
- *Green thing* – spiritual life. *"They will still bear fruit in old age, they will stay fresh and green"* (Psalm 92:14 *NIV*). *"...the righteous will thrive like a green leaf"* (Proverbs 11:28). *"But blessed is the man who trusts in the LORD, whose confidence is in him. He will be like a tree planted by the water that sends out its roots by the stream. It does not fear when heat*

comes; its leaves are always green. It has no worries in a year of drought and never fails to bear fruit" (Jeremiah 17:8 *NIV*).

- The men without *"the seal of God in their foreheads"*- referrers to those that did not keep the Sabbath. Unlike Sunday, which in the near future will be the mark of the beast for the final days, Saturday has always been the seal or mark of loyalty to God. The attack was directly intended against the Catholic Church. The Christians hiding in the mountains who kept the true Sabbath holy were not to be touched.

These invaders were not to touch anybody who kept the Sabbath holy, regardless of their status in society. Their targets were specifically those that had attacked them previously during the Crusades (named that way because of the use of the cross on their banners). The Crusades were expeditions of armies undertaken after taking a solemn vow, to "deliver (in reality, to conquer for the pope)" the Holy Places, such as Jerusalem, from Mohammedan control.

5And to them it was given that they should not kill them, but that they should be tormented five months: and their torment was as the torment of a scorpion, when he striketh a man. 6And in those days shall men seek death, and shall not find it; and shall desire to die, and death shall flee from them.

The torment was to last five months or 150 days that in Bible prophecy is 150 years. The intent was not to kill but to cause suffering, to torture. It was so fastidious that those people victimized preferred to be killed rather than been submitted to those conditions.

7And the shapes of the locusts were like unto horses prepared unto battle; and on their heads were as it were crowns like gold, and their faces were as the faces of men. 8And they had hair as the hair of women, and their teeth were as the teeth of lions. 9And they had breastplates, as it were breastplates of iron; and the sound of their wings was as the sound of chariots of many horses running to battle. 10And they had tails like unto scorpions, and there were stings in their tails: and their power was to hurt men five months.

The scorpions are mentioned three times in this chapter for emphasis to indicate how bothersome these invaders were. Again, these three last trumpets deal with how the beast power suffered setbacks by the powers of the earth- at that times the Muslims. The *crowns like gold* refer to their turbans. They also wore long hair and breastplates like those that the prophecy indicated. Although they had a common cause, they were not united until the 13th century when Othman consolidated the tribes and became their king, founding the Ottoman Empire.

God's plan was to use them to distract the Catholic power from persecuting those that wanted to have freedom of religion. Five months are 150 days, which in prophecy represent 150 years. What marked the beginning of period of torment? "Othman first entered the territory of Nicomedia on the 27th day of July, 1299." (Gibbon.) Adding 150 years to this date brings us to July 27th, 1449, when the period of this trumpet ends.

"The calculations of some writers have gone upon the supposition that the period should begin with the foundation of the Ottoman Empire; but this is evidently an error; for they not only were to have a king over them, but were to torment men five months. But the period of torment could not begin before the first attack of the tormentors, which was, as above [stated], July 27, 1299." *Uriah Smith, The Prophecies of Daniel and Revelation, pages 504 & 505.*

11And they had a king over them, which is the angel of the bottomless pit, whose name in the Hebrew tongue is Abaddon, but in the Greek tongue hath his name Apollyon.

In Job 26:6, Proverbs 15:11 and Proverbs 27:20 Abaddon (אבדון *'abaddown*) is translated as destruction. Apollyon in Greek means destructor. The Strong's Concordance identifies Apollyon with Satan, probably due to the words of Jesus registered in John 10:10: *"The thief cometh not, but for to steal, and to kill, and to destroy...."* The mission of the Saracens was to attack the idolaters; this is, the Catholic Church with their many statues, which they considered as idols. In the message to the church of this time period, Thyatira, Jesus told John to write: *"Behold, I will cast her into a bed, and them that commit adultery with her* ***into great tribulation****, except they repent of their deeds* (Revelation 2:22). Worshipping idols is spiritual adultery.

[12]One woe is past; and, behold, there come two woes more hereafter.

[13]And the sixth angel sounded, and I heard a voice from the four horns of the golden altar which is before God,

The sixth trumpet describes how the Turks conquered the Eastern Roman Empire.

That is the altar of incense mentioned in chapter 8:3. Was something going to happen in this period that needed Jesus' intercession? Much indeed. This period would witness the discovery and colonization of America, the French Revolution, the war of independence in the United States and the proliferation of atheistic ideas in many places, all of which would influence the final events in the history of this world. To counteract atheism Jesus inspired His church to create the Bible societies and the start of modern missions. He also raised men in different parts of the world to study the prophecies, with the result of thousands renovating their faith and commitment to His cause.

[14]Saying to the sixth angel which had the trumpet, Loose the four angels which are bound in the great river Euphrates.

"Loose the four angels which are bound"- Nowhere before did we find bound angels, which indicates that these are not heavenly angels. In chapter 20, we do find that Satan is going to be bound for 1,000 years (Revelation 20:2), so these four angels are either fallen angels or instruments in the hands of Satan to do his work of hate and destruction. The chapter does show other angels that do not come from heaven. We must remember that the word angel means messenger and the context opens the door to understand which kind of angels John is referring to. Uriah Smith explains it very clearly:

"The Four Angels.--These are <u>the four principal sultanies</u> of which the Ottoman Empire was composed, located in the country watered by the Euphrates. These sultanies were situated at Aleppo, Iconium, Damascus, and Bagdad. Previously they had been restrained; but God commanded, and they were loosed."

[What happened at the end of the 150 years that opened the doors for the next power to arise?]

"Late in the year 1448, as the close of the 150-year period approached, John Palaeologus died without leaving a son to follow him on the throne of the Eastern Empire. His brother Constantine, the lawful successor, would not venture to ascend the throne without the consent of the Turkish sultan. Ambassadors therefore went to Adrianople, received the approbation of the sultan, and returned with gifts for the new sovereign. Early in the year 1449, under these ominous circumstances, Constantine, the last of the Greek emperors, was crowned" (Smith-*The Prophecies of Daniel and Revelation, page 506).*

15And the four angels were loosed, which were prepared for an hour, and a day, and a month, and a year, for to slay the third part of men.

"To slay the third part of men"- In the comment of chapter 8:6,7 we saw that the frequent reference to "the third" (of the waters, the third of men and the third of the trees) represented the three sections into which Constantine divided his empire for his three sons. Each one of these last three trumpets deals with the fall of one section of the Roman Empire. This "third part" is related to the fall of Constantinople, the last stand for the old empire (the Greek part of it). Until then, the city had withstood attacks by many enemies but its walls had proven impregnable. Then a founder deserted to the side of the sultan Mahomet and was asked to cast a cannon capable of bringing down the walls. The artisan went to work and very soon the city was simultaneously attacked on all sides with the powerful new weapons and Constantinople succumbed to the armies of the sultan.

"The calculation which follows, founded on this starting point, was made and first published in a work entitled, *Christ's Second Coming,* by Josiah Litch, in 1838." *Ibid. 505.*

One hour= 15 days

One day= 1 year

A month= 30 years

A year= 360 years

Total= 391 years and 15 days. This period started July 27th, 1449. Adding 391 to 1449 would bring us to the year 1840. The 15 days added to July 27th would end August 11th of that year. When Josiah Litch published his interpretation of this prophecy in 1838 and then in early 1840, agnostics and atheists all over the United States laughed at him. Pastor Litch had indicated that in the same way that the Ottoman Empire had begun- without bloodshed- it would end. In those times, the sultan was having conflicts with Mehemet Ali, pasha of Egypt who had destroyed his army and taken his fleet. The sultan asked for the intervention of the Four Great Powers of that time, Prussia, Russia, Austria and England (all Christian nations), who, taking over the negotiations, gave an ultimatum to the pasha to surrender the fleet and return the territories that belonged to the sultan. When the news came August 12th that the sultan had requested the intervention of the aforementioned nations and that the ultimatum had been delivered to the pasha the day before (August 11th), many of the former unbelievers wrote letters of apology and indicated their desire to know more about the Bible that so accurately predicted these events. From that time on Turkey was under the protection of the Christian allies. "The London Morning Herald, after the capture of St. Jean dAcre, speaking of the state of things in the Ottoman empire, says: 'We have dissipated into thin air the prestige that lately invested as with a halo the name of Mehemet Ali. We have in all probability destroyed forever the power of that hitherto successful ruler. But have we done aught to restore strength to the Ottoman Empire? We fear not. We fear that the sultan has been reduced to the rank of a puppet; and that the sources of the Turkish empires strength are entirely destroyed.

"If the supremacy of the Sultan is hereafter to be maintained in Egypt, it must be maintained, we fear, by the unceasing intervention of England and Russia. . .'" (Josiah Litch- *The Three Wo Trumpets*).

"His Excellency, Rifat Bey, Musleshar for foreign affairs, has been dispatched in a government steamer to Alexandria, to communicate the ultimatum to the Pacha." [Moniteur Ottoman, Aug. 22, 1840.]

"The question now comes up, when was that document put officially under the control of Mehemet Ali?

"By the French steamer of the 24th, we have advices from Egypt to the 16th. The Turkish government steamer, which had reached Alexandria on the11th, with the envoy rifat bey on board, had by his (the Pachas) orders been placed in quarantine, and she was not released from it till the 16th. . . however. . .on the very day [August 11, 1840] on which he had been admitted to pratique, the above named functionary had had an audience of the Pacha, and had communicated to him the command of the Sultan, with respect to the evacuation of the Syrian province, appointing another audience for the next day, when, in the presence of the consuls of the European powers, he would receive from him his definite answer, and inform him of the alternative of his refusing to obey; giving him the ten days which have been allotted him by the convention to decide on the course he should think fit to adopt." The London Morning Chronicle, Sept. 18, 1840.

"According to previous calculation, therefore, ottoman supremacy did depart on the eleventh of August [1840] into the hands of the great Christian powers of Europe" (Josiah Litch- *The Three Wo Trumpets*).

16And the number of the army of the horsemen were two hundred thousand thousand: and I heard the number of them.

Many had tried to understand this large number but the interpretation that I consider more reasonable is that this is the total of the armies through the duration of this power. "Many *correctly* suggested that the 200,000,000 warriors described in Revelation 9:16, were figurative and inclusive of all Islamic warriors and sympathizers throughout the centuries-long war against non Islamic territories" (Charles H. Clever, *The Decline of Islamic Supremacy as Predicted in the Bible*).

17And thus I saw the horses in the vision, and them that sat on them, having breastplates of fire, and of jacinth, and brimstone: and the heads of the horses were as the heads of lions; and out of their mouths issued fire and smoke and brimstone. 18By these three was the third part of men killed, by the fire, and by the smoke, and by the brimstone, which issued out of their mouths.

Now the prophet is shown scenes far away in the distant future and he makes his best effort to describe what he sees which had not being invented yet. In contrast, when Daniel was probably shown the discoveries and inventions of modern era (like TV's, computers, robots, etc.) and all he could write was that science would multiply. "The first part of this description may have reference to the appearance of these horsemen. Fire, representing a color, stands for red, 'as red as fire' being a frequent term of expression; jacinth, or hyacinth, for blue; and brimstone, for yellow. These colors greatly predominated in the dress of these warriors; so that the description, according to this view, would be accurately met in the Turkish uniform, which was composed largely of red, or scarlet, blue, and yellow. The heads of the horses were in appearance as the heads of lions, to denote their strength, courage, and fierceness; while the last part of the verse undoubtedly has reference to the use of gunpowder and firearms for purposes of war, which were then but recently introduced. As the Turks discharged their firearms on horseback, it would appear to the distant beholder that the fire, smoke, and brimstone issued out of the horses' mouths." *Ibid.*

19For their power is in their mouth, and in their tails: for their tails were like unto serpents, and had heads, and with them they do hurt.

"The inference is therefore well supported that they used firearms on horseback, accurately fulfilling the prophecy, according to the illustration above referred to." *Ibid.*

20And the rest of the men which were not killed by these plagues yet repented not of the works of their hands, that they should not worship devils, and idols of gold, and silver, and brass, and stone, and of wood: which neither can see, nor hear, nor walk:

Although there are millions of sincere Catholics in the world, God does not approve of them to kneel before the statues found in their churches. The great majority of them bow down to those idols without knowing that they are worshipping devils and not

Christ or the saints to whom they address their prayers and light their candles. *"God overlooked the times when people didn't know any better. But now he commands everyone everywhere to turn to him and change the way they think and act"* (Acts 17:30 *GW*). Many, however, are fully aware that God does not want statues in their churches and yet promote their use. Growing up as a Catholic, my mother and I used to bow before the images and pray, but the Bible clearly indicates that statues cannot see us or hear what we say: *"Their idols are silver and gold, the work of men's hands. They have mouths, but they speak not: eyes have they, but they see not: They have ears, but they hear not: noses have they, but they smell not: They have hands, but they handle not: feet have they, but they walk not: neither speak they through their throat. They that make them are like unto them; so is every one that trusteth in them"* Psalm 115:4-8). David counsels: *"Ye that fear the LORD, trust in the LORD: he is their help and their shield"* (115:11). Isaiah adds: *"They that make a graven image are all of them vanity; and their delectable things shall not profit; and they are their own witnesses; they see not, nor know; that they may be ashamed. Who hath formed a god, or molten a graven image that is profitable for nothing?"* (Isaiah 44:10) *"Behold, they are all vanity; their works are nothing: their molten images are wind and confusion"* (Isaiah 41:29). The Catholic Encyclopedia reads: "There is indeed 'one mediator of God and man, the man Christ Jesus'. But He is our mediator in His quality of our common Redeemer; He is not our sole intercessor nor advocate, nor our sole mediator by way of supplication. In the eleventh session of the Council of Chalcedon (451) we find the Fathers exclaiming, 'Flavianus lives after death! May the Martyr pray for us!' If we accept this doctrine of the worship of the saints, of which there are innumerable evidences in the writings of the Fathers and the liturgies of the Eastern and Western Churches, we shall not wonder at the loving care with which the Church committed to writing the sufferings of the early martyrs, sent these accounts from one gathering of the faithful to another, and promoted the veneration of the martyrs." No place in the Scriptures tells us that we should or could pray to the saints. Although many of them probably lived a commendable life, only the intercession of someone completely holy can be accepted by our holy God.

I used to pay regular visits to the cathedral in my city and on probably two occasions, we went to another catholic church because my mother had made a promise. Unfortunately, my mother and I were, sorry to say it, praying to the air. This particular church made a good business selling medals, statues, prayer cards and other religious artifacts. Some argue that the statue is a representation and the prayer goes to the saint in heaven. Let me respectfully ask you a question: If you have a problem, and are granted permission and direct access to the President of the nation to present your issue, why stop at his secretary's desk to ask her to solve your problem? Wouldn't that be an insult to the President? Or, would you tell your problem to a picture or a statue of the President? God has granted us direct access to His throne and as a loving Father, He is anxiously waiting for us to come to Him. *"Let us therefore come boldly unto the throne of grace, that we may obtain mercy, and find grace to help in time of need"* (Hebrews 4:16). The Scriptures do not support to pray to any other than to God Himself.

21 Neither repented they of their murders, nor of their sorceries, nor of their fornication, nor of their thefts.

This very well describes the sinister side of the Catholic orders such as the Jesuits, the most powerful secret service in the world with license to kill and accustomed to steal. Their motto is "the end justifies the means." No relationship is sacred to them; neither have they respected any political authority, so they even kill their own families if they depart from the mother church or even presidents of nations. For more on this, see chapter 13 and my commentary on Daniel chapter 7.

REVELATION 10

Bitter honey

[1]*And I saw another mighty angel come down from heaven, clothed with a cloud: and a rainbow was upon his head, and his face was as it were the sun, and his feet as pillars of fire:*

This is a vision of Jesus similar to what John described in chapter one. This is undoubtedly, Jesus.

[2]*And he had in his hand a little book* ***open****: and he set his right foot upon the sea, and his left foot on the earth,*

This little book has a message to be taught to all the earth-continents and islands. This book is not the same as the one mentioned in chapter 5:1. The word used there is βιβλίον (bib-lee'-on), and means book or scroll. The word used by John here is βιβλιαρίδιον (bib-lee-ar-id'-ee-on), which is a booklet or little book. This little book has been identified as the book of Daniel, which was to be sealed until the time of the end and it is now specifically shown as open.

[3]*And cried with a loud voice, as when a lion roareth: and when he had cried, seven thunders uttered their voices.* [4]*And when the seven thunders had uttered their voices, I was about to write: and I heard a voice from heaven saying unto me, Seal up those things which the seven thunders uttered, and write them not.*

It is possible that what John heard was meant for him only. The seven thunders are mentioned only in this passage. It is not clear what they represent. It is evident that what they said was not necessary for our salvation and that is why we were not allowed to know what John heard.

[5]*And the angel which I saw stand upon the sea and upon the earth lifted up his hand to heaven,* [6]*And sware by him that liveth for ever and ever, who created heaven, and the things that therein are, and*

the earth, and the things that therein are, and the sea, and the things which are therein, that there should be time no longer:

This verse refers to time prophecies. At the time when the second coming message was being preached, only one time prophecy remained to be fulfilled: the 2,300 years prophecy of Daniel 8:14 that it was about to be fulfilled.

[7]But in the days of the voice of the seventh angel, when he shall begin to sound, the mystery of God should be finished, as he hath declared to his servants the prophets.

Mystery of God finished- Paul wrote asking for prayers to help him communicate *"the mystery of the gospel"* (Ephesians 6:19). This phrase from John indicates the finalization of the preaching of the gospel. This is the time of the church of Philadelphia when the world missions were established and flourishing. Those early missionaries opened the doors for the final push in the preaching of the gospel to every creature on the earth. See comment on chapter three and 11:15.

[8]And the voice which I heard from heaven spake unto me again, and said, Go and take the little book which is open in the hand of the angel which standeth upon the sea and upon the earth. [9]And I went unto the angel, and said unto him, Give me the little book. And he said unto me, Take it, and eat it up; and it shall make thy belly bitter, but it shall be in thy mouth sweet as honey. [10]And I took the little book out of the angel's hand, and ate it up; and it was in my mouth sweet as honey: and as soon as I had eaten it, my belly was bitter.

What book was this? The historical context can help us find out. The previous chapter in Revelation refers to the year 1840. The book of Daniel was to be sealed until the time of the end and then *"the wise shall understand"* (Daniel 12:10). Another vision of a book with similar details to this chapter is found in Ezekiel 2:8-3:5: *"'Son of Man, you are to listen to what I tell you. You are never to be rebellious like they are: a rebellious group. Now, open your mouth and eat what I'm giving you.' As I watched, all of a sudden there was a hand being stretched out in my direction! And there was a scroll being unrolled right in front of me! Written on both sides were lamentations, mourning, and cries of grief. Then he told me, 'Son of Man, eat! Eat what you see—this scroll—and then go talk to the house of Israel.' So I opened my mouth and he fed me the scroll. Then he told me, 'Son of Man, fill your stomach and digest this scroll that I'm giving you.' So I ate it, and it was like sweet honey in my mouth. Then he told me, 'Son of Man, go to the house of Israel and tell them what I have to say to them, because you're not going to a people whose speech you cannot understand or whose language is difficult to speak. Instead, you're going to the house of Israel"* (International Standard Version). This message was given to the church, not to outsiders.

What kind of message could have been sweet as honey for John? Imagine that you are he. You met Jesus at an early age, in your teens. You were probably not older than 14. You used to rest on his shoulder. Remember that? You observed Him in his daily efforts to reach and elevate mankind. You saw Him healing the sick, multiplying food, walking on the water, calming the storm, casting out demons, forgiving sins, giving sinners a second chance, teaching love and forgiveness and raising the dead. You spent special time with Him as part of the three disciples' inner circle and saw miracles that no other disciple saw, like the transfiguration. Then one night Jesus was arrested and you followed Him and saw the mob and soldiers beating, mocking, spitting and crowning Jesus with thorns. He then was given to be crucified and you watched Him die. Three days later, you were so joyful when you saw Him raised from the dead! But your joy lasted only 40 more days because He ascended to heaven, and since, you have not walk with Him again. By now, 66 long years have passed. What would be as sweet as honey for you? His second coming! What could be bitter? That He does not come when expected.

This message was preached with power in different parts of the word in the first half of the 19th century by men that had studied the prophecies of Daniel and Revelation. Manuel de Lacunza, a Jesuit priest representing himself as a converted Jew and using the pen-name Juan Josafat Ben-Ezra for his writings, wrote a book entitled *"La venida del Mesías en gloria y majestad (The Coming Of the Messiah In Glory And Majesty)"* that soon was distributed throughout many countries, including England and the United States. Then a real Jewish convert, Dr. Joseph Wolff, "the missionary to the world," began to proclaim the Lord's soon coming first as a Catholic convert and then as a Protestant. "During the twenty-four years from 1821 to 1845, Wolff traveled extensively: in Africa, visiting Egypt and Abyssinia; in Asia, traversing Palestine, Syria, Persia, Bokhara, and India. He also visited the United States, on the journey thither preaching on the island of St. Helena. He arrived in New York in August, 1837; and after speaking in that city, he preached in Philadelphia and Baltimore, and finally proceeded to Washington. Here, he says, 'on a motion brought forward by the ex-President, John Quincy Adams, in one of the houses of Congress, the House unanimously granted me the use of the Congress Hall for a lecture which I delivered on a Saturday, honored with the presence of all the members of Congress, and also of the bishop of Virginia, and the clergy and citizens of Washington. The same honor was granted to me by the members of the Government of New Jersey and Pennsylvania, in whose presence I delivered lectures on my researches in Asia, and also on the personal reign of Jesus Christ.' "The *Great Controversy* (1888), pages 360,361.

"Dr. Wolff traveled in the most barbarous countries, without the protection of any European authority, enduring many hardships, and surrounded with countless perils. He was bastinadoed and starved, sold as a slave, and three times condemned to death. He was beset by robbers, and sometimes nearly perished from thirst. Once he was stripped of all that he possessed, and left to travel hundreds of miles on foot through the mountains, the snow beating in his face, and his naked feet benumbed by contact with the frozen ground. Thus, he persevered in his labors until the message of the Judgment had been carried to a large part of the habitable globe. Among Jews, Turks, Parsees, Hindus, and many other nationalities and races, he distributed the Word of God in these various tongues, and everywhere heralded the approaching reign of the Messiah. In his travels in Bokhara, he found the doctrine of the Lord's soon coming held by a remote and isolated people. The Arabs of Yemen, he says, 'are in possession of a book called 'Seera,' which gives notice of the coming of Christ and his reign in glory, and they expect great events to take place in the year 1840.' 'In Yemen I spent six days with the Rechabites. They drink no wine, plant no vineyards, sow no seed, live in tents, and remember the words of Jonadab, the son of Rechab. With them were the children of Israel of the tribe of Dan, . . . who expect, in common with the children of Rechab, the speedy arrival of the Messiah in the clouds of heaven.'" *Ibid.,* 362.

It is said that some 700 Anglican priests joined in the preaching of the glorious message of the soon return of Jesus. The message of the wonderful hope was preached in Russia, France, Switzerland and Scandinavia by a Lutheran Minister named Bengal.

In the United States, William Miller, a Baptist farmer got convinced after many years of deep personal Bible study that Jesus was going to return soon. It is estimated that he preached 4,500 sermons in different parts of the United States to crowds of up to 10,000 eager listeners. His followers diligently studied the Scriptures. Almost entire nights were often devoted to earnest searching of the prophecies of Daniel, Matthew and Revelation. They searched for the truth as for hidden gems. Miller preached all over the nation the glorious message of a soon coming Savior. Unfortunately, his associates put pressure on him to establish a day for that event and when Jesus did not return that day, many got discouraged and left the movement.

And so it was the experience of the believers during the last part of the period of Philadelphia. They made the mistake of assigning dates for the return of Jesus. First, they announced that His return would happen in 1843, then in the spring of 1844, and finally, October 22, 1844. Farmers did not harvest their crops and others gave away their properties. The anxiously expected day came and they gathered in groups to read the Scriptures, to praise God and enthusiastically wait for the last trump to sound. Those in houses and churches were looking out the windows, hoping to see a little black cloud like the hand of a man just as in times of Elijah. Others were in the open, also gazing at the sky in anticipation of the encounter with their God, but the hours went by.... midnight came and a new day dawned. Jesus had not come and they were crushed. The One that was more precious to them than gold did not return the day they thought He would.

They were wrong when they chose a day, because the Scripture shows that no one knows the day or the hour, except the Father. They could have saved the heartache. However, God allowed this to happen to try them so only those whose hearts were sincere would remain and spread the gospel worldwide. Those that had joined the movement out of fear of being lost, and not for pure love for Jesus, left to never again return. "It was in the Lord's order that this disappointment should come, and that hearts should be revealed." E.G. White, *Selected Messages Book 2, page, 108. "Because thou hast kept the word of my patience, I also will keep thee from the hour of temptation, which shall come upon all the world, to try them that dwell upon the earth"* (Revelation 3:12). Difficult times are approaching that will require from us a faith capable of withstanding persecution, hunger and delay. We need to strive to be found worthy to be in the presence of the Lamb. There is nothing of course, which can recommend us before a Holy God, because we are extremely sinful, but if we are covered by the robe of righteousness of our Lord and Savior, we will be granted ample entrance into the kingdom.

There were two other prophets, besides John, that tasted the Word and found it pleasant. And like John, they too experienced bitterness. The first one was Jeremiah. *"Thy words were found, and I did eat them; and thy word was unto me the joy and rejoicing of mine heart: for I am called by thy name, O LORD God of hosts"* (Jeremiah 15:16). Then he asked: *"Why is my pain perpetual, and my wound incurable...?"* (Jeremiah 15:18). Ezekiel also mentions a book given him to eat (Ezekiel 3:1-5). It was also sweet like honey like John's but later the prophet is shown experiencing bitterness (verse 14). We all have mountaintop experiences followed by valleys of challenges and even depression. Sometimes we wonder where God is when all this happens. We cannot pretend to grasp the meaning of everything that touches our lives, but we can let the hand of God guide us through. In eternity, we will see that what we thought to be curses, were instruments in the hands of our wise God to make us stronger and to get us closer to Him. It we trust Him even when we only see darkness surrounding us, He will take us to new pastures and refreshing waters. Then one day, soon, He will take us home with Him and after knowing the answers to our perplexities, we will praise God for we will know that He was always near.

The preaching of the second coming of Christ did not reach the whole world as it should have because the majority of the preachers opposed to the message. "Ministers who would not accept this saving message themselves hindered those who would have received it. The blood of souls is upon them. Preachers and people joined to oppose this message from heaven and to persecute William Miller and those who united with him in the work. Falsehoods were circulated to injure his influence; and at different times after he had plainly declared the counsel of God, applying cutting truths to the hearts of his hearers, great rage was kindled against him, and as he left the place of meeting, some waylaid him in order to take his life. But angels of God were sent to protect him, and they led him safely away from the angry mob. His work was not yet finished." *Early Writings*, 235. Just like it happened with the glorious preaching of the second coming of Jesus, millions of souls will perish thanks to the efforts of their religious leaders to keep them from knowing the truth of the Sabbath. This is very well described in this verse: *"Those who guide these people lead them astray. Those who are guided by them will be destroyed"* (Isaiah 9:16).

11And he said unto me, Thou must prophesy again before many peoples, and nations, and tongues, and kings.

Now that only the sincere people had been left after the disappointment, those that remained were commanded to continue the work of preaching the gospel to all creatures in the world. These are the people represented as the three angels in chapter 14 *"...having the everlasting gospel to preach unto them that dwell on the earth, and to every nation, and kindred, and tongue, and people"* (Revelation 14:6).

REVELATION 11

Dead but not for long

Chronologically, verses 3-13 from this chapter should precede chapter 10 because they describe things that happened almost half a century before the great disappointment. Chapter 10 and 11:1-14 constitute a parenthesis between the sixth and seventh trumpets. In chapter 10:11, John is told: *"Thou must prophesy again before many peoples, and nations, and tongues, and kings."* In chapter 11:15 we see the result of that preaching: *"The kingdoms of this world are become the kingdoms of our Lord, and of his Christ; and he shall reign for ever and ever."* Both chapters deal with the apparent defeat of the divine plans but indicate that God is in control and we must continue our march preaching the gospel to all nations.

[1]And there was given me a reed like unto a rod: and the angel stood, saying, Rise, and measure the temple of God, and the altar, and them that worship therein.

The prophet Zechariah also wrote about an angel taking measurements- of Jerusalem's walls (Zechariah 2:2) but was told not to because God would be its protector. Evidently, there was a perceived need of rebuilding the walls of the city for the sake of safety. John, however, was told to measure the temple, the altar and the worshippers. Obviously, God wants to rebuild the spiritual relationship that had been unstable in the last days' church in order to prepare His people for the final events.

Let us explain the symbolism:

Angel- We already discussed that angel means messenger. This angel here is Jesus himself. In verse three, it shows that this angel gives power to His two witnesses. Common angels do not give power and do not have witnesses. Witnesses give witness about Jehovah. We testify of the Creator; never about the creature.

Measure- Matthew comes to our help quoting Jesus: *"Judge not, that you be not judged. For with what judgment you judge, you will be judged; and with the measure you use, it will be measured back to you"* (Matthew 7:1,2 NKJV). To measure means *"to Judge."*

Reed like a rod for measuring- the rod then is the standard used to measure. It is interesting that the New Living Translation uses the word *standard* for *measure*. What is the standard to be used in the judgment? Let us ask James. *"So speak ye, and so do, as they that shall be judged by the law of liberty"* (James 2:12). The Ten Commandments are the standard for the judgment.

Ezekiel also mentions the measuring of the temple. In chapter 40, he describes a measuring that took place *"in the beginning of the year, in the tenth day of the month"* (verse one). The Jewish nation had two calendars; the civilian and the religious. If Ezekiel was referring to the civilian calendar, then it was on the seventh month of the Jewish calendar and thus would be the Day of Atonement. Jewish scholars refer to the Day of Atonement as a day of judgment.

The first two verses of Revelation 11 refer back to the great disappointment day of chapter 10 because that was the start of the investigative judgment in the year 1844. Since John is evidently pointing to a work of judgment, and judgment is related to atonement, we should look at its origin in the Old Testament. In the book of Leviticus, we find instructions regarding the cleansing done on the Day of Atonement. It was a day in which their souls had to be afflicted. In other words, they had to confess and repent of all their sins so they could be forgiven. At the present time, Jesus is doing a cleansing work in heaven while the Holy Spirit is doing the same in the heart of the believers on earth. We must cooperate with the Holy Spirit in that cleansing of the temple of the soul. The following chart illustrates the relationship between the work of the priest in Leviticus and that of our High Priest Jesus in the heavenly sanctuary:

Revelation 11:1	Leviticus 16
Measure the temple	The sanctuary was cleansed - verse 16
Measure the altar	The altar was cleansed - verse 18
Measure the worshipers	The people (worshipers) got cleansed - verse 17

"For on that day shall the priest make an atonement for you, to cleanse you, that ye may be clean from all your sins before the LORD...And he shall make an atonement for the holy sanctuary, and he shall make an atonement for the tabernacle of the congregation, and for the altar, and he shall make an atonement for the priests, and for all the people of the congregation" (Leviticus 16:30,33). The sanctuary cleansing was an act of judgment to declare them forgiven from the sins committed the previous year.

Everything about the worship and the worshippers is examined here. What a responsibility for the preachers! They must *"Preach the word; be instant in season, out of season; reprove, rebuke, exhort with all longsuffering and doctrine"* (2 Timothy 4:2). They must be faithful and teach only the undiluted truth. There is no place for entertainers behind the pulpit. Neither is the pulpit a political forum. It is not for unconverted people to address the congregation. For that, they can rent a hall somewhere else. The pulpit is to teach sinners the way back to God and saints on how to live a godly life. We need to hear the unadulterated Word of God. He wants His preachers to speak His will and not what the people want to hear. A real preacher is not accountable to whoever pays his salary, but to God Himself and he will be responsible for the blood of his listeners if he is not faithful and do not put any effort in waking them up from their slumber. *"When I say unto the wicked, Thou shalt surely die; and thou givest him not warning, nor speakest to warn the wicked from his wicked way, to save his life; the same wicked man shall die in his iniquity; but his blood will I require at thine hand"* (Ezekiel 3:18). The listeners must follow the guidance of the Holy Spirit to implement in their lives what is said from the pulpit. The book of Joel has a great recommendation for us 21st century Christians to follow:

"Therefore also now, saith the LORD, turn ye even to me with all your heart, and with fasting, and with weeping, and with mourning: And rend your heart, and not your garments, and turn unto the LORD your God: for he is gracious and merciful, slow to anger, and of great kindness, and repenteth him of the evil. ... Blow the trumpet in Zion, sanctify a fast, call a solemn assembly: Gather the people, sanctify the congregation, assemble the elders, gather the children, and those that suck the breasts: let the bridegroom go forth of his chamber, and the bride out of her closet. Let the priests, the ministers of the LORD,

weep between the porch and the altar, and let them say, Spare thy people, O LORD, and give not thine heritage to reproach, that the heathen should rule over them: wherefore should they say among the people, Where is their God?" (Joel 2:12-17).

What kind of music do we use in our services? Satan was the director of the heavenly choir and orchestra. He knows which notes to play to hypnotize you and make you believe that the music you are hearing is filling you up. You leave church on a cloud. Solemn music no longer appeals to you and you find it boring. I have news for you. The first intention of music is not to fill you up; it is to glorify God. When you sing to glorify Him for His majesty, power and mercy, you are filled with joy and peace. I see more and more music that appeal to the senses and I see the singers moving their bodies sometimes in sensual contortions proper of what a common worldly person would do with non-sacred music. Christian artists are treated in the way that rock stars are treated. By the way, I cannot imagine Jesus or His disciples playing or listening to "Christian" rock. For me that is an oxymoron. The rhythm and the lyrics used in today's musical selections appeal to the base instincts in human nature. It is common also to hear and observe sensuality in the performance. Why do we have to imitate the world? We know what happened when the early church brought paganism into their temples. It remained to this day and changed the pure church into Babylon the mother of harlots. Why her daughters are called harlots? Because they too brought the world into the church. Today Christians fill the dance halls, the theaters, the racetracks, amusement parks, etc. and spend thousands of dollars entertaining themselves but give only a dollar for offering. In spite of all those distractions, they feel emptiness in their hearts.

Most of the TV programs that we watch are detrimental to our relationships. Take for example the sitcoms in which the husband is almost 100% of the time portrayed as an irresponsible, careless, cheating, lying man; what is commonly called a "jerk." After sometime watching that kind of programs, the wife will start to look at her real life husband under a different unfavorable light, projecting the ugly personality of the TV actor into her husband. I told a sitcom-addicted wife that her preferred programming would affect her marriage and she said it would not. A few months later, she filed for divorce, resulting in two miserable lives that once were happy before she became a sitcom TV junkie. I am very sure you all have heard about the violence scenes that our children are exposed to in TV and how this is affecting them as they grow older. There is a marked increase in violent crimes that can be tracked down to the kind of programs felons watched as they grew up. Most everyone wants to have a big screen, high-resolution TV with cable or satellite and rent the latest thriller (or chick flick). Then we do not want to live with the results. Imitating what the world does only invites the devil to take control of our "homes." Do we have to live a boring life to be a Christian? Of course not! When you are in communion with Christ, you will find a deeper satisfaction in other activities that will not imprint the world's marks on your character to ruin it for eternity- and you will have a better chance to save your children too.

John, who once was young and before knowing Christ wanted to enjoy what the world of his times had to offered, wrote: *"Love not the world, neither the things that are in the world. If any man loves the world, the love of the Father is not in him. For all that is in the world, the lust of the flesh, and the lust of the eyes, and the pride of life, is not of the Father, but is of the world. And the world passeth away, and the lust thereof: but he that doeth the will of God abideth for ever"* (1 John 2:15-17). Solomon tried everything and almost lost his salvation, to the point that he even worshipped and build temples to idols. Today we have other idols of our making. We might no longer memorize Bible verses but surely, we know who won the Oscars and who the star of the latest movie is.

"Measuring the Church of God.--The grand judgment is taking place, and has been going on for some time. Now the Lord says, Measure the temple and the worshipers thereof. Remember when you are walking the streets about your business, God is measuring you; when you are attending your household duties, when you engage in conversation, God is measuring you. Remember that your words and actions are being daguerreotyped [photographed] in the books of heaven, as the face is reproduced by the artist on the polished plate.

"Here is the work going on, measuring the temple and its worshipers to see who will stand in the last day. Those who stand fast shall have an abundant entrance into the kingdom of our Lord and Savior Jesus Christ. When we are doing our work, remember there is One that is watching the spirit in which we are doing it. Shall we not bring the Savior into our everyday lives, into our secular work and domestic duties? Then in the name of God we want to leave behind everything that is not necessary, all gossiping or unprofitable visiting, and present ourselves as servants of the living God." (See Revelation 20:12, 13; 1 Peter 4:17; 2 Peter 1:10, 11). *S.D.A. Bible Commentary Vol. 7, page 972*

2But the court which is without the temple leave out, and measure it not; for it is given unto the Gentiles: and the holy city shall they tread under foot forty and two months.

The Bible teaches that the judgment would commence with the believers. *"For the time is come that **judgment must begin at the house of God**: and if it first begin at us, what shall the end be of them that obey not the gospel of God?"* (1 Peter 4:17). The judgment of the wicked will take place at the end of the thousand years (Revelation 20) and the result of that judgment will happen outside the city where the temple will be.

Forty-two months are 1,260 days, which in prophetic time is 1,200 years (Ezekiel 4:6). This represents the time during the dark ages when the Scriptures were forbidden to the common people.

3And I will give power unto my two witnesses, and they shall prophesy a thousand two hundred and threescore days, clothed in sackcloth.

Sackcloth was a symbol of humiliation, of pain.

"a thousand two hundred and threescore days"- The previous verse indicates that the gentiles would tread under foot the holy city. This refers to the dominion of papal Rome- and trampling under foot was a practice of imperial Rome (see Daniel 7:7) which it succeeded. The time of that hegemony was to be 42 months. Verse three says that the two witnesses would be prophesying 1,260 days, which is exactly 42 months. Both verses are referring to the same period of time from 538 AD to 1798 AD (1,260 years). The Lord obviously wants to emphasize the duration of the dark ages, when only a few privileged were able to afford a Bible, which usually became chained to a wall.

[4]These are the two olive trees, and the two candlesticks standing before the God of the earth.

This passage is similar to Zechariah 4:2-6 where it mentions the olive trees and candlesticks. Olive trees produce olive oil; the candlesticks in the sanctuary were also full of olive oil, a symbol of the Holy Spirit. When the prophet was asked about the meaning of the symbols and could not give an answer, he heard this explanation:

"Then he answered and spake unto me, saying, this is the word of the LORD unto Zerubbabel, saying, not by might, nor by power, but by my Spirit, saith the LORD of hosts."

[5]And if any man will hurt them, fire proceedeth out of their mouth, and devoureth their enemies: and if any man will hurt them, he must in this manner be killed. [6]These have power to shut heaven, that it rain not in the days of their prophecy: and have power over waters to turn them to blood, and to smite the earth with all plagues, as often as they will.

Due to the mention of the lack of rain from heaven and the plagues, some people have identified the two witnesses with Moses and Elijah. However, the passage also mentions fire that *"proceedeth out of their mouth"* which does not match the character of the work of any of these prophets. The work of both prophets was localized: Elijah in Israel and Moses in Egypt. These two prophets from Revelation 11, on the other hand, have a worldwide work to do. In the light of the passage from Zechariah, the 1,260 years of their restricted witnessing and the worldwide reach of these two witnesses, we could safely conclude that they represent the inspired Word of God- both the Old and the New Testaments. They are presented as dressed on sackcloth- a symbol of humiliation, which is a well-fitting description of how the Word of God was despised on behalf of tradition during the Dark Ages. During those years, having just a portion of the Scriptures was enough to guarantee the arrest or even the death of the possessor. Superstition was highly regarded instead of the light of the truth. By keeping the people in darkness regarding the Scriptures, the church secured its unquestionable tyrannical authority. It was not the Scriptures that brought darkness to that repressive period of human history, but the lack of knowledge of it. Once the Bible started to be distributed worldwide without restrictions, real science took the place of superstition. Unfortunately pseudo science also appeared- namely anything that promotes the evolutionary theory as a fact when it is as laughable as the absurdities of superstition, being based only on suppositions and fabricated evidence. See commentary of chapter three.

Now, is all science bad? Is the Bible anti-science? Before Christopher Columbus went on his first trip west to prove that the earth was round, he read Isaiah 40:22. *"It is he that sitteth upon the circle of the earth..."* The verse uses the Hebrew word "chuwg" to indicate the shape of the earth: a circle. More accurately, the Hebrew word means globe. This is significant because a globe is longer than it is wide, just as the earth is. The distance between the poles is larger than when measured across the equator.

The Bible, even though was influenced by the belief of some of its writers, has valid scientific data that was not validated for centuries, making it to be far ahead of its time. For example, it mentions the rain cycle in Job 36:27: *"He draws up the drops of water, which distill as rain to the streams."* It talks about the movement of the winds and their influence in the weather in Job 37:9: *"Out of the south cometh the whirlwind: and cold out of the north."* Centuries before Galileo was born, Job wrote that God gave weight to the wind (Job 28:25). The Bible has many valid scientific pieces of information that are worth digging. It also talks about the best ways to take care of our bodies. It shows that the original factory diet was vegetarian (Genesis 1:29; 3:18), that it is not good to consume alcohol (Proverbs 23:31-*"Look not thou upon the wine"*) and that consuming too much sweet stuff is not good (Proverbs 25:27 *"It is not good to eat too much honey"*).

Many read the Scriptures with a critical and skeptical eye because they do not know how accurate its scientific declarations and prophecies are. Only a book inspired by a real God can make the claim to open the curtain to the future, like this book of Revelation. Studying the prophecies with an open mind will help you have faith on an instant creation. Too bad many accept evolution (coincidence, accidents, afterthoughts) as true when it is so much easier and logical to believe on a God that speaks and things are created instantly (design, planning, care).

[7]And when they shall have finished their testimony, the beast that ascendeth out of the bottomless pit shall make war against them, and shall overcome them, and kill them. [8]And their dead bodies shall lie in the street of the great city, which spiritually is called Sodom and Egypt, where also our Lord was crucified.

According to this passage, at the end of the 18th century, the two witnesses will have no life. The city where they would lie had characteristics of Sodom (immorality) and Egypt (atheism). *"And Pharaoh said, Who is the LORD, that I should obey his voice to let Israel go? I know not the LORD, neither will I let Israel go"* (Exodus 5:2). Was there a country at the end of that century in which these two characteristics were present? It was France during its reign of terror. The Scriptures were forbidden and religion was abolished. The first of the European nations to recognize the papacy centuries before was the first one to turn its back on it.

where also our Lord was crucified- In persecuting those that believe the gospel, France crucified Jesus in the person of His followers, just as Saul was doing when he stoned Stephen and incarcerated the other believers. Whatever is done against a follower of Jesus, He takes it personal: *"...for he that toucheth you toucheth the apple of his eye"* (Zechariah 2:8).

[9]And they of the people and kindreds and tongues and nations shall see their dead bodies three days and an half, and shall not suffer their dead bodies to be put in graves.

In 1793, the French assembly enacted a law abolishing religion and replacing it with the "goddess" of reason. France was the first nation that by decree of its legislative body declared that there is no God. For three and a half years, the nation suffered terrible civil unrest and thousands died under the guillotine (even its inventor, whose head was the first one to roll to test the device) or languished in filthy prisons. The official count is 17,000 dead and at least 300,000 arrested. Three and a half years later the same body adopted a resolution that overturned the previous decree and granted tolerance to the Holy Scriptures. The civilized world had contemplated with apprehension the terrible results obtained by disregarding the Holy Scriptures and men then recognized that the ways of God and His Word are the only way to guarantee the stability of society.

There was in those times a young man who, after seeing the abuses of the Catholic Church, turned into an unbeliever and became one of the leaders of the French Revolution. His name was Voltaire. He once said that he was tired of listening that twelve men established the Christian religion and that he would prove that one man would be enough to destroy it, referring to himself. I heard that the building where he pronounced those words was later used to distribute Bibles. Today the Scriptures have been translated into more than 1,000 languages and dialects and the Bible is the greatest best selling book of all times.

France also presented the characteristic that distinguished Sodom the most. During the Revolution it was manifested such a degraded and corrupt moral condition that can be compared to the one which caused the destruction of the cities of the plain. The sacred contract of marriage was reduced to a mere civil arrangement of transitory character, which any two people could celebrate or dissolve at their will. The practice of divorce inspired by demons has spread now to all nations carrying a curse from generation to generation, degrading in turn the whole society of which it was supposed to be the column to uphold it.

The seed that for centuries the church had planted on the soil of its eldest daughter was producing the bitterest fruit. For over a thousand years, the Church had oppressed the citizens and kept them under the slavery of fear, ignorance and superstition. It had persecuted men and women of the most noble character and intelligence for the sole crime of reading the Scriptures. The blood of the Huguenots and others was now ready to be avenged. At the very beginning of the revolution, the priests that in other times trained their parishioners to track down and hunt Protestants, were now the first ones to be arrested and sent to the gallows as slaves or to lose their heads before a blood thirsty populace. In the very place where the first martyrs of the Reformation were burned at the stake in the previous century, there was used the first guillotine of the Revolution.

[10]And they that dwell upon the earth shall rejoice over them, and make merry, and shall send gifts one to another; because these two prophets tormented them that dwelt on the earth.

they that dwell upon the earth – Notice that it does not say "all that dwell upon the earth," because Protestant nations, such as the United States and England, did not join in the rejoicing.

There was rejoicing at the capital of France and singing and dancing in other countries when they heard the news. This reminds me of the scenes of Palestinians celebrating when they heard the news of the destruction of the World Trade Center in September 11th, 2001, when close to 3,000 lives, including children and even some of their own people, were lost. In their ignorance, they rejoiced on an evil and senseless act because their leaders tell them that America is evil. How fast they take American help when they suffer an earthquake! Just days before Jesus was crucified, when the Priests were plotting His assassination, He approached Jerusalem and stop to look at it. He knew what voluntary ignorance could do. The leaders of the Jewish nation were turning the people against their only hope. *"He came closer to the city, and when he saw it,* ***he wept over it****, saying, "If you only knew today what is needed for peace! But now you cannot see it! The time will come when your enemies will surround you with barricades, blockade you, and close in on you from every side. They will completely destroy you and the people within your walls; not a single stone will they leave in its place,* ***because you did not recognize the time when God came to save you****!"* (Luke 19:41-44- Contemporary English Version). The Israelites heard prophet after prophet telling them the will of God. Of them, some were killed, others rejected and persecuted. Now Jesus Himself had come to His vineyard to seek fruit, giving a final chance. Like a hen that gathers her chick for protection before imminent danger, Jesus pleaded with the Jewish nation to keep them from destruction by the Roman armies, but they rejected His invitation (Matthew 23:37). God is giving you dear reader the truth of how to be saved, His true Sabbath and many other precious truths. Do not make His heart cry by rejecting the light that will set you free.

For centuries, He sent His faithful servants to the French nation to invite them to repent, but they preferred to listen to the fables of the Catholic Church. Had they hid the divine counsel, not a single drop of blood would have been shed. The religion of Christ has never been popular but it is the only guarantee of peace and freedom for nations and individuals.

[11]And after three days and an half the spirit of life from God entered into them, and they stood upon their feet; and great fear fell upon them which saw them. [12]And they heard a great voice from heaven saying unto them, Come up hither. And they ascended up to heaven in a cloud; and their enemies beheld them. [13]And the same hour was there a great earthquake, and the tenth part of the city fell, and in the earthquake were slain of men seven thousand: and the remnant were affrighted, and gave glory to the God of heaven. [14]The second woe is past; and, behold, the third woe cometh quickly.

the tenth part of the city fell – The tenth is a very accurate number because it refers to the fall of one of the nations that formed after the Roman Empire collapsed: France- the eldest and favorite daughter of the papacy. Daniel chapter two indicated that ten kingdoms would come out of the fourth great world empire (Rome).

When the French Assembly reverted its previous decree, it also encouraged Protestants and Jews to celebrate services and read the Scriptures, thus granting them religious liberty, which they did not have before the Revolution. When Satan tries to destroy God's influence, he always ends up losing more. In this case, his triumph lasted only three and a half years when he got to use his subjects to outlaw the Bible. However, when the three and a half years ended, there was a renewed interest not only in studying the Bible but also in translating it and distributing it to foreign countries. This helped create the Bible societies, which sent the light of the Gospel to the darkest area of the world and inspired countless men and women to leave the comfort of their homes to become missionaries overseas. Many of them never came back home but with the offering of their lives they planted a seed that to this day is still bearing fruit for the kingdom of heaven. See commentary on Revelation chapter 3.

What was God's intention in allowing the French Revolution? First, it slowed down the Catholic Church in its quest to destroy the

Protestants. By inflicting the mortal wound to the papacy in 1798, the Church had to temporarily stop inflicting wounds to others so it could lick its own. Second, the French Revolution was a significant step towards doing away with the monarchic style of government, which was Rome's favorite, because it was easier to manipulate one man (the king) than a whole cabinet with dissenting ideas. Third, the ideas that eventually inspired the Revolution also motivated the patriots in the United States to seek independence from the crown of England. The principles of modern democracy owe a great debt to the French Revolution. Democratic governments promote freedoms for their citizens that otherwise are not enjoyed under Rome's dictatorship. One has only to look at the Catholic-trained leaders of Latin America (Fidel Castro) and Europe (Hitler and Mussolini) to comprehend the results of allowing the Church's teachings to permeate the affairs of the state.

Atheists in our times, contrary to what the majority of Christians believe, play a very important role in protecting the true church from religious persecution when they oppose the union of church and state. In the days of our founding fathers, the good relations between church and state were not a problem because they understood the importance of tolerance, themselves coming from nations that persecuted minorities with different beliefs. Today we find religious bigots trying to force their beliefs down people's throats having an agenda to use the government to advance their cause. Can God use unbelievers to fulfill His eternal plans? Sure, He can. All over the Bible, we see pagans helping God's children. We find Abraham making alliances with pagan neighbors. Solomon recurred to the king of Tyre to provide materials for the new temple. Cyrus set the Israelites free from the Babylonian captivity. Three times in the book of Acts, the Romans interceded to protect Paul from the Jewish fanatics. We must remember that according to Daniel 3, the union of church and state can only bring tyranny. The union of church and state had its origin in Nimrod's mind. He was the founder of Babylon, whose religion has influenced all the pagan religions of the world.

The second beast of Revelation 13 will be the result of what Protestants are pursuing today: run the government. They want to make and impose laws because they have seen how secular the nation has become. Instead of fulfilling the great commission of preaching the from-the-inside-out-life-changing-gospel, they want to impose their ideals on people (from the outside in). That is not God's way. If it were, He would have instructed the disciples to attempt to overthrow the Roman government. Instead, He sent them to preach God's love to the nations that were perishing for lack of that knowledge. Although many Christians are well intentioned in their desire to have a Christian government at all levels, the end result will be persecution of minorities and oppressive and intolerant laws. Unknowingly, they are giving the reigns to the first beast, the one that for 1,260 years had the world in darkness and created the inquisition; the one responsible for the killing of over 60 million people just because they dared to believe different (upholding the truth) and they were not even violent people. Thousands of them were even killed in their sleep. A great example of this abuse of power was the massacre of St. Bartholomew on August 24, 1572. "Suddenly—and without warning—the devilish work commenced. Beginning at Paris, the French soldiers and the Roman Catholic clergy fell upon the *unarmed* people, and blood flowed like a river throughout the entire country. Men, women, and children fell in heaps before the mobs and the bloodthirsty troops. In one week, almost 100,100 Protestants perished. The rivers of France were so filled with corpses that for many months no fish were eaten. In the valley of the Loire, wolves came down from the hills to feed upon the decaying bodies of Frenchmen. The list of massacres was as endless as the list of the dead!

"Many were imprisoned—many sent as slaves to row the King's ships—and some were able to escape to other countries. The massacres continued for centuries. The best and brightest people fled to Germany, Switzerland, England, Ireland and eventually America and brought their incomparable manufacturing skills with them. France was ruined. Wars, famine, disease and poverty finally led to the French Revolution—the Guillotine—the Reign of Terror—the fall of the Roman Catholic Monarchy—atheism—communism etc., etc....

And what did the church do? "When news of the Massacre reached the Vatican there was jubilation! Cannons roared—bells rung—and a special commemorative medal was struck—*to honor the occasion!* The Pope commissioned Italian artist Vasari to paint a mural of the Massacre—which *still* hangs in the Vatican!" http://www.reformation.org/bart.html

How easy these Protestant Christians forget the words of Jesus: *"My kingdom is not of this world..."* (John 18:36).

Would the two witnesses (the Old and New Testaments) ever be "killed" again? The message of the gospel is presently being proclaimed freely worldwide and it is represented in Revelation 14 in the work of the three angels. They are no longer dressed in sackcloth but exalted everywhere. Now the radio and TV programs proclaiming freedom to the masses reach all nations through the satellites and the internet. The time will come, however, when evidently there would no Bibles be found. Therefore, I believe it is possible that new legislation will be enacted against the authoritative Word of God. *"Behold, the days come, saith the Lord GOD, that I will send a famine in the land, not a famine of bread, nor a thirst for water, but of hearing the words of the LORD: ... they shall run to and fro to seek the word of the LORD, and shall not find it."* (Amos 8:11,12). Careless Christians will try to find answers and comfort due to the worlds' crisis but will no longer find Bibles. These are the ones portrayed as foolish in the parable of the ten virgins. They procrastinated when they had so many opportunities to be acquainted with their Bible but found it boring and preferred to watch TV or "do something fun" instead. Now is the time to memorize the wonderful Bible promises. The Bible should be appreciated for what it is: the Word of the Living God. It is His love letter that can satisfy the hunger and thirst of the neediest of humans.

15And the seventh angel sounded; and there were great voices in heaven, saying, The kingdoms of this world are become the kingdoms of our Lord, and of his Christ; and he shall reign for ever and ever.

Chapter 10 contains a passage that sheds light on this verse and vice versa.

Revelation 10:7	Revelation 11:15
But in the days of the voice of the seventh angel,	*And the seventh angel sounded*
when he shall begin to sound, the mystery of God should be finished	*The kingdoms of this world are become the kingdoms of our Lord, and of his Christ*

As mentioned before, the mystery of God is the preaching of the gospel to the entire inhabited world (chapter ten). The finishing of the great commission will cause that all the kingdoms will finally become the Lord's at the end of the judgment.

In Daniel chapter seven, we see Jesus approaching the throne of God and is given the kingdom. *"I saw in the night visions, and, behold, one like the Son of man came with the clouds of heaven, and came to the Ancient of days, and they brought him near before him. And there was given him dominion, and glory, and a kingdom, that all people, nations, and languages, should serve him: his dominion is an everlasting dominion, which shall not pass away, and his kingdom that which shall not be destroyed"* (Daniel 7:13, 14). It is important to notice that the reception of that kingdom is found in the context of the scene of judgment. Jesus did not have the kingship while on this earth. *"He said therefore, A certain nobleman went into a far country to receive for himself a kingdom, and to return"* (Luke 19:12). Jesus will receive the kingdom at the end of the work of judgment. Verse 18 of this same chapter of Revelation refers to the judgment of the dead, which of course started with Abel, the first church member that died. At the end of the judgment, when all the cases are decided, Jesus will remove His priestly garments and change into his kingly robes. Then He will lead His heavenly troops for the battle of Armageddon (Revelation 19:11-16).

Daniel 7	Revelation 11 and 20
The judgment scene- The Judge sat and the books are opened- verse 10	Time to judge the dead and the books are opened - Revelation 11: 18; 20:12
The Son of Man receives the kingdom- Verse 14	The kingdom becomes Christ's- Revelation 11:15
"His dominion is an everlasting dominion, which shall not pass away, and his kingdom that which shall not be destroyed"- Verse 14	*"he shall reign for ever and ever"* - Revelation 11:15

16And the four and twenty elders, which sat before God on their seats, fell upon their faces, and worshipped God, 17Saying, We give thee thanks, O LORD God Almighty, which art, and wast, and art to come; because thou hast taken to thee thy great power, and hast reigned.

The heavenly host can hardly wait for the inauguration of the kingdom. Six thousand years of cosmic conflict will soon come to an end and the universe again will be at peace. God will restore everything to a pre-sin condition and only notes of harmony and love will be heard. I look forward to that day too.

18And the nations were angry, and thy wrath is come, and the time of the dead, that they should be judged, and that thou shouldest give reward unto thy servants the prophets, and to the saints, and them that fear thy name, small and great; and shouldest destroy them which destroy the earth.

The nations were angry- The greatest conflicts in the history of this world were to be expected at the time of the end. In the 20th century, we suffered WWI, WWII, the Korea conflict, the Vietnam war, the wars in the Middle East, and now in the 21st we are still battling the war on terrorism while also the nations of Iran and North Korea are defying the world with a possible nuclear bomb. Never before in history did we see so many lives lost as we saw in the past century. "The calamities by land and sea, the unsettled state of society, the alarms of war, are portentous. They forecast approaching events of greatest magnitude. The agencies of evil are combining their forces and consolidating. They are strengthening for the last great crisis. Great changes are soon to take place in our world, and the final movements will be rapid ones." *Last Day Events*, page 11.

Thy wrath is come- This last generation of Christians seems to be out to defy everything that God wants them to stand for. Principle has been sacrifice on the altar of public opinion, of what is politically correct, of what is acceptable by society. Instead of fulfilling the divine commission of converting and elevating mankind to God's ways, the church has been steadily converting itself and being accommodating to the world. We now have, not only gay marriages and partnerships, but also openly gay and lesbian ministers. We have alcohol consumption, drugs, promiscuity (girlfriend and boyfriend moving in together), dancing and all kinds of activities that are not sanctioned by the Bible but by the world. Regarding this, Isaiah 5:20 reads: *"Woe unto them that call evil good, and good evil; that put darkness for light, and light for darkness; that put bitter for sweet, and sweet for bitter!"* How can we teach the world that we have something better from God if we lower His standards that He entrusted us to share with mankind and come down to the world's degrading level? Living in sin does not bring peace; only heartache and emptiness. No wonder there are so many cases of depression and even suicide among Christians and the rate of divorce is identical to that of the world! *"Ye adulterers and adulteresses, know ye not that the friendship of the world is enmity with God? whosoever therefore will be a friend of the world is the enemy of God"* (James 4:4). Why would we want to go back to the mud where we were rescued from, our past way of life? Are we addicted to pain and suffering? *"For if after they have escaped the pollutions of the world through the knowledge of the Lord and Saviour Jesus Christ, they are again entangled therein, and overcome, the latter end is worse with them than the beginning"* (2 Peter 2:20). *"Love not the world, neither the things that are in the world. If any man loves the world, the love of the Father is not in him. For all that is in the world, the lust of the flesh, and the lust of the eyes, and the pride of life, is not of the Father, but is of the world. And the world passeth away, and the lust thereof: but he that doeth the will of God abideth for ever"* (1 John 2:15 -17). So, why is the wrath of God going to be manifested? Because of all the sins that are sanctioned by the Christian community while pretending to represent Christ. *"Mortify therefore your members which are upon the earth; fornication, uncleanness, inordinate affection, evil concupiscence, and covetousness, which is idolatry: For which things' sake the wrath of God cometh on the children of disobedience"* (Colossians 3:5,6). Is it worth it to remain faithful to Biblical principles in a world were the Word of God is despised and discredited as authoritative? If you are a committed Christian, the world will be observing you and you might be surprised because of the many who will claim to have made it to the kingdom of heaven influenced by your good example.

the time of the dead, that they should be judged- This is the judgment mentioned in verses one and two of this chapter when John was told to measure the worshipers. As mentioned before, it is the same scene of judgment from the book of Daniel: *"A fiery stream issued and came forth from before him: thousand thousands ministered unto him, and ten thousand times ten thousand stood before him: the judgment was set, and the books were opened"* (Daniel 7:10). Notice that according to Revelation 22:11 and 12 the reward is mentioned after the judgment. How can a person be considered worthy of enjoying the heavenly bliss if his life is not examined first? If you go to school, do you get your diploma before you take the final exam? Why preachers are so prompt to place the dead in heaven as soon as they die during funeral services? Many times those that they are so quick to put in heaven beat their wives the night before or committed embezzlement of funds, or cheated some other way. The judgment will determine who is worthy of eternal life and who deserves to be deprived of it. When Jesus returns, He will give the due reward to everyone of His followers. *"And, behold, I come quickly; and my reward is with me, to give every man according as his work shall be"* (Revelation 22:12). It is clear that no one is enjoying heaven or suffering in the flames of hell as soon as he or she dies. People die and wait on their graves until the resurrection at the final day. Notice how Jesus mentions the judgment before the resurrection in this passage of John: *"And hath given him authority to execute judgment also, because he is the Son of man. Marvel not at this: for the hour is coming, in the which all that are in the graves shall hear his voice, And shall come forth; they that have done good, unto the resurrection of life; and they that have done evil, unto the resurrection of damnation"* (John 5:27-29). Notice also that Jesus clearly indicates that people are in their graves, not in heaven or hell. The reward will be given in the resurrected bodies. There is no such thing as a separate spiritual entity that goes to enjoy heaven or suffer hell after we die. The reward, whichever it will be, will also be given on the surface of this earth, not on any ethereal place: *"Behold, the righteous shall be recompensed in the earth: much more the wicked and the sinner"* (Proverbs 11:31).

destroy them which destroy the earth – Never before in history did we suffer so many environmentally induced diseases as in the 20th and 21st centuries. Cancer is supposed to affect one in every two men and one in every three women during their lifetime and some people will have recurrences. We are on this earth as stewards (managers, administrators) and as such, we are responsible for how we preserve and protect our entrusted resources. Technology- although not perfect- has provided us with some tools to save water, electricity and gas. Not letting the water running during a shower or shave, observing energy-saving practices with our electric devices, buying fuel-efficient vehicles, avoiding soil, air and water contamination, buying or making organic cleaners (and even shopping for organic foods), recycling, composting, can all be small effective steps that we all can contribute to have a better environment for us and our children.

[19]*And* ***the temple of God was opened in heaven****, and there was seen in his temple the ark of his testament: and there were lightnings, and voices, and thunderings, and an earthquake, and great hail.*

The temple in heaven- When Moses was in the dessert with the children of Israel, he was instructed to make a sanctuary and to do it according to the model shown him on the mount (Exodus 25:8,40). The type was in the desert; the antitype was in heaven- more on this ahead. Every element in that place of worship represented Jesus:

- The altar of sacrifice- The cross where Jesus would die shedding His blood
- The laver- the water is associated with purification, thus a fitting symbol of the blood of Jesus that cleanses us all (Psalm 26:6; Ezekiel 36:25; Ephesians 5:26; 1 John 1:9)
- The table of showbread- Jesus is the bread of life. John 6:48
- The candlestick- Jesus is the light of the world. John 8:12
- The altar of incense- The righteousness of Jesus mixed with our prayers to make them ascend to God as a pleasant fragrance. Revelation 8:3,4
- The ark of the covenant- Where the shekinah glory was manifested. The ark contained the two tables of the moral law, which demanded our death *("the wages of sin is death"-* **not hell**- Romans 6:23). The high priest, a human himself was to present blood on the golden plate above the commandments once a year. The law demanded his life as a sinner, but the blood "intervened" and he was able to finish the yearly cleansing ritual and walk alive from the tabernacle. In similar manner, when the wrath of God was about to fall on this rebel world, Jesus came and placed Himself in the middle, suffering the wrath against sin on our behalf to guarantee our salvation (Romans 5:9).

If we could take an aerial view of the tabernacle, we could notice that the arrangement of the items in it shaped a cross, indicating how Jesus would die. Even in that detail, we can see that everything in the sanctuary and the prophecies were fulfilled in Jesus' life and death. No doubt, He is the Messiah.

The outside of the sanctuary itself was a symbol of Jesus' incarnation. It was covered with dark, unattractive skins. *"For he shall grow up before him as a tender plant, and as a root out of a dry ground: he hath no form nor comeliness; and when we shall see him, there is no beauty that we should desire him"* (Isaiah 53:2). As humans, we are attracted to external beauty but God looks at the heart (1 Samuel 16:7) and that is the attitude that God wanted us to have when Jesus came to dwell among us. We must be attracted to the beauty of His character and likewise treat our fellow human beings with equal dignity regardless of their physical appearance.

Paul wrote that the sanctuary in the desert was a symbol of the real one not made of this creation (Hebrews 8:2; 9:11). Jesus is our High Priest in the heavenly sanctuary. There He intercedes on our behalf presenting His blood to cover our confessed sins. Some people deny that there is a sanctuary in heaven but it is clearly mentioned in different other passages in both the Old and New Testaments:

- *"The LORD is in <u>his holy temple</u>, the LORD's throne <u>is in heaven</u>: his eyes behold, his eyelids try, the children of men"* (Psalm 11:4).
- *"For he hath looked down from the height of <u>his sanctuary; from heaven</u> did the LORD behold the earth"* (Psalm 102:19).
- *"Then the priests the Levites arose and blessed the people: and their voice was heard, and their prayer came up to <u>his holy dwelling place [temple]</u>, <u>even unto heaven</u>"* (2 Chronicles 30:27).
- *"And another angel came out of the <u>temple which is in heaven</u>, he also having a sharp sickle"* (Revelation 14:17).
- *"And after that I looked, and, behold, <u>the temple of the tabernacle of the testimony in heaven</u> was opened"* (Revelation 15:5).
- *"And the seventh angel poured out his vial into the air; and there came a great voice out of <u>the temple of heaven</u>, from the throne, saying, It is done"* (Revelation 16:17).

What is Jesus doing there? When He ascended to heaven, He became our intercessor as we already mentioned, but Daniel 8 and 9 point to an additional role that He assumed starting in 1844 at the end of the 2,300 years. He started a work of judgment that needs to be done before He returns to determine the reward (Revelation 22:12). He is presiding as a judge (John 5:22 & 27). Please see my comment on the book of Daniel chapters 7-9 for more detailed information.

there was seen in his temple *the ark of his testament* - Why is it important that John saw the ark of His testament or covenant? It is because "Christian" preachers claim that the Ten Commandments were for the Jewish nation only and no longer binding for New Testament believers. Let us compare the cities where preachers teach that the law was for the Jews. Detroit and Pontiac- both cities in Michigan, USA, have some streets (like Woodward Avenue in Detroit) lined up with so many churches that visitors could conclude that they must be heavenly. However, they are in the top ten in crimes in the whole nation. Now, let us consider Loma Linda, California where 97% of inhabitants believe that the Ten Commandments are still binding. They had never made the list of even the 500 most affected cities by crime. What makes the difference? In the first example, there is no restrain. Since according to these preachers in error teach, the "law of God has been abolished" or "it was for the Jews" or "was nailed to the cross," there is a sense that all other laws are to be disregarded. See the crime statistics comparison between Loma Linda:

Violent crime index in 2010

Loma Linda: 70.5
U.S. Average: 222.7

http://www.city-data.com/crime/crime-Loma-Linda-California.html#ixzz26aB17wRL

and Detroit:

Violent crime index in 2010

Detroit: 1,059.6
U.S. Average: 222.7

http://www.city-data.com/crime/crime-Detroit-Michigan.html#ixzz26aBVMt1y

Although factors such as size of the city, unemployment, education level and other factors play a role, we cannot forget that the moral backbone is important and preachers have the responsibility to teach the truth about the Sabbath and the other Commandments as still being valid for all mankind.

The tables of the Law were kept in the ark. There, at the heart of it, was the commandment to **remember** to keep the Sabbath holy. Many argue that the Sabbath was of temporary duration because it is not mentioned in the writings of the apostles. To that, I answer again that it was not necessary to remind them of the commandment that was meant to be remembered by the believers." Why in the world God would have to repeat a commandment that He specifically told us not to forget? What it matters is that Jesus, His followers after His death, and Paul in the book of Acts all kept the Sabbath holy. Besides, that argument is very lame because it is base on assumptions, and forgetting that the whole Bible is its own context. If in Revelation, the last book of the Bible, none of the commandments is mentioned specifically, we cannot assume that they were done with. The gospel of John was the last book of the Bible to be written (not Revelation) and mentions the Sabbath 11 times. Had the Sabbath been abolished, I am sure John would have known it and made efforts to clearly present the news in his book. Being the last disciple alive, he would have called the seventh day of the week "the old Sabbath," making clear that it was no longer binding and Sunday had taken its place.

Satan is using the Christian leaders to proclaim that the Sabbath was only for the Jewish people and Christians now are to keep Sunday. There are so many contradictions in those preachers that amazes me how the congregations do not realize that they are being taken for a ride- to a point of no return! If the Commandments are no longer binding, why worry about being honest and not lying? Why is killing wrong? After all, both the fourth and sixth Commandments are part of the same Law. The Sabbath was never changed by Jesus. His custom was to go to the synagogue (the church of His time) and worship every Sabbath (Luke 4:16). His ministry lasted three and a half years; so He went to church during that time for 150 Sabbaths. The Scriptures do not record Him worshiping or authorizing worshiping in any other day. Pagans in the time of Jesus worshiped on Sunday in honor of Mitra.

If it has a pagan origin then it is a satanic idea. Why worship on the day created by Satan? The proof of the eternal requirement to keep the seventh day Sabbath is in the fact that it will be observed in the new earth. *"For as the new heavens and the new earth, which I will make, shall remain before me, saith the LORD, so shall your seed and your name remain. And it shall come to pass, that from one new moon to another, and from one Sabbath to another, shall all flesh come to worship before me, saith the LORD"* (Isa 66:22,23). What kind of God would be so impulsive that first required to keep the seventh day and then the first, and in the new earth, go back to the seventh? For me He would be inconsistent and unreliable. What if he does the same with His decision to save me, changing His mind? This will give such insecurity to believers that would be like pulling the petals of a daisy: "He loves me, He loves me not." I am so grateful that He does not change *"For I am the LORD, I change not..."* (Malachi 3:6).

In regards to the true Sabbath, it is a very clear matter; it could not possibly be more black and white: the seventh day Sabbath is the day God wants me to keep and Sunday is not. It does not matter who tells me to keep Sunday sacred. My pastor will not save me, neither my parents or spouse or friends. This is not about being legalistic either. I keep the Sabbath holy to spend the specific time with Jesus that He asked me to spare for Him, not to be saved. He saved me on the cross before I knew about the Sabbath. It is a matter of loyalty and being able to be faithful even in what some consider "little things." Many spiritualize the Sabbath and say that they have a daily Sabbath rest in Jesus. What a lame excuse for not obeying. Is being obedient being legalistic? If your boss asks you for a report, is it legalistic to make the report for him? So, why is it legalistic to observe the Sabbath when I do not mean to keep it to be saved but to be in communion with God?

Now, let us consider the term "legalism."

The term indicates that someone pretends to be saved by obedience, instead of by faith. This word describes the attitudes and practices of the Jews after they returned from their Babylonian exile. They recognized that the reason why they were taken captives from their land was that they violated the commandments, specifically, the 4th (rest on the Sabbath day) and the first two (idolatry). The rabbis decided to create laws that would keep the Israelites saved from further national disgrace. Today, orthodox Jews abstain from certain kinds of labor during the day of rest:

"Observant Jews (primarily orthodox Jews) consider electricity to be a form of fire. These Jews do not turn on lights, ovens, televisions, radios and other electrical appliances on the Sabbath. Instead, prior to the start of the Sabbath, they often plug their electrical appliances into special 'Shabbat clocks' which turn the lights, air conditioners, ovens, on and off at pre-set times." http://judaism.about.com/od/sabbathdayshabb2/f/electricity.htm

As you can see, they got carried away by their tradition (flipping a switch is not a sin), making the Sabbath, a day meant to relax with friends and family and above all, a day to get closer to their Creator, a terrible burden. That is why in Matthew 23: 4 Jesus said: *"For they bind* ***heavy burdens and grievous to be borne****, and lay them on men's shoulders; but they themselves will not move them with one of their fingers."* Jeremiah 8:8 (NIV) shows God's disapproval of what the scribes were already doing even before the exile: *"How can you say, 'We are wise, for we have the law of the LORD,' when actually the lying pen of the scribes has handled it falsely?"* The religious leaders felt that they had the right to create laws and impose them on the people just as if those "commandments of men" were the will of God.

In Jesus' times, the Israelites could not walk more than 1,000 steps because they would be considered to be working on the Sabbath. To get around that rule, they could walk backwards a few steps and then they could walk 1,000 more forward. If any Jewish person had a cold, he could not bring a handkerchief because it would be equivalent to carrying a load. When God forbade lighting a fire on the Sabbath, the Israelites were in the desert. Being in such environment would have required to probably walk for miles to find dry wood (remember, trees are seldom found in a desert), then they would have to walk back to the camp, position the wood and kindling in place and then rub probably one stone against another to try to produce a spark. This whole process would have taken them 3 to 4 hours- probably per meal. They would be so tired and so late for worship that they would stay in their tents and go nowhere, whining all day. The Sabbath was given as a day to worship, to relax (weekly vacation), to observe nature with the family so they could learn from their loving Creator, to take care of the sick, to learn how they could surrender their difficulties, temptations and challenges in the hand of a loving God and thus gain rest for their troubled souls.

The Bible does not teach salvation by works- not even in the Old Testament- as some preacher$ assert. When the Jewish people asked Jesus which works they should do, *"Jesus answered and said unto them, This is the work of God,* ***that ye believe on him*** *whom he hath sent"* (John 6:29). That is right; the work for our salvation is to believe. We are saved by grace through faith (Ephesians 2:8). However, the majority of people stop there. The context continues: *"For we are his workmanship, created in Christ Jesus* ***unto good works****, which God hath before ordained that we should walk in them."* Those works are not executed to be saved but as the verses indicates, God expects us to show our faith trough our actions. *"....the tree is known by his fruit"* (Matthew 12:33), *"Produce fruit in keeping with repentance"* (Matthew 3:8) and James added:

[17] *"Even so faith, if it hath not works, is dead, being alone.* [18]*Yea,*
a man may say, Thou hast faith, and I have works: shew me thy
faith without thy works, and I will shew thee my faith by my works.
[19]*Thou believest that there is one God; thou doest well: the devils*
also believe, and tremble. [20]*But wilt thou know, O vain man, that*
faith without works is dead? [21]*Was not Abraham our father justified*
by works, when he had offered Isaac his son upon the altar? [22]*Seest*
thou how faith wrought with his works, and by works was faith
made perfect? [23]*And the scripture was fulfilled which saith, Abraham*
believed God, and it was imputed unto him for righteousness: and he
was called the Friend of God. [24]*Ye see then how that by works a man*
is justified, and not by faith only. [25]*Likewise also was not Rahab the*
harlot justified by works, when she had received the messengers, and
had sent them out another way? [26]*For as the body without the spirit is*
dead, so faith without works is dead also" (James 2:17-26).

I must repeat, we are not saved by works, but the works inspired by the Holy Spirit are evidence to the world that Jesus lives in us. *"I am crucified with Christ: nevertheless I live; yet not I, but Christ liveth in me: and* ***the life which I now live in the flesh I live by the faith of the Son of God****, who loved me, and gave* *himself for me"* Galatians 2:20. As he also wrote: *"But by the grace of God I am what I am: and his grace which was bestowed upon me was not in vain; but I laboured more abundantly than they all: yet not I,* ***but the grace of God*** *which was with me"* (1 Corinthians 15:10). Dr. Ivan Blazen, a professor from Loma Linda University in California explained it this way in an interview: "what we do for God is a **reaction to His Action**." The same Holy Spirit that guides you to Christ is the same one that produces those fruits of obedience (Philippians 2:13).

"But because God was so gracious, so very generous, here I am. And I'm not about to let his grace go to waste. Haven't I ***worked hard trying to do more*** *than any of the others? Even then, my work didn't amount to all that much.* ***It was God giving me the work to do, God giving me the energy to do it****. So whether you heard it from me or from those others, it's all the same: We spoke God's truth and you entrusted your lives"* (1 Corinthians 15:10 The Message).

"...or in Jesus Christ neither circumcision availeth any thing, nor uncircumcision; but ***faith which worketh by love****"* Galatians 5:6.

And we cannot forget Acts 5:32 *"And we are his witnesses of these things; and so is also the Holy Ghost, whom God hath* ***given to them that obey him****."* It makes me sad to know that those that call me legalist for keeping the Commandments cannot receive the real Holy Spirit for being disobedient to God. They were weighted in balance and were found wanting (Daniel 5). Jesus said: *"If ye love me, keep my commandments."* (John 14:15) and: *"Ye are my friends, if ye do whatsoever I command you"* (John 15:14).

Illustration: Let us say that a father has two sons. One obeys his every command. He obeys because of the loving and trusting relationship between them. For him, obeying his father is not a burden because he loves his father. The other son reasons: "I do not have to obey my father. He knows that I love him and he will love me no matter what. I will inherit anyways." If you were the parent of these two, which one will make you feel appreciated and honored, not to mention, grateful to have such a son?

Jesus also spoke about a father with two sons in the Bible. The father asked both to go and work in the fields. One said yes but never showed up to work. The other had said that he would not go, but ended up going to work. Which one of these two did Jesus said earned the favor of the father? The one that obeyed **because he loved** his father.

I imagine that not killing other people is not considered legalism. Not stealing (being honest) is not called legalism. But eating healthy by limiting fats, not smoking or using drugs, avoiding gluttony and limiting the consumption of sweets, keeping the Sabbath holy (resting, relaxing) it is considered legalism. These practices are just part of the owner's manual instructions.

Whoever told you that I am a legalist, for eating healthy and observing the day of rest specified by God, instead of a man made day of rest, is trying to sell you a skunk while making you believe that it is a rabbit. I am not legalist but the Bible shows that those that are saved by faith are directed by the Spirit to bear fruits, and the law is written in their hearts, which programs them to delight in doing God's will. In contrast, *"the sinful mind is hostile to God. It does not submit to God's law, nor can it do so"* (Romans 8:7 NIV). I always wonder why those that keep Sunday are never called legalist.

You see, a legalist is someone that pretends to earn God's favor by doing things. On the other hand, a Christian obeys because he is saved, not to be saved (Ephesians 2:8-10). What I find amusing is that a Christian can be considered legalist for doing what God expects them to do (keep the Sabbath holy), but they do not consider legalism to expect obedience from their children or from their employees at work or even from the soldiers in our armed forces. After all, obeying the parents is part of the same law. The Bible teaches in Romans, Galatians and Hebrews that Jesus set us free from sin, its condemnation, slavery, the curse of the law and from death. However, it also teaches that He never came to set us free from obedience. He told the woman caught in adultery: "go and sin no more." In other words, since sin is the transgression of the law (1John 3:4), what He said was: "go and do not break the law again." Do you think that Jesus was going to ask an impossibility from her? Never. When Jesus gives a command, He also enables the mortal being to comply with that command. It is only when we try to obey on our own strength that we fail because in our flesh we only have an inclination to do evil. In Christ, we are free to render obedience out of love and gratitude. If a person is released from prison for a crime that he committed, is that person free to go out and break the law, reasoning that now is free? Now all the more must he be careful to keep himself on the good side of the law and stay away from prison.

Now, let us go back to the Sabbath. In chapters two and three I explained some of the verses being used to "prove" that the Sabbath was for the Jews and that the law was nailed to the cross. It is very important that we get acquainted with the Scriptures so we are not deceived. Very soon, we will be faced with a choice whether or not we accept the mark of the beast. The majority of the pastors will be encouraging their congregations to accept it and the flock will accept the mark just because their pastors said so. Right now when a person is told the truth, the most common excuses are:

- I need to ask my pastor- wrong answer- ask your Bible. The pastor is a human being subject to err. According to Paul, the majority of preachers is in the profession for monetary or other kind of gain and corrupts the Word of God. *"For we are not as many, which corrupt the word of God: but as of sincerity, but as of God, in the sight of God speak we in Christ"* (2 Corinthians 2:17). The Contemporary English Version translates the verse like this: *"A lot of people try to get rich from preaching God's message. But we are God's sincere messengers, and by the power of Christ we speak our message with God as our witness."* Jesus was constantly contradicted by the religious leaders of his days. Together with His disciples, He was a minority. Many of the people that believe in His teachings did not break up with the false teachers because *"they loved the praise of men more than the praise of God"* (John 12:43). In like manner, prestige (fame) and money are the motivation that many preachers have to keep teaching error when they already know the truth. It surely seems great for modern day preachers to be popular in TV and have a mega church, but they are driving their congregations down to hell with them.
- That is not what my pastor told me- What is the Holy Spirit telling you through the Bible?

- My pastor told me that the Sabbath is for the Jews- Jesus said: *"...The Sabbath was made for man, and not man for the Sabbath"* (Mark 2:27). The Sabbath was made for ALL mankind not for the Jews. When the Sabbath was kept for the first time, it was by God Himself to spend time with Adam and Eve (Genesis 2:1-3) the very first day after they were created. I hope you listen to Jesus; He will never lead you astray.

If your pastor is not telling you according to the truth, you need Jesus as your new pastor. Read your Bible and take notes. Find a good concordance. Please, even compare what I am presenting here with your Bible (see Acts 17:11). Your salvation will depend greatly on what you do with the resources God put in your hands.

REVELATION 12

A woman with splendid clothing

[1]*And there appeared a great wonder in heaven; a woman clothed with the sun, and the moon under her feet, and upon her head a crown of twelve stars:*

The woman is a symbol of the church (Isaiah 37:22; Song of Solomon 6:10). This woman contrasts that of Revelation 17 known as the great whore. Being dressed with the sun and having the moon under her feet has been interpreted as being dressed with the sunlight of the New Testament with the moon representing the Old Testament. Just like the moon does not have a light of its own but reflects the sun's, so the Old Testament shadows point to their glorious fulfillment in the New Testament.

The word crown is translated from the Greek στέφανος (stephanos), which was a prize in the public games and was worn as a symbol of honor. It was the crown of the victors. The twelve stars have been interpreted as the twelve apostles.

This chapter shares some common elements with chapter eleven. For example:

Chapter 11	Chapter 12
"they ascended up to heaven"	The woman is shown in heaven
The 2 witnesses (Old and New Testament)	The sun and the moon (Old and New Testament)
they shall prophesy a thousand two hundred *and* threescore days, clothed in sackcloth.	And the woman fled into the wilderness… that they should feed her there a thousand two hundred *and* threescore days.
And after three days and an half the Spirit of life from God entered into them, and they stood upon their feet	And the earth helped the woman

[2] *And she being with child cried, travailing in birth, and pained to be delivered.*

If we did not serve the God that we have learned to trust and love, this verse would simply have read: "and being pregnant, the time came for her to deliver." However, our God cares and shows it by inspiring John to use the word βασανίζω (bas-an-id'-zo), which means "to torture: - pain, toil, torment." Even in childbirth when a woman would think the whole world could care less for her terrible anguish and pain, God assures her that He is by her side. Her agony strikes a cord of sympathy in the heart of God. *"I will be glad and rejoice because of your constant love. You see my suffering; you know my trouble"* (Psalm 31:7 *Good News Bible*). I remember my late mother with gratitude. Being nine months pregnant with her first child, she was taken to the hospital in the city in the night and the personnel in turn forgot about the poor country girl. When the first shift "found" her in the morning, she was in a puddle of blood and amniotic fluid. I am glad that God was with her through her travail because that baby was me. God will also be with you even through the painful teenage years of your child (when you probably prefer the childbirth pains over the emotional anguish that he or she is giving you) if you trust Him. He knows all your troubles and challenges as a parent and His hand is ready to help you. He cares for your problems of the daily life and promises to be with you always to the very end.

[3] *And there appeared another wonder in heaven; and behold a great red dragon, having seven heads and ten horns, and seven crowns upon his heads.*

These crowns are different from the one worn by the woman. The word used here comes from the Greek διάδημα (dee-ad'-ay-mah)- a "diadem" (as bound about the head). That is the crown of kings. This crown is usually inherited, not earned. Not all kings have deserved to wear a crown for their behavior is far from honorable. A Biblical example is Jeroboam, one of the kings that got Israel astray from God.

Dragon- Was is a dragon? Mythology worldwide speaks of dragons and flying serpents. We find them from China to Mexico and all over in between. Although I must admit that some con artists have falsified "evidence," it is also true that on the other hand, evolutionists have also falsified fossils to "prove" evolution. However, people that we consider credible, such as the explorer

Marco Polo, have described strange creatures that do not resemble at all what we see in our modern world. Of the creatures that he saw in China, Polo wrote: "The jaws are wide enough to swallow a man, the teeth are large and sharp, and their whole appearance is so formidable that neither man, nor any kind of animal can approach them without terror." (Polo, Marco, *The Travels of Marco Polo*, 1961, pp. 158-159). Scientists want us to believe that these creatures became extinct 60 million years ago and were not contemporary with man. If any such evidence is found, they try to discredit it and even hide it from the general public. Many times unbelievers have claimed that some city or place did not exist because it has not been found. That is no conclusive proof that it was not a real place. For example, many claimed that Ur, the city of Abram was a myth- until it was found and even the tablets in the city mention the Bible character. They said the same about the Hittites- until their cities were found. In the same way, they claim that no human and dinosaur's remains have been found together. If I saw a dinosaur close by, there is no way you will find my remains by his. I would run as far as I could and hide in a cave until the beast disappears and I can be sure I will not be his lunch. I will wait and in due time God will allow the evidence to show. When this happens, I will be the one laughing- although I must admit that I feel sorry for those believing the fallacies of evolution. Regardless of the inaccuracy of carbon dating, they still insist that the dinosaurs lived over 60 million years ago. Time will tell and it is on our side.

What about the Bible? Were dinosaurs in Noah's ark? When we speak of the ark, we usually think of adult animals being housed for over a year. I have thought about nine reasons why the animals in the ark were young and small, opening the possibility that dinosaurs were in the ark too:

1. The Bible uses the word nests in the description of the ark, indicating that the creatures taken by Noah were young.
2. They would need less food
3. They would produce less waste
4. They would be less aggressive
5. They would need less space
6. They would be easier to handle
7. They would adapt better to the new environment

8. Noah and his family would have more free time (feeding and cleaning less) and more fun with the animals during the long stay in the ark.
9. Being young, the animals would have more reproductive years left to repopulate the planet.

The Bible does mention creatures that do not resemble any creature alive that we know of today. They are called leviathan and behemoth. In some passages, the translators used the word serpent.

The description of these creatures in the book of job indicates that they were terrible and inspired fear. That is why John is presented with the image of a dragon to represent Satan- complete with tail. The first one that Job mentions was the behemoth.

"Look at Behemoth, which I made along with you. It eats grass as cattle do. Look at the strength in its back muscles, the power in its stomach muscles. It makes its tail stiff like a cedar. The ligaments of its thighs are intertwined. Its bones are bronze tubes. They are like iron bars. Behemoth is the first of God's conquests. <u>Its maker approaches it with his sword</u>....*Though the river flows powerfully against it, it's not alarmed. It's confident even when the Jordan rushes against its mouth. Can anyone blind its eyes or pierce its nose with snares?"* (Job 40:15-19,23,24 *God's Word*).

Which animal could be as formidable as the behemoth? Certainly, it was not any known today, as some declare erroneously that it was a hippopotamus. I have never seen a hippo with a tale like a cedar. Then the book of Job mentions the leviathan:

"Can you pull Leviathan out of the water with a fishhook or tie its tongue down with a rope? Can you put a ring through its nose or pierce its jaw with a hook?... *Can you fill its hide with harpoons or its head with fishing spears?... Certainly, any hope of defeating it is a false hope. Doesn't the sight of it overwhelm you? No one is brave enough to provoke Leviathan. Then who can stand in front of me?...I will not be silent about Leviathan's limbs, its strength, or its graceful form. Who can skin its hide? Who can approach it with a harness? Who can open its closed mouth? Its teeth are surrounded by terror. Its back has rows <u>of scales that are tightly sealed</u>. One is so close to the*

other that there is no space between them. Each is joined to the other. They are locked together and inseparable. When Leviathan sneezes, it gives out a flash of light. Its eyes are like the first rays of the dawn. Flames shoot from its mouth. Sparks of fire fly from it. Smoke comes from its nostrils like a boiling pot heated over brushwood. Its breath sets coals on fire, and a flame pours from its mouth. Strength resides in its neck, and power dances in front of it. ... Its chest is solid like a rock, solid like a millstone. The mighty are afraid when Leviathan rises. Broken down, they draw back. A sword may strike it but not pierce it. Neither will a spear, lance, or dart. It considers iron to be like straw and bronze to be like rotten wood. An arrow won't make it run away. Stones from a sling turn to dust against it. It considers clubs to be like stubble, and it laughs at a rattling javelin. Its underside is like sharp pieces of broken pottery. It stretches out like a threshing sledge on the mud. It makes the deep sea boil like a pot. It stirs up the ocean like a boiling kettle. It leaves a shining path behind it so that the sea appears to have silvery hair. Nothing on land can compare to it. It was made fearless" (Job 41:1-33 *God's Word*). This is definitely not the description of a crocodile as some suppose. It was a ferocious creature, for sure now extinct that inspired terror and was indomitable.

Isaiah 27:1 calls this creature a serpent and a dragon just like this chapter of Revelation. *"In that day the LORD with his sore and great and strong sword shall punish leviathan the piercing serpent, even leviathan that crooked serpent; and he shall slay the dragon that is in the sea."* Therefore, this was a deep-sea creature that no man could conquer- unlike a crocodile or a hippopotamus- a creature that could breathe fire and smoke, with practically impenetrable and indestructible skin and that only its Maker could strike dead. Likewise, no man can fight Satan, who lives among the sea of people, on his own because there is no moral strength in us to fight him. The dragon is too strong for us and only the Lord can destroy him with His double-edged Sword.

4 And his tail drew the third part of the stars of heaven, and did cast them to the earth: and the dragon stood before the woman which was ready to be delivered, for to devour her child as soon as it was born.

According to verse 9, the dragon is Satan. Those stars are heavenly angels that joined him in his rebellion against God. What was his sin? Isaiah indicates that Satan was pompous and self-exalted. He dared to covet the position of God, at least that of Christ. *"How art thou fallen from heaven, O Lucifer, son of the morning! How art thou cut down to the ground, which didst weaken the nations! For thou hast said in thine heart, **I** will ascend into heaven, **I** will exalt my throne above the stars of God: **I** will sit also upon the mount of the congregation, in the sides of the north: **I** will ascend above the heights of the clouds; **I** will be like the most High"* (Isaiah 14:12-14). Five times, he used the pronoun "I," with the last one uncovering his real purpose: to be like God, but not in character; only in power and authority. All the conflicts between good and evil center on the issue of worship:

Event	Issue
War in heaven	Satan wanted to be worshipped
Fall of man	Worship- whom they trusted and obeyed
Temptation of Christ	Satan wanted to be worshipped by Jesus
Mark of the beast	Worship day- Sabbath of God vs. Sunday of man

The chapter starts with a cosmic battle describing how evil first appeared in the universe. It ends showing that the battle will end at the level of the human heart when Satan makes his last efforts to fight against those that- like once he did- *"keep the commandments of God"* (verse 17). He knows that those beings are going to occupy the place that he voluntarily relinquished when he rebelled against God and he, as selfish as always, wars against them with the attitude: "if I cannot enjoy it, nobody will." God has provided everything needed for you to enjoy heaven. Just like in the case of Eve in the Garden, it will ultimately be up to you whom you are going to believe and where you will spend eternity (although the word properly applies to only one choice).

Drew- σύρω (soo'-ro) – to trail: - ***drag***, draw, hale.

Cast- βάλλω (bal'-lo) – to throw (in various applications, more or less violent or intense): - arise, cast (out), strike, throw (down), **thrust**.

Satan dragged and thrust the angels. From those two words, I infer that the deception of Satan, like any other deception, bruised the soul of those that accepted it. *"For none of us liveth to himself, and no man dieth to himself"*, wrote Paul (Romans 14:7). Satan's eloquent reasonings cause the lost of one third of the heavenly angels. Just because Satan was a non-conformist and was outspoken in his dissatisfaction, the perversion of his "right" to speak has caused disgrace to all the universe and dishonor to himself, once the most exalted angel. It is marvelous to live in a society where there is freedom of expression, where we can speak up our minds on whatever subject we deem proper. However, when our comments can produce doubt, discouragement and disappointment in those that listen our comments, we join the ranks of Satan by doing his work. We need to pray like David to put a guard to our mouths. *"Set a watch, O LORD, before my mouth; keep the door of my lips"* (Psalm 141:3). Although we have the freedom to speak, not always what comes from our mouths is water of life but often produces a bitterness that dries the soul of others. Sometimes what we speak is just like a drop of cyanide diluted in water. I would not drink a cup of water if I know there is cyanide for poison is not to be trusted. Nevertheless, I am conscious that I myself have been guilty of spilling poison with my words. The most lamentable part of that is that I cannot take back the words I pronounced. How can I undo what I have done? I can only pray that God intervene and will bring healing. When we speak, we should remember the words of Jesus regarding the fruit of our lips. *"And he said, that which cometh out of the man, that defileth the man. For from within, out of the heart of men, proceed evil thoughts, adulteries, fornications, murders, Thefts, covetousness, wickedness, deceit, lasciviousness, an evil eye, blasphemy, pride, foolishness: All these evil things come from within, and defile the man."* (Marcus 7:20-23).

There is no safe way to erect ourselves as judges over others- which we do when we criticize- even what could be construed as a seemingly innocent comment could unleash a chain of events that could cause great damage. *"For in many things we offend all. If any man offend not in word, the same is a perfect man, and able also to bridle the whole body.... Even so, the tongue is a little member, and boasteth great things. Behold, how great a matter a little fire kindleth! And the tongue is a fire, a world of iniquity: so is the tongue among our members, that it defileth the whole body, and setteth on fire the course of nature; and it is set on fire of hell... But the tongue can no man tame; it is an unruly evil, full of deadly poison. Therewith bless we God, even the Father; and therewith curse we men, which are made after the similitude of God. Out of the same mouth proceedeth blessing and cursing. My brethren, these things ought not so to be"* (James 3:2,5,6, 8-10). David's approach was *"...I said, I will take heed to my ways, that I sin not with my tongue: I will keep my mouth with a bridle, while the wicked is before me"* (Psalm 39:1). Let us not be a stumbling block for Jesus' little ones and *"Let the words of my mouth, and the meditation of my heart, be acceptable in thy sight, O LORD, my strength, and my redeemer"* (Psalm 19:14).

The third part of the stars of heaven- that was the quantity of angels that joined Satan in his rebellion; it gives me relief to know that there are twice more faithful angels than rebels (2/3 vs. 1/3).

5 *And she brought forth a man child, who was to rule all nations with a rod of iron: and her child was caught up unto God, and to his throne.*

The woman is shown at the point in church history when the type meets the antitype, for that child is Jesus, born from the Jewish nation as promised, from the seed of Abraham. *"...in thee shall all the families of the earth be blessed"* (Genesis 12:3). On his deathbed, Jacob blessed his children and said: *"The sceptre shall not depart from Judah, nor a lawgiver from between his feet, until Shiloh come; and unto him shall the gathering of the people be"* (Genesis 49:10). Shiloh was a nickname of the Messiah. Balaam, the corrupt prophet added: *"I shall see him, but not now: I shall behold him, but not nigh: there shall come a <u>Star out of Jacob</u>, and a Sceptre shall rise out of Israel, and shall smite the corners of Moab, and destroy all the children of Sheth"* (Numbers 24:17). For centuries, the Jewish nation looked forward to the coming of the glorious Messiah, but when He came, they rejected and crucified Him because He did not fulfill their expectations. They wanted a military hero to set them free from the Romans, without realizing that being slaves of sin was the worst oppression that they were under and only Jesus could set them free.

The phrase "to rule" – from the Greek ποιμαίνω (poy-mah'ee-no) does not convey the idea of a tyrant, but rather, it communicates a tender leadership. It means "to tend as a shepherd."

6 *And the woman fled into the wilderness, where she hath a place prepared of God, that they should feed her there a thousand two hundred and threescore days.*

See comment on verse 14.

7 *And there was war in heaven: Michael and his angels fought against the dragon; and the dragon fought and his angels,*

Michael, the only archangel mentioned in the Bible, was the leader of the angels, although He was not an angel Himself as many, based on tradition- not on the Bible- are made to believe. If He were an angel, the text would read: "Michael and the other angels." In that way, there would be no doubt as to his nature. I considered the correct understanding of this subject to be so important that I dedicated the next few pages to analyze it.

Who is Michael?

Before reading this section, I suggest that you rid your mind of prejudice and pray that the Holy Spirit guide your understanding. Notice that the evidence is from the Bible not from "I think" or "I believe" or "this is the opinion of." If the Bible speaks, I believe it.

Who is Michael? The name means, "Who is like God?" Paul presents Jesus as *"being in the form of God"* (Philippians 2:6), *"the image of the invisible God"* (Colossians 1:15) and *"the express image of His person"* (Hebrews 1:3). He is the only being that is like God. He is not created. Jesus is the Creator Himself.

"Jude (verse 9) declares that Michael is the (definite article-indicates that there is only one) Archangel. This word signifies 'head, or chief, angel,' and in our text, Gabriel calls Him 'one (the margin reads, *the first*) of the chief princes.' There can be but one archangel, and hence it is manifestly improper to use the word in the plural as some do. The Scriptures never so use it. In 1

Thessalonians 4: 16, Paul states that when the Lord appears the second time to raise the dead, the voice of the archangel is heard. Whose voice is heard when the dead are raised?-The voice of the Son of God. (John 5: 28.) Putting these scriptures together, they prove that the dead are called from their graves by the voice of the Son of God, that the voice which is then heard is the voice of the Archangel [no creature has power over death], proving that the Archangel is the Son of God, and that the Archangel is called Michael, from which it follows that Michael is the Son of God. In the last verse of Daniel 10, He is called "your Prince," and in the first of Daniel 12, "the great Prince which stands [see Acts 7:55] for the children of thy people," expressions which can appropriately be applied to Christ, but to no other being." Uriah Smith in *The Prophecies of Daniel*, page 129.

In Greek, the word archangel appears only **twice** and in both cases is called the archangel, indicating that there is only one. Archangel means ruler of the angels.

There are three Hebrew words translated as angel. The First one, mal'âk (pronounced mal-awk') is also the most common. It means messenger and also a prophet, king or angel. The second is elôhîym (pronounced el-o-heem') and means God, great, judge, and mighty. This one is translated for angel only in Psalm 8:5. The third one is 'abbîyr (pronounced ab-beer') and it is translated as angel, mighty one, strong (one). Is it a coincidence that Jesus is called prophet, king, God, judge and mighty one also? The word angel in the New Testament comes from the Greek angelos (aggelos) and means messenger.

In the Old Testament, there were occasions when an angel appeared to some people and was worshipped or treated as Deity. If this were a common angel, he would not have accepted any homage from man. When John was so impressed by an angel that wanted to worship him, he was not allowed to do it: *"And I fell at his feet to worship him. And he said unto me, See [thou do it] not: I am thy fellow servant..."* (Revelation 19:10). Let us see Exodus 3:2, 4-6. *"and the Angel of the Lord appeared to him [Moses] in a flame of fire out of the midst of a bush...God called to him out of the midst of a bush...And He said, Draw not nigh hither: put off thy shoes from off thy feet, for the place whereon thou standest is holy ground.*

Moreover He said, ***I am the God of Abraham****...*" at first, we see the Angel of the Lord, but when He speaks, reveals himself as God.

Let us see Joshua 5: 13-15 where Joshua thinks that he sees a soldier, but He identifies Himself as the leader of the angels:

13 *"And it came to pass, when Joshua was by Jericho, that he lifted up his eyes and looked, and, behold, there stood a man over against him with his sword drawn in his hand: and Joshua went to him, and said to him, Art thou for us, or for our adversaries?*

14 *And he said, Nay; but as captain of the host of the LORD am I now come. And Joshua fell on his face to the earth, and did worship, and said to him, What saith my Lord to his servant?*

15 *And the captain of the LORD'S host said to Joshua, Loose thy shoe from off thy foot; for the place whereon thou standest is holy. And Joshua did so."*

Here we can see that Joshua worshipped Him and called Him Lord. Also, the ground was called holy. Only the presence of God himself can make a place holy. The captain of the host is the Archangel, one that can be worshipped and is called Lord, one that makes holy the ground where He appears. We can see that this Archangel is not a creature. He is the Lord, the Creator.

Then, we have Manoah asking the name of the Angel (it was a common pagan belief that knowing the secret name of a deity, gave power over that deity, sort of like a genie).

"And the angel of the LORD said to him, Why askest thou thus after my name, seeing it is secret? So Manoah took a kid with a meat offering, and offered it upon a rock to the LORD: and the angel did wonderously; and Manoah and his wife looked on. For it came to pass, when the flame went up toward heaven from off the altar, that the angel of the LORD ascended in the flame of the altar. And Manoah and his wife looked on it, and fell on their faces to the ground [an act of worship]. But the angel of the LORD did no more appear to Manoah and to his wife. Then Manoah knew that he was an angel of the LORD." And Manoah said to his wife, We shall surely die, because we have seen God" (Judges 13:18-22).

First, Manoah was told that the mane of the angel was "secret." The word for secret in Hebrew is pâlîy' and can be translated also as wonderful. Where else did we see that word? In Isaiah 9:6 where the Messiah is called "wonderful (Hebrew 'pele')." Both words are from the same root. The angel was saying "I am the one whose name is Wonderful, Admirable." Second, Manoah and his wife worshiped Him and they were not prohibited from doing so. Third, and more important, He was called God.

Genesis 16:7-13 presents the Angel of the Lord talking to Agar. Let us read verses 10-13:

"And the angel of the LORD said to her, I will multiply thy seed exceedingly, that it shall not be numbered for multitude. [can a simple angel, a creature, make such a promise?] And the angel of the LORD said to her, Behold, thou art with child, and shalt bear a son, and shalt call his name Ishmael; because the LORD hath heard thy affliction. And he will be a wild man; his hand will be against every man, and every man's hand against him; and he shall dwell in the presence of all his brethren. And she called the name of the LORD that spoke to her, Thou GOD seest me: for she said, Have I also here looked after him that seeth me?"

She called the angel God. If this were a mistake, the Bible would have omitted it. God would not allow it to be registered so we could be misled. That specific angel was Jesus pre-incarnated.

Malachi 3:1 says that *"the Lord will come to his temple, even the messenger [Hebrew angel] of the covenant, whom ye delight in."* The Hebrew word for messenger in this verse is mal'âk, and we already presented that it means angel. In other words, the Angel of the Covenant is called Lord.

When Abraham was asked to sacrifice his son, the angel talked to the father of the faithful in first person and called himself The Lord (Genesis 22:15,16):

"And the angel of the LORD called to Abraham out of heaven the second time, And said, By myself have I sworn, saith the LORD, for because thou hast done this thing, and hast not withheld thy son, thine only son..."

Now, why is Jesus presented as an angel? That is easy to answer. Do you remember Hebrews 1:1,2?

"God, who at sundry times and in divers manners spoke in time past to the fathers by the prophets, Hath in these last days spoken to us by his Son..."

Jesus is the spokesman of the Trinity. That is why He is presented as an angel (messenger). It is a matter of role-playing and not a matter of status. He is also presented as a lion and a lamb for the same reason. Michael is Jesus, "who is like God." Jesus is not an angel, but the commander of the angels. "The president of the United States is the 'chief' of the armed forces of his country. That does not make him a soldier. The fact that the archangel is the chief of the entire angelic host does not imply that He is a created being." Henry Feyerabend, *Daniel Verse by Verse* page 154.

For more biblical information on this topic, log on to www.amazingfacts.org and enter Michael in the search box.

[8] *And prevailed not; neither was their place found any more in heaven.*[9] *And the great dragon was cast out, that old serpent, called the Devil, and Satan, which deceiveth the whole world: he was cast out into the earth, and his angels were cast out with him.*

Four times this chapter mentions that the Devil was cast out:

Rev 12:9- *the great dragon was cast out*

Rev 12:9- *he was cast out into the earth, and his angels were cast out with him*

Rev 12:10- *the accuser of our brethren is cast down*

Rev 12:13- *the dragon saw that he was cast unto the earth*

The emphasis is to assure us that he no longer has access to heaven to expose your sins before God and accuse you of not deserving to enter heaven. Remember that after all, Satan's attitude is, if he cannot be there, why would you?

Deceiveth- πλανάω plan-ah'-o- means to go astray, deceive, err, seduce, wander, be out of the way.

10 And I heard a loud voice saying in heaven, Now is come salvation, and strength, and the kingdom of our God, and the power of his Christ: for the accuser of our brethren is cast down, which accused them before our God day and night.

Among the woes of Revelation, there are plenty of reasons for celebration. All of them center on Jesus' victory over evil. However, His victories are not His alone. Whenever He overcomes, we receive great benefits. In this case, the accuser is no longer allowed to enter heaven to claim us for himself. We must remember that although it seems that evil triumphs, the ultimate victory will be the Lord's.

11 And they overcame him by the blood of the Lamb, and by the word of their testimony; and they loved not their lives unto the death.

We, as sinners were completely separated from God. He sent Jesus to reunite us to Him. We were the offenders, but God loves us so much that He took it upon Himself to take the first step for that reconciliation to be a reality. On our own power, we cannot overcome temptations, but God showed us a way out: the blood of the Lamb. When the accuser wants to make you depressed because of your sins, remember that Jesus shed His precious blood to purchase your pardon and set you free. Remember that through that blood you can also overcome the Devil and all that he wants to throw at you.

The word testimony comes from the Greek μαρτυρία (mar-too-ree'-ah) and means "record, report, testimony, witness." It comes from μάρτυς (mar'-toos) the word for martyr. To those that encounter death in the service of the Master, He promises that *"whosoever will lose his life for my sake, the same shall save it"* (Luke 9:24) and *"he that hateth his life in this world shall keep it unto life eternal"* (John 12:25). Sometimes death is a blessing in disguise for the victim and for others. For example, death can "seal" a person for salvation, since dead people do not sin. This would have been the case with King Hezekiah. He was told that he would die. At that time, he was faithful to God so he could have died saved. However, he bargained with God to extend his life. During those extra years, he departed from God and it almost cost his salvation. There are other times when the death of an individual opens the doors for others to be saved. Although Steven was stoned by Saul and his followers (Acts chapter 7), his death was undoubtedly an important element in the future conversion of his killer into Paul the apostle. I remember a church in Añasco, Puerto Rico that got started after a church member died. Her eight children accepted Bible studies, joined the church and started a new and vibrant congregation. She did not live to see any of her children follow her steps when she was alive and surely died disappointed, but her death made her offspring reflect and surrender their lives to their mother's Savior. Unlike the non-believers that die without hope, we have the sure promises of God that we will have eternal life and who knows, the seed that he have planted all our lives might bring more fruit that when we lived. Have you ever gone to the funeral home for the viewing of a Christian? Did you notice the peace and even the smile in his or her face? A Christian dies with hope, which brings joy and peace. A non-believer dies thinking: "this is it. I am going to die in a few seconds and there is nothing else." I prefer to die as a believer with a smile on my face because I know that not only is God real, but also His promises will be kept and I am going to rise again to eternal life when Jesus returns.

They loved not their lives unto the death – Death is just like falling asleep (John 11) and from the time we die until we resurrect to go to heaven it will seem like we blinked. Those that think that killing a follower of Jesus gives them victory over us are in for a big surprise. Our blood will seal our destiny for eternity in heaven for we love more Jesus than our temporary lives on this earth.

[12] *Therefore rejoice, ye heavens, and ye that dwell in them. Woe to the inhabiters of the earth and of the sea! For <u>the devil is come down unto you</u>, having great wrath, because he knoweth that he hath but a short time.*

This verse clarifies the others that indicate that the Devil was cast down to earth. That phrase indicates his defeat. Here it is clear that the Devil came to this earth on his own looking for followers for his cause. Unfortunately, after being defeated in heaven, he won the two votes (Adam and Eve) on the earthly elections and became an absolute tyrant.

He hath but a short time – Now, that is a great reason for celebration. Soon the Devil will be no more. It was 2,000 years ago when John wrote these words but compared to eternity, it is indeed a very short time.

13 *And when the dragon saw that he was cast unto the earth, he persecuted the woman, which brought forth the man child.*

The dragon is said to be Satan (Revelation 12:9) but his chief instrument in making war against Jesus and His followers during the first centuries of the Christian era was the Roman Empire. He influenced Herod to try to put the Savior to death. The dragon primarily represents Satan but in a secondary sense, it is a symbol of pagan Rome. This enmity between the woman and Satan was prophesied in the book of Genesis chapter three: *"And I will put enmity between thee and the woman, and between thy seed and her seed; it shall bruise thy head, and thou shalt bruise his heel"* (verse 15). When Jesus died on the cross, He sealed Satan's destiny, thus wounding him on the head. Paul described it this way: *"Forasmuch then as the children are partakers of flesh and blood, he also himself likewise took part of the same; that through death he might destroy him that had the power of death, that is, the devil"* (Hebrews 2:14). The Devil will not live forever. We will see the Bible proof in chapter 20.

14 *And to the woman were given two wings of a great eagle, that she might fly into the wilderness, into her place, where she is nourished for a time, and times, and half a time, from the face of the serpent.*

A time, and times, and half a time – A time is one year, times is two years and half a time is six months. The Jewish calendar had 360 days. This time described here is the same 42 months that the holy city would be *"tread under foot"* and it's also the *"thousand two hundred and threescore days"* when the two witnesses would prophesy *"clothed in sackcloth"* in chapter 11. This period refers to the time (538 AD to 1798 AD) when the popular church oppressed, persecuted and killed those that dared to believe the Bible and keep the Sabbath holy. The message to the church of Thyatira applies to this time. There was among the church leaders tolerance and even the promotion of idolatry and immorality. The history of the popes is full of examples of corruption, tyranny and oppression. Even the papal throne had its price. Many popes had mistresses and placed their illegitimate sons in positions of leadership in the church. Worst of all were the bulls written to create the crusades and the inquisition, killing millions of innocent men, women and even babies.

15 And the serpent cast out of his mouth water as a flood after the woman, that he might cause her to be carried away of the flood.

Cast out of his mouth – Since the false church did not have its own army (cheaper that way, so it could accumulate the riches described in chapter 18), it ordered the kings of the nations to do the dirty job. They followed the model of the Jewish authorities when they brought Jesus to Pilate to be executed. The Pharisees did not want to contaminate themselves by entering in the pagan palace and depended on the Romans to kill Jesus. So the popes in many occasions just commanded the civil authorities to send their armies after the Protestants. The water shown here is a symbol of the multitudes (Revelation 17:15) that the false church sent to fight the real church, here represented by a woman.

16 And the earth helped the woman, and the earth opened her mouth, and swallowed up the flood which the dragon cast out of his mouth.

Revelation 11 and 12 have a striking similitude with the experience of the Israelites leaving Egypt:

Exodus	Revelation 11 & 12
The Israelites were oppressed as slaves in Egypt	In Revelation 11 the true witnesses suffered oppression in spiritual Egypt
A child was born (Moses) that would become a ruler but the dragon* wanted to kill him as soon as he was born	The dragon wanted to kill the child that was to become a ruler (Jesus) as soon as he was born
The Israelites applied blood of a lamb to their doors when they were set free	The brethren overcame Satan (were set free) by the blood of the Lamb. V. 11
God took the Israelites on eagles wings- Ex. 19:4	To the woman were given two wings of a great eagle

The Israelites headed for the wilderness	The woman was to fly to the wilderness. V.14
Pharaoh and the Egyptian army followed the Israelites to kill them in wrath. Ex. 14:5,9	The serpent cast water (multitudes) to kill the woman. "For the Devil came down to you, having great wrath, knowing that he has but a little time." V.12. "the dragon... persecuted the woman who bore the man *child*." V. 13
The Egyptian army drowned	The earth swallowed up the flood
The Israelites were fed in the desert	The woman was fed in the wilderness. V. 14
Enemies attacked the Israelites on the way to Canaan	"And the serpent cast out of his mouth water like a flood after the woman, so that he might cause her to be carried away by the river." V. 15
Satan raised enemies from within to destroy the unity and sanctity of the children of God (Datan and his followers). The earth opened up and swallowed up the enemy	"And the earth opened its mouth and swallowed up the river which the dragon cast out of his mouth." V.16
They received the Ten Commandments	They are those that keep the commandments. V. 17
A remnant entered the promised land (original adults died in the desert)	A remnant is left

*Pharaoh is compared to a dragon: *"Speak, and say, Thus saith the Lord GOD; Behold, I am against thee, Pharaoh king of Egypt, the great dragon ...."* (Ezekiel 29:3).

[17] And the dragon was wroth with the woman, and went to make war with the remnant of her seed, which keep the commandments of God, and have the testimony of Jesus Christ.

Since the army sent against the church failed its commission, Satan takes matters into his own hands and wars against the remnant. Why are they called remnant? The word is translated from the Greek λοιποί (loy-poy'), which means, "remaining ones, which remain, remnant, residue, rest." In other words, through seductions like those presented by Balac on the suggestion of Balaam, threats and deceiving miracles, Satan will manage to ensnare the majority of Christians. Remember how he approached Jesus in the desert?

He told Jesus: *"All these things will I give thee, if thou wilt fall down and worship me"* (Matthew 4:9). After studying the human nature and every individual since birth, demons know each human's weakness and those things that made us fall in the past will be presented in abundance to those that profess to follow Christ, to snatch if it were possible, even the elect. Daily we are confronted with our share of temptations. Being a Christian does not exempt any of us from troubles- They seem to multiply for some when becoming believers. If you do not have trials and challenges it could be because Satan already got you, but you can be set free by Christ. Having difficulties in this world is not a proof that we are Christians, but woe unto him who do not suffer at all.

How is the war waged against the commandment-keeping remnant of believers? If we look at Jesus' life, we can have a clear idea of what to expect. His enemies concocted lies and spoke half-truths against Him. He was criticized for everything He did- not even His brothers believed in Him. Wherever He went, He suffered contradiction. Jesus was also victim of physical abuses. He was beaten, flocked, spat on, and finally crucified. It was no different with His followers. Of His eleven disciples and Paul, only John died a natural death. All the rest died assassinated. Paul records his own experience: *"Are they ministers of Christ? (I speak as a fool) I am more; in labours more abundant, in stripes above measure, in prisons more frequent, in deaths oft. Of the Jews five times received I forty stripes save one. Thrice was I beaten with rods, once was I stoned, thrice I suffered shipwreck, a night and a day I have been in the deep; In journeyings often, in perils of waters, in perils of robbers, in perils by mine own countrymen, in perils by the heathen, in perils in the city, in perils in the wilderness, in perils in the sea, in perils among false brethren; In weariness and painfulness, in watchings often, in hunger and thirst, in fastings often, in cold and nakedness"* (2 Corinthians 11:23-27). However, Paul was more concerned for the salvation of the people than for the treatment that he was receiving while preaching the good news: *"Beside those things that are without, that which cometh upon me daily, the care of all the churches. Who is weak, and I am not weak? Who is offended, and I burn not?"* (2 Corinthians 11:28,29).

The true church to which all the disciples were affiliated was considered <u>a sect</u>. *"But this I confess unto thee, that after* ***<u>the Way</u>***

***which they call a sect**, so serve I the God of our fathers, believing all things which are according to the law, and which are written in the prophets"* (Acts 24:14 ASV). The Greek word αἵρεσις means heresy, sect. Today the church that keeps the Commandments is called a cult. Yes, popular preachers, for lack of Biblical arguments against the truth recur to name calling as it would a bullish child in a playground, envious of whom he calls a nerd. So the true church of the last days will suffer verbal insults from those that are supposed to be watchmen; from those responsible to tell their congregations of the imminent disaster that is coming upon this earth. Instead of joining those that believed and followed the truth, they dedicate their time in radio, TV, the internet and the written word to launch attacks against those that uphold the bloodstained banner of the truth. *"Thou hast given a banner to them that fear thee, that it may be displayed because of the truth"* (Psalm 60:4). All the popular TV preachers have been shown the truth but they refuse to accept it because they fear to lose their influence and audience, not to mention their income. They show to love the glory of men more than they love God. But Jesus said: *"If ye love me, keep my commandments"* (John 14:15).

"The dignitaries of church and state will unite to bribe, persuade, or compel all classes to honor the Sunday. The lack of divine authority will be supplied by oppressive enactments. Political corruption is destroying love of justice and regard for truth; and even in free America, rulers and legislators, in order to secure public favor, will yield to the popular demand for a law enforcing Sunday observance. Liberty of conscience, which has cost so great a sacrifice, will no longer be respected. In the soon-coming conflict we shall see exemplified the prophet's words: 'The dragon was wroth with the woman, and went to make war with the remnant of her seed, which keep the commandments of God, and have the testimony of Jesus Christ.' Revelation 12:17.

"The apostle John in vision heard a loud voice in heaven exclaiming: 'Woe to the inhabiters of the earth and of the sea! For the devil is come down unto you, having great wrath, because he knoweth that he hath but a short time.' Revelation 12:12. Fearful are the scenes which call forth this exclamation from the heavenly voice. The wrath of Satan increases as his time grows short, and his work of deceit and destruction will reach its culmination in the time of trouble." *The Great Controversy*, page 592

Satan aims to cause suffering so people blame God and turn their backs on Him. Everywhere we see calamities such as hurricanes, tornadoes, earthquakes, epidemics, man-made disasters like the BP oil spill in the gulf of Mexico, etc. It seems like he does not take a month off so we can recuperate from one disaster when the next one hits. The enemy of our souls is preparing the nations to lay the blame on those that keep the Commandments of God.

The seventh day Sabbath is at the center of those despised Ten Commandments. It was never abolished, neither was it changed into Sunday. If your preacher tells you that the Sabbath was for the Jews and Christians are not obligated to keep it, in spite of the overwhelming Biblical evidence on favor of the Sabbath, you better think twice about going back to that church. How come the other nine commandments are not for the Jews? For the sake of your soul, take Jesus' side regardless of how popular the preacher is. In the times of Jesus, the high priests Annas and Caiaphas were very popular, but both asked for Jesus to be crucified. Being in the wrong side of the conflict will bring terrible results. There were two groups of people when Jesus went before Pilate: two of His scared disciples and the bloodthirsty mob. That crowd had listened to His teachings and witnessed His miracles. Just a few days before, Jesus had the triumphal entry in Jerusalem and the multitudes followed Him with songs and exclamations of joy. Now they were claiming for His crucifixion. Their leaders went against the Bible counsel that they knew well: *"Thou shalt not raise a false report: put not thine hand with the wicked to be an unrighteous witness. Thou shalt not follow a multitude to do evil; neither shalt thou speak in a cause to decline after many to wrest judgment"* (Exodus 23:1,2). How easy it is to follow the crowd to do the wrong thing even when we know better. Very soon, you and I will be confronted with a choice of loyalties. Satan is in control of the apostate churches (the harlots of Revelation 17:5) but God has a small number of believers that follow Him faithfully. Either we follow Jesus and keep the real Sabbath holy, or we follow the majority to worship in the wrong day and thus turn our backs on our loving Savior. It will be a matter of a heaven to win and a hell to shun. No, keeping the Sabbath will not save us because that will be a legalistic claim. However, Jesus

Notice how she is called mother of God and also that people ask her to intercede on their behalf in life and death. It is argued that a mother has authority over her son. This means that she can command God. Why not pray to Jesus? Because Catholicism teaches that His death on the cross left Jesus without mercy and sinners now need to go to Mary for help. This can be read repeatedly in the Catholic book *The Glories of Mary* authored by one of Rome's saints. I remember that when reciting the rosary there were several more Hail Mary's than Our Father's (10:1). Also, when going to the confessionary, I was given more Hail Marys than Our Fathers to pray for my penance. Unfortunately, this good woman that was a servant of God has been exalted even to the level of God to the point of saying now that Mary is our co-redeemer and mediator. The Bible shows only one redeemer and one mediator: both in the person of Jesus alone (1 Timothy 2:5).

The second theological exaltation came in the First Vatican Council (December 1869–October 1870), convoked by Pope Pius IX. It was convened to deal with contemporary problems that were eroding the authority of the church. The Pope feared that the rising influence of rationalism, liberalism, and materialism could threaten the very existence of the church and they needed to counter attack those before it was too late. When the doctrine of the Immaculate Conception was approved, there was an attempt to also proclaim the infallibility of the pope but it was successfully opposed then. Now, at the urging of Pius IX the dogma was approved. This happened in July 18, 1870 by a margin of 533 votes to 2. The dogma, controversial since its inception and of course not Biblical, teaches that the pope is preserved free from error when he teaches a doctrine concerning faith or morals to be taught by the whole church. This dogma came, not from the delegates, but from the pope himself, always hungry for self-exaltation. By declaring himself non-erring, he placed himself at the same level of God. This doctrine contributed to restore the lost prestige and authority of the popes since then and it is playing a mayor role in the healing of the wound.

Following these dogmas that healed the religious phase, the popes worked hard to get recognition from political leaders. In 1929, Benito Mussolini and Pope Pius XI signed the Lateran Treaty, which again made Roman Catholicism the official state religion of Italy. It also granted the Vatican the right to govern itself, becoming a country within a country. This began the political phase of the process of the healing of the deadly wound. Ever since, the world has a more favorable opinion of the Catholic Church and is becoming again a religious and political power, having ambassadors in many Nations of the world and receiving theirs in exchange. However, it will be the second beast of Revelation chapter 13 who will accomplish the healing when the image of the beast is formed and legislation is enacted to favor the Catholic Church. It will not be until the church gains dominion over all the kingdoms of the earth that the wound will be healed.

The Catholic power has been growing through the 20th century and will continue during this new 21st until the whole world falls under its "charm." The church is dictating its will and the governments are happy to please it. In some instances, the church has used its influence to place people in power that can later be of service to the church. To illustrate this, let me show what happened in Germany in the first half of the 20th century. Eugenio Pacelli, who later became known as Pope Pius XII (the Pope during World War II) had negotiated a concordat (agreement between the church and the government) with Hitler in 1933 that opened the doors for him to become dictator. Had not been for the bullying influence of Pacelli, then still a papal nuncio, over the German Catholic leaders, Hitler would have not been able to come to power. In other words, the Catholic Church put and later kept Hitler on power. Pacelli saw in Hitler the champion that the church needed to fight its battles and destroy every one that opposed Catholicism or was not willing to become Catholic. When he became pope in 1939, he had already shown disdain for the Jews. Some people believe that Hitler's holocaust was an assignment from the pope to the Führer whom he called protector of the church. So why were the Jews sent to die in concentration camps? The reason is simple: they have managed to maintain the knowledge of the true Sabbath (Saturday). As long as there is one group of people that keeps the Sabbath holy, Satan and his agents will try to destroy it by any means possible. Satan's final wrath will be directed towards the group that will keep all the Ten Commandments (Revelation 12:17), which of course includes the Sabbath.

Since the plans of the church to return to absolute power failed again with the defeat of Germany, the papacy resorted once more to diplomacy and a fake friendship with the world's most influential people. Rome always likes to move among the powerful and influential individuals because this is a shortcut to reach the masses. This is also an strategy to earn the common citizens trust. If their leader trusts them, then the citizens will likely trust them too. Now is courting every US president and the most prominent world leaders. Chapters 17:2 and 18:3,9 of Revelation indicate its preference to go directly to "kings of the earth". One way or another, Rome wants to exert world dominion again and crush anyone that opposes. How are they working towards that goal now? With covert operations in the background while presenting a face of innocence and good will to the world.

Is there any threat to our national security coming from Rome? America's power is based on its economy. The attack on the Twin Towers in September 11th, 2001 showed how fast a catastrophe could make the stock market drop. The Catholic Church has the American economy in its hands by placing key people in the Federal Reserve Board most important posts. They are in charge of handling the nation's economy. The chairman's decisions of modifying the interest rates directly affect how the stock goes up or down. One brusque or careless movement from the Fed could send investors into a panic frenzy. This could contribute to create the biggest depression in history. The recent approach of the Fed to print paper money for which there is no gold to guarantee its value is driving away investors from the once mighty dollar to more secured assets such as oil, gold and natural resources, and even invest in other countries currency. This paper money printed out of thin air- how it is called by the economists- is producing inflation and devaluation of the dollar, which lost 40% of its value in about ten years. I am convinced that the crisis brought by the collapse of the housing market was just an experiment of what could be done in the future to bring America to its knees. The rest of the world will follow because we know very well that when America sneezes, everyone else gets a cold. We know also that whoever has the gold makes the rules. It was said before the end of the cold war that Rome had more gold than the USA and the former USSR (Russia and its satellites) combined. Why is the Vatican secretly plotting against America? Because the nation holds two of the principles that Rome hates the most: freedom of religion and separation of church and state. According to this chapter of Revelation both will be lost soon. Such is the goal of the papacy and they are using their enormous resources of riches and intelligence (Jesuits) to accomplish it.

Another way in which the Catholic Church is sabotaging our society is by placing their agents into the most important positions in the press to control what is published. In other words, we are getting our news censored. One example of how we get our information through a filter is regarding the new encyclopedias entries on the Inquisition. Old encyclopedias dedicated even whole pages to the subject. The new ones hardly mention it, thus eliminating unfavorable views of the church that could cripple its influence on our affairs. As mentioned earlier, it is now forbidden in Canada to distribute the book *The Great Controversy* (but at least you can still read it for free in the internet). Gradually they are becoming the hand rocking the cradle of future generations of Americans. The present generation of youth does not investigate things on their own. Just as they enjoy fast food devoid of nutrition and fiber, they can be categorized as the summary data generation. The least information the better for them, as long as they are amused with "cool" entertainment. Ron Paul, former U.S. presidential candidate, referring to the importance of education to the freedoms we enjoy as citizens, wrote: "An educated public is an essential ingredient of a free society. Ambitious governments would have far greater difficulty implementing schemes that undermine liberty and prosperity where they faced with an informed and vigilant population."

With the churches uniting and the political and economical crisis boiling in all continents causing panic, the stage is being set now for a powerful <u>one-world church</u> to promote a <u>one-world government</u> of which the pope will be head. The world is now looking to the pope for solutions to the crisis that their governments have been unable to solve. If they only knew that, most of the biggest crisis have been the result of Catholic sabotage. This world really needs a Savior to rescue it from the impending debacle but Jesus is the only one that can really provide a solution; others- the pope included- will serve only their own interests.

The following material (until verse 13:4) was written by Avro Manhattan in his book *The Vatican's Holocaust*, a book that I am sure very soon will disappear:

Extreme Oath of the Jesuits

"When a Jesuit of the minor rank is to be elevated to command, he is conducted into the Chapel of the Convent of the Order, where there are only three others present, the principal or Superior standing in front of the altar. On either side stands a monk, one of whom holds a banner of yellow and white, which are the Papal colors, and the other a black banner with a dagger and red cross above a skull and crossbones, with the word INRI, and below them the words IUSTUM, NECAR, REGES, IMPIOUS. The meaning of which is: It is just to exterminate or annihilate impious or heretical Kings, Governments, or Rulers. Upon the floor is a red cross at which the postulant or candidate kneels. The Superior hands him a small black crucifix, which he takes in his left hand and presses to his heart, and the Superior at the same time presents to him a dagger, which he grasps by the blade and holds the point against his heart, the Superior still holding it by the hilt, and thus addresses the postulant:'

Superior:

"My son, heretofore you have been taught to act the dissembler: among Roman Catholics to be a Roman Catholic, and to be a spy even among your own brethren; to believe no man, to trust no man. Among the Reformers, to be a reformer; among the Huguenots, to be a Huguenot; among the Calvinists, to be a Calvinist; among other Protestants, generally to be a Protestant, and obtaining their confidence, to seek even to preach from their pulpits, and to denounce with all the vehemence in your nature our Holy Religion and the Pope; and even to descend so low as to become a Jew among Jews, that you might be enabled to gather together all information for the benefit of your Order as a faithful soldier of the Pope. You have been taught to insidiously plant the seeds of jealousy and hatred between communities, provinces, states that were at peace, and incite them to deeds of blood, involving them in war with each other, and to create revolutions and civil wars in countries that were independent and prosperous, cultivating the arts and the sciences and enjoying the blessings of peace. To take sides with the combatants and to act secretly with your brother Jesuit, who might be engaged on the other side, but openly opposed to that with which you might be connected, only that the Church might be the gainer in the end, in the conditions fixed in the treaties for peace and that the end justifies the means. You have been taught your duty as a spy, to gather all statistics, facts and information in your power from every source; to ingratiate yourself into the confidence of the family circle of Protestants and heretics of every class and character, as well as that of the merchant, the banker, the lawyer, among the schools and universities, in parliaments and legislatures, and the judiciaries and councils of state, and to be all things to all men, for the Pope's sake, whose servants we are unto death.

"You have received all your instructions heretofore as a novice, a neophyte, and have served as co-adjurer, confessor and priest, but you have not yet been invested with all that is necessary to command in the Army of Loyola in the service of the Pope. You must serve the proper time as the instrument and executioner as directed by your superiors; for none can command here who has not consecrated his labors with the blood of the heretic; for "without the shedding of blood no man can be saved." Therefore, to fit yourself for your work and make your own salvation sure, you will, in addition to your former oath of obedience to your order and allegiance to the Pope, repeat after me---

The Extreme Oath of the Jesuits:

"1, _ now, in the presence of Almighty God, the Blessed Virgin Mary, the blessed Michael the Archangel, the blessed St. John the Baptist, the holy Apostles St. Peter and St. Paul and all the saints and sacred hosts of heaven, and to you, my ghostly father, the Superior General of the Society of Jesus, founded by St. Ignatius Loyola in the Pontificate of Paul the Third, and continued to the present, do by the womb of the virgin, the matrix of God, and the rod of Jesus Christ, declare and swear, that his holiness the Pope is Christ's Vice-regent and is the true and only head of the Catholic or Universal Church throughout the earth; and that by virtue of the keys of binding and loosing, given to his Holiness by my Savior, Jesus Christ, he hath power to depose heretical kings, princes, states, commonwealths and governments, all being illegal without his sacred confirmation and that they may safely be destroyed. Therefore, to the utmost of my power I shall and will defend this doctrine of his Holiness' right and custom against all usurpers of the heretical or Protestant authority whatever, especially the Lutheran of Germany, Holland, Denmark, Sweden, Norway, and the now pretended authority and churches of England and Scotland, and branches of the same now established in Ireland and on the Continent of America and elsewhere; and all adherents in regard that they be usurped and heretical, opposing the sacred Mother Church of Rome. I do now renounce and disown any allegiance as due to any heretical king, prince or state named Protestants or Liberals, or obedience to any of the laws, magistrates or officers.

"I do further declare that the doctrine of the churches of England and Scotland, of the Calvinists, Huguenots and others of the name Protestants or Liberals to be damnable and they themselves damned who will not forsake the same.

"I do further declare, that I will help, assist, and advise all or any of his Holiness' agents in any place wherever I shall be, in Switzerland, Germany, Holland, Denmark, Sweden, Norway, England, Ireland or America, or in any other Kingdom or territory I shall come to, and do my uttermost to extirpate the heretical Protestants or Liberals' doctrines and to destroy all their pretended powers, regal or otherwise.

"I do further promise and declare, that notwithstanding I am dispensed with, to assume my religion heretical, for the propaganda of the Mother Church's interest, to keep secret and private all her agents' counsels from time to time, as they may entrust me and not to divulge, directly or indirectly, by word, writing or circumstance whatever; but to execute all that shall be proposed, given in charge or discovered unto me, by you, my ghostly father, or any of this sacred covenant.

"I do further promise and declare, that I will have no opinion or will of my own, or any mental reservation whatever, even as a corpse or cadaver (perinde ac cadaver), but will unhesitatingly obey each and every command that I may receive from my superiors in the Militia of the Pope and of Jesus Christ.

"That I may go to any part of the world withersoever I may be sent, to the frozen regions of the North, the burning sands of the desert of Africa, or the jungles of India, to the centers of civilization of Europe, or to the wild haunts of the barbarous savages of America, without murmuring or repining, and will be submissive in all things whatsoever communicated to me.

"I furthermore promise and declare that I will, when opportunity present, make and wage relentless war, secretly or openly, against all heretics, Protestants and Liberals, as I am directed to do, to extirpate and exterminate them from the face of the whole earth; and that I will spare neither age, sex or condition; and that I will hang, waste, boil, flay, strangle and bury alive these infamous heretics, rip up the stomachs and wombs of their women and crush their infants' heads against the walls, in order to annihilate forever their execrable race. That when the same cannot be done openly, I will secretly use the poisoned cup, the strangulating cord, the steel of the poniard or the leaden bullet, regardless of the honor, rank, dignity, or authority of the person or persons, whatever may be their condition in life, either public or private, as I at any time may be directed so to do by any agent of the Pope or Superior of the Brotherhood of the Holy Faith, of the Society of Jesus.

"In confirmation of which, I hereby dedicate my life, my soul and all my corporal powers, and with this dagger which I now receive, I will subscribe my name written in my own blood, in testimony thereof; and should I prove false or weaken in my determination, may my brethren and fellow soldiers of the Militia of the Pope cut off my hands and my feet, and my throat from ear to ear, my belly opened and sulphur burned therein, with all the punishment that can be inflicted upon me on earth and my soul be tortured by demons in an eternal hell forever!

"All of which, I, _, do swear by the Blessed Trinity and blessed Sacraments, which I am now to receive, to perform and on my part to keep inviolable; and do call all the heavenly and glorious host of heaven to witness the blessed Sacrament of the Eucharist, and witness the same further with my name written and with the point of this dagger dipped in my own blood and sealed in the face of this holy covenant."

"(He receives the wafer from the Superior and writes his name with the point of his dagger dipped in his own blood taken from over his heart.)

"Superior: 'You will now rise to your feet and I will instruct you in the Catechism necessary to make yourself known to any member of the Society of Jesus belonging to this rank. In the first place, you, as a Brother Jesuit, will with another mutually make the ordinary sign of the cross as any ordinary Roman Catholic would; then one cross his wrists, the palms of his hands open, and the other in answer crosses his feet, one above the other; the first points with forefinger of the right hand to the center of the palm of the left, the other with the forefinger of the left hand points to the center of the palm of the right; the first then with his right hand makes a circle around his head, touching it; the other then with the forefinger of his left hand touches the left side of his body just below his heart; the first then with his right hand draws it across the throat of the other, and the latter then with a dagger down the stomach and abdomen of the first. The first then says Iustum; and the other answers Necar; the first Reges. The other answers Impious.' (The meaning of which has already been explained.) 'The first will then present a small piece of paper folded in a peculiar manner, four times, which the other will cut longitudinally and on opening the name Jesu will be found written upon the head and arms of a cross three times. You will then give and receive with him the following questions and answers:

"Question —From whither do you come? Answer — The Holy faith.

Q. —Whom do you serve?

A. —The Holy Father at Rome, the Pope, and the Roman Catholic Church Universal throughout the world.

Q. —Who commands you?

A. —The Successor of St. Ignatius Loyola, the founder of the Society of Jesus or the Soldiers of Jesus Christ.

Q. —Who received you? A. —A venerable man in white hair.

Q. —How?

A. —With a naked dagger, I kneeling upon the cross beneath the banners of the Pope and of our sacred order.

Q. —Did you take an oath?

A. —I did, to destroy heretics and their governments and rulers, and to spare neither age, sex nor condition. To be as a corpse without any opinion or will of my own, but to implicitly obey my Superiors in all things without hesitation of murmuring.

Q. —Will you do that? A. —I will.

Q. —How do you travel? A. —In the bark of Peter the fisherman.

Q. —Whither do you travel? A. —To the four quarters of the globe.

Q. —For what purpose?

A. —To obey the orders of my general and Superiors and execute the will of the Pope and faithfully fulfill the conditions of my oaths.

Q. —Go ye, then, into all the world and take possession of all lands in the name of the Pope.

He who will not accept him as the Vicar of Jesus and his Vice-regent on earth, let him be accursed and exterminated.'"

The preceding shows with gory details the true spirit of the beast and gives us an idea of what will happen, not if, but <u>when</u> the church and state will unite, thanks to the efforts of...probably even <u>your own pastor</u>.

4And they worshipped the dragon which gave power unto the beast: and they worshipped the beast, saying, Who is like unto the beast? who is able to make war with him?

Following the beast is clearly rendering tribute to Satan. The phrase "<u>Who is like unto the beast</u>" echoes the praises from Moses and David: *"<u>Who is like unto thee, O LORD</u>, among the gods? Who* *is like thee, glorious in holiness, fearful in praises, doing wonders?"* (Exodus 15:11). *"Who is this King of glory? The LORD strong and mighty, the LORD mighty in battle"* (Psalm 24:8). This is because Satan always wants that which belongs to God.

In chapters two and twelve we saw how, since the beginning of the Christian church, Satan has made war against the Ten Commandments. It is not going to be any different now that we approach the end of the history of this world.

Remember that when Adam and Eve sinned against God in the Garden of Eden, they broke five Commandments (see chapter two)? Worshipping of the beast will also violate five of the Ten Commandments. The following table shows how in just this chapter of Revelation, the four Commandments that honor God are broken by the beast and his followers and also the sixth Commandment:

Commandment of God	Worship of the beast
1st -Thou shalt have no other gods before me – Exodus 20:3	"All the world...worshipped the beast"- Revelation 13:3,4
2nd -Thou shalt not make unto thee any graven image, or any likeness – Exodus 20:4	They make an image to the beast –Revelation 13:14
3rd -Thou shalt not take the name of the LORD thy God in vain – Exodus 20:7	He opened his mouth in blasphemy against God-Revelation 13:6
4th -Remember the Sabbath day, to keep it holy – Exodus 20:8	"And he causeth all, both small and great, rich and poor, free and bond, to receive a mark [a false day of worship] in their right hand, or in their foreheads"- Revelation 13:16
6th -Thou shalt not kill – Exodus 20:13	"as many as would not worship the image of the beast should be killed" –Revelation 13:15

The preceding table proves the fulfillment of Paul's prophecy in 2 Thessalonians 2:4: *"Who opposeth and exalteth himself above all that is called God, or that is worshipped; so that he as God sitteth in the temple of God, shewing himself that he is God."* Through the beast, Satan accomplishes what he dreamed of in heaven: to be worshiped by other creatures as if he were God (Isaiah 12:12-14).

[5]And there was given unto him a mouth speaking great things and blasphemies; and power was given unto him to continue forty and two months.

The Biblical definitions of blasphemy are:

1. being a man, pretending to be God (John 10:33) and:
2. claiming authority to forgive sins (Mark 2:7; Luke 5:21).

The Catholic Church fits both since the priests practice absolution of sins and the Pope is deified. In many writings, the pope is placed even above God. One of those claims is that the pope can even modify divine laws. Therefore, if the pope sees a law that he does not like, he can change it or even do away with it completely. Regarding the claim of the authority to forgive sins, Liguori wrote in his book *Duties and Dignities of the Priest*, the following: "The greatness of the dignity of a priest is also estimated from the high place that he occupies. The priesthood is called, at the synod of Chartres, in 1550, the seat of the Saints. Priests are called Vicars of Jesus Christ, because they hold his place on earth. 'You hold the place of Christ,' says St. Augustine to them; 'you are therefore His lieutenants.' In the Council of Milan, St. Charles Borromeo called priests the representatives of the person of God on earth. And before him, the Apostle said: For Christ we are ambassadors, God, as it were, exhorting by us. When He ascended into Heaven, Jesus Christ left His priests after Him to hold on earth His place of mediator between God and men, particularly on the altar. 'Let the priest,' says St. Laurence Justinian, 'approach the altar as another Christ.' According to St. Cyprian, a priest at the altar performs the office of Christ. When, says St. Chrysostom, you have seen a priest offering sacrifice, consider that the hand of Christ is invisibly extended. The priest holds the place of the Savior Himself, when, by saying 'Ego te absolvo,' he absolves from sin. This great power, which Jesus Christ has received from His eternal Father, He has communicated to His priests. 'Jesus,' says Tertullian, 'invests the priests with His own powers.' To pardon a single sin requires all the omnipotence of God. 'O God, Who chiefly manifestest Thy almighty power in pardoning and showing mercy,' etc., says the holy Church in one of her prayers. Hence, when they heard that Jesus Christ pardoned the sins of the paralytic, the Jews justly said: Who can forgive sins but God alone. But what only God can do by

His omnipotence, the priest can also do by saying 'Ego te absolvo a peccatis tuis;' for the forms of the Sacraments, or the words of the forms, produce what they signify."

Some other blasphemous teachings and practices are:

- Infant baptism- The Bible is clear that we must hear the gospel and believe it (Mark 16:16), then repent, before being baptized. Babies do not qualify for baptism, since none of the requisites is present. Why baptizing infants? Because if babies are allowed to grow up and given a choice if they want to be Catholics, many will not become one. By being baptized in infancy, they are automatically Catholic and they grow up with a sense of loyalty and obligation towards the Mother Church. Definitely not the way God deals with sinners. He gives us freedom of choice.
- The mass- This is when the priest offers the bread and wine and pretends that it changes into the real flesh and blood of Jesus by a process of transubstantiation. "When the priest pronounces the tremendous words of consecration, he reaches up into the heaven, brings Christ down from His throne, and places Him upon our altar to be offered up again as the victim for the sins of man. It is a power greater than that of monarchs and emperors. It is greater than that of saints and angels, greater than that of Seraphim and Cherubim. Indeed, it is greater than the power of the Virgin Mary. While the blessed virgin was the human agency by which Christ became incarnate a single time, the priest brings Christ down from heaven, and renders Him present on our altar as the eternal victim for the sins of man-not once, but, a thousand times! The priest speaks and lo! Christ the eternal and omnipotent God, bows His head in humble obedience to the priest's command. Of what sublime dignity is the office of the Christian priest who is thus privileged to act as the ambassador and the vicegerent of Christ on earth. He continues the essential ministry of Christ - he teaches the faithful with the authority of Christ, he offers up again the same sacrifice of adoration and atonement which Christ offered on Calvary. No wonder that the name which spiritual writers are especially fond of applying to the priest is that of 'alter Christus.' For the

priest is and should be another Christ" (*Faith of Millions*, by Reverend John A. O'brien, pages 270,271). "But our wonder should be far greater when we find that in obedience to the words of his priests—-HOC EST CORPUS MEUM—-God Himself descends on the altar, that He comes wherever they call Him, and as often as they call Him, and places Himself in their hands, even though they should be His enemies. And after having come, He remains, entirely at their disposal; they move Him as they please, from one place to another; they may, if they wish, shut Him up in the tabernacle, or expose Him on the altar, or carry Him outside the church; they may, if they choose, eat His flesh and give Him for the food of others. 'Oh, how very great is their power,' says St. Laurence Justinian, speaking of priests. 'A word falls from their lips and the body of Christ is there substantially formed from the matter of bread, and the Incarnate Word descended from Heaven, is found really present on the table of the altar! Never did Divine goodness give such power to the Angels. The Angels abide by the order of God, but the priests take Him in their hands, distribute Him to the faithful, and partake of Him as food for themselves.'" -Liguori, *Duties and Dignities of the Priest*, p. 26 "And **God himself is obliged to abide by the judgment of his priest** and either not to pardon or to pardon, according as they refuse to give absolution, provided the penitent is capable of it." -Liguori, *Duties and Dignities of the Priest*, p.27. "Hence priests are called the parents of Jesus Christ: such is the title that St. Bernard gives them, for they are the active cause by which He is made to exist really in the consecrated Host. Thus the priest may, in a certain manner, be called the creator of his Creator, since by saying the words of consecration, he creates, as it were, Jesus in the Sacrament, by giving Him a Sacramental existence, and produces Him as a victim to be offered to the eternal Father. As in creating the world it was sufficient for God to have said, Let it be made, and it was created—-He spoke, and they were made—-so it is sufficient for the priest to say, 'Hoc est corpus meum,' and behold the bread is no longer bread, but the body of Jesus Christ. 'The power of the priest,' says St. Bernardine of Sienna, 'is the power of the Divine person; for the transubstantiation of the bread requires as much power as the creation of the world.' And St. Augustine has written, 'O venerable sanctity of the hands! O happy function of the priest! He that created [if I may say so] gave me the power to create Him; and He that created me without me is Himself created by me!' 'As the Word of God created Heaven and earth, so,' says St. Jerome, '**the words of the priest create Jesus Christ**.'"-Liguori, *Duties and Dignities of the Priest.*

Paul wanted to make clear that **the sacrifice of Jesus was done once and for all**: *"And every priest standeth daily ministering and offering oftentimes the same sacrifices, which can never take away sins: But this man, after he had offered one sacrifice for sins for ever, sat down on the right hand of God... For* ***by one offering*** *he hath perfected forever them that are sanctified... Now where remission of these is,* ***there is no more offering for sin****"* (Hebrews 10:11,12,14 & 18). These verses render the "sacrifice of the mass" as null and void. The sacrifice of Christ on Calvary was enough to pay for our sins and no more sacrifice is needed, much less thousands of times a day around the world.

- Papal infallibility- Only God is infallible: *"God forbid: yea, let God be true, but every man a liar; as it is written, That thou mightest be justified in thy sayings, and mightest overcome when thou art judged"* (Romans 3:4). The popes claim to have inherited Peter's throne but forget that he was fallible. Soon after he confessed Jesus as God, he opposed to Jesus' plan to go to Jerusalem. When Jesus was arrested, he took a sword to cut off the head of a servant- fortunately, he only cut off his ear and Jesus healed the man. Jesus did not approve the use of violence against the enemies. However, popes through the ages persecuted and ordered to kill those that dared to believe differently. Later on during Jesus' trial, Peter denied his Savior three times. Years later Paul reprimanded him for playing favorites with the Jews while rejecting the gentiles. Was he infallible? Evidently not! Much less his supposed successors. So much evil was in Rome, that Dante placed the pope in hell in his *Divine Comedy.* Martin Luther, a devout monk in his first visit to Rome, concluded that if there was really a hell, it must have been located in the Vatican due to the great corruption sponsored by the popes. Old history books faithfully document the sins of incest, adultery, simony, homosexuality, illegal appropriation, assassinations and many other evil acts committed by those that pretended to represent their pure Master Jesus.

- The ascension of Mary to heaven- Not mentioned in the Bible. This idea has its origin in the pagan goddess Semiramis ascension to heaven. The Israelites were condemned by God for their devotion to the queen of heaven, known by different names. *"The children gather wood, and the fathers kindle the fire, and the women knead their dough, to make cakes to the queen of heaven, and to pour out drink offerings unto other gods, that they may provoke me to anger"* (Jeremiah 7:18- see also Jeremiah 44:17-19,25). The teaching of the exaltation of Mary to heaven and the titles and attributes given to her are no accident. Given the existence of female goddesses in cultures around the world, the Marian cult can be the glue that will attract non-Christian worshippers to the Catholic faith. After all, the church attracted the pagans in the first centuries in that way. The statues of the pagan gods were renamed to reflect the new Christian heroes and thus facilitate the transition to the new state religion. As we will see in this same chapter and then in chapter 17, there is going to be a one-world religion, having the pope as its head. Pope John Paul II held various meetings with leaders of different world religions in an effort to find common ground for unity. He even had prayers together with them in different parts of the world. Pope Benedict has continued those meetings. One of the ways in which the arch deceiver is preparing the ground for the unity of faiths is through the virgins apparitions. Even prominent leaders of the New Age movement are claiming sightings of the Virgin through their meditations. Wiccans have a long list of goddesses from around the world that they compare to the Virgin (Hera, Ashtoreth, Astarte, Athena, Frigg, Isis, Ishtar, Asherah, Juno (Dove), Athor, Inanna, etc.). Among the Chinese, they venerate Guan Yin. In English, she is called Goddess of Mercy. She is known by other names among other oriental cultures, considering her as one who hears the cries of the suffering and helps those in need. The late pope John Paul II dedicated himself to the devotion of the Virgin, in his case, the Black Madonna. This virgin, being black, will appeal to many non- white cultures, such as the Hindu, since one of their deities is also black. For those that do not worship a female deity, Mary has a great appeal too, such as among the Muslim, since the Koran praises Mary for her faith. The bond will not be based on Christ, but on the common false doctrines and the miracles, many of which are being done by the "Virgin." People from many faiths worldwide are claiming to be healed by her and will not take long to group them together under one banner. If they only knew that is not the real Mary who is appearing to them!

- The intersession of Mary and the saints- The only way to the Father is through Jesus. *"For there is one God, and one mediator between God and men, the man Christ Jesus"* (1 Timothy 2:5). If the Virgin misplaced Christ when He was 12 years old under her care, and could not find Him for three days, how could she care for all the millions praying to her simultaneously? Such multitasking is not possible for human beings to accomplish. There is no doubt that Mary was a special person, a chosen vessel to bring the Son of God to this world as a member of the human family. She did a wonderful job in raising Him in the midst of a wicked town (Nazareth). Regardless of these facts, her role was limited to the motherhood of Jesus. There is no Biblical proof that she (or any of the so-called saints) was chosen to be an intercessor. As the previously cited verse makes it very clear, such a job belongs to Christ alone. Paul, writing to the Hebrews, said: *"Seeing then that we have a great high priest, that is passed into the heavens, Jesus the Son of God, let us hold fast our profession. For we have not an high priest which cannot be touched with the feeling of our infirmities; but was in all points tempted like as we are, yet without sin. Let us therefore come boldly unto the throne of grace, that we may obtain mercy, and* ***find grace*** *to help in time of need"* (Hebrews 4:14 -16). Who is sitting on that throne? It is God Himself. According to this passage, we all have direct access to God's throne. We do not need a priest, a saint or even a pope to find grace and forgiveness. Jesus identified Himself as the door and the way (John 10:9; 14:6). That means clearly

> that the only way to heaven, to obtain salvation, not to be lost, to avoid hell, is ONLY through Jesus Christ. *"Therefore being justified by faith, we have peace with God through our Lord Jesus Christ: By whom also we have access by faith into this grace wherein we stand, and rejoice in hope of the glory of God"* (Romans 5:1, 2).

Now, I want to submit some quotes from the book *The Glories Of Mary* by St. Alphonsus Liguori, 1931 edition:

Page 30: "To honor this Queen of Angels is to gain eternal life...." The Bible says "He that hath the Son hath life..." (1 John 5:12).

Page 36: "And if Jesus is the King of the universe, Mary is also its Queen." The concept of a queen of heaven had its origins in ancient Babylon, with Semiramis. Jeremiah wrote in chapters 7 & 44 of his book "burn incense to the queen of heaven, ..."

Page 38: "...the Eternal Father gave the office of judge and avenger to the Son, and that of showing mercy ... to the Mother.'"

A passage from the Psalm that the book of Hebrews applies to Jesus, was forcibly applied to Mary: *"God hath anointed thee with the oil of gladness."* Forcing the Scriptures to say what we want is not God's way to interpret them.

Page 43: "the door through which sinners are brought to God'." John 10:7,9 says that Jesus is the door.

Page 80: "Mary is our life." Jesus said: "I am ...the life."

Page 83: "Sinners receive pardon by the intercession of Mary alone." "For there is one God and one Mediator between God and men, the man Christ Jesus" (1 Timothy 2:5).

Page 93: says the she withholds "the arm of her Son from falling on sinners." Daniel 4 teaches that nobody can restrain the hand of the Lord.

Page 137: "Many things- says Nicephorus,- are asked from God, and are not granted: they are asked from Mary, and are obtained." Jesus told His disciples to ask in His name (John 14:13,14;15:7,16;16:23,24 &26). *"Ask and ye shall receive."*

Page 153: "...'Let us not imagine that we obscure the glory of the Son by the great praise we lavish on the mother; for the more she is honored, the greater is the glory of her Son.' ...."

"...St. Laurence Justinian asks, "How can she be otherwise than full of grace, who has been made the ladder to paradise, the gate of heaven, the most true mediatress between God and man?" John1:51 shows that Jesus is the ladder.

"Saint Bonaventure expressly calls her "Mary, the most faithful mediatress of our salvation" And St. Laurence Justinian asks, "How can she be otherwise than full of grace, who has been made the ladder to paradise, the gate of heaven, the most true mediatress between God and man?" John 1:51 shows that Jesus is the ladder.

Page 155: "We should have all through Mary." See comments about the quote in page 137.

Page 174: "Let us... venerate this divine Mother ...that we should receive every good thing from her hand."- James 1:17: "Every good gift ...comes down from the Father..."

Page 181: "At the command of Mary, **all obey, even God**."..."Yes, Mary is omnipotent." What a blasphemy; that God obeys Mary? And she is omnipotent?

Page 238: "To thee, O Lady, are committed the keys and treasures of the kingdom of heaven." Jesus has the keys (Revelation 1:18;3:7).

Page 246: "...'Frequently our petitions are heeded sooner when we address ourselves to Mary the Queen of Mercy, than when we go directly to Jesus who as King of Justice is our Judge' " Is she more powerful than Jesus, or is it that He doesn't love us enough anymore?

Page 256: "...How can the Son refuse to hear his Mother when she shows him ... the breast that gave him suck?" What a sick thought! This quote probably came from a pervert.

Page 256: "...our salvation is in her hands, and depends on her.' "Referring to Jesus, the Bible says: *"Nor is there salvation in any other name under heaven given among men by which we must be saved"* (Acts 4:12).

The preceding quotes showed that this deified woman it is not the same Mary of the Scriptures. This one is the "resurrected" Semiramis. If the real Mary were alive now, she would be horrified seeing people glorifying her, giving her attributes of God.

Now, back to our list of blasphemous teachings:

- The confessional- this became the best source of income from the nobility in Europe through blackmailing. Nowhere in the Bible are we taught to confess our sins to a man. David made that very clear: *"I acknowledged my sin unto thee, and mine iniquity have I not hid. I said, I will confess my transgressions unto the LORD; and thou forgavest the iniquity of my sin. Selah"* (Psalm 32:5). The disciples, including Peter, never told a sinner: "your sins are forgiven." The only authority given to them by God was to tell the sick: "get up and walk."
- Purgatory- a pagan idea that crept in the church. "In Egypt, substantially the same doctrine of Purgatory was inculcated. But when once this doctrine of Purgatory was admitted into the popular mind, then the door was opened for all manner of priestly extortions. Egyptian prayers for the dead ever go hand in hand with Purgatory; but no prayers can be completely efficacious without the interposition of the priests; and no priestly functions can be rendered unless there be special pay for them. Therefore, in every land we find the pagan priesthood 'devouring widows' houses' and making merchandise of the tender feelings of sorrowing relatives, sensitively alive to the immortal happiness of the beloved dead." (Alexander Hislop, *The Two Babylons*, pages 167-168). This doctrine teaches that if the person was not too evil in life but did not have enough merits to enter directly into heaven, when he/she dies will go to a temporary place of torment to purge the sins and then be granted the entrance into Paradise. This could require even hundreds of years. The catechism reads: "All who die

in God's grace and friendship, but still imperfectly purified, are indeed assured of their eternal salvation; but after death they undergo purification, so as to achieve the holiness necessary to enter the joy of heaven. The Church gives the name Purgatory to this final purification..." *(Catechism p.268, para #1030, 1031).* The church teaches that the parishioners can buy indulgences to get their loved ones out of purgatory faster. The Bible teaches that we stay in the grave until Jesus returns with the reward and nowhere in the Scriptures mentions purgatory. It says, regarding rescuing a loved one: *"They that trust in their wealth, and boast themselves in the multitude of their riches; None of them can* ***by any means*** *redeem his brother,* ***nor give to God a ransom for him****: (For the redemption of their soul is precious, and it ceaseth for ever:) That he should still live for ever, and not see corruption"* (Psalm 49:6-9).

- Hell- the Biblical definition of hell is very different from what it is taught. Plato's ideas are accepted and preferred over what the Bible says. See comment on chapter 20 for the Biblical concept of hell.
- Indulgences- This is buying forgiveness in advance and getting out of purgatory sooner. Some people in the times of Luther bought these documents and then decided to commit a crime. When the authorities came to arrest them, they turned back to prison empty handed because the criminals had bought forgiveness in advance and had the document that granted exoneration sometimes for the rest of their lives. This practice funded the construction of the pope's palace in the Vatican. Again, we cannot buy God's favor with money.
- The rosary- came from the Babylonians. Jesus taught that we should not repeat prayers. *"But when ye pray, use not vain repetitions, as the heathen do: for they think that they shall be heard for their much speaking"* (Matthew 6:7). When Jesus offered the model prayer (Our Father- or Pater Noster), He meant to present it as an example of how to address God in prayer, not that we have to repeat it verbatim. God is not to be approached with the fear experienced by the superstitious pagans. We can approach God with confidence because He loves us. When we pray,

we should talk to Him like when we converse with a dear friend.

- Penance- this is kind of salvation by works when the Bible teaches that we are saved by faith only *"For by grace are ye saved through faith; and that not of yourselves: it is the gift of God: Not of works, lest any man should boast"* (Ephesians 2:8,9). What a marvelous God we serve! We are sinful, worthless, selfish, arrogant and rebellious people and still God bestows His incredible love on us and grants us free salvation. This is the best example of giving something for nothing. If I were God, I would not find even one person worthy of heaven and salvation- much less myself. But since He is the one who is God, He sees possibilities in you and me and through faith, He wants us to accept and enjoy His salvation. He wants us home with Him and He sent Jesus to pay the penalty for our sins. Our debt has been paid- we need no penance.
- The sacraments- not Biblical. Our entrance to heaven is faith in Jesus- and that comes from God.
- Abstaining from meat on Fridays- a pagan custom to honor Dagon
- Lent- this pagan custom was to honor Tammuz. Ezekiel 8:14 mentions the *"women weeping for Tammuz."* This was done for 40 days and ended in the spring when they believed he resurrected from the dead. It was easy for the Catholic Church to bring this doctrine aboard because Jesus was resurrected in the spring.
- Celibacy- If Peter is the model for the popes, they are not following him faithfully because He was married (Matthew 8:14) and even brought his wife along in his trips (1 Corinthians 9:5).
- The pope as representative of Christ- "The Pope is not only the representative of Jesus Christ, he is **Jesus Christ himself**" -*Catholic National* July 1895.

6 *And he opened his mouth in blasphemy against God, to blaspheme his name, and his tabernacle, and them that dwell in heaven.*

To blaspheme his name – maligning His name with doctrines such as hell and purgatory and persecuting dissenters to death. If instead of killing dissenters, it would have treated them kindly, there would be a lot less atheists in the world.

And his tabernacle – The Bible teaches that Jesus is our advocate in the heavenly sanctuary. *"Now of the things which we have spoken this is the sum: We have such an high priest, who is set on the right hand of the throne of the Majesty in the heavens; A minister of the sanctuary, and of the true tabernacle, which the Lord pitched, and not man"* (Hebrews 8:1,2). Rome never teaches the sinner to look up to Jesus but to the saints and priests. However, they are fallen human beings just as we are and they are powerless to save or help anyone. Besides, they are in their graves until Jesus returns in glory. Our prayers ought to be directed to Jesus alone in the heavens.

7And it was given unto him to make war with the saints, and to overcome them: and power was given him over all kindreds, and tongues, and nations.

This period of tyrannical dominion lasted from 538 AD until 1798 AD. There is a recurrent mentioning of the persecution in Daniel and Revelation. The sad part is not the persecution but who is doing the persecuting. In chapter 17, we will see John's amazement when he discovers that we are dealing with an evil power pretending to be the real and true church. Some believers might die in the last persecution. However, no one will die if their death would not bring souls to God.

8And all that dwell upon the earth shall worship him, whose names are not written in the book of life of the Lamb slain from the foundation of the world.

Book of life- mentioned in relation to those that believe. Moses was the first one that mentioned the book (Exodus 32:32).

Lamb slain from the foundation of the world – Sin did not take God by surprise so He would frantically have to improvise a solution. It is evident then that in the heavenly courts the question was brought up: "If man sins, what will be done?" God, as sovereign, could do anything He pleased with the rebellious creature. He could have destroyed it and start all over again, but then all His other creatures would obey out of fear. He could, on the other hand, let the sinner go with a slap on the hand. Then all the other creatures would not have taken Him seriously and disobedience would have been rampant. The solution came from Jesus. He offered Himself to rescue mankind by taking the punishment deserved by the sinner. Therefore, before the world was created, He saw the desperate condition brought by sin and having you and me in His heart, provided for our salvation.

[9]If any man have an ear, let him hear.

Not wanting that anyone perish, He invites us to <u>pay attention</u> to the thing that really matters: eternal life in the presence of God.

[10]<u>He that leadeth into captivity shall go into captivity</u>: he that killeth with the sword must be killed with the sword. Here is the patience and the faith of the saints.

Here it is described how the wound was inflicted on the head of the beast. The pope was taken captive in 1798 AD by orders of Napoleon Bonaparte and died in exile the following year putting an end to the 1260 years of tyrannical dominion.

Here is the patience and the faith of the saints- This phrase is also found in chapter 14:12, where it is amplified and explained. There the verse explains that those who have the patience of the saints are the ones that keep the commandmends. The beast does not like the Ten Commandments and has always been against them, especially the fourth one which requires the observance of the seventh day Sabbath and the second, which forbids the veneration of statues.

[11]And I beheld another beast coming up out of the earth; and he had two horns like a lamb, and he spake as a dragon.

Now the prophet is shown another power that, with the passing of time, would assist the fallen beast to get up on its feet again. This beast is not like all those in Daniel and the previous one here in chapter 13 that came up from the sea. It comes up from the earth. We saw that the sea represents densely populated areas, such as the nations of Europe. In contrast, this new beast comes from a sparsely populated region. It has two horns like a lamb, indicating youth, unlike the ram from Daniel eight. Notice that this second beast has no crowns. This is because it is neither a king nor a pope. It is a republic. There was only one powerful nation (a republic) starting during those days of the mortal wound: the United States of America. After this verse in chapter 13, this power is never again referred to as a beast, but as the false prophet (see Revelation 16:13; 19:20; and 20:10) due to this nation being the crib of many of the Protestant religions with worldwide influence, but apostate in their doctrines.

But the prophecy indicates that this new power speaks as a dragon, indicating great authority, influence and power. It is going to be an imposing power that no one would dare to challenge and everyone will follow. Through legislation, this power would speak with the arrogance of a dragon. There have been many attempts to modify the United States constitution to pave the way for the church to impose their dogmas on the people. By God's grace, the rights of minorities have been preserved and we still have freedom of expression and of the press. Right now, we are enjoying the protection assured by the First Amendment: "Congress shall make no law respecting an establishment of religion, or prohibiting the free exercise thereof; or abridging the freedom of speech, or of the press; or the right of the people peaceably to assemble, and to petition the Government for a redress of grievances."

But that is about to change soon. Presenting many excuses such as protecting our nation from terrorism, coming in clear about political contributions (the disclose act of 2010), the preservation of the family, etc., bills have been introduced that will make it very easy to overthrow the constitution on behalf of a totalitarian form of government. It no longer be a "we the people" document or a democratic government but one in which the powers will be more concentrated on one person. Unfortunately, this person will be a puppet of Romanism.

The U.S. Constitution guarantees that the privilege to the rights to **habeas corpus,** regarded among the basic protections of individual liberty, "shall not be suspended, unless when in cases of **rebellion** or invasion the public safety may require it." Since the remnant will refuse to keep a man-made day of rest, they will be considered rebellious and thus stripped of this right.

[12]*And he exerciseth all the power of the first beast before him, and causeth the earth and them which dwell therein to worship the first beast, whose deadly wound was healed.*

At the time this will happen, the deadly wound would have completely healed. It is still in the process of healing. It will be healed when the churches unite and the nations decide to follow the beast. Very soon, legislation would be introduced, approved and signed into law to honor the beast by the keeping of Sunday as the official day of rest.

All the power of the first beast – This second beast will obtain that power when the religious right gets the reigns of the government. The first beast got to world dominion united with the civil powers. Daniel chapter three should be studied to see the deadly results of the marriage of church and state. In the narrative of that chapter, we see the power of the state legislating religion. The government was ordering that every person had to worship when they said the people should worship. There was even a death penalty for those that did not submit to the order. A similar arrangement is coming not only to America but also to the entire world. What is established here will be implemented in the rest of the nations. John wrote that this power (the United States) will cause (force) the earth (all the nations) to worship the beast. As the superpower, United States is policing the world with the backing of the United Nations. Even communist China and former cold war era enemy Russia are recently voting as the US requests them to do. When the world has common troubles, they come together to find solutions and all the nations are now looking up to the United States as the nation that can solve mankind's problems.

If Jesus wanted us to be involved in politics, He would have told His followers clearly that they had to run for office or fight to occupy positions of authority. It is not wrong to vote or even to have a government position. What is wrong is to use the civil power to legislate or to enforce anyone's religious views upon others. It is clear in Paul's writings that instead of trying to be in control, we must submit ourselves to the authorities, as established by God. *"Put them in mind to be subject to principalities and powers, to obey magistrates, to be ready to every good work"* (Titus 3:1). *"Let every soul be subject unto the higher powers. For there is no power but of*

God: the powers that be are ordained of God. Whosoever therefore resisteth the power, resisteth the ordinance of God: and they that resist shall receive to themselves damnation. For rulers are not a terror to good works, but to the evil. Wilt thou then not be afraid of the power? do that which is good, and thou shalt have praise of the same: For he is the minister of God to thee for good. But if thou do that which is evil, be afraid; for he beareth not the sword in vain: for he is the minister of God, a revenger to execute wrath upon him that doeth evil. Wherefore ye must needs be subject, not only for wrath, but also for conscience sake. For for this cause pay ye tribute also: for they are God's ministers, attending continually upon this very thing" (Romans 13:1-6). There are many groups now putting pressure on our lawmakers to legislate their religious agenda, which will curtail the rights of minorities. Once these laws are enacted, intolerance and persecution will follow. Rome has not changed and will request the authorities to impose steep penalties (even the death penalty) against those that do not accept her dogmas. Our role as Christians is to obey the law not to make it.

[13]*And he doeth great wonders, so that he maketh fire come down from heaven on the earth in the sight of men,* [14]*And deceiveth them that dwell on the earth by the means of those miracles which he had power to do in the sight of the beast; saying to them that dwell on the earth, that they should make an image to the beast, which had the wound by a sword, and did live.*

The Protestant church members base much of their faith on the performance of miracles. God wants us to pay attention to the truth not to miracles. *"Then said I unto him, Except ye see signs and wonders, ye will not believe"* (John 4:48). Chapters 16 and 19 of Revelation clearly identify the source of the miracles brought by this beast: *"For they are the spirits of devils, working miracles, which go forth unto the kings of the earth and of the whole world, to gather them to the battle of that great day of God Almighty"* (Revelation 16:14). *"And the beast was taken, and with him the false prophet that wrought miracles before him, with which he deceived them that had received the mark of the beast, and them that worshipped his image...."* (Revelation 19:20). Those so call miracles are usually temporary and the benefits tend to disappear within 24 hours of the healing. I have witnessed those miracles myself and I know that something happened to those people healed during the service. I also noticed when visiting them afterwards that they returned to their previous condition and were told that they lacked faith to hold the miracle. Nonsense! If the miracles had been from God, it would have remained a healing, not a reversion to the previous state. Naaman the Syrian did not lose his new baby skin, neither any of those healed by Jesus or His disciples lost what they received as a gift from heaven. That is why we are told: *"Beloved, believe not every spirit, but try the spirits whether they are of God: because many false prophets are gone out into the world"* (1 John 4:1).

Notice how that second beast is also called "the false prophet." That title represents the apostate Protestantism in the USA. They will extend the hand to the original beast and enact laws favoring it. There are many Protestant church leaders applying pressure to have Sunday laws passed at the local and national level. Although there are some of those laws in the books of some states, they are not generally enforced at the present time. They are known as blue laws because they were originally written in blue paper. Very soon, no one will be able to go shopping on Sunday or even mow their lawn or do their laundry. The day of rest will be enforced with the excuse of strengthening the family. Then, only those that keep Sunday as if it was holy will be able to do transactions.

The true believers will find themselves in a very difficult situation. However, God will provide for those that trust Him in the same way He did it for the Israelites in the desert and for Elijah when he was in hiding. We must learn to trust Him now before the difficult times come. *"Behold, the LORD'S hand is not shortened, that it cannot save; neither his ear heavy, that it cannot hear"* (Isaiah 59:1). Every day He blesses us in many ways. He provides our food, enable us to work so we can earn a living, gives us sunshine, rain, clothing, friends, family, and even some of us have a car, a house and other properties. When we are sick, He can heal us, when we are poor, He can provide for our needs, when we are troubled, He can intervene on our behalf. *"...God is our refuge and strength, a very present help in trouble"* (Psalm 46:1). Yes, difficult times are coming but *"What shall we then say to these things? If God be for us, who can be against us?"* (Romans 8:31).

Your relationship with God now will determine the outcome of the trial that is to affect every inhabitant of this planet. We need to learn to trust God unconditionally in relatively good times so we can be 100% on His side and remain loyal to Him. A good way to do this is to write down those special times when against all odds, the hand of God came to your rescue, so in the future your faith will be strengthened by reading how God has guided your in the past.

an image to the beast – In the same way that the original beast exerted its power trough the power of the state, the image would be the result of the union of the church and the state. Influent religious leaders are pushing their government representatives to submit to their religious ideologies. On the other hand, the sacred pulpits are being lent to politicians to spread their messages and get followers. The church is compromising with the powerful politicians in order to influence the making of the laws, so the church can have the moral control of the nation.

15*And he had power to give life unto the image of the beast, that the image of the beast should both speak, and cause that as many as would not worship the image of the beast should be killed.*

That "life" will be given through legislation, when the laws to keep Sunday holy will be enforced. This power does not play around and we will see the demonic power in action when these laws are approved. How different that spirit from that of Christ! As a dragon, this power imposes the death penalty for not worshipping the image of the beast. How sad that the nation that used to boast of religious liberty would be brought so low as to coerce people's consciences to keep an spurious day of worship. Jesus taught His disciples how to deal with those of different faiths, including those that reject the message of salvation and the messenger. *"And John answered and said, Master, we saw one casting out devils in thy name; and <u>we forbad him, because he followeth not with us</u>. And Jesus said unto him, Forbid him not: for <u>he that is not against us is for us</u>"*. Later on, during the journey to Jerusalem, the Samaritans rejected Jesus and His disciples asked permission to destroy them with fire just like the Catholic Church would be doing centuries later. Rome could have worked with the Protestants. Instead, she burned them up. Read His response: *"And it came to pass, when the time was come that he should be received up, he steadfastly set his face to go to Jerusalem, And sent messengers before his face: and they went, and entered into a village of the Samaritans, to make* *ready for him. And they did not receive him.... And when his disciples James and John saw this, they said, Lord, wilt thou that we command fire to come down from heaven, and consume them, even as Elias did? But he turned, and rebuked them, and said, Ye know not what manner of spirit ye are of. For the Son of man is not come to destroy men's lives, but to save them. And they went to another village"* (Luke 9:49-56). The spirit that burns others at the stake is not the Spirit of Christ!!! It is clearly the behavior of those possessed by the spirit of Satan. Jesus' solution was to go to another village and leave those people alone. Rome is incapable to do that because it is thirsty for blood (Revelation 17:6) and cannot tolerate competition.

***16**And he causeth all, both small and great, rich and poor, free and bond, to receive a mark in their right hand, or in their foreheads:*

The mark on the hand implies salvation by works, while the mark on the forehead implies a conscious submission. Notice two things here:

1. The mark on the hand is mentioned first, which implies that these people are used to believe that they should do something to help in their salvation. These represent Catholics and the multitude of different religions of the world that believe in salvation by works.
2. The mark on the forehead is mentioned in second place to indicate those that actually believe that salvation is by faith (which is correct) and will accept Sunday (which is wrong) by blind faith. These are the people that follow the dictates of their pastors without questioning if the Bible backs their claims. These Christians are described at the time when Jesus returns: *"Not every one that saith unto me, Lord, Lord, shall enter into the kingdom of heaven; but he that doeth the will of my Father which is in heaven. Many will say to me in that day, Lord, Lord, have we not prophesied in thy name? and in thy name have cast out devils? And in thy name done many wonderful works? And then will I profess unto them, I never knew you: depart from me, ye that work iniquity"* (Matthew 7:21-23). There are so hypnotized by the miracles (and the tongues) that they do not bother to read their Bibles on their own to compare what they see or hear with God's Word. I was blessed that when I witnessed some of

those miracles I had the Word of God to let me know that it was not the power of God but of the Devil, for the next day the "miracle" had disappeared. The lame was limping again and the paralyzed muscles were crippled like before. Not even the repaired molars remained fixed. Notice also how the element of works is implied in that passage.

17And that no man might buy or sell, save he that had the mark, or the name of the beast, or the number of his name.

Many believe, with an erroneous theological application, that we will receive a microchip implanted in our hands that will enable us to process transactions for goods and services. Although I do not believe the mark is a microchip for the reasons that I will explain in the comment of verse 18, I do not discount that it could be used by the government to track our movements and actions. At the present time, there is talk about using the chip to track the health history of patients. Since the Bible does talk about the mark of the beast and mentions the location to be in the hand or forehead, the makers of the RFID chip introduced it as a way to track potentially lost animals. Since they have successfully proven the device usefulness with pets returned to the owners, now they are touting the potential benefits of the chip being used in humans. For example, a person with Alzheimer's could be tracked if finds his/her way out of the safety of the house, a kidnapped child could be rescued and returned to his/her loving parents, etc. It will definitely end many kinds of crime, such as prostitution, illegal gambling, kidnappings, many robberies, home invasions, assaults and illegal drug usage because the implementation of such a system will eliminate cash. As a cashless society, every worker will receive a credit that he could redeem to buy groceries or anything else that now uses a credit or debit card. However, I believe that although it could be implemented, this is a distraction so people will not consider which is the real mark of the beast. The radio frequency chip is an electronic device, not a mark.

Right now all our credit cards transactions are being tracked. We can no longer keep our privacy. Every book we read, the kind of food we buy, the movies that we rent, all of it can become known by any interested party in the government and not only the credit card issuing company. Some states, with the excuse of avoiding insurance fraud allow the use of tracking devices in the insured vehicles. Did you know that new vehicles contain a "black box" just like an airplane? For now, it is programmed to tell your driving habits in case that you are involved in an accident. For example, it will let investigators know if you hit the brakes before the crash, the speed at which you were traveling, if the ABS and other safety systems were activated, if you failed to maintain the vehicle properly, etc. When we use GPS devices to find an address, we tracked ourselves. When you buy a GPS device and register it for the warranty, your name is linked to it and you are no longer an anonymous user innocently looking for an address. You already know that your phone calls can be tracked to get a location of where you are calling from (even cell phones). And you also know that your conversations can be tapped and text messages can be retrieved. Not to mention that emails that we sent as private can be retrieved and read. Erased hard drives can be recovered. Cities are installing cameras capable of distinguishing facial features- as to identify criminals and terrorists. New "smart" cameras capable of interpreting actions are being installed in airports and other public places. They are even sold to the public. We are moving towards a society where Big Brother will know exactly where we are at all times, who our friends are, our buying habits, who gets our money and we will be categorized by our ideologies, in complete disregard of the freedoms granted in the constitution. If our movements had tracked in that way in the 1940's right after WWII, the population would have resisted those measures, accusing the government of becoming a communist state. However, these changes have come to happen slowly so we can get used to them and not be scared. We have completely lost our right to privacy under the pretext of protecting our freedoms. It appears now that the first right to go away is the freedom of speech. It is being as if going back to the Middle Ages, when people could not express their opinion for fear of been tried without a lawyer, tortured and executed.

Is the inquisition going to return? Probably not as we know it, burning people at the stake, but the spirit will be the same. Just like in those times, those that follow God wholeheartedly will be considered as enemies of the State, as fanatics, terrorists, bigots, closed-minded, as a threat to the well-being of society. They will be seen as the scum of the earth and they will decide to get rid of them just because they do not submit, in the same way that the three Hebrews refused to worship the statue made by the king of Babylon. In the end times, the statue (image) of Babylon (the Catholic Church) will be erected and everyone will be told to worship it. It is possible that there are going to be a few martyrs, but the majority will be kept completely protected by powerful angels that will take them to the mountains just like when they rescued Lot from Sodom. Here we see a parallel with the terrible abomination of they gay lifestyle in our days, whose supporters attack the Bible and occupy the pulpit as preachers. Very soon, they will suffer the divine judgments too for their defiant attitude. God's angels will be sent to rescue His children on time and, like lot, they will be taken to the refuge on the mountains (Isaiah 33:16).

Hans Küng, in his book *The Catholic Church*, wrote in pages 96, 97: "Aroused by a zeal to eradicate the heretical threats, bishops and popes, kings and emperors prepared what would then fill many of the most terrible pages of church history under the dreaded name of the Inquisition- the systematic legal persecution of heretics by a church court (*inquisition haereticae pravitatis*), which enjoyed the support not only of the secular power but also of broad groups among the people, who <u>often eagerly looked forward to the execution of heretics</u>. The Inquisition would become an essential characteristic of the Roman Catholic Church....

"Heretics condemned by the church were to be handed over to secular judgment- for a fiery death or at least to have their tongues cut out. ...Church authorities alone could decide on matters of faith, and <u>no freedom of thought and speech was allowed</u>. Innocent IV, in particular, a great lawyer pope, went one step further. He authorized the Inquisition also to allow torture by secular authorities in order to extract confessions. The physical torments this caused for the victims of the Inquisition beggars any description.

"Only the Enlightenment would remove the barbarism of torture and the stake for heretics, but the Roman Inquisition would continue under a different name (holy office; Congregation for the Doctrine of Faith), and even today its proceedings accord to medieval principles. The proceedings against someone who is suspected or accused are secret. No one knows who the informants are. There is no cross-examination of witnesses, nor are there any experts. The proceedings are kept closed, so that any knowledge of the preliminaries is prevented. Accusers and judges are identical. Any appeal to an independent court is ruled out or is useless, for the aim of the proceedings is not to discover the truth but to bring about unconditional submission to Roman doctrine, which is always identical with the truth....There is no question that such an Inquisition mocks both the gospel and the generally accepted sense of justice today, which has found expression in the declarations of human rights."

that no man might buy or sell- Do we have any reason to doubt that God will not be able to provide? Didn't God provide for the Israelites in the dessert and for Elijah when he was running from the wicked queen? Didn't Jesus provide for the two great multitudes, one been over 5,000 (Jews) and the other over 4,000 (gentiles)? *"Behold, the LORD'S hand is not shortened, that it cannot save; neither his ear heavy, that it cannot hear"* (Isaiah 59:1). *"Behold, the eye of the LORD is upon them that fear him, upon them that hope in his mercy; To deliver their soul from death, and to keep them alive in famine"* (Psalm 33:18,19). *"Young lions may go hungry or even starve, but if you trust the LORD, you will never miss out on anything good"* (Psalm 34:10 *CEV*). Satan is portrayed as a lion in the first book of Peter (5:8), so the lions in this verse are his followers. They will suffer hunger in the time of the great tribulation. It sounds ironic that those that will be permitted by law to buy or sell will go hungry and those forbidden to do transactions will have food, but <u>God will in no way abandon His children</u>. How true ring the words of David: *"A little that a righteous man hath is better than the riches of many wicked"* (Psalm 37:16). We should never be worried about being able to find food for our children in those few days of the great tribulation. We have God's promises and He always keeps His word. *"I have been young, and now am old; yet have I not seen the righteous forsaken, nor his seed* [children] *begging bread"* (Psalm 37:25). Chapter 16 indicates that the last plagues will cause hunger among the wicked because the sun will scorch everything. They will not have water either because the rivers will turn into blood. The real irony is that what they plan for the children of God is precisely what they will get for themselves- no food or water. Their retribution will be according to the cruelty of their hearts.

[18]*Here is wisdom. Let him that hath understanding count the number of the beast: for it is the number of a man; and his number is Six hundred threescore and six.*

Why the mark of the beast is not a microchip? First of all, the beast is a spiritual power, since it requires adoration. The mark must be of a spiritual nature and be related to adoration- Sunday fits this requirement perfectly like nothing else. Second, the person also must have the name of the beast. In other words, the person must belong to the institution that the beast represents. It must have accepted the teachings and chosen loyalty to the beast. When the churches unite, all the members, regardless of their present religious affiliation, will be grouped under the Catholic umbrella. Third, the mark is directly related to the name of the beast that must be added up. This means that the numeric value of the letters of the title or name of the beast when added up will be 666. There are however, many ways to obtain this sum.

***Titles that add to 666*:**

Before we analyze the titles or names, I want to mention that if we add the first 6 letters in the Latin alphabet that have a numerical value, the sum will be 666 (six is number of imperfection, represents man, in contrast with 7, which is the number that represents perfection and represents God). Those letters are I=1, V=5, X=10, L=50, C=100, D=500. In ancient times, the numeral 1000 was written "CIO," with the "O" being shaped by two opposite "C's." The use of the M is from more recent use. The U and the V have the same value.

1) Teitan= Satan (ancient Greek).

τ	300
ε	5
ι	10
τ	300
α	1
ν	50
=	666

Satan is the originator of the revolt against God, and the invisible head of the mystery of iniquity. In the same way as Christ dwells with his people and is their king, thus also Satan's dwelling is in Babylon.

Note: Daniel 7:25 mentions a power that is going against God, persecutes His people and changes His law. The meaning of the word "against" in Hebrew, describes one that appears to be on the side of God, but in reality is a constant traitor. Revelation 17:4 describes that same power having in its hand wine of fornication, that is nothing else than the mix of the truth of God with the error of paganism. What is that wine?-her false doctrines. She has given to the world a false Sabbath instead of the Sabbath of the fourth commandment, and has repeated the falsehood that Satan first told Eve in Eden--the natural immortality of the soul. Many errors she has spread far and wide, "But in vain they do worship me, **teaching for doctrines the commandments of men**" (Matthew 15:9).

Now we will expose that power that pretends to be a Christian church:

2) Romiit= Roman kingdom (Hebrew).

ρ 200
ο 6
μ 40
ι 10
ι 10
τ 400
= 666

It is undeniable the fact that the Catholic Church is a great kingdom, and above all, calls itself holy mother, Catholic, apostolic and Roman.

"For the first seventeen hundred years of the papacy, then, and in a very real sense, it could fairly be said that the Pope was Rome, and Rome was the Pope." Malachi Martin *The Keys of this Blood*, page 118

Romiti, or the Roman Man is:

Ρ 200
ο 6
μ 40
ι 10
τ 400
ι 10
= 666

3) Latin basileia = Latin kingdom (Greek).

λ	30
α	1
τ	300
ι	10
ν	50
β	2
α	1
σ	200
ι	10
λ	30
ε	5
ι	10
α	1
=	666

Both the Roman empire and the Catholic church, are Latin kingdoms and Latin is the official language of Romanism.

4) Italika ekklesia-- Italian church (Greek).

ι	10
τ	300
α	1
λ	30
ι	10
κ	20
α	1
ε	5
κ	20
κ	20
λ	30
η	8
σ	200
ι	10
α	1
=	666

The Catholic Church has its headquarters in Italy, from where it masters the world, as says in Rev. 17:18. Therefore, it is clear that the Italian church is not what pretends to be, but it fulfils the prophecy regarding the antichrist.

Note: the ETA, transliterated as an e with accent, has a value of 8, without it, it is transliteration of the epsilon and it is worth 5. This is only applied to the titles in Greek.

5) Lateinos = Latin speaking man (Greek).

λ	30
α	1
τ	300
ε	5
ι	10
ν	50
ο	70
ς	200
=	666

It is a very old custom that the pope speaks in Latin in the meetings and councils before the cardinals. The papal bulls are also written in Latin.

Below will be analyzed some titles of the "Latin speaking man."

6) Dux cleri -captain of the clergy (Latin).

D	500
u	5
x	10
C	100
l	50
e	0
r	0
i	1
=	666

This is one of the tittles with which the pope is known, as leader of the clergy (priestly Catholic class).

7) Vicarius Filii Dei = Vicar of the Son of God (Latin).

V	5
i	1
c	100
a	0
r	0
i	1
u	5
s	0

The only Vicarius or representative that Jesus left on the earth was the Holy Spirit, the one who is God (Jn.14:26; Acts 5:3,5). When the papacy is applied this title, it is fulfilling the prophecy that indicated that the antichrist would make itself God (2Tes.2:3,4). Pope Leo XIII declared "we occupy on this earth the place of God Almighty" (The Great Encyclical Letters of Leo XIII, Page 164). "The title of the Pope of Rome is Vicarius Filii Dei and if you take the letters of his title which represent Latin numerals and add them together they come to 666." *Our Sunday Visitor,* Nov. 15, 1914. The word "Anti" in Greek means one that takes the place of another or that is a substitute. Vicarius is, likewise, according to the *American Heritage Dictionary,* a substitute, thus antichrist is a substitute of Christ and when the pope claims to be the vicar of Christ is just admitting to be the antichrist. Antichrist = Vicarius Filli Dei.). Pope John Paul II wrote in *Crossing the threshold of Hope.* "The Pope is considered the man on earth who **represents the Son of God**, who 'takes the place' of the Second Person of the omnipotent God of the Trinity." The title Vicarius Filii Dei applied to the pope is found in Lucius Ferraris, *Prompta Bibliotheca* on the entry Papa (pope).

Modern Catholics deny the use of the triple crown with the title Vicarius Filii Dei, but there are many witnesses' accounts of the existence of such title of authority.

F	0
i	1
l	50
i	1
i	1

D	500
e	0
i	1
=	666

Let us read what a Catholic publication has to say about this: *"What are the letters supposed to be in the Pope's crown, and what do they signify, if anything?*

"The letters inscribed in the Pope's mitre are these: *Vicarius Filii Dei*, which is the Latin for the Vicar of the Son of God. Catholics hold that the church, which is a visible society, must have a visible head. Christ, before His ascension into heaven, appointed St. Peter to act as His representative. Upon the death of Peter the man who succeeded to the office of Peter as Bishop of Rome, was recognized as the head of the Church. Hence to the Bishop of Rome, as head of the Church, was given the title 'Vicar of Christ.'

"Enemies of the Papacy denounce this title as a malicious assumption. But the Bible informs us that Christ did not only give His Church authority to teach, but also to rule. Laying claim to the authority to rule in Christ's spiritual kingdom, in Christ's stead, is not a whit more malicious than laying claim to the authority to teach in Christ's name. And this every Christian minister does." April 18th, 1915 edition of *Our Sunday Visitor*.

The above comments are wrong because: a) Jesus left the Holy Spirit to be in his place (John 16:7), b) Jesus is the head of the church (1 Corinthians 11:3; Ephesians 1:22; 4:15;5:23; Colossians 1:18;2:10), c) Peter is not the Rock; is Jesus (1 Corinthians 10:4). Peter himself acknowledged that Christ is the Rock. *"Be it known unto you all, and to all the people of Israel, that by the name of Jesus Christ of Nazareth, whom ye crucified, whom God raised from the dead, even by him doth this man stand here before you whole. This is the stone which was set at nought of you builders, which is become the head of the corner"* (Acts 4:10,11). "Wherefore also it is contained in the scripture, Behold, I lay in Sion a chief corner stone, elect, precious: and he that believeth on him shall not be confounded. Unto you therefore which believe *he is* precious: but unto them which be disobedient, the stone which the builders disallowed, the same is made the head of the corner, And a stone of stumbling, and a rock of offence, *even to them* which stumble at the word, being disobedient: whereunto also they were appointed" (1 Peter 2:6-8).

8) Ludovicus= vicarious chief of the court of Rome (Latin).

L	50
u	5
d	500
o	0
v	5
i	1
c	100
u	5
s	0
=	666

9) Paulo V Vice Deo- Paulo V vicar of God (Latin). The pope that adopted this title governed between the years 1605-1621.

P	0
a	0
u	5
l	50
o	0
V	5
V	5
i	1
c	100
e	0
D	500
e	0
o	0
=	666

10) **IOANES PAVLVS SECVNDO**=John Paul II

I	1
o	0
a	0
n	0
e	0
s	0

P 0
a 0
u 5
l 50
u 5
s 0

S 0
e 0
c 100
u 5
n 0
d 500
o 0
= 666

11) Vicarius generali Dei in terris= general vicar of God on earth (Latin).

V= 5
i= 1
c= 100
a= 0
r= 0
i= 1
u= 5
s= 0

G= 0
e= 0
n= 0
e= 0
r= 0
a= 0
l= 50
i= 1

D= 500
e= 0
i= 1

i= 1
n= 0

T= 0
e= 0
r= 0
r= 0
i= 1
s= 0
666

The following two titles have a great relationship to the untruthful rest day and the origin of its observance:

12) Stur - was the secret God of the mystery-religion of Babylon. This word is Aramaic and it should be pronounced satur.

S = 200
t = 60
u = 400
r = + 6
666

The Bible calls Catholicism Babylon and it was precisely this group that imposed the observance of the day of the sun as rest day in the council of Laodicea. Catholicism is nothing else than the religion - mystery of Stur or Nimrod (=rebel) resuscitated. From Stur was derived Saturn, called son of the sun by the Romans. By Persian influence, the Romans were worshipping the sun on **Sun**days.

Archeological evidence has been found that shows that the adoration to the sun - god was important part of the religion - mystery of Babylon. The untruthful church of chapter 17 of Revelation, presented as an impure woman, is called mystery, Babylon the great - and those that have heard the rosary (the author grew up with it)- have heard several times the word mystery. We know about these mysteries among many proclaimed by the Catholic Church:

- The mystery of the Church
- **The mystery of faith**

From the rosary, we find mysteries from beginning to end:

The 5 Joyful Mysteries

- The *Mystery* of the Annunciation
- The *Mystery* of the Visitation
- The *Mystery* of the Birth of the Lord
- The *Mystery* of the Presentation in the Temple
- The *Mystery* of Finding Jesus in the Temple

The 5 Sorrowful Mysteries

- The *Mystery* of the Agony in the Garden
- The *Mystery* of the Scourging at the Pillar
- The *Mystery* of the Crowning with Thorns
- The *Mystery* of Jesus carrying his cross
- The *Mystery* of the Crucifixion

The 5 Glorious Mysteries

- The *Mystery* of the Resurrection
- The *Mystery* of the Ascension of Our Lord
- The *Mystery* of the Descent of the Holy Spirit
- The *Mystery* of the Assumption of the Blessed Virgin
- The *Mystery* of the Coronation of the Blessed Virgin as Queen of Heaven

13) The tables that follow were on the back of some amulets used by priest worshipers of the sun. Any line of these vertical tables added vertically or horizontally, gives as a result 111. If this number is multiplied by the quantity of vertical or horizontal lines (6), gives as product 666. If all the numbers from 1 to 36 are added, this also gives 666. Here are the tables:

1	32	34	3	35	6
30	8	27	28	11	7
20	24	15	16	13	23
19	17	21	22	18	14
10	26	12	9	29	25
31	4	2	33	5	36

6	32	3	34	35	1
7	11	27	28	8	30
19	14	16	15	23	24
18	20	22	21	17	13
25	29	10	9	26	12
36	5	33	4	2	31

Stur was the secret name of Nimrod, founder of Babylon and its first king (Gen.10:8-12). After his death, he was venerated as a god.

"She (the church) took the pagan **Sun**day and converted it to the Christian **Sun**day... And thus, pagan **Sun**day, devoted to balder [other name for the sun-god] became the Christian **Sun**day devoted to Jesus" (Catholic World, March of 1894, Page 809).

The book Unfolding the Revelation, by R.A. Anderson, contains photos and more information about these amulets in page 126.

Though the minds are affected by a supernatural somnolence such as the one that engulfed the disciples the night of the arrest of Jesus, it is possible to find evidence of the worship of the sun-god in modern liturgy:

1) Head shaved in round that is used by the Roman leaders and that it was specifically forbidden by God in Leviticus 19:27 ("You shall not round the corners of your heads,"), because it was a practice of the followers of Nimrod.
2) The round form of the communion bread (when Jesus parted the bread, it did not remain round- try it at home, please) it is a copy of the communion bread that the Egyptian priests were using to adore their sun-god Amon - ra.
3) The black priestly clothes are only an imitation of the clothes that the priests of Baal were using, in whose service, the sun was largely honorable. The priestly clothes that are used while offering the mass, were the same ones used by the Roman priests in their idolatrous service.
4) Nowhere in the Bible is presented Jesus or any of His disciples with a halo on their heads. This usage had its origin in the halo that Circe, the Roman goddess daughter of the sun, had over her head.

As we have seen, the 666 has to do with the observance of **Sun**day as well as with the power that changed it for the real day of rest. Now we will analyze the language in which the New Testament was written originally. There are only two words in the Biblical Greek whose sum is 666. They have been related to Catholicism during all its history, since by thus to say it, describe two of its principal characteristics.

14) Paradosis = tradition (Greek).

π=	80
α=	1
ρ=	100
α=	1
δ=	4
ο=	70
σ=	200
ι=	10
ς=	200
	666

"We Catholics...have precisely the authority for keeping **Sun**day holy instead of Saturday... we followed the tradition in this matter" (Clifton Tracts, volume 4, Page 15). In his Dies Domini letter, Pope John Paul II wrote: "The spiritual and pastoral riches of Sunday, as it has been handed on to us by tradition, are truly great." "You break the commandment of God [Saturday] for your tradition [**Sun**day]" (Mathew I5:2,3).

15) euporia=wealth (Greek)- according to how it appears in Acts 19:25. In Revelation 18 it is used the word emporoi (vers.3,11,15 and 23) that is translated merchants and comes from the same root as euporia.

ε=	5
υ=	400
π=	80
ο=	70
ρ=	100
ι=	10
α =	1
	666

As Ralph Woodrow wrote in his excellent book, *Babylon Religious Mystery Ancient and Modern* (page 160), "The wealth, that characterized the Babylon of Revelation 17, corrupted the honesty (there were occasions in which the ecclesiastic charges were sold) and the tradition corrupted the doctrine, making it wine of fornication."

16) Benediktos, the name of Pope Benedict adds up to 666 in Greek:

β=	2
ε =	5
ν =	50
ε =	5
δ=	4

ι=	10
κ=	20
τ=	300
ο=	70
ς=	200
	666

What about the Bible? It is not a coincidence that the only New Testament passage that contains three sixes refers to an action of apostasy. The passage is John 6:66, which reads: *"Thereupon many of His disciples left Him and went away, and no longer associated with Him"* (1912 Weymouth New Testament). It is very possible that the people that stopped following Jesus and turned their backs on Him were those that were later chanting "crucify Him" before Pilate. The book The Great Controversy in Spanish, in page 666, contains these sentences that we can connect with this passage from John: "As the storm approaches, a large class who have professed faith in the third angel's message, but have not been sanctified through obedience to the truth, abandon their position and join the ranks of the opposition. By uniting with the world and partaking of its spirit, they have come to view matters in nearly the same light; and when the test is brought, they are prepared to choose the easy, popular side. Men of talent and pleasing address, who once rejoiced in the truth, employ their powers to deceive and mislead souls. They become the most bitter enemies of their former brethren. When Sabbath keepers are brought before the courts to answer for their faith, these apostates are the most efficient agents of Satan to misrepresent and accuse them, and by false reports and insinuations to stir up the rulers against them" (page 608 in English).

Catholics have tried to fabricate ways to come up with other names' sum, but it had resulted in falsehoods, since they force the sum, in order to distract the attention from Vicarius Filii Dei totaling 666. The following 3 paragraphs are an example:

"Some will suggest that the book of Revelation was written only for those living at the time, and that 666 most probably applies to Caesar Nero, who ruled Rome from 54 to 68 AD, rather than someone from latter centuries. This point of view, which suggests Revelation was historic rather than prophetic, is known as *preterism*, and is commonly held by the Catholic Church. So, just how is Nero linked to 666?

"The preterist takes a relatively uncommon form of Nero's name, Nero Caesar or Caesar Nero, and adds an "n", resulting in Neron Caesar. Next, the Latin is transliterated into Aramaic, resulting in *nrwn qsr,* which when using the numeric equivalent of the letters, then adds up to 666 as follows:

Nun	=	50
Resh	=	200
Waw	=	6
Nun	=	50
Qoph	=	100
Samech	=	60
Resh	=	200
		666

"There is a problem though with the above calculation. According to the rules of Jewish numerology, known as *gematria,* when the letter Nun appears a second time in a word, it is known as a "Final", and takes the value of 700.* So to be precise, NRWN QSR actually adds up to 1316 and not 666."

*Source: Behind Numerology, by Shirley Blackwell Lawrence, copyright 1989, published by Newcastle Publishing Co., Inc., North Hollywood, California, ISBN 0-87877-145-X, page 41. This is a quote from the Internet site of Michael Scheifler (http://www.aloha.net/~mikesch).

Some say that the number in Revelation 13 is 616, not 666 based on some ancient Bible manuscripts. However, Irenæus [A.D. 120-202] attributes the 616 to only a copyist error (*Against Heresies: Book V Chapter XXX.*). *Ibid.*

"Therefore shall ye lay up these my words in your heart and in your soul, and bind them for a sign upon your hand, that they may be as frontlets between your eyes [forehead]" (Deuteronomy 11:18).

When can we know for sure that the image of the beast has been formed?

"When the leading churches of the United States, uniting upon such points of doctrine as are held by them in common, shall influence the state to enforce their decrees and to sustain their institutions, then **Protestant America will have formed an image of the Roman hierarchy**, and the infliction of civil penalties upon dissenters will inevitably result.

"The beast with two horns 'causeth [commands] all, both small and great, rich and poor, free and bond, to receive a mark in their right hand, or in their foreheads: and that no man might buy or sell, save he that had the mark, or the name of the beast, or the number of his name.' Revelation 13:16, 17. The third angel's warning is: 'If any man worship the beast and his image, and receive his mark in his forehead, or in his hand, the same shall drink of the wine of the wrath of God.' 'The beast' mentioned in this message, whose worship is enforced by the two-horned beast, is the first, or leopard-like beast of Revelation 13-the papacy. The 'image to the beast' represents that form of apostate Protestantism which will be developed when the Protestant churches shall seek the aid of the civil power for the enforcement of their dogmas. The 'mark of the beast' still remains to be defined." *The Great Controversy*, 444-445. Right now, there is a very strong push to make the government submit to the control of the church. Jesus told us to beware of wolves dressed on sheep's clothes (Matthew 7:15).

REVELATION 14

A triple invitation

[1]*And I looked, and, lo, a Lamb stood on the mount Sion, and with him an hundred forty and four thousand, having his Father's name written in their foreheads.*

Mount Sion or Mount Zion- Where is that mount where John sees the 144,000? Again, we just have to look elsewhere in the Bible for clarification. *"But ye are come unto mount Sion, and unto the city of the living God, <u>the heavenly Jerusalem</u>, and to an innumerable company of angels"* (Hebrews 12:22). John is contemplating them now in the presence of God in heaven. As also verse three indicates, they are singing before the elders and the creatures that are around the heavenly throne inside the New Jerusalem, which is presented in chapter 21 as descending on this earth from heaven.

For a detailed analysis of the 144,000, see chapter 7. This time John sees the group after the great tribulation in the presence of the Lamb. What characterizes them now is that they are shown as having their Father's name written on their foreheads. The Strong's Concordance has this note on the word name (Greek *onoma*): "the name is used for everything which the name covers, everything the thought or feeling of which is aroused in the mind by mentioning, hearing, remembering, the name, i.e. for one's rank, authority, interests, pleasure, command, excellences, deeds etc." The name is a representation of the character. Through the daily surrendering of their will to God, the 144,000 have participated of the divine nature and the result is that their characters reflect the one of their heavenly Father.

[2]*And I heard a voice from heaven, as the voice of many waters, and as the voice of a great thunder: and I heard the voice of harpers harping with their harps:*

This is the powerful word of Jesus Himself (Revelation 1:15). But the voice here is not to inspire terror, because it is accompanied by the sweet and melodious sound of harps.

[3]*And they sung as it were a new song before the throne, and before the four beasts, and the elders: and no man could learn that song but the hundred and forty and four thousand, which were redeemed from the earth.*

The redeemed have a new song of deliverance to sing before the throne, a song that not even the angels can sing because it is unique to the experience of this group, which points to the great liberation performed in their behalf when they were going through the great tribulation. Which song is this? *"And they sing the song of Moses the servant of God, and the song of the Lamb, saying, Great and marvelous are thy works, Lord God Almighty; just and true are thy ways, thou King of saints"* (Revelation 15:3). When Moses saw the chariots and the whole army of Pharaoh drown in the Nile River, he composed a song that retold the Israelites experience. By faith, he looked into the future to a time when the redeemed will be in heaven and wrote: *"Thou in thy mercy hast led forth the people which thou hast redeemed: thou hast guided them in thy strength unto thy holy habitation...Thou shalt bring them in, and plant them in the mountain of thine inheritance, in the place, O LORD, which thou hast made for thee to dwell in, in the Sanctuary, O LORD, which thy hands have established"* (Exodus 15:13). Notice that Moses' song refers to God's mountain (Sion), to God's habitation and to the Sanctuary. Everything in the book of Revelation points to Christ- and He deserves all the glory. However, all elements in Revelation continuously show the church, concluding with the 144,000 because they are those that Jesus will come to rescue. It is the love story between Christ and His bride.

[4]*These are they which were not defiled with women; for they are virgins. These are they which follow the Lamb whithersoever he goeth. These were redeemed from among men, being the first fruits unto God and to the Lamb.*

Not defiled with women- Women in the Bible are a symbol of a church. The virtuous woman of chapter 12 represents the true church, while the harlot woman of chapter 17 represents the corrupt one. Isaiah 4:1 mentions the "women" of the final days: *"And in that day seven women shall take hold of one man, saying, We will eat our own bread, and wear our own apparel: only let us be called by thy name, to take away our reproach."* This is the interpretation:

Seven- represents totality (in some other contexts, perfection)

The women- the last day churches

The man- Jesus

The bread- the word of God

The apparel- the robe of righteousness

The name- the name Christian

The false churches of the end time will have only a name relationship with Jesus, but it will be just a title. They will be preaching their own non-Biblical messages and reject the righteousness of Jesus. They have a name that make believe that they are alive but in reality are dead. *"Not every one that saith unto me, Lord, Lord, shall enter into the kingdom of heaven; but he that doeth the will of my Father which is in heaven. Many will say to me in that day, Lord, Lord, have we not prophesied in thy name? and in thy name have cast out devils? and in thy name done many wonderful works? And then will I profess unto them, I never knew you: depart from me, ye that work iniquity"* (Matthew 7:21-23). The 144,000 will not allow the false doctrines of those churches contaminate their beliefs. Since they will not commit spiritual fornication, they will be considered virgins.

[5]*And in their mouth was found no guile: for they are without fault before the throne of God.*

How could it be that after having sinned so many thousands of times these human beings can be seen as faultless? Didn't David commit adultery and ordered the assassination of an innocent man? This man not only sinned but also tried to cover his tracks. Yet, God referred to him as His servant and a man after His own heart. Let us compare two passages of the New Testament to help us understand how this can happen:

Colossians 1:22- referring to the Christians:	Hebrews 7:26- referring to Jesus:
"In the body of his flesh through death, to present you holy and unblameable and unreproveable in his sight"	*"Such a high priest meets our need—one who is holy, blameless, pure, set apart from sinners, exalted above the heavens."*

What the Bible says about how God sees Jesus, it applies also to how God sees repented believers. What happens is that Jesus' life takes the place of our lives. When God the Father looks towards us, He sees Jesus' record of 33- ½ years without sin. He does not see your failures (see Romans 3:10-18), your sins or rebellions; only the perfect life of Jesus that takes the place of yours. See, Jesus did not only die to take away your sins. He also died to share the record of His perfect life with you, so when your name is called up in judgment, it is His life the one that is scrutinized and not yours. You will be declared acquitted and given the right to dwell in heaven with God. That is how the 144,000 are said to be without fault before God. That is what He wants for you.

[6]*And I saw another angel fly in the midst of heaven, having the everlasting gospel to preach unto them that dwell on the earth, and to every nation, and kindred, and tongue, and people,*

As we studied in chapter 1, the word angel means messenger. In Daniel 7, the beasts with wings represented the celerity (speed) of their movements. In Revelation 11, the two witnesses are called up to heaven, indicating exaltation. Here we have an urgent heavenly message being brought to every corner of the planet. This is the final push of the great commission given by Jesus to His disciples to preach the Gospel to every creature. God has allowed mankind to reach an advanced level of scientific advances that are being utilized to reach the most remote corners of the earth. In countries closed to the Gospel, His messages get through short wave radios, the internet and satellite TV- literally flying in the midst of heaven. Very soon, the last post of darkness will be reached with the glorious light of the Gospel of Jesus Christ and He will return.

What is the gospel? It is defined by Paul in his first letter to the Corinthians 15:1-4: *"Moreover, brethren, I declare unto you the gospel which I preached unto you, which also ye have received, and wherein ye stand; By which also ye are saved, if ye keep in memory what I preached unto you, unless ye have believed in vain. For I delivered unto you first of all that which I also received, how that Christ died for our sins according to the scriptures; And that he was buried, and that he rose again the third day according to the scriptures."* Writing to the Romans, Paul added: *"For I am not ashamed of the gospel of Christ: for it is the power of God unto salvation to every one that believeth; to the Jew first, and also to the Greek. For therein is the righteousness of God revealed from faith to faith: as it is written, The just shall live by faith"* (Romans 1:16-17). For Paul this was the subject of his preaching. *"For I determined not to know any thing among you, save Jesus Christ, and him crucified"* (1 Corinthians 2:2).

This is a gospel of equality; for there is no difference among those that accept it. "There is neither Jew nor Greek, there is neither bond nor free, there is neither male nor female: for ye are all one in Christ Jesus" (Galatians 3:28). This message gives dignity to the oppressed and freedom even to those that lack it physically. The value of the elements that compose the human body (carbon, calcium, magnesium, phosphorus, iron, copper, etc.) cost less that $10.00. However, God placed such an infinite value on human beings that He sent His own Son to purchase them with His precious blood. Even though John 3:16 says that God sent Jesus, it was a voluntary offering by Him. The Father did not force Jesus to do it. *"Then said I, Lo, I come (in the volume of the book it is written of me,) to do thy will, O God" (Hebrews 10:7). He laid down His life on His own: "Therefore doth my Father love me, because I lay down my life, that I might take it again. No man taketh it from me, but I lay it down of myself. I have power to lay it down, and I have power to take it again. This commandment have I received of my Father"* (John 10:17-18). If you really wonder about the value of a human, look at Calvary and you will see it clearly. It is worth so much, that Jesus gave His own sinless life to redeem us. What do you appreciate more, a dollar coin that you found on the grass on your backyard or one that you worked harder than usual to earn? Both are dollars and if the same design and year, they have the same face value. However, the quarter that we sweat to earn seems more valuable. I was given a carved elephant a few years ago. It is on a shelf close to where

I am writing this. Next to it is a dog that I carved. The wood is so hard that I broke several blades on it. I placed more value, of course, on the one that took me hours of effort to shape. For Christ, who struggled and suffered indescribable agony to save your soul, you are precious. In the Garden of Gethsemane he sweat blood knowing what awaited Him. Looking into the future He saw you condemned to eternal death if He did not take your sins on Him as if He were the one who committed each one of them.

Many years ago, a schoolteacher left the students alone in the classroom. When he returned he discovered that one of the children had made a non-flattering drawing of him on the blackboard. He started to ask who did it and got only silence. He kept asking while raising his voice. One of the students, perhaps scared to have the whole class punished if the guilty was not found, pointed to a little, skinny and sickly child. The teacher had a stick on his hand and was about to swing it on the boys' back when another student screamed: "I did it teacher, it was me." The teacher, by now very angry, repeatedly hit the student very hard until he was on the floor. The real guilty child was the little fellow, but this other child had pity on him and took the punishment on his place. That day they became best friends. Doesn't it move you to see Jesus hanging on the cross suffering for what you have done, taking the punishment for your sins that you deserve so you can walk free and unpunished? Behold the Lamb of God taking away your sins so you can be free indeed. That is the gospel message being preached all over the world. It is the message of a compassionate God that could not suffer to have you lost forever.

It is interesting that just as it is presented here in the book of Revelation, Paul also sees a relationship between the gospel and the judgment: *"In the day when God shall judge the secrets of men by Jesus Christ according to my gospel"* (Romans 2:16).

Rev 14:6	The gospel to all nations
Rev 14:7	The hour of judgment

Romans 2:16	The gospel preached by Paul
	God will judge according to the gospel

The Gospel is preached to the entire world first, and if rejected, then those that take the grace of God for granted will be judged. This is exactly how it happened in the garden of Eden. God promised a Savior (the gospel incarnated) and then spoke of the hardships that awaited the human race. This was as well the approach in the times of Noah, when he preached 120 years, giving his audience twelve decades of opportunity. It was also the case in times of Abraham when he sent the angels to the impenitent city of Sodom, but even the future sons in law refuse the offer of mercy. This word is getting ripe for the day of judgment but God is still sending warnings. The perils abound more in the cities because the psychology of the masses influence many to follow the few that corrupt them. "Life in the cities is false and artificial. The intense passion for money getting, the whirl of excitement and pleasure seeking, the thirst for display, the luxury and extravagance, all are forces that, with the great masses of mankind, are turning the mind from life's true purpose. They are opening the door to a thousand evils. Upon the youth they have almost irresistible power" (Country Living 5-6 -1905). These days it is very difficult to distinguish between the Christian youth and those that do not serve Him, due to the lax attitude of the parents who, instead of fulfilling their parental duties, they allowed the TV and video games to raise their precious children. Very soon, Jesus would not be able to wait any longer in order to save His children.

7 *Saying with a loud voice, Fear God, and give glory to him; for the hour of his judgment is come: and worship him that made heaven, and earth, and the sea, and the fountains of waters.*

This verse contains a few elements that should be discussed:

- Loud voice- it is essential that everybody listens.
- Fear and glorify God for the hour of His judgment is come- We are to reverence and respect God. He should occupy the first place in our hearts. Having this attitude daily will help us to be prepared for the judgment. This is the same judgment mentioned in Daniel chapter 7 in which Jesus comes before the Father. The Bible teaches that Jesus is the judge, the witness, the lawyer and his life record takes the place of ours in the judgment if we are reconciled with Him.
- Worship the Creator- The historic context of this passage refers to the preaching of the three angels' message during the 19th century before Darwin published his *Origin of*

Species book. God is not taken by surprise and wanted the world to have the opportunity to know the truth before being exposed to the error (I would prefer to say the non-sense) of evolution.

I grew up being taught that evolution was a fact, although they still called a "theory." The absurdity of an idea that proposes that we evolved from inferior forms of life over a period of millions of years has been taught unchallenged in schools at all levels, even in Christian settings. Let us say for example that it took only a year to develop a lung (by the way we have two of those, two kidneys, two eyes, ears, arms, legs, making us symmetric inside and out- whatever we have only one of, is usually in the middle and always in the most optimal position and location). How long could we have survived without breathing air? What about the time that it took to develop a liver, a pancreas, a stomach, or a spleen? Could we have survived without any vital organ, waiting for some strange influence to discover that a specific organ was needed? How those organs came to be? Did they just start to appear and suddenly started doing a determined function? How did the cells become specialists (brain cells, liver cells, skin cells, etc.). How many attempts were made to produce viable mammals? What if one or more of those organs was not completely functional- like a heart with only one cavity? Or what if the circulatory system did not have veins and arteries and the blood was all the same, without separating oxygenated blood from the blood with CO2? How long would it have taken to have the blood too saturated, making live unsustainable?

Now, Let us imagine that a completely functional monkey appeared in what we know as Spain. How could it have found a compatible mate with the chromosomes needed to produce a like creature? Keep in mind that at that time there were no dating websites to connect them. What about if the other functional monkey was of the same sex? How long would they have to wait until a complementary sex monkey would be produced? When did the reproductive organs appear? And what about how to keep the "baby" alive? How long it took to discover the need for mammary glands? Why there are so many species with male and female- and with compatible DNA to make reproduction possible? We see male and female in birds, reptiles, mammals and even fish. Is all of this coincidence? It took Thomas Alba Edison 2,000 attempts to make a functional light bulb. How many tries did it take to have all the species that we have today? Failure to reproduce alike creatures would be equivalent to extinction without an external hand to continue guiding the effort until reaching that eureka moment. It would be enough for the first couple of a species to die without viable offspring to completely eliminate via total extinction their kind from this planet. This could eliminate the hope of ever contemplating that kind of creature under the sun again.

And what about the human female enjoyment of copulation? For the male, the desire for the female makes a big difference because without it, there could not be fertilization of the female eggs to produce the next generation if he does not have that craving. However, for the female, that is utterly useless unless a loving Creator wanted her to have a pleasure conductive to increasing her happiness. Otherwise, It would have sufficed to only have the instinct of reproduction, just as the animals, many of which have a season for mating, when the females are on heat (like with mammals), or if the season is the correct one like with salmon and other creatures. Once accomplished, they do not see action again until the next season comes around. The fact that women enjoy sex shows that there is a Creator that cares about them. Evolution (if any creature could endure the wait to have every organ working as needed) would have given them no enjoyment because it would not have been functional.

Time after time, it has been discovered that the great findings that "prove" evolution have been hoaxes. All those "ancestors" were modified bones and even pig bones to make people believe that those humanoids were ancient humans. Time after time, all those "proofs" of evolution have been found to be hoaxes, either fabricated or from species not related to humans.

What about carbon and other methods of dating? They have been proven unreliable many times. For example, it is said that the upper layers of the Grand Canyon show an older age than the bottom ones. Could we know how old is this planet by the quantity of people living in it? How long would it take to the human population to grow to the seven plus billion that we have today? "A tremendous change occurred with the industrial revolution:

whereas it had taken all of human history until around 1800 for world population to reach one billion, the second billion was achieved in only 130 years (1930), the third billion in less than 30 years (1959), the fourth billion in 15 years (1974), and the fifth billion in only 13 years (1987). During the 20th century alone, the population in the world has grown from 1.65 billion to 6 billion." http://www.worldometers.info/world-population/. Going backwards, we can see that it has not taken more than 4,500 years of growth, which takes us back to the time of the flood. Some estimate that by that time, the world population could have easily surpassed a billion, given that the lifespan was a lot longer, allowing to reproduce for centuries instead of just decades as it is in our days.

Meanwhile, the perfection of our human body is ignored as an evidenced of design. How many millenniums took for a nose to appear? So we were breathing only cold air until then? When did we get a mouth? How did we eat until then? How was it determined that we needed teeth, saliva and a tongue to properly process the food we needed for fuel? What happened with the food until we got a stomach? How did the stomach get to learn how to process that food? How did food with all necessary nutrients to sustain life appear in the world? What if no trees or plants would have "popped" out of the ground or plankton in the seas? How oxygen would be produced? How those trees knew how to produce seed in order to reproduce an identical fruit-bearing tree? After the stomach was done with the digestion- assuming that there was also a pancreas and a liver to produce the necessary enzymes, what happened with the waste? Did it come out the mouth until the body produced the two intestines? How did we get a heart and how blood circulation was designed to bring in oxygen and carry out the waste gas?

Evolution teaches that we developed how we are now over millions of years. Since evolution cannot be real, then there had to be a brain that orchestrated those changes on that original cell in order to accomplish the marvels that we know today. Doesn't it make sense that everything followed a well-organized plan from a designer?

How come bees appeared to help plants and trees reproduce? They are very organized too and know the cardinal points, which allow the explorers to convey an exact location and distance to the workers for the source of food. How come we have a cycle of rain and the water just do not disappear into space? What about the distance from the sun and the moon to the earth? This planet is at the perfect distance from the sun to permit life. The moon produces the tides needed by the ecology of the oceans at the distance that it is from earth. How come the earth goes around the sun in 365 days and a few minutes, year after year and it always takes the same time? What about the laws of nature, like the gravity laws? Are those laws coincidence? How all these facts are voluntarily ignored and the fallacies of evolution with all the deceit from the "scientists" and philosophers are exalted? For many decades, it was taught in schools that the appendix was a vestigial organ from when we were monkeys. Now it has been discovered that it serves a function. I do not think that common sense and real analytical logic are being used by evolutionists- only voluntary and blind ignorance. The probabilities that all of these things on this planet are a coincidence are so astoundingly impossible that it requires less faith to believe that there was a plan and a designer that orchestrated all of this, as we know it.

When I had just turned 16 years old, I was managing the family business. We were about 40 small merchants operating under one roof. My father had just passed away a month before my birthday and my mother has gone to help in what she could. In a slow time, I went around and saw fresh "green" lima beans. I immediately bought them for my mother to cook (and she was a great cook!). When she looked at them, she was infuriated and took the beans and me to the merchant that sold them to me. She was resentful that he took advantage of a minor who had just lost his father. She was not an educated woman, having attended only a first grade of elementary school, but she was no dummy. The merchant had soaked the beans to make them swell and look like fresh. It so happened that my mother noticed holes in them, characteristic of insect boring, which happens to the dry beans, not fresh green ones. The apologetic merchant gave me the money back and I never saw him selling "fresh lima beans" again.

Evolutionists have done the same by teaching their fallacies to young, defenseless developing minds. With evolution has come the greatest moral decay in the history of humanity because by taking God out of the picture, we are only animals, whose only purpose in life is to reproduce. Without a Superior Being to which we are accountable for our moral decisions, we run in frenzy to do what it pleases us ("if it feels good, do it") and society degenerates more and more instead of evolving to a superior condition. When evolution started to be taught in schools, the biggest offenses committed by the students were chewing gum and making paper planes. Now children rape, sell drugs and bring guns to school to kill fellow students and teachers. Where will it all end, if not in total chaos?

This verse is parallel to Revelation 3:14 where it talks about the church of Laodicea, which covers the period of 1844 to the end of the world. There it refers to Jesus as *"the beginning of the creation of God."* The word "beginning" refers to Him as the originator or Creator. God knew what Darwin was going to do, as He knew about Cyrus and other Bible characters even before they were born. He knows also about our actions and motives long before we commit them. We need to pray for His guidance, so our actions can be positive and constructive.

8And there followed another angel, saying, Babylon is fallen, is fallen, that great city, because she made all nations drink of the wine of the wrath of her fornication.

For over 1,500 years, Babylon has oppressed the true children of God while claiming to be the true church. Now the time of reckoning has come. It will fall because it mingled the truth with fables and made the world drink of the resulting wine.

9And the third angel followed them, saying with a loud voice, If any man worship the beast and his image, and receive his mark in his forehead, or in his hand, 10The same shall drink of the wine of the wrath of God, which is poured out without mixture into the cup of his indignation; and he shall be tormented with fire and brimstone in the presence of the holy angels, and in the presence of the Lamb:

A good and wise parent never disciplines his children for misbehavior if they were not taught beforehand what the unacceptable behavior was. Our loving heavenly Father has not left us in the dark regarding what is necessary to know. He has told us the truth including which day we should worship and desires that we escape harmless from Babylon. In chapter 20, we will discuss how and when that punishment takes place.

Very soon, the three angels' message will be preached to all earth and the Sunday laws will be enforced. However, as prophesied by Zechariah 13:8, 9, not all those in the church will remain in it. There is going to be a sifting. *"And it shall come to pass, that in all the land, saith the LORD, two parts therein shall be cut off and die; but the third shall be left therein. And I will bring the third part through the fire, and will refine them as silver is refined, and will try them as gold is tried: they shall call on my name, and I will hear them: I will say, It is my people: and they shall say, The LORD is my God."* The refining fire is burning the rubbish, preparing our characters to make them worthy of the kingdom. However- and this is the tragic part- many that are half-converted will separate themselves from the fold and join the ranks of the enemy. "When the law of God is made void the church will be sifted by fiery trials, and a larger proportion than we now anticipate, will give heed to seducing spirits and doctrines of devils. Instead of being strengthened when brought into strait places, many prove that they are not living branches of the True Vine; they bore no fruit, and the husbandman taketh them away." *Selected Messages*, book 2, 368. We must be faithful to God in these relatively calmed times so we can remain in the fold when the hard times come.

11 And the smoke of their torment ascendeth up for ever and ever: and they ***have*** *no rest day nor night, who worship the beast and his image, and whosoever receiveth the mark of his name.*

The smoke that ascends forever and ever has caused much confusion to many people. This is a figurative language and must be understood from the point of view that hell is not what people think it is. We must take this and every other confusing passage at the light of the rest of the Bible. Truth must harmonize on its own and be complimentary of other Biblical teachings- not contradictory.

First, observe that the verb "have" is in the present tense. Isaiah wrote that *"the wicked are like the troubled sea, when it cannot rest, whose waters cast up mire and dirt"* (Isaiah 57:20). The wicked cannot have peace living apart from the source of peace, joy and real love. They do not have a relationship with the only One that can resolve their problems. They have no faith and are always worrying and fearful, not to mention that are never satisfied in any situation. Nothing they try can satisfy the emptiness of their hearts. Eventually, they will cease to exist. Not out of revenge but out of love. How could this be? Humans apart from God cannot achieve happiness because they are motivated by selfishness. We strive for people and circumstances to make us happy and when it does not happen, we head for divorce court and other such extremes. In God's kingdom, everybody will find his/her happiness in looking out for the good of the others. The unbelievers will not find happiness in heaven and their selfish behavior would not be for the good of the other inhabitants. They will always be complaining and fighting, perpetuating the unhappiness and suffering from this world. Heaven will not be heavenly with their attitude and actions. They will always be against God and everything that represents his character such as purity and unselfish love. God cannot force anyone to be saved and the sad time will come when He will have to pull the plug on the majority of humans, due to their own choices.

Now, lets go back to the smoke and review some similar passages:

> *"And when the men of Ai looked behind them, they saw, and, behold, <u>the smoke</u> of the city <u>ascended up to heaven</u>, and they had no power to flee this way or that way: and the people that fled to the wilderness turned back upon the pursuers"* (Joshua 8:20).

> *"The sword of the LORD is filled with blood, it is made fat with fatness, and with the blood of lambs and goats, with the fat of the kidneys of rams: for the LORD hath a sacrifice in Bozrah, and a great slaughter in the land of Idumea... It shall not be quenched night nor day; <u>the smoke thereof shall go up for ever</u>: from generation to generation it shall lay waste; none shall pass through it for ever and ever"* (Isaiah 34:6,10).

> *"As smoke is driven away, so drive them away: as wax melteth before the fire, so let the wicked perish at the presence of God"* (Psalm 68:2). The smoke here obviously ends when the wicked perish, for what good is it to burn something lifeless and irresponsive?

If we go to Idumea now, we see no smoke. Once the fire fulfills its purpose, there is no more smoke. Likewise, it will be when the wicked are consumed. The smoke will stop ascending. We will discuss this in more detail in chapter 20, where I show Biblical proof- some of which your church leader might not be revealing to you, just as mine was doing until I read the Bible on my own. For now, I ask you to be patient until we get to that chapter so we continue with the building blocks of Revelation.

[12]Here is the patience of the saints: here are they that keep the commandments of God, and the faith of Jesus.

The saints are really patient, seeing everyday with pain in their hearts how mankind destroys itself more and more. However, not all is lost. As in times of Elijah, He has a people that keep His commandments and honor Him in spite of ridicule and persecution. For them the commandments are a delight. Lets read David's opinion in Psalm 119:

> *"[45] And I will walk at liberty: for I seek thy precepts. [46]I will speak of thy testimonies also before kings, and will not be ashamed. And I will delight myself in thy commandments, which I have loved... [56]This I had, because I kept thy precepts... [92]Unless thy law had been my delights, I should then have perished in mine affliction... [95]The wicked have waited for me to destroy me: but I will consider thy testimonies... [97]O how love I thy law! it is my meditation all the day. [98]Thou through thy commandments hast made me wiser than mine enemies: for they are ever with me. [99]I have more understanding than all my teachers: for thy testimonies are my meditation. [100]I understand more than the ancients, because I keep thy precepts.*

> *[101]I <u>have refrained my feet from every evil way</u>, that I might keep thy word."*

However, keeping the commandments is not all that characterizes God's children. They love sinners in spite of how they are treated by them: *"Rivers of waters run down mine eyes, because they keep not thy law"* (Psalm 119:136). They pray for the sinners to repent and get to know Jesus as their friend and Savior. They plead with them with tears hoping to see them in heaven. They fast, praying for their salvation. When Jesus was about to be crucified, He stood to look at the city of Jerusalem and said these sad words: *"O Jerusalem, Jerusalem, thou that killest the prophets, and stonest them which are sent unto thee, how often would I have gathered thy children together, even as a hen gathereth her chickens under her wings, and ye would not!"* (Matthew 23:37). In spite of their crimes against His messengers of mercy, Jesus wanted nothing less than to save them. He is been trying to reach your heart too. Is He still waiting outside of it? He does not force His entry but you can invite Him in. Your life will never be better once He is invited in as Lord and Savior.

Many claim that the Ten Commandments were nailed to the cross and are no longer binding. Really? So it is OK to kill, steal, commit adultery, envy, lie and disobey our parents? No reasonable mind will admit that it is now admissible and correct to do those things. So what is the Bible talking about in Ephesians and Galatians- the two misunderstood passages regarding the law?

The Bible mentions more than one law. There were civil laws, health laws, the Moral law and the ceremonial law. Let us compare the last two:

The Moral law (the 10 Commandments)	The ceremonial law
1. It is a real law (James 2:8) 2. It was written by God on stone (Exodus 24:12; 31:18) 3. It was placed in the arc (Exodus 40:20) 4. It was to be magnified by Jesus (Isaiah 42:21; Matthew 5:17) 5. It is immutable and eternal (Psalm 111:7,8; 119:152) 6. It is perfect (Psalm 19:7) 7. Is spiritual (Romans 7:14) 8. Is a delight to obey it (Psalm 119:77) 9. He who obeys it is happy (James 1:25) 10. It is a law of freedom (James 2:11,12) 11. It is holy, just and good (Romans 7:12)	1- It was a ritual law (Ephesians 2:15) 2- It was written by Moses on a book (Deut. 31:24) Galatians 3:10 refers to this law. 3- It was placed by the arc (Deut. 31:24) 4- It was abolished by Jesus (Ephesians 2:15) 5- It was mutable (Hebrews 10:1) 6- It did not make anything perfect (Hebrews 10:1,3,4) 7- It is carnal (Hebrews 7:16) 8- It is a yoke (Gal. 5:1) 9- He who obeys it is not happy (Galatians 3:10;5:1-6) 10- It was a "yoke of bondage." (Galatians 5:1)

The purpose of the preceding table is to prove that the law of the 10 Commandments is different from the one that required circumcision and the sacrifice of animals. This later one was the one abolished by Jesus (nailed to the cross) and it is known as the ceremonial law. This law included the observance of days that for their ritual meaning were called sabbaths but did not necessarily fall on the 7th day of the week (rather, they fell on specific days of the month). Leviticus 23 can help us to clarify the difference.

"Speak unto the children of Israel, saying, In the seventh month, <u>in the first day of the month</u>, shall ye have a sabbath, a memorial of blowing of trumpets, an holy convocation. ...[27]<u>Also on the tenth day</u> of this seventh month there shall be a day of atonement: it shall be an holy convocation unto you; and ye shall afflict your souls, and offer an offering made by fire unto the LORD. [34]Speak unto the children of Israel, saying, The fifteenth day of this seventh month shall be

the feast of tabernacles for seven days unto the LORD. [35]*On the first day shall be an holy convocation: ye shall do no servile work therein.* [36]*Seven days ye shall offer an offering made by fire unto the LORD: on the eighth day shall be an holy convocation unto you; and ye shall offer an offering made by fire unto the LORD: it is a solemn assembly; and ye shall do no servile work therein.* [39]*Also in the fifteenth day of the seventh month, when ye have gathered in the fruit of the land, ye shall keep a feast unto the LORD seven days: on the first day shall be a sabbath, and on the eighth day shall be a sabbath."* Leviticus 23:24,27,34-36 & 39. Here we have that these Sabbaths fell on specific days of the month and were not tied to the weekly cycle. They were to be observed on the 1st, 8th, 10th and 15th days of the seventh month.

Now notice that verse 38 clearly indicates that these Sabbaths were *"**Beside** the Sabbaths of the LORD."* These sabbath days had a symbolic meaning that pointed to Christ's sacrifice and ministry. Since they were a symbol or shadow, they were to expire, as Paul wrote: *"Let no man therefore judge you in meat, or in drink, or in respect of an holyday, or of the new moon, or of the sabbath days:* [17]*Which are a shadow of things to come; but the body is of Christ"* (Colossians 2:16,17). Those ceremonial sabbaths were a shadow because the sacrifices offered those days were a symbol of Jesus. The Sabbath of the Ten Commandments cannot be considered a shadow because there was no shedding of blood. It only points to the need to rest and it was a day to commune with God.

Besides, how could anyone in clear conscience, claim that Jesus contradicted himself? He declared that He would not abolish the law but rather exalt it: *"The LORD is well pleased for his righteousness' sake; he will magnify the law, and make it honorable."* (Isaiah 42:21). This passage complements the words of Jesus found in Matthew 5:17: *"Think not that I am come to destroy the law, or the prophets: I am not come to destroy, but to fulfill."*

Some verses to consider:

Matthew 5:18,19 *"For verily I say unto you, **Till heaven and earth pass**, one jot or one tittle shall in no wise pass from the law, till all be fulfilled. Whosoever therefore shall break **one** of these least commandments, and shall teach men so, he shall be called the least* *in the kingdom of heaven: but whosoever shall do and teach them, the same shall be called great in the kingdom of heaven."* Did heaven and earth already passed? No. Has any part of the law then has changed? Not at all. Only in some preachers' minds.

Rev 12:17 *"And the dragon was wroth with the woman, and went to make war with the remnant of her seed, which* ***keep the commandments of God****, and have the testimony of Jesus Christ."* Satan does now make war against those whom he already has in his pocket. His war is against those that are faithful to God and keep His law- not to be saved, for we are saved by grace only- but out of gratitude and in His strength.

Romans 3:31 *"Do we then make void the law through faith? God forbid: yea,* ***we establish the law****."* If we (Paul included) establish (= confirm, corroborate, validate, approve, sanction, ratify, endorse) the law, how come so many preachers (yours probably included) teach that the law was abolished?

Psalm 119:152 *"Concerning your testimonies, I have known of old that you have* ***founded them for ever****."* If they were founded forever, they were not to be abolished at the cross! Therefore, what was abolished was some other law that no longer had usefulness after the cross- it was the one pointing to the supreme sacrifice of Christ- the ceremonial law.

Romans 7:7 *"What shall we say then? Is the law sin? God forbid. Not, I had not known sin, but by the law: for I had not known lust, except the law had said, Thou shalt not covet."*

Romans 7:22 *"****For I delight in the law of God*** *after the inward man."*

James 1:25 *"But whoever looks into the* ***perfect law of liberty****, and continues therein, he being not a forgetful hearer, but a doer of the work, this man will be blessed in his deed."*

James 2:10-12 *"For* ***whosoever shall keep the whole law, and yet offend in one point, he is guilty of all****. For he that said, Do not commit adultery, said also, Do not kill. Now if you commit no adultery, yet if you kill, you become a transgressor of the law. So* *speak you, and so do, as they that* *shall be* ***judged by the law of liberty***." Notice that the standard of the judgment will be the Ten Commandments and twice it is called *"law of liberty."* Keeping that law in the power of Christ guarantees our freedom. Can a person caught after committing a crime be free? No, he will spend a good time in prison. We are free if, depending on the divine strength to render obedience, keep each one of those commandments, not to be saved, but out of gratitude for having been saved.

If James calls the commandments *"law of liberty"*, he obviously is not referring at all to the temporary ceremonial law that required sacrifices and was a burden. If I do not kill, lie, or cheat on my wife I am free. If I steal or kill someone, I am not free because I will feel bad and fear that I will be caught. Keeping the law gives me total freedom. You might say that you cannot keep the law. Can I have your permission to ask you, in the presence of your boss if you ever stole anything, even a paper clip, from work? Hopefully, your answer would be "I have not stolen anything from my employer." There you have it: you have the power to choose if you want to do what is right. If you exercise the power to chose, God will enable you to obey the Ten Commandments.

Did you notice that those who say that the 10 commandments are no longer valid or were only for the Jews still consider that killing, adultery and stealing are wrong, while they reject the only commandment that starts with "**Remember**?" All of them are part of the Decalogue. To say that a law that was called eternal in Psalm 119:152 has a temporary section (the Sabbath part that some say now we should keep **SUN**day), would be equivalent to declare that a man was granted eternal life but his right hand is mortal. It is either ALL eternal or not eternal at all, since eternal and temporary exclude each other like light and darkness.

The ceremonial law was temporary (a shadow) because it pointed towards Jesus' first advent and His sacrifice to pay the penalty of our sins.

The Moral Law is eternal because it is a reflection of the character of God and we cannot do away with it. It is a sign of loyalty to our Creator. Which side would you chose?

*[13]And I heard a voice from heaven saying unto me, Write, **<u>Blessed are the dead which die in the Lord from henceforth</u>**: Yea, saith the Spirit, that they may rest from their labours; and their works do follow them.*

Daniel 12 discusses the lot of those that die during this time in history. This passage corresponds to the period of Laodicea as we mentioned above. Those that died from 1844 on will be part of a special resurrection just before Christ returns. Let me explain. Both the Old and the New Testaments mention the resurrection of the righteous. However, the Scriptures indicate that there will be more than one. For example, if we compare Daniel 12 and John 5, we can see that both passages point to different events. Daniel speaks of a special resurrection separate from the general resurrection on the final day of human history of which John writes.

Daniel 12:2	John 5:28,29
*"And **<u>many</u>** of them that sleep in the dust of the earth shall awake, some to everlasting life, and some to shame and everlasting contempt."*	*"Marvel not at this: for the hour is coming, in the which **<u>all</u>** that are in the graves shall hear his voice, And shall come forth; they that have done good, unto the resurrection of life; and they that have done evil, unto the resurrection of damnation."*

Notice that the passage in Daniel speaks about MANY that will be resurrected, while John is referring to ALL. "Many" indicates just a few compared with the all. There are two additional passages that must be taken into consideration:

> *"Jesus saith unto him [the wicked high priest], Thou hast said: nevertheless I say unto you, Hereafter **<u>shall ye see</u>** the Son of man sitting on the right hand of power, and coming in the clouds of heaven"* (Matthew 26:64). The only way for them to see Jesus return in the clouds is if they are alive- resurrected – to witness that event.
>
> *"Behold, he cometh with clouds; and every eye shall see him, and **<u>they also which pierced him</u>**: and all kindreds of the earth shall wail because of him. Even so, Amen"* (Revelation 1:7).

Before Jesus' return, the wicked that were involved in His crucifixion will be resurrected to behold Him in His glory. In addition, the believers that died in this era of atheism and materialism will be raised up from their graves to behold their beloved Savior return. This special resurrection will be a reward for them. They will join the saints alive, the 144,000 that are coming from the great tribulation. Then all the redeemed from the previous centuries will be resurrected in the general resurrection of the righteous. Describing that moment, Paul wrote: *"For the Lord himself shall descend from heaven with a shout, with the voice of the archangel, and with the trump of God: and the dead in Christ shall rise first: Then we which are alive and remain shall be caught up together with them in the clouds, to meet the Lord in the air: and so shall we ever be with the Lord"* (1 Thessalonians 4:16-17). Jesus has left an open invitation for you and me. He wants to take us home with Him (John 4:1-3) for ages with no end. We will study about that heavenly dwelling in chapter 21.

14And I looked, and behold a white cloud, and upon the cloud one sat like unto the Son of man, having on his head a golden crown, and in his hand a sharp sickle.

This verse describes Jesus in His second coming. Now Jesus is shown sitting but it will not be on His throne of grace (Hebrews 4:16) but on His throne of Glory. Mercy can no longer be offered to the sinner. Now Jesus has come to claim those that have been faithful, many of whom were persecuted for His sake, to take them home with Him (John 14:1-3). There is going to be a great celebration in heaven as the processional host of the redeemed goes through the gates of the promised new city (Hebrews 11:10,16;13:14). *"Open ye the gates, that the righteous nation which keepeth the truth may enter in"* (Isaiah 26:2).

*15And another angel came out of the temple, crying with a loud voice to him that sat on the cloud, Thrust in thy sickle, and reap: for **the time is come** for thee to reap; for the harvest of the earth is ripe.*
16And he that sat on the cloud thrust in his sickle on the earth; and the earth was reaped.

This is the harvest of the saved. God is not subject to anything that He created but He does things on time. When the time came to set the Hebrews free from slavery, He called Moses; to redeem mankind, He sent Jesus on time (Gal. 4:4) and now He will reap His harvest on time. We cannot delay our decision to follow Him. We too, must be on time for that divine appointment.

[17]*And another angel came out of* ***<u>the temple which is in heaven</u>****, he also having a sharp sickle.*

This is a different sickle, also sharp, but in this case, it will be used to harvest a different fruit.

[18]*And another angel came out from the altar, which had power over fire; and cried with a loud cry to him that had the sharp sickle, saying, Thrust in thy sharp sickle, and gather the clusters of the vine of the earth; for her grapes are fully ripe.*

The ripeness refers to the setting of the character. This time the harvest is of grapes. This passage is similar to Joel 3:13: *"Put ye in the sickle, for the harvest is ripe: come, get you down; for the press is full, the fats overflow; for their wickedness is great."* Isaiah wrote about a vineyard that God planted. Since He provided everything necessary for it to be productive, He expected good grapes from it. Instead, it produced bad fruit (Isaiah 5:1,2,7). When God expected love, harmony, obedience and righteousness, His people produced violence. As God gave Israel in the past time to repent, so He is doing it today with the inhabitants of this world, hoping that they *"Bring forth fruit that is consistent with repentance [let your lives prove your change of heart]* (Matthew 3:8 Amplified Bible). How do we produce good fruit? This is such an important matter that Jesus Himself answered it. John 15:4, 5 says: *"Abide in me, and I in you. As the branch cannot bear fruit of itself, except it abide in the vine; no more can ye, except ye abide in me. I am the vine, ye are the branches: He that abideth in me, and I in him, the same bringeth forth much fruit: for without me ye can do nothing."* The secret is to abide in Jesus. How do we abide? We do it by daily communion and surrendering of our wills to His will. There must be a connection so the divine sap will run through our souls and bring life. No connection can happen if we are always in a hurry and do not take time to spend it with God. Most people just offer a quick prayer in the morning and even a shorter one before going to bed and do not even remember Him in between. After making dinner for his wife, a romantic husband asked his beloved mate of eleven years if she missed him that day. Her answer crushed him: "I was so busy that I did not remember you." They eventually divorced. How do you think God feels if we go about our daily business and do not think about Him? We need to be in love with Jesus. Not only to think about Him, but singing praises to Him in our hearts with gratitude for the forgiveness of our sins and the promise of eternal salvation. *"Praise the LORD, my soul, and never forget all the good he has done: He is the one who forgives all your sins, the one who heals all your diseases, the one who rescues your life from the pit, the one who crowns you with mercy and compassion, the one who fills your life with blessings so that you become young again like an eagle"* (Psalm 103:2-5 *GW*).

Eternal life is worth it and spending time with God in prayer, meditation and Bible study is crucial to accomplish our union with Him. We must develop a close relationship with Him or face total separation. That relationship will bring us from abiding to obedience, which will come naturally and without hidden motives- for we are not saved by obeying but by believing. *"If ye keep my commandments, ye shall <u>abide</u> in my love; even as I have <u>kept my Father's commandments</u>, and abide in his love"* (John 15:10). Verse 12 above shows that those saints living in the end times will keep the commandments of God.

However, there is a group that will not abide: *"If a man abide not in me, he is cast forth as a branch, and is withered; and men gather them, and cast them into the fire, and they are burned"* (John 15:6). This group is represented in Matthew 25 as the 5 foolish virgins and in Matthew 22 as the man without the wedding garment. These people pretended to follow Jesus but their relationship with Him was superficial and a mere formalism. There was no change in the heart, no fruits to bring glory to God. They had a religion of convenience and did not submit their wills to God. They were not connected, so there was no life in them. These people go to church occasionally but the principles of the church do not get in them. They pick and choose whatever they want to believe and keep. These are described by Paul as *"Having a form of godliness, but denying the power thereof: from such turn away"* (2 Timothy 3:5). How sad to notice them absent from church and finding that they went to the beach or that they were at a party the night before and slept in, instead of going to the house of God to worship Him and commune with the saints. Sometimes they get full of alcohol instead of the Holy Spirit. They can tell you the latest style or Hollywood gossip but cannot tell you a memory verse. They wear all kinds of jewelry but their heart is devoid of the fruit of the spirit- the only adornment approved by God. They do not realize that being almost saved is the same as being totally lost. These are the people that say that they do not need to go to church to have a relationship with Jesus, when we find Jesus Himself going to church every week (Luke 4:16) in spite that Matthew 23 reads that His church was full of hypocrites! If we are to follow Christ, our hearts cannot be divided. Jesus expressed this principle clearly in the sermon of the mount: *"No man can serve two masters: for either he will hate the one, and love the other; or else he will hold to the one, and despise the other. Ye cannot serve God and mammon"* (Matthew 6:24).

Have you ever been troubled in your mind wondering what can you do after you find yourself in a self-dug hole with no possible way out? You probably think: "I have probably gone too far. My life is a mess and I do not think God is even interested in me." By reading the 15th chapter of the gospel of Luke, we can clearly see that God IS interested in you personally. In the same way that the woman counted every coin, God counts every human being and is not a number. He knows us individually by name and knows our joys and heart aches. If you are thinking that you probably have gone too far for Him to reach you, rejoice because the very fact that you think that way is proof that you have not gone too far- your conscience is still alive. If your life is a mess, ask the prodigal son how was his. He was not only a mess spiritually and emotionally but tending pigs made him physically a mess too. However, when the father saw him returning home, the Bible says that *"when he was yet a great way off, his father saw him, and had compassion, and ran, and fell on his neck, and kissed him"* (verse 20). In Jesus' culture, it was not proper for men over 30 to run. Much less to greet someone ungrateful that snubbed him years before. However, this father was different and anxious so he ran to receive him. The son was covered in dust and sweat after walking many miles for days to return home and surely smelled bad because of his job taking care of pigs in the mud. In spite of all that, his father hugged him and kissed him. Friend, no matter the mess you are or have been in, God the Father will take you back. If you have never had a relationship with Him, do not hesitate to come to Him for He is waiting for you to take your first baby step in response to His invitation.

[19]*And the angel thrust in his sickle into the earth, and gathered the vine of the earth, and cast it into the great winepress of the wrath of God.*

Chapter 19:11-16 shows Jesus as a rider coming to the winepress were the wicked will be punished. Of course, this is figurative language. It is not the will of God that any man perishes but that everyone accepts the gift of eternal life through the sacrifice of Jesus and be saved. However, God respects our free will. Before the whole universe, it will be proven that everyone had the chance to be saved. Only those that chose to be lost will be lost. They went against their consciences and moral judgment with full knowledge that they were constantly reaching for the forbidden fruit.

[20]*And the winepress was trodden without the city, and blood came out of the winepress, even unto the horse bridles, by the space of a thousand and six hundred furlongs.*

When the Jewish nation rejected Jesus and took Him to be crucified, He suffered "without the gate" of the city. Likewise, the wicked that reject Jesus will also suffer "without the city" (Hebrews 13:12). According to Revelation 20, the wicked will surround the city, the New Jerusalem, and then they will be punished for their rebellion. Describing that time, Isaiah indicates the pain in the heart of God when He will have to destroy the wicked: *"For the LORD shall rise up as in mount Perazim, he shall be wroth as in the valley of Gibeon, that he may do his work, his strange work; and bring to pass his act, his strange act. Now therefore be ye not mockers, lest your bands be made strong: for I have heard from the Lord GOD of hosts a consumption, even determined upon the whole earth. Give ye ear, and hear my voice; hearken, and hear my speech. Doth the plowman plow all day to sow? doth he open and break the clods of his ground?"* (Isaiah 28:21-24). God is by nature a creator, a life giver. For Him to destroy His creation is a strange act. In the same way that the plowman does not work all day, God's call to repentance will not last forever either. The time when the Holy Spirit was attempting to plant the seeds of truth and calling us to convert will soon be over. The heart gets hardened after resisting the calls of mercy, to the point that the small, still voice can no longer be heard. May God be able to reach our hearts and obtain a positive response from each of us before is too late.

REVELATION 15

Seven ways to make the wicked mad

[1]And I saw another sign in heaven, great and marvellous, seven angels having the seven last plagues; for in them is filled up the wrath of God.

The plagues are God's preliminary punishment of the wicked for their rejection of his offer of salvation, for trampling the Sabbath and oppressing His people. It is preliminary because their real punishment will be given to them at the end of the millennium.

[2]And I saw as it were a sea of glass mingled with fire: and them that had gotten the victory over the beast, and over his image, and over his mark, and over the number of his name, stand on the sea of glass, having the harps of God.

This scene presents the children of God as if they were already in heaven. The reason for this is that at this time, they are already sealed. Until recently, the angels had been *"holding the four winds of the earth, that the wind should not blow on the earth, nor on the sea, nor on any tree..."* until the servants of God are sealed in their foreheads (Revelation 7:1-3).

[3]And they sing the song of Moses the servant of God, and the song of the Lamb, saying, Great and marvellous are thy works, Lord God Almighty; just and true are thy ways, thou King of saints.

When the children of God crossed the Red Sea, Moses sang a song of triumph, recognizing the bountiful mercy and protection of God. See comment on chapter 14:3.

[4]Who shall not fear thee, O Lord, and glorify thy name? for <u>thou only art holy</u>: for all nations shall come and worship before thee; for thy judgments are made manifest.

Only God has inherent holiness. The thought that He is holy and we all are sinners should inspire us to worship our Creator God.

Worship is an action that connects us to Him. *"God is a Spirit: and they that worship him must worship him in spirit and in truth"* (John 4:24). Our worship of God is not due to fear to be destroyed, but rather it comes from the profound gratitude for the gifts of life and redemption. God does not gain with our acts of worship; it benefits us. We are released from the bondage of self-centeredness.

[5]And after that I looked, and, behold, the temple of the tabernacle of the testimony in heaven was opened:

This verse refers to the heavenly sanctuary in the same way that it is described by Moses in the Old Testament, giving us another proof that this is a literal building like the one that God ordered to be built according to the model shown him at the mountain (Exodus 25:8,40). Jesus is ministering in that temple right now, celebrating a work of judgment. The time will come when the last person will be judged and the time of grace will end. According to Hebrews 4:16, Jesus is now on the throne of grace. At this present time, the door is till open, but the time will come when He will pronounce the words "it is finished" and He will be back on His throne of glory. When this happen, the human race will have no intercessor. This means that both Jesus and the Holy Spirit will cease interceding for the impenitent mankind. Right now, the Holy Spirit pleads with the sinners to repent so He can lead them to Jesus to obtain salvation. Very soon, that voice that speaks to our hearts will be silent and sinners will wish for another chance, which unfortunately for them, will never get. They saddened the Holy Spirit and neglected to prepare for the kingdom of heaven. Now there will be no more hope for the sinner. Why are they rejected? It will be because what they will experience will be remorse, not repentance. We can see an example of both reactions in the lives of Judas and Peter. Judas, being remorseful for betraying Jesus, hung himself; Peter, because he loved Jesus, went out and cried bitterly for his sin. He cried because he had just denied the best of friends. Peter went on to become a great preacher who brought thousands of souls to Christ. True repentance produces reformation, a changed life. The wicked however, will feel sorry for themselves, fearing the divine retribution; they will not be sorry for their rebellion against God or their sins against their fellow men.

[6]And the seven angels came out of the temple, having the seven plagues, clothed in pure and white linen, and having their breasts girded with golden girdles. [7]And one of the four beasts gave unto the seven angels seven golden vials full of the wrath of God, who liveth for ever and ever.

The plagues serve two purposes:

- to punish the wicked for their rebellion and:
- to distract the wicked from persecuting the saints while they prepare to meet their beloved Savior.

[8]And the temple was filled with smoke from the glory of God, and from his power; and no man was able to enter into the temple, till the seven plagues of the seven angels were fulfilled.

This verse points to the time when there will not be an intercessor because no one could enter into the temple. Jesus' intercession for the fallen race has come to and end. The judgment is finished. The time of grace has ended. Now it is when the words from Revelation 22:11 apply: *"He that is unjust, let him be unjust still: and he which is filthy, let him be filthy still: and he that is righteous, let him be righteous still: and he that is holy, let him be holy still."* When Jesus died on the cross, the gates of heaven became wide opened for whoever would accept His offer of salvation. Although it was the cruelest day in the history of mankind because the creator was crucified by His creatures, it was also the most glorious because our debt was paid by His death. Now it comes the saddest day so far for the unrepentant sinners, when the door of grace is shut closed forever and no longer can they be saved. They had reached the point of no return. This is the time described in the parable of the ten virgins. Many will knock the door that now will be closed to never again open. They had wasted the precious opportunities graciously granted to them and now they are without God and without hope. They had decided to turn their backs on the only One that could shield them from the terrible times ahead described in chapter 16. May God find us worthy of being at His side.

Revelation 16

Part 1: The first 6 plagues

Chapter 15 of Revelation indicates that the time of grace and salvation will come to an end when Jesus finishes his work in the heavenly sanctuary. Right now, the four angels mentioned in chapter 7 are holding the winds of strife until Jesus finishes His work and the saints are sealed. John saw that the "angel took the censer, and filled it with fire of the altar, and cast it into the earth: and there were voices, and thunderings, and lightnings, and an earthquake" (Revelation 8:5). Chapter 15:8 shows the result of this action: "And the temple was filled with smoke from the glory of God, and from his power; and no man was able to enter into the temple, till the seven plagues of the seven angels were fulfilled." There will be no more intersession in the heavenly sanctuary. No more appeals to repent will be given by the Holy Spirit. At this time the gospel would have been preached all over the world (Matthew 24:14) and every human being would have had the opportunity to make a choice for God and His truth or for the fables of the popular preachers. At the present time there are *"Multitudes, multitudes in the valley of decision: for the day of the LORD is near in the valley of decision"* (Joel 3:14). When the last person is reached, then everybody either will be sealed (Revelation 7), as in the case of the righteous, or received the mark of the beast (Revelation 13), as in the case of those that reject the truth. After that time, the children of God will not sin anymore and the wicked will not have any more chances to repent. This is how John expressed it: "He that is unjust, let him be unjust still: and he which is filthy, let him be filthy still: and he that is righteous, let him be righteous still: and he that is holy, let him be holy still" (Revelation 22:11). When the plagues fall on the wicked, they will refuse to repent and will become more rebellious. Verse 8 says, "they refused to repent and glorify"; in verse 11: they "cursed the God of heaven" and in verse 21 again "they cursed God on account of the plague of hail". Like Pharaoh in the times of Moses, their hearts will become hardened and that is why they could not be saved. Ahaz had the same reaction: *"In his time of trouble King Ahaz became even more unfaithful to the LORD"*

(2 Chronicles 28:22). It will be their own choice to be lost, because they will not want to recognize God. Rather, they will hate Him.

This will mark the end of the pre-advent judgment and the beginning of the time of trouble (Daniel 12:1) since the Holy Spirit will not be restraining the wicked any longer and the false religions will not tolerate the presence of the just. The saints will go through the purifying fire and, like the 3 Hebrews in the fiery furnace, the fire will just make their characters shine. "Many shall be purified, and made white, and tried; but the wicked shall do wickedly" (Daniel 12:10a). Jesus compared the time of his return with the time of Noah. God said then that His Spirit would not content with man forever (Genesis 6:3). This is when the 4 angels will stop restraining the winds of strife (Revelation 7). Those whose names are written in the book of life have heard and obeyed the call from Jesus to come out of Babylon: "And I heard another voice from heaven, saying, Come out of her, my people, that ye be not partakers of her sins, and that ye receive not of her plagues" (Revelation 18:4).

While the wicked will be suffering the calamities of the seven last plagues, the righteous will be going through the great tribulation (Daniel 12:1; Revelation 7:14). The intent of the tribulation is to prepare God's children for the second coming. If we go back to Revelation 3 and read the description of the spiritual condition of the church of the last days, we will have an idea of why this is necessary. The church that claims to be waiting for her Master is so linked to the world that it can hardly be seen a difference between a worldly person and a believer. It will be necessary to submit the material through the fire to make it heaven-worthy. *"Now if any man build upon this foundation gold, silver, precious stones, wood, hay, stubble; Every man's work shall be made manifest: for the day shall declare it, because it shall be revealed by fire; and the fire shall try every man's work of what sort it is"* (1 Corinthians 3:12,13). *"And it shall come to pass, that in all the land, saith the LORD, two parts therein shall be cut off and die; but the third shall be left therein. And I will bring the third part through the fire, and will refine them as silver is refined, and will try them as gold is tried: they shall call on my name, and I will hear them: I will say, It is my people: and they shall say, The LORD is my God"* (Zechariah 13:8,9). That period of time will impact the two groups differently:

The wicked	The righteous
Will suffer the seven last plagues	Will go through the great tribulation
Physical suffering	Mental anguish
End of time of grace for them- no savior, no angels	Powerful holy angels surround them
The Holy Spirit no longer pleads with them	They will get the seal of God by the Spirit

The anguish of the righteous is not due to the wicked persecuting them or fear of receiving the plagues. They want to make sure that there is no unconfessed sin that could separate them from their beloved Savior and Friend Jesus.

During the time when the plagues fall upon the impenitent inhabitants of the earth, the children of God will be protected. God will hide them and send His powerful angels to protect them. This will be a good time to carefully study and even memorize Psalms 37 & 91, since their messages apply specifically to that difficult time soon to come. *"The wicked plotteth against the just, and gnasheth upon him with his teeth. The LORD shall laugh at him: for he seeth that his day is coming. The wicked have drawn out the sword, and have bent their bow, to cast down the poor and needy, and to slay such as be of upright conversation. Their sword shall enter into their own heart, and their bows shall be broken"* (Psalm 37:12-15). *"The wicked watcheth the righteous, and seeketh to slay him. The LORD will not leave him in his hand, nor condemn him when he is judged"* (Psalm 37:32,33). At the end of that inspiring psalm, we find this jewel: *"But the salvation of the righteous is of the LORD: he is their strength in the time of trouble. And the LORD shall help them, and deliver them: he shall deliver them from the wicked, and save them, because they trust in him"* (Psalm 37:39,40). There are not going to be martyrs at that time. "If the blood of Christ's faithful witnesses were shed at this time, it would not, like the blood of the martyrs, be as seed sown to yield a harvest for God. Their fidelity would not be a testimony to convince others of the truth; for the obdurate heart has beaten back the waves of mercy until they return no more. If the righteous were now left to fall a prey to their enemies, it would be a triumph for the prince of darkness. Says the psalmist: "In the time of trouble He shall hide me in His pavilion: in the secret of His tabernacle shall He hide me." Psalm 27:5. Christ has spoken: 'Come, My people, enter thou into thy chambers, and shut thy doors about thee: hide thyself as it were for a little moment, until the indignation be overpast. For, behold, the Lord cometh out of His place to punish the inhabitants of the earth for their iniquity.' Isaiah 26:20, 21." *The Great Controversy*, 1950 edition, page 634.

We have nothing to fear from the future if we trust the God that saved us in so many wonderful ways and provided for our needs in the past. Lets see now the wonderful promises of Psalm 91:

1. *He that dwelleth in the secret place of the most High shall* ***abide under the shadow of the Almighty****.*
2. *I will say of the LORD,* ***He is my refuge and my fortress****: my God;* ***in him will I trust****.*
3. *Surely* ***he shall deliver thee from the snare of the fowler, and from the noisome pestilence****.*
4. *He shall cover thee with his feathers, and* ***under his wings shalt thou trust****: his truth shall be thy shield and buckler.*
5. ***Thou shalt not be afraid for the terror by night****;* ***nor for the arrow that flieth by day****;*
6. ***Nor for the pestilence that walketh in darkness****;* ***nor for the destruction that wasteth at noonday****.*
7. *A thousand shall fall at thy side, and ten thousand at thy right hand; but* ***it shall not come nigh thee****.*
8. *Only with thine eyes* ***shalt thou behold and see the reward of the wicked****.*
9. ***Because thou hast made the LORD, which is my refuge****, even the most High, thy habitation;*
10. ***There shall no evil befall thee****,* ***neither shall any plague come nigh thy dwelling****.*
11. ***For he shall give his angels charge over thee, to keep thee in all thy ways****.*
12. ***They shall bear thee up in their hands****, lest thou dash thy foot against a stone.*
13. *Thou shalt tread upon the lion and adder: the young lion and the dragon shalt thou trample under feet.*
14. ***Because he hath set his love upon me, therefore will I deliver him: I will set him on high, because he hath known my name****.*
15. *He shall call upon me, and I will answer him:* ***I will be with him in trouble****;* ***I will deliver him****, and honour him.*
16. *With long life will I satisfy him, and* ***shew him my salvation****.*

The Bible tells us to hide for a little while (Isaiah 26:20- quoted below) also to wait for the time of trouble with confidence (Habakkuk 3:16).

According to Luke 21:11, there will be famines before Jesus' return. The world will experience hunger probably due to the terrible natural disasters that will occur. The Bible also indicates that the world economy will collapse, since even the gold and silver will loose their value (see Isaiah 2:20). That is probably why there will be restrictions as to whom will be able to obtain goods and only those with the mark of the beast will be able to purchase, since that will be the sign of allegiance to their cause. As Jesus said in the sermon of the mount, the gentiles love those that love them, so the meager resources that will be found during the difficult times ahead will be shared only with those that pledge allegiance to the beast. However, the righteous will have their needs supplied, just like the Israelites in the dessert received their daily provision of manna and water. David wrote: *"I have been young, and now am old; yet have I not seen the righteous forsaken, nor his seed begging bread."* Isaiah 33:16, referring to the righteous says that: *"He shall dwell on high: his place of defence shall be the munitions of rocks: bread shall be given him; his waters shall be sure."* This passage promises that we will have a refuge, food and water to drink (remember that the wicked will have blood to drink- water will taste a lot better and without the smell).

Although some of the plagues sent against the deities of Egypt are similar to these mentioned in Revelation, there are also differences. Furthermore, just like there are parallels between the visions within the book of Daniel, there are also certain parallels between the seven trumpets and the seven last plagues in Revelation.

Trumpets	Plagues
Earth-hail and fire mingled with blood- Revelation 8:7	**Earth**- noisome and grievous sore- Revelation 16:2
Sea- third part of the creatures which were in the sea, and had life, died- Revelation 8:8,9	**Sea**-it became as the blood of a dead man: and every living soul died in the sea-Revelation 16:3
Rivers and fountains- many men died of the waters- Revelation 8:11	**Rivers and fountains**- they became blood- Revelation 16:4

Sun, moon, stars- part of them was darkened-Revelation 8:12	**Sun**- men were scorched with great heat- Revelation 16:9
Darkness, bottomless pit- sun and the air were darkened by the smoke of the pit- there were **painful** scorpion stings- Revelation 9:2, 5,1**0**	**Darkness** on throne of the beast- his kingdom was full of darkness and there was **pain**-Revelation 16:10
River Euphrates- the four angels were loosed, which were prepared for...the army of the horsemen- Revelation 9:15,16	**River Euphrates** the water thereof was dried up, that the way of the kings of the east might be prepared- Revelation 16:12
Loud voices- The kingdoms of this world become our Lord's- and there were lightnings, and thunderings, and an earthquake, and great hail- Revelation 11:15-19	**A loud voice**: "It is done"- And there were thunders, and lightnings; and a great earthquake, and there fell upon men a great hail out of heaven- Revelation 16:17-21

Although the first and fourth lines have differences, the remaining elements are very similar.

Now Let us read the description of the plagues.

[1] *And I heard a great voice out of the temple saying to the seven angels, Go your ways, and pour out the vials of the wrath of God upon the earth.* The time has come to *"destroy them which destroy the earth"* (Revelation 11:18). This world will soon reach 6,000 years of sin and rebellion. Babylon had *"made all nations drink of the wine of the* ***wrath*** *of her fornication"* (Revelation 14:8) and now is her turn to drink. The cup of the wrath of God is full.

[2] *And the first went, and poured out his vial upon the earth; and there fell a noisome and grievous sore upon the men which had the mark of the beast, and upon them which worshipped his image.*

This plague is on the skin of the wicked that refused to accept the mark of God (Sabbath) and accepted the spurious mark (Sunday).

[3] *And the second angel poured out his vial upon the sea; and it became as the blood of a dead man: and every living soul died in the sea.* [4] *And the third angel poured out his vial upon the rivers and fountains of waters; and they became blood.*

These two plagues are directed to the waters and their fountains. It is similar to the plague in Egypt that changed the water of the Nile into blood. If the wicked affected by the first plague want to wash their sores, they will only have blood to do it. That they will also be thirsty is an understatement.

5 And I heard the angel of the waters say, Thou art righteous, O Lord, which art, and wast, and shalt be, because thou hast judged thus.

6 For they have shed the blood of saints and prophets, and thou
hast given them blood to drink; for they are worthy. 7 And I heard
another out of the altar say, Even so, Lord God Almighty, true and righteous are thy judgments.

The Catholic Church did not tolerate any perceived threat to its power. Whoever dared not followed their heretic teachings was branded as a heretic himself and condemned to lose all his properties, tortured and finally killed. *"And I saw the woman drunken with the blood of the saints, and with the blood of the martyrs of Jesus: and when I saw her, I wondered with great admiration"* (Revelation 17:6).

Psalm 56:8 indicates that God keeps a record of the tears we shed. Now we can see that He also keeps track of the blood of His saints. He cares about each one of us as a loving parent would.

8 And the fourth angel poured out his vial upon the sun; and power was given unto him to scorch men with fire. This plague will force the wicked to look for caves because up to some depth they are naturally cool. That is why John wrote that they will be close to the mountains and rock formations when Jesus comes back. *"And said to the mountains and rocks, Fall on us, and hide us from the face of him that sitteth on the throne, and from the* ***wrath*** *of the Lamb"* (Revelation 6:16). How hot will the sun burn? Isaiah 30:26 says that it will be seven times hotter. So, both groups will be in the mountains at this time of the fourth plague. However, just as it happened when Saul was persecuting David and were in the same mountain simultaneously, the righteous will never fall in the hands of the wicked (1 Samuel 23:26-29).

[9] And men were scorched with great heat, and blasphemed the name of God, which hath power over these plagues: and they repented not to give him glory.

How sad that even in the middle of the divine judgments they will refuse to repent. Instead, they will become more rebellious. Their pride stiffened their knees so they will recognize no other god than themselves.

[10] And the fifth angel poured out his vial upon the seat of the beast; and his kingdom was full of darkness; and they gnawed their
tongues for pain, [11] And blasphemed the God of heaven because of
their pains and their sores, and repented not of their deeds.

This plague is specific for the beast power. It is clear that they are the same ones that received the first one because it mentions their sores. Again, they chose to remain impenitent and blaspheme the Creator that gave them life.

Part 2: Earth's Final Battle - Armageddon

"And the sixth angel poured out his vial upon the great river Euphrates; and its water was dried up, that the way of the kings of the east might be prepared. And I saw <u>three unclean spirits</u> like frogs come <u>out of the mouth of the dragon</u>, and out of the mouth <u>of the beast</u>, and out of the mouth <u>of the</u> <u>false prophet</u>. For <u>they are the spirits of devils</u>, <u>working miracles</u>, which go forth unto the kings of the earth and of the whole world, to gather them to the battle of that great day of God Almighty. Behold, I come as a thief. Blessed is he that watches, and keeps his garments, <u>lest he walks naked, and they see his shame</u>. And he gathered them together into a place called in the Hebrew tongue Armageddon" (Revelation 16:12-16).

come out of the mouth- What comes out of the mouth? Doctrines, blasphemies and guidance.

lest he walks naked, and they see his shame- Adam and Eve were dressed with the glory of God. Psalm 8:5 in Hebrew reads: "Thou... hast <u>encircled</u> [or dressed] him with glory." They were covered with the light of the righteousness of Jesus just like when Moses left the presence of God. When the first couple was created, they were physically naked but were dressed with the divine light. When they sinned, that light abandoned them. That is the nakedness that made them feel ashamed just as it will happen with those that reject the light of the true Sabbath in the final days.

Revelation chapter 14 presents the redeemed reunited as the result of responding to the messages of the three angels, which appeals to both, the intellect and the heart. In chapter 16, the wicked are gathered by the message of the 3 unclean spirits. That message is mostly visual because it is based in miracles.

God's message	Satan's message
Presented as proclaimed by 3 angels	Proclaimed by 3 unclean spirits
Goes to everybody so they can chose by themselves	Presented to the powerful, so they impose it on the people
Accepted by faith- mark on forehead	By works- applied on hand and forehead

This battle is spiritual. There are not going to be found any weapons in the hands of the children of God. In fact, the battle is between the forces of evil and God. The righteous will not have to fight. It is going to be more than enough to have God on their side. *"If God is for us, who can be against us?"* (Romans 8:31).

The word *Armageddon* appears only once in the Bible, contributing to make its meaning obscure. Many people use that fact to put together horror stories regarding the "rapture" and trying to position the battle in the Middle East, in the Valley of Megiddo. That valley is named 11 times- (all in the Old Testament) and it is never assumed in those passages that it will be the place for the final battle between good and evil. The word is probably derived from two Hebrew words; har (mountain) and *mow`ed* (destruction, assembly, congregation). It is very likely that the meaning is "mountain of assembly or congregation" or "mountain of destruction." The Strong's Concordance says that the name is a symbol. Isaiah 14:13 uses *har mow`ed* to identify the place where God has His throne. That is the place that Satan coveted.

But, could God congregate all the seven billions of people on earth in that little valley? Hal Lindsey, in his book *The Late Planet*

Earth, mentions that in the battle of Armageddon, 200 million Chinese soldiers will be congregated in that valley. In his opinion, the armies of the most powerful nations will also be congregated in that little space. This valley, by the way, is only about 300 square kilometers. The only way to fit all those people there is to pile them up like melons in the market or stack them up like boxes in a warehouse. Unfortunately, Mr. Lindsey's conclusion is not based on the solid foundation of the Scriptures but on shaky suppositions.

It is often overlook the fact that, <u>Megiddo is a **valley**</u> and <u>the Bible speaks about a **mountain**</u>. It is not safe to force the Bible to say something that it never said. The Bible is very clear about the place where the wicked will be punished. Solomon wrote: *"Behold, the righteous shall be <u>recompensed **in the earth**</u>: much more the wicked and the sinner."* It is clear that the Holy Scripture does not mention a place of torment as some place in outer space, but it is relevant also that they will be punished on the earth- not in a valley. The whole earth will be the place for that battle.

There is another Bible passage that could help us to build on this idea. In Daniel 2:35 says: *"Then was the iron, the clay, the brass, the silver, and the gold, broken to pieces together, and became like the chaff of the summer threshing floors; and the wind carried them away, that no place was found for them: and the stone that smote the image <u>**became a great mountain**</u>, and filled <u>the whole earth</u>."* Here we see a great mountain (har) that covers the whole earth and it causes the destruction of all the kingdoms (kingdoms are composed of people). It is when Jesus comes that all the people will be congregated before Him. He will send His angels to separate the sheep from the goats; the wheat from the tares.

Mount Carmel is so close to Megiddo that some people even call it mount Megiddo. It was there that the children of Israel saw the power of God in times of Elijah and also where the false religious leaders were punished. At that time, those leaders were not allowed to make fire descend from heaven, but now, the false prophet will be allowed to do it, to help congregate the nations of the world against their Creator. Some theologians believe that Mount Carmel will be the place for the punishment of the wicked, but I see that the events-not the place- only as a symbol of when God intervenes to save His children.

Three unclean spirits- The last triumvirate in the history of this world will be shaped by the spiritual manifestations in the churches. The Catholic Church left the doors wide opened when adopted the non-biblical teaching of the immortality of the soul. After that, they allowed the mix of local superstitions with their doctrines. For example, in Haiti it is common to find altars to demons filled with statues of the saints. I met a former Catholic priest who at the same time was a witch. The same can be observed in other countries in the Caribbean. Protestant churches, also adopting the false belief of the immortal soul, allowed other cultures to permeate their churches. For example, Christians practice yoga, check their horoscopes, get their palms read, purchase Ouija boards for their children and hold new age beliefs. By not studying the Scriptures to check those practices against what God teaches, the delusion has taken over their minds producing blindness and preparing the way to receive further deceptions. The last element is spiritism, for now just crawling into the churches via the above-mentioned practices that Christians see as an "entertainment," but that brings hell itself dragged behind. Spiritism teaches life after death and, though it claims not being religious, it is found in a syncretistic relationship with churches all over the world, especially in the Americas. I once held in my hand a copy of the book *The Gospel According to Spiritism* by Allan Kardec, in which it shows that they believe in God and hold Jesus in high honor (although not seen as Divine). This pretend belief makes them look more innocent to Christians, but beware: the devils also believe. *"You believe that there is one God. That's fine! The demons also believe that, and they tremble with fear"* (James 2:19 *GW*). We cannot let our guard down and we must be always vigilant to discern the teachings that we are exposed to, so we are not led astray. *"Be sober, be vigilant; because your adversary the devil, as a roaring lion, walketh about, seeking whom he may devour"* (1 Peter 5:8). As time goes by, there are more and more manifestations of the supernatural and people of all nations become more curious and more open to explore these phenomena. Spiritism is going to be the glue that will bring about the ultimate coalition- one whose bewitched followers will believe will bring progress to the human race. Unfortunately, there is light that in reality is darkness: *"So be sure that your light isn't darkness"* (Luke 11:35 *CEV*).

Some beliefs and practices of spiritism through which they appeal to different classes and cultures:

- "God is the Supreme Intelligence, first cause of all things. God is eternal, immutable, immaterial, unique, omnipotent, supremely just and good... The Universe is God's creation. It encompasses all rational and non-rational beings, both animate and inanimate, material and immaterial.... All the Laws of Nature are Divine Laws because God is their author. They cover both the physical and moral laws. Jesus is the Guide and Model for all Humankind. The Doctrine He taught and exemplified is the purest expression of God's Law"- http://www.spiritist.us- these principles appeal to Christians whose guards are down for lack of studying their Bibles. An spiritist is a person who believes that the spirits of the dead communicate with the living
- Healing touch- very common in today's "natural" approach to healing
- Hypnotism
- Belief in Karma
- Belief in reincarnation—though not into animals as Hindus believe
- Belief in life in other worlds with varying degrees of advancement- this facilitates the demonic manifestations of "flying saucers." I must admit that I saw one flying from east to west before I gave my heart to Christ. Once I became a Christian, all the strange manifestations disappeared. Having my feet on the Rock protected me from being fooled by the devil.

Notice how verse 14 indicates who the main target of the spirits is: *"For they are the spirits of devils, working miracles, which go forth unto the kings of the earth and of the whole world, to gather them to the battle of that great day of God Almighty."* Spiritism, unlike voodoo, appeals to the intellectual and the powerful. These, on time will force their followers and subjects to go along with the instructions given by the spirits. The world is getting used to the frequent apparitions of "dead saints" such as the Virgin Mary (and I suspect that soon Mother Theresa and John Paul II will follow). To top it off, Satan's most powerful delusion will be the impersonation of Christ in the very last days. That is why He advised not to believe when some will bring the news that He has returned. *"Then if any man shall say unto you, Lo, here is Christ, or there; believe it not. For there shall arise false Christs, and false prophets, and shall shew great signs and wonders; insomuch that, if it were possible, they shall deceive the very elect. Behold, I have told you before. Wherefore if they shall say unto you, Behold, he is in the desert; go not forth: behold, he is in the secret chambers; believe it not. For as the lightning cometh out of the east, and shineth even unto the west; so shall also the coming of the Son of man be" (Matthew 24:23-27).* Only those who know their Bibles and wholly trust God to supply their every need will be able to resist the temptation and not be deceived. Did you read your Bible today?

God's advise is found in Deuteronomy 18:10-12 (*English Standard Version*): *"There shall not be found among you anyone who burns his son or his daughter as an offering, anyone who practices divination or tells fortunes or interprets omens, or a sorcerer or a charmer or a medium or a necromancer or one who inquires of the dead for whoever does these things is an abomination to the LORD. And because of these abominations the LORD your God is driving them out before you."* We cannot venture into Satan's enchanted territory and expect to be untouched. If you are curious about the spirit world, leave it alone. There is no safety in going there because it is like when Eve left the safety of her husband's company and went to where the devil was. If you go there, you might never get out.

"And the sixth angel poured out his vial upon the great river Euphrates; and its water was dried up, that the way of the kings of the east might be prepared.

The drying up of the river Euphrates reminds me of something similar that happened centuries ago, when Cyrus conquered Babylon. That city was so secured that the inhabitants believed it would never be conquered. They were surrounded by two thick walls, the Euphrates river passed under those walls providing plenty of water for all their needs, they had enough food in storage to last 20 years, and the irrigation system helped to provide them with fresh crops to replace what they were eating. For all those reasons, they felt that they were invincible. But their conquerors reasoned that if the river was giving them life and support, it could also be used to bring ruin to the city.

This was done by one of Cyrus' generals who put his soldiers to dig a long ditch to deviate the waters of the river. The prophecy of Isaiah 45:1 was fulfilled that night: *"Thus saith the LORD to his* ***anointed****, to Cyrus, whose right hand I have held, to subdue nations before him; and I will loose the loins of kings, to open before him the double gates; and* ***the gates shall not be shut****."* The guards were so drunk in the celebration that King Belshazzar had that night that they forgot to close the gates that secured the entrance where the water entered the city. Those gates were designed to allow the water to go through, but not people- if they were closed. Noticed also that Cyrus is called anointed, which means *Messiah*. He was also commanded by God to set the captives in Babylon free. By bringing freedom from bondage to the children of Israel, Cyrus became a type of Christ, our Messiah, who very soon will intervene to save us from the oppression of spiritual Babylon.

The meaning of this is that very soon those (the "river" of people) that back up and support spiritual Babylon will abandon her: "And the ten horns which thou sawest upon the beast, these shall hate the whore, and shall make her desolate and naked, and shall eat her flesh, and burn her with fire" (Revelation 17:16).

three unclean spirits... out of the mouth of the dragon... of the beast... and... of the false prophet... they are the spirits of devils, working miracles- Unclean spirit is another name for demon. In Mark chapter 5, we find a man in the cemetery possessed by an unclean spirit. There are other passages that also mention them. Here are two cases:

"And it shall come to pass in that day, saith the LORD of hosts, that I will cut off the names of the idols out of the land, and they shall no more be remembered: and also I will cause the prophets and the unclean spirit to pass out of the land" (Zechariah 13:2). Notice that the passage mentions idols, prophets and unclean spirits. Babylon is full of idols, it will be jointed to the false prophet and it has become "habitation of devils" (Revelation 18:2).

"And in the synagogue there was a man, which had a spirit of an unclean devil, and cried out with a loud voice" (Luke 4:33). It is common to find the unclean spirits talking. Satan seduced Eve to sin by talking. *"Now the Spirit speaketh expressly, that in the latter times some shall depart from the faith, giving heed to seducing spirits, and doctrines of devils"* (1 Timothy 4:1). So, what will come out of the mouth of the dragon, the beast and the false prophet in the last days will be doctrines of devils, false teachings, and the wine of Babylon. It is evident that whatever comes out will provide unity. What kind of manifestations we have seen in later decades that are bringing these three powers together? The dragon represents the spiritist movement that began in New York in March 31st, 1848 in the house of Margaretta and Katie Fox, and spread like a wild fire through the entire world. Although later in life they denounced before the press that all had been a fraud, the spiritualist movement was already too strong to hold it back and now we see millions following mediums and psychics. One of the most famous of the later ones was Jeane Dixon. Her predictions of the assassinations of John F. Kennedy and Martin Luther King made believers out of former skeptics, even among so-called Christians, who should know better. However true those two predictions were, her prophecies failed most of the time. The reason for this is that they did not come from God, the only One who knows the future. One of her predictions was regarding the birth of a new messiah somewhere in the Middle East. She even gave the time and date of his coming to this world: 7:00 AM on February 5, 1962. Her prediction indicated that before the end of the 20th century, all mankind would be united under him. As we know, that never happened.

Another of the ways in which the demons manifested themselves in the 19th century was through the use of tongues, or glossolalia in spiritist centers. From there, "the gift" went to a Pentecostal church where it was considered a manifestation of the Holy Spirit of God and spread like a wild fire throughout Protestant churches. After this movement spread to other Protestant denominations, such as Baptists, Presbyterians and Methodists, Catholics started to also speak in tongues- specifically in 1967. Consequently, the Charismatic movement was born and received papal recognition. The International Catholic Charismatic Renewal Services (ICCRS) was approved by the Holy See as a private association of the faithful with a juridical personality to promote catholic charismatic renewal. Protestants, who normally would be suspicious of Catholics and even correctly associated their church with the beast of Revelation 13, now embraced them and called them brothers, marveling that they too got the "spirit." In the 1800's, the Catholic priest Father Charles Chiniquy, wrote in his *50 years in the Church of Rome* book:

"Americans! you are sleeping on a volcano, and you do not suspect it! You are pressing on your bosom a viper which will bite you to death, and you do not know it. Rome is the great danger ahead for the Church of Christ, and you do not understand it. It is ignorance which paves the way to the triumph of Rome in the near future. It is that ignorance which paralyzes the arm of the Church of Christ, and makes the glorious word 'Protestant' senseless, almost a dead and ridiculous word. For who does really protest against Rome? - Where are those who sound the trumpet of alarm?

"When Rome is striking you to the heart by cursing your schools, and wrenching the Bible from the hands of your children, how few dare go to the breach and repulse the audacious and sacrilegious foe! Why so? Because modern Protestants have forgotten what Rome was, what she is, and what she will forever be: the most irreconcilable and powerful enemy of the Gospel of Christ. The monster Church of Rome, who shed the blood of your forefathers, is still at work today at your very doors, to chain your people to the feet of her idols."

Although there are many God-fearing, genuine Christians among the Catholic churches, most of their leadership have sinister motives in their attempts to unite with Protestants. Their tongue speaking is many times faked, since they have been trained to speak in tongues- so I personally heard former Bishop Alberto Rivera say.

The tongues movement has been sweeping the religious world regardless of the core of believes held by the different churches. So, could it be possible that the real Holy Spirit of God be working in all those different denominations? Not likely. Those preachers' sermons either are a repent or go to hell message or a feel good speech. The Holy Spirit cannot inspire any of them, for the former is not Biblical and the latter makes people to procrastinate and do not confess and depart from their sins. In spite of their doctrines being so different from one church to another they all claim to be guided by the Spirit. All those churches claim to have the truth. The followers of the Charismatic movement chose to ignore the clear words of Jesus: *"Howbeit when he, the Spirit of truth, is come, he will guide you into all truth..."* (John 16:13). It is not possible to receive the Spirit and persevere in error. He cannot guide a church to conclude that salvation is by works and another that salvation is by grace. He cannot teach that baptizing infants is right and another church to baptize only after the person can comprehend the doctrine; they were to be taught and then be baptized (Matthew 28:19) Mark adds that the person must believe before being baptized (16:16). What we have in the Charismatic movement is babel (confusion). *"For God is not the author of confusion, but of peace, as in all churches of the saints"* (1 Corinthians 14:33). If these believers have been guided by the Holy Spirit for so many decades, they would have undoubtedly come to the same doctrinal conclusions based on the Word of God under the guidance of the Holy Spirit.

Could it be possible that these tongues are all of divine origin? Again, not likely. The tongues spoken by the disciples in the day of Pentecost were known languages. This is evident by reading the passage found in the book of Acts. When God wants to emphasize a point, He mentions it three times and it was precisely three times that the story in Acts mentions the pilgrims in Jerusalem hearing the message of the apostles in their own language. *"Now when this was noised abroad, the multitude came together, and were confounded, because that every man heard them speak in his own language. And they were all amazed and marvelled, saying one to another, Behold, are not all these which speak Galilaeans? And how hear we every man in our own tongue, wherein we were born? Parthians, and Medes, and Elamites, and the dwellers in Mesopotamia, and in Judaea, and Cappadocia, in Pontus, and Asia, Phrygia, and Pamphylia, in Egypt, and in the parts of Libya about Cyrene, and strangers of Rome, Jews and proselytes, Cretes and Arabians, we do hear them speak in our tongues the wonderful works of God"* (Acts 2:6-11). The gift of tongues was given as a resource to accomplish the task of preaching the gospel. Acts 2:8 says that those present there HEARD the disciples speak in their

OWN LANGUAGES "in which they were born." It is easy to embrace preconceived ideas and ignore what is so clearly mentioned in the Bible, repeating what this or that preacher said. We should not relieve men regardless of how holy they seem to be. Human beings are not perfect and often they misunderstand the Scriptures. We must only believe a "thus saith the Lord." In that chapter of Acts, we are taught that the gift of tongues has the purpose of reaching the lost so they can look to their Savior, who was crucified for their sins, so they can be saved. The tongues are never presented in the Bible as evidence that the person is saved. If the tongues are an evidence of salvation, Why does the Bible says that <u>whoever believes will be saved</u>, but it never says that whoever speaks in tongues will be saved?

Today's tongue speakers pronounce words that neither them nor their fellow church members understand. Some even go as far as teaching that if a person does not speak in tongues, he or she has not been born again and therefore is not a real Christian. How come we never read that Jesus spoke in tongues? After all, the Bible teaches that He was full of the Holy Spirit (Acts 10:38). God never designed for the gift of tongues to become the proof to authenticate a religious experience. Jesus said two very important identifiers what would witness to the world that a person was His real follower. The first one is genuine love: *"This is how <u>everyone will know</u> that you are my disciples, <u>if you have love for one another</u>"* (John 13:35 *International Standard Version*). The second is the fruit of the person's life: *"<u>You will know them by their fruit</u>. Grapes aren't gathered from thorns, or figs from thistles, are they? In the same way, every good tree produces good fruit, but a rotten tree produces bad fruit. A good tree cannot produce bad fruit, and a rotten tree cannot produce good fruit. Every tree that doesn't produce good fruit will be cut down and thrown into a fire. So by their fruit you will know them.' 'Not everyone who keeps saying to me, 'Lord, Lord,' will get into the kingdom from heaven, but only the person who keeps doing the will of my Father in heaven. Many will say to me on that day, 'Lord, Lord, we prophesied in your name, drove out demons in your name, and performed many miracles in your name, didn't we?' Then I will tell them plainly, 'I never knew you. Get away from me, you who practice evil!'"* (Matthew 7:16-23 *ISV*). The greatest authority in the whole universe- Jesus Himself- never mentioned the gift of tongues and much less made it a proof of genuine conversion. Are we going to believe in Christ or the corner preacher? The Bible is our only safeguard to avoid falling for the delusions of these last days, because Satan will try to seduce even the elect (Matthew 24:24). John advised: *"Dear friends, don't believe all people who say that they have the Spirit. Instead, test them. See whether the spirit they have is from God, because there are many false prophets in the world"* (1 John 4:1 *GW*).

Paul taught in his writings that other gifts of the Spirit are more relevant to the church. In the list found in his first letter to the Corinthians, the tongues take last place: *"And there are diversities of operations, but it is the same God which worketh all in all. But the manifestation of the Spirit is given to every man to profit withal. For to one is given by the Spirit the word of wisdom; to another the word of knowledge by the same Spirit; To another faith by the same Spirit; to another the gifts of healing by the same Spirit; To another the working of miracles; to another prophecy; to another discerning of spirits; to another divers kinds of tongues; to another the interpretation of tongues"* (1 Corinthians 12:6-10). The phrase "to profit withal" means for the common good, to help others. If the person that speaks in tongues is only benefitting himself, then it is very likely that it is not the real gift of tongues. In the Pentecostal or Charismatic churches, the members pray to be able to speak in tongues. However, Paul taught that the gift is given by the Holy Spirit <u>as He deems it necessary</u>: *"But all these worketh that one and the selfsame Spirit, dividing to every man severally <u>as he will</u>"* (1 Corinthians 12:11). It is not up to us to dictate to the Holy Spirit which gift we are going to receive from Him. In the same chapter, Paul wrote a list of the gifts of the Spirit in order of relevance: *"And God hath set some in the church, <u>first</u> apostles, <u>second</u>arily prophets, <u>third</u>ly teachers, after that miracles, then gifts of healings, helps, governments, diversities of tongues"* (1 Corinthians 12:28). Why so much emphasis in the gift of tongues when it is <u>listed last</u>? Then he clearly states that not all believers speak in tongues: *"Have all the gifts of healing? do all speak with tongues? do all interpret?"* (1 Corinthians 12:30).

There are some important points written regarding the subject of tongues in the church setting. For example, the gift of prophecy, one of the characteristics of the last time true church (Revelation 12:17 & 19:10), is more important than speaking in tongues. *"I would that ye all spake with tongues, but rather that ye prophesied: for greater is he that prophesieth than he that speaketh with tongues, except he interpret, that the church may receive edifying"* (1 Corinthians 14:5). In the same chapter, Paul set the ground rules for tongue speaking in church, which unfortunately are not being followed:

"For if the trumpet give an uncertain sound, who shall prepare himself to the battle? So likewise ye, except ye utter by the tongue words easy to be understood, how shall it be known what is spoken? for ye shall speak into the air" (1 Corinthians 14:8).

"Yet in the church I had rather speak five words with my understanding, that by my voice I might teach others also, than ten thousand words in an unknown tongue" (1 Corinthians 14:19).

"Wherefore tongues are for a sign, not to them that believe, but to them that believe not: but prophesying serveth not for them that believe not, but for them which believe. If therefore the whole church be come together into one place, and all speak with tongues, and there come in those that are unlearned, or unbelievers, will they not say that ye are mad? But if all prophesy, and there come in one that believeth not, or one unlearned, he is convinced of all, he is judged of all" (1 Corinthians 14:22-24). According to this passage and Acts chapter 2, the church is not the correct setting to speaking in tongues because that is not the place with the major amount of unbelievers. When the disciples spoke in tongues, they were not confined to a building with fellow believers. They were in the open with the multitudes that could be benefited with their gift. There were people with spiritual hunger that needed to be satisfied.

"If any man speak in an unknown tongue, let it be by two, or at the most by three, and that by course [by turn]*; and let one interpret. But if there be no interpreter, let him keep silence in the church; and let him speak to himself, and to God"* (1 Corinthians 14:27,28). This is the most fragrantly ignored instruction regarding the gift of tongues as I have observed in my visits to those churches. In these church services members start turning around unaware of their surroundings, women lift their skirts, men, women and children roll on the floor, and some even break their necks or backs falling hard on the church pews (I know of one such deaths). Could we consider

these irreverent, indecent and even deadly occurrences as genuine manifestations of the Holy Spirit? My experiences have taught me that Paul's counsel was not heeded: *"Let all things be done decently and in order"* (1 Corinthians 14:40).

Another method these demons are using to unify the apostates is through *"working miracles."* One can hardly turn the TV on Sunday morning without finding a few channels dedicated to show a healing service, where people being "healed" fall backwards and many times have to be carried away by the platform ushers because they lose conscience. Those fake miracles are mesmerizing the multitudes, who sincerely believe that they are of heavenly origin. If they only were willing to study their Bibles and let the Holy Spirit illuminate their understanding, they would realize how hard Satan has been working to get them lost- in their own churches. Yes, Satan too goes to church and is the first one to be there and usually stays for the whole service. I have read the Bible from cover to cover and have been unable to find one passage in which Jesus healed a person in a theatrical manner, specially falling backwards, unconscious to the point of having to take the person away. Only one young person who had been demon possessed looked like dead but was not taken away. He remained in the presence of the Healer and soon opened his eyes and was returned to his father completely healed.

Part 3: The last plague

17And the seventh angel poured out his vial into the air; and there came a great voice out of the temple of heaven, from the throne, saying, It is done.

God has a great master clock to run His salvation program. When Jesus was born, He came right at *"the fullness of the time"* (Galatians 4:4). His daily planner has checkmarks that emphasize His goals accomplished. When Jesus was dying on the cross, He said: *"It is finished."* Not only was mankind's redemption accomplished when Jesus died but also Satan's destiny was decided. It was at that moment that Satan was finally cast out from heaven (Revelation 12:11, 13). Until then, he had access to the presence of God (Job 1:6; 2:6) where he was the accuser of the brethren (Revelation 12:10). Now this voice comes out of the heavenly temple, from the throne of God, with the final "It is done." I believe that voice to be Jesus' because only He as the High Priest would have the authority to pronounce them. This marks the end of the investigative judgment.

18*And there were voices, and thunders, and lightnings; and there was a great earthquake, such as was not since men were upon the earth, so mighty an earthquake, and so great.*

This resembles the time when the Ten Commandments were given to ancient Israel at Mount Sinai. *"And it came to pass on the third day in the morning, that there were thunders and lightnings, and a thick cloud upon the mount, and the voice of the trumpet exceeding loud; so that all the people that was in the camp trembled"* (Exodus 19:16). However, this last time, it is not about giving the law to the people; now it is the time to settle accounts with those that trespassed that law. Jesus said: *"Whosoever therefore shall break one of these least commandments, and shall teach men so, he shall be called the least in the kingdom of heaven: but whosoever shall do and teach them, the same shall be called great in the kingdom of heaven"* (Matthew 5:19).

19And *the great city was divided into three parts, and the cities of the nations fell: and great Babylon came in remembrance before God, to give unto her the cup of the wine of the fierceness of his wrath.*

Why was the city divided into three parts? Because it was composed of a triple alliance: the beast, the dragon and the false prophet (see verse 13). The common purpose that brought them together (to fight the children of God and the Sabbath) no longer binds them due to the plagues.

20*And every island fled away, and the mountains were not found.*

The topography of the planet had been changed by the previous earth destruction through the flood. Now it is going to happen again. *"Behold, the LORD maketh the earth empty, and maketh it waste, and turneth it upside down, and scattereth abroad the inhabitants thereof"* (Isaiah 24:1). The last earthquake will not be like any other that humans had felt in the past: *"The earth is utterly broken down, the earth is clean dissolved, the earth is moved exceedingly. The earth shall reel to and fro like a drunkard, and shall be removed like a cottage; and the transgression thereof shall be heavy upon it; and it shall fall, and not rise again"* (Isaiah 24:19,20). The new earth is going to be restored to its original glory and perfect beauty without precipices or even islands. Peter seems to indicate that the original earth was a mass of land in the middle of the waters: *"For this they willingly are ignorant of, that by the word of God the heavens were of old, and the earth standing out of the water and in the water"* (2 Peter 3:5). The New International Reader's Version renders Peter's words this way: *"...His word separated the earth from the waters. And the waters surrounded it...."* If we take a world map and try to put the landmasses together, we can see that they seem to have been connected at one time. Some scientists believe that the American continents were one with Europe and Africa and that they depart from each other about one centimeter per year.

21And there fell upon men a great hail out of heaven, every stone about the weight of a talent: and men blasphemed God because of the plague of the hail; for the plague thereof was exceeding great.

That plague was long coming. Here we see a God that does not improvise. He has planned every detail of His interventions in human affairs. He asked the patriarch job: *"Hast thou entered into the treasures of the snow? or hast thou seen the treasures of the hail, Which I have reserved against the time of trouble, against the day of battle and war?"* (Job 38:22, 23). The weight of the hail is approximately 70 pounds. Some believe that it will be even heavier. Whatever survived the previous plagues, it is not likely to survive this one. Again, it seems to be of short duration because Job mentions the time to be a day. This one seems to be universal in scope because it falls "upon men." As I wrote earlier, the purpose of the final plagues is not only to punish the wicked; it accomplishes distracting them from persecuting the saints that are now in the mountains (Isaiah 33:16) examining their hearts and preparing to encounter their beloved Savior. Like on the night before the exodus from Egypt, the saints will be hiding: *"Come, my people, enter thou into thy chambers, and shut thy doors about thee: hide thyself as it were for a little moment, until the indignation be overpast"* (Isaiah 26:20). When the Israelites were about to receive the Law, they were told to prepare for that event: *"And the LORD said unto Moses, Go unto the people, and sanctify them today and tomorrow, and let them wash their clothes, And be ready against the third day: for the third day the LORD will come down in the sight of all the people upon mount Sinai"* (Exodus 19:10,11). The saints will be doing serious heart searching to encounter their God. Have you experience a daily walk with God and are preparing to meet Him soon? *"Therefore thus will I do unto thee, O Israel: and because I will do this unto thee,* ***<u>prepare to meet thy God</u>****, O Israel"* (Amos 4:12). And now, at the end of this plague, is when Jesus will return to save His people. He went to prepare a place for you (John 14:1-3). He wants to take you home to enjoy the things that He has prepared for you. *"But as it is written, Eye hath not seen, nor ear heard, neither have entered into the heart of man, the things which God hath prepared for them that love him"* (1 Corinthians 2:9).

REVELATION 17

A woman of ill reputation

[1]*And there came one of the seven angels which had the seven vials, and talked with me, saying unto me, Come hither; I will shew unto thee the judgment of the great whore that sitteth upon many waters:*
[2] *With whom the kings of the earth have committed fornication, and the inhabitants of the earth have been made drunk with the wine of her fornication.*

It is worth to remember that some prophecies still need historical events to happen in order to be understood and interpreted properly. Although my present convictions are expressed in this comment, I must admit that I am observing the worlds' events at the light of this passage and do not pretend to be dogmatic in its interpretation, hoping for more light. The first verse here indicates that John is transported into the future when *"the great whore"* is going to be punished. So this prophecy is not to be analyzed from the historical point of view of John's times, around 96 AD, but around the time of the end, which started in 1798. It is also worth to notice that this chapter is sandwiched between chapter 16, where the last evil alliance is formed and then collapses after a short stint in supreme power, and chapter 18 where the final collapse of the whore is amplified and described in details.

With whom the kings of the earth have committed fornication - It seems that the leaders of the nations all want to follow the pope's guidance and to mediate when there are conflicts. Even the late Sadam Hussein asked for the pope's intervention during a time of crisis. Since Ronald Reagan, every USA president has had audiences with the pope early on in their administration. It is as if the President were asking the pope how to run the affairs of the nation, just as it was in the middle ages.

An image Google search can show many pictures of American Presidents meeting with the popes as equals and even Obama bowing to Pope Benedict XVI.

Why does the Bible compare the false church with a whore or prostitute? It is because of its power of seduction. *"For a whore is a deep ditch; and a strange woman is a narrow pit. She also lieth in wait as for a prey, and increaseth the transgressors among men"* (Proverbs 23:27,28). The exterior architecture of the buildings, the stunning decoration of the interior, the statues in spiritual, mystic poses, the elaborate service, the reverent silence, the solemn music, the incense aroma, the flicker of the candles, the clothing of the priests, the cavernous size of the cathedrals, the processions, all contributes to the awe effect in the worshipper and so he/she falls as prey like a fish in a net. Solomon, whose lust made him fall in idolatry, wrote extensively against the perils of falling for a seductress. He wrote: *"Let not thine heart decline to her ways, go not astray in her paths. For she hath cast down many wounded: yea, many strong men have been slain by her. Her house is the way to hell, going down to the chambers of death"* (Proverbs 7:25-27). *"And I find more bitter than death the woman, whose heart is snares and nets, and her hands as bands: whoso pleaseth God shall escape from her; but the sinner shall be taken by her"* (Ecclesiastes 7:26). God gave many millions around the world the strength and knowledge to escape; He can help you as well before it is too late.

[3]So he carried me away in the spirit into the wilderness: and I saw a woman sit upon a scarlet coloured beast, full of names of blasphemy, having seven heads and ten horns.

As we discussed in chapter 12, a woman represents a church (see 2 Corinthians 11:1,2). This church is riding the beast, symbol of the state. This indicates that the church will influence the government to legislate according to what the church understands how the laws should be. The government will be just a puppet of the state. The previous great alliance of church and state lasted over a thousand years. We know that period as the middle ages when people were kept in ignorance and those intelligent enough to illustrate the populace were ostracized (Galileo, for example). Millions were killed using the sword of the state. In the 20th century, there was an attempt to restore the union of the church and the state. At that time, the church acted behind the curtains and the Third Reich ran the show. Millions more died but not as many as during the Dark Ages. Very soon, the union will be universal; all the world's governments will be subjects of the beast and persecution of minorities will soon follow.

This woman is not the true church of God, although it pretends to be it. As we studied Isaiah chapter four, verse one earlier, we saw what is wrong with this church other than what it says in this chapter of Revelation. Let us see it again:

"And in that day seven women shall take hold of one man, saying, We will eat our own bread, and wear our own apparel: only let us be called by thy name, to take away our reproach."

Symbolism:

- Seven- totality (all the last day churches)
- Women- Churches of the time of the end
- One man- Jesus, the Son of Man
- Own bread- Their own doctrines (paganism mixed with Christianism)
- Own apparel- Their own righteousness, not that of Jesus
- Only let us be called by your name- Only the name is Christian for their doctrines are not biblical, such as Sunday keeping, immortality of the soul, a pagan diet (eating scavenger animals that God called unclean), infant baptism, etc.

Christian churches today have only the name because they have departed from the truth and have become as apostates as the mother church from where all their Protestant founders departed. Now they criticize Luther, Calvin and all the founders of their respective churches saying that they took things too seriously and were fanatics. In other words, the reformers over-reacted. Regarding the issue of justification, Protestants and Catholics could not have been more apart five centuries ago. Protestants then taught that salvation is a free gift of God who saves the sinner by grace through faith (Ephesians 2:8). This means that there is nothing the sinner can do to earn or deserve salvation. In contrast, Catholics teach that we are saved by works and monetary offerings (sorry, no Bible text because it is not Biblical). Now it is said that the difference between Protestants and Catholics was just a problem of semantics. These modern "theologians" forget the abuses, persecutions and crimes committed by the Roman church and believe that she is sorry and has changed. Let Rome have the government backing and legislative support and we will be back in the Middle Ages (when church and state were united). Carnage of minorities will follow this union. Rome was and will ever be a wolf among the sheep. The union of this particular church and the state is an aberration before God.

full of names of blasphemy – names such as "holy mother," "the original church," "the church that Jesus founded." How could Jesus have founded a church that insists in teaching non-Biblical doctrines, that exalts tradition over the Scriptures and persecutes and kills those that teach the truth?

Blasphemies are just one of the elements that remind of the beast of Revelation 13. The following table draws a comparison between both beasts:

Revelation 13	Revelation 17
Has seven heads and ten horns -13:1	Has seven heads and ten horns -17:3
Has a mouth speaking blasphemies -13:5	Beast is full of blasphemous names -17:3
Received a mortal wound -13:3	Was in the bottomless pit -17:8
His deadly wound was healed- 13:3	Shall ascend out of the bottomless pit -17:8
All the world wondered after the beast -13:3	They that dwell on the earth shall wonder -17: 8
Attracts those "whose names are not written in the book of life of the Lamb slain from the foundation of the world" -13:8	Those "whose names were not written in the book of life from the foundation of the world" wonder when they behold it -17:8

Differences between the beasts of Revelation 13 and 17

Revelation 13	Revelation 17
Does not have any color	It is "a scarlet coloured beast"- 17:3
The sea beast has crowns on its horns - 13:1	Does not have any crowns
The beast comes out of the sea - 13:1	Comes out of the abyss - 17:8
The beast represents the political and religious powers together	This beast represents the political power and the woman the religious

Comparison between the woman and the beast:

The woman	The beast
arrayed in purple and scarlet colour-verse 4	scarlet coloured beast- verse 3
the woman reigneth over the kings of the earth- verse 18	The kings "give their power and strength unto the beast-" verses 13,17
The woman has a "cup in her hand full of abominations and filthiness of her fornication-" verse 4	The beast was "full of names of blasphemy-" verse 3

Obviously, the woman cannot ride the Beast and at the same time be the beast, so even though there are a few similar characteristics between the beast and the woman, they are different entities. The woman shares characteristics with the beast because it inherited the kingdom and paganism from the Roman Empire.

The woman sits on the beast (verses 1,3), on seven mountains, and also sits on the waters (verse 15). She also "reigneth over the kings of the earth" which is another way to say that she sits on them as she does on the waters.

4And the woman was arrayed in colour, and decked with gold and precious stones and pearls, having a golden cup in her hand full of abominations and filthiness of her fornication:

Spiritual fornication is the mixing of false doctrines with a little bit of the truth. The greatest of the blasphemies of spiritual Babylon is that the popes pretend to be God- as prophesied in 2 Thessalonians 2:4: *"Who opposeth and exalteth himself above all that is called God, or that is worshipped; so that he as God sitteth in the temple of God, shewing himself that he is God."* See chapter 13 for more on this subject. The word "sitteth" used by Paul is related to the word used by John in this chapter of Revelation 17 where it refers to the harlot sitting on the scarlet beast. What was the cup in the woman's hand used for? *"For all nations have drunk of the wine of the wrath of her fornication, and the kings of the earth have committed fornication with her, and the merchants of the earth are waxed rich through the abundance of her delicacies"* (Revelation 18:3). The false Babylonian doctrines were used to benumb the spiritual senses of the nations and make them believe on a false system of salvation by works, contrary to the plan of God of free salvation by the blood of Christ.

Comparison between the women in Revelation 12 and 17:

Revelation 12- The pure woman	Revelation 17- The corrupt woman
A woman clothed with the sun -12:1- no jewelry	Decked with gold and precious stones and pearls -17:4
"Upon her head a crown of twelve stars" -12:1	On her forehead "*was* a name written, MYSTERY, BABYLON THE GREAT, THE MOTHER OF HARLOTS AND ABOMINATIONS OF THE EARTH" 17:5
This woman was persecuted- 12:13-17	This woman persecuted the other. "The woman drunken with the blood of the saints, and with the blood of the martyrs of Jesus" -17:6

decked with gold and precious stones and pearls- The pure woman of chapter 12, who represents the true church is covered with light; this one with jewelry. It was never God's plan that Christians deck themselves in jewelry but with a noble character. Peter wrote: *"Whose adorning let it not be that outward adorning of plaiting the hair, and of wearing of gold, or of putting on of apparel; But let it be the hidden man of the heart, in that which is not corruptible, even the ornament of a meek and quiet spirit, which is in the sight of God of great price"* (1Peter 3:3,4). Christians should strive to be all-natural without artificial ingredients. After all, why spend the money in self-gratification, in order to produce envy on others, instead of helping those in need, which will give us all a more restful sleep?

purple and scarlet – the colors of the popes and cardinals. The scarlet color is a symbol of sin (Isaiah 1:18) and the color of the blood shed by the Catholic Church. These church leaders differ from the high priest in the old testament in which the colors of their clothing do not include blue, a representation of the Ten Commandments (Numbers 15:38-40), of which they dared to change two.

having a golden cup in her hand – the cup of the mass. The 100 lira coin has a woman (as a symbol of the church) holding a cup (for the mass).

The inscription on the reverse side of the coin reads in Italian "CITTA DEL VATICANO", which means *City of Prophecy*, since Vatican means divination or prophecy. Notice also that she is standing on top of the word FIDES (faith), which is trapped. This indicates that she is above faith, since for the church, salvation is based on the mass, the intercession of the saints and works and not on faith as the Bible teaches so clearly (see Ephesians 2:8).

See the detail showing the sun dawning out of the cup:

Photo by author.

Observe how the official Vatican coin fulfills the description of the prophecy of a woman holding a cup.

[5]And upon her <u>forehead</u> was a name written, MYSTERY, BABYLON THE GREAT, THE MOTHER OF HARLOTS AND ABOMINATIONS OF THE EARTH.

The Roman church involves all her rites in mysteries, such as the mysteries of the rosary, as discussed in chapter 13. It is called the mother of harlots since all the Protestant churches that came from her have apostatized and have become like her (see next paragraph). Now they want to extend the hand of reconciliation to the mother church and "come home." These churches whose founders died as martyrs upholding the glorious truths of righteousness by faith (Sola Fide), Christ alone (Solus Christus) and the Bible only (Sola Scriptura), now listen to doctrines from the old serpent from Eden. *"Now the Spirit speaketh expressly, that in the latter times some shall depart from the faith, giving heed to seducing spirits, and doctrines of devils"* (1 Timothy 4:1). *"For the time will come when they will not endure sound doctrine; but after their own lusts shall they heap to themselves teachers, having itching ears"* (2 Timothy 4:3).

How sad that the consciences of preachers are being seared for the love of prestige and money and their congregations do not want to hear the truth- only what makes them feel comfortable.

THE MOTHER OF HARLOTS- When a church embraces abominations (false doctrines, wrong way of worship), it becomes a harlot: *"Cause Jerusalem to know her abominations"..."Thou didst trust in thine own beauty, and playedst the harlot"* (Ezekiel16:2,15). The Protestant churches that came out of Babylon have all apostatized by uniting with the world. Three hundred years ago, it was easy to distinguish a worldling from a Protestant. The former cursed, had no hope or real joy. The latter rejoiced even in the midst of terrible trials, his language was pure; he did not drink, smoke, or participated in anything that could separate him from his beloved Savior and Lord. Today the line of distinction is almost unnoticeable. Modern Christians fill the casinos and other houses of pleasure, their speech no longer has the purity and sweetness of heaven, they complain all day long, making others around miserable and they seem to have lost their hope in front of life's vicissitudes. Their behavior is no different from that of their neighbors and associates and their continuous involvement in politics in the quest for power leaves so much to be desired. Today it seems that the agenda is no longer to preach the gospel but to promote a political platform or to get a candidate elected. Instead of the world turning to the church for answers, the church has been converted to the world by vain compromises with the excuse to attract worldlings into the church (just as the Catholic mother did in the third and fourth centuries, which resulted in an influx of paganism into the church). So now, we can certainly say that modern Protestant churches are harlots like their mother.

It is never safe to sacrifice the quality of the service rendered to God for the quantity of people joining the ranks of His church. Even though He wants all humans to be saved, He also wants His rules to be followed, since this is the school where we train for life beyond the skies. Our attitudes, words, behavior and customs must be such that people will be drawn to Christ. The pulpit is sacred and not for entertainers or politicians. Do not take me wrong; God wants us to enjoy life and have a good laugh here and there. It is that everything has a time and place. The church is portal of heaven and we must be reverent in it so we can listen what God has to tell our souls when we are there. The church must be the place from where words of life satisfy thirsty souls and hungry spirits. It is the place where heaven and earth come together in reconciliation, where the sinner learns that the Creator really cares for his needs and well-being to the point of self-sacrifice on his behalf.

6And I saw the woman drunken with the blood of the saints, and with the blood of the martyrs of Jesus: and when I saw her, I wondered with great admiration.

I wondered with great admiration - For John it was very difficult to understand how a church that pretends to follow Christ and be the real true original church founded by Jesus, persecutes and kills the saints of God- by the millions! This false church is also guilty of sheltering pedophile priests, of selling indulgences that even "cover" uncommitted sins, of popes fathering illegitimate children, of selling the high offices in the church, of plotting to commit political assassinations (see comment on chapter 13), of making impious alliances with Mussolini, Hitler and the likes and imposing its doctrine by force on indians in Latin America and other places, among its many crimes.

7And the angel said unto me, Wherefore didst thou marvel? I will tell thee the mystery of the woman, and of the beast that carrieth her, which hath the seven heads and ten horns. 8The beast that thou sawest was, and is not; and shall ascend out of the bottomless pit, and go into perdition: and they that dwell on the earth shall wonder, whose names were not written in the book of life from the foundation of the world, when they behold the beast that was, and is not, and yet is.

9And here is the mind which hath wisdom. The seven heads are seven mountains, on which the woman sitteth.

here is the mind which hath wisdom - This phrase connects this woman with the beast of Revelation 13:18. *"Here is wisdom. Let him that hath understanding count the number of the beast: for it is the number of a man; and his number is Six hundred threescore and six."*

Verse 18 indicates that the woman is a city: *"the woman which thou sawest is that great city, which reigneth over the kings of the earth."* Which city has been known for centuries to be established over seven mountains? The only one is Rome, the city of the seven hills. The word "sitteth" is translated from the Greek κάθημαι (*kath'-ay-mahee*) and can also be translated as "reside" or dwell."

The names of these seven hills are: Aventine, Palatine, Capitoline, Caelian, Quirinal, Viminal and Esquiline. Although Vatican Hill is not one of the seven, it was included within the protective wall of the city in times of Pope Leo around the year 850 AD. The seat (cathedra) of the Roman Church is St. John Lateran on the Caelian Hill. Known as the Patriarchate, it was the Pope's official residence until the fifteenth century. The Concordat of 1929 granted the Lateran Palace as an extra territorial part of the Vatican. In fact, there was a medal struck by Pius XI that portrays both the Lateran Palace on the left side and St. Peter's Basilica on the right, side to side. Notice also the cup with the communion wafer shaped as the sun.

It is interesting that the name of the hill where the Vatican sits is called Vaticanus- a combination of *Vatic* and *anus*. The first word means divination or prophecy, while the second means either hill or the old woman of prophecy. Thus, Vaticanus can be translated as "hill of prophecy" or the "old woman of prophecy" and in both ways can be applied to the Catholic Church.

The Vatican is easily recognized in pictures by the design of St. Peter's Square pictured below, having a giant obelisk in the center. "The obelisk which comes from Heliopolis, Egypt, where it was built by the Pharaoh Mencares in 1835 BC in honor of the sun, was brought to Rome in 37 BC by the Emperor Caligula (37-41) and erected in the circus he built. Here it was silent witness of the martyrdom of St. Peter and of many other Christians. In 1586 Sixtus V had it moved to the center of St. Peter's Square." http://saintpetersbasilica.org/Exterior/Obelisk/Obelisk.htm. Noticed how the website mentions the relationship of the obelisk with pagan customs (astrology): "It is also a sun dial, its shadows mark noon over the signs of the zodiac in the white marble disks in the paving of the square. The obelisk rests upon four couchant lions, each with two bodies whose tails intertwine." "On the top...was placed a bronze emblem of Pope Sixtus containing a relic of the cross."

The Vatican- Observe the eight solar rays coming from the obelisk in the center of St. Peter's Square just as also was found in pagan illustrations regarding their sun deity with the stars of Ishtar. The obelisk was originally transported from Egypt by a Roman emperor, where it had been erected in honor of pagan deities. The church ordered it transferred to the actual location in the middle of St. Peter's Square. "Today, thirty obelisks are still standing or have been erected, about fourteen of which are in Rome (they were first consecrated by exorcism and crowned with a cross)..." http://www.thewatchman.co.za/Obelisk.html. The above illustration was photographed from an old engraving. Author unknown.

Regarding the word "mountain," Jeremiah 51:25 identifies the symbol with Babylon: *"Behold, I am against thee, O destroying mountain, saith the LORD, which destroyest all the earth: and I will stretch out mine hand upon thee, and roll thee down from the rocks, and will make thee a burnt mountain."* We must remember that Babylon was on a plain, so the mountain was a symbol of it as a kingdom. Daniel chapter two shows the kingdom of God as a mountain.

[10]And there are seven kings: five are fallen, and one is, and the other is not yet come; and when he cometh, he must continue a short space.

These kings represent world powers. The five fallen ones at the time when John was shown this vision were Babylon, Medo-Persia, Greece, Pagan Rome, and Papal Rome. He saw this vision at the period when the papacy had fallen. At the time of the vision, United States was ("and one is"). The seventh is the union of the three unclean spirits from chapter sixteen in the time of the end (one world order). Of the seventh power, it is said that he *"must continue a short space."* This would match with the declaration found in verse twelve of this chapter about the horns that will *"receive power as kings one hour with the beast."*

Another interpretation is that the seven kings were the forms of Roman government that existed between the Seven Hills of Rome. The list varies among interpreters. One of them is: Kings, Consuls, Decemvirs, Dictators, Triumvirs, Emperors, and Popes. William Miller wrote a slightly different list of Roman type of government under the Republic: senatorial, tribunate, consular, decemvir, and triumvirate. These five were fallen in John's time. One is, (when John wrote his prophecy,) imperial, with the latest form not yet come, kingly, which would refer to the pope kind of leadership. Although this interpretation seems to have some merit, I still prefer the former because Rome was just one power in a succession of nations that antagonized the people of God throughout the ages. Since our understanding of Revelation is based on Daniel, we must adhere to the fact that the later always spoke of kingdoms and not forms of government.

The following table gives us some of the most common interpretations. Time will tell which- if any of them- is right. I consider that there is not enough light to make an informed decision as to the correct interpretation. So, even though after decades studying the subject I have my preference, I do not want to be dogmatic and give the weight of the gospel to it. In matters where there is not sufficient light we must abstain from being too narrow, risking to mislead truth seekers. Since knowing this is no crucial for anyone's salvation, I think that we should respect each other's opinions and keep an open mind waiting for more light to be granted in heaven's time.

The Seven Headed Beast

Heads	#	1st Interpretation	2nd Interpretation	3rd Interpretation	4th Interpretation	5th Interpretation
Five powers are fallen	1	Egypt	Babylon	Babylon	Babylon	Babylon
	2	Assyria	Medo-Persia	Medo-Persia	Medo-Persia	Medo-Persia
	3	Babylon	Greece	Greece	Greece	Greece
	4	Medo-Persia	Rome	Rome	Rome	Rome
	5	Greece	Papal Rome	Papal Rome	Papal Rome	Papal Rome
One is	6	Historic Rome	France during Revolution	France during Revolution	Wounded Papal Rome	Wounded Papal Rome
One is yet to come and is of the eight	7	Papal Rome	Revived Papal Rome	United States and Revived Rome	United States	United States
	8	Revived Papal Rome	Revived Papal Rome	Satan impersonating Christ	Revived Papal Rome	Future coalition including the papacy

The first interpretation is a leaky cistern that does not hold water because in no part of Revelation we can find Assyria and

Egypt is mentioned only as a symbol of the conditions in France during the Revolution in chapter 11.

It is my belief that just as the chapter began with the woman riding the beast, it must also end including the woman as part of the eighth power because the subject of the passage is her condemnation.

See http://amazingdiscoveries.tv/media/133/220-a-woman-rides-the-beast/

http://www.youtube.com/watch?v=Qi7rzZrjmyc&sns=fb

One of the greatest difficulties in dealing with this passage is that interpreters are not sure if John was seeing into the future, being transported through time in vision, or if he was being shown the sixth head in the politico-historical situation in his days. The best argument in this case is flawed with elements of speculation. Through the many years dedicated to the study of this subject, I have changed my mind with respect to the interpretation of the last three heads. More recently, I prefer the 5th interpretation more, though some argue that the United States does not fit the bill on the context of the other nations. It is being argued that the previous nations were enemies of the children of God all throughout history. However, Medo-Persia was friendlier by setting the Babylonian captives free and providing for the rebuilding of the temple. Some enemies are more effective at working from within. The US has done more damage to the church by secularizing the nation, which eventually permeated the church. Now the line of demarcation between the holy and the unholy cannot be distinguished. Both Christians and worldlings participate of the same pleasures and vices. Christians drink, smoke, dance, do drugs, gamble and the divorce rate is just like the world's. What I consider important is that we are prepared for whatever conditions lay ahead for us by maintaining a daily communion with our Father in heaven, so regardless of who our enemy is, we can be protected.

11And the beast that was, and is not, even he is the eighth, and is of the seven, and goeth into perdition.

The beast, instrument of Satan, uses the number eight to contrast Jesus. The letters of the name of Jesus add up to 888 in Greek. Eight is the number of the Savior. He was raised from the dead in the eight day, the Sabbath being the seventh of the week. This passage talks about the beast that was and is not, evidently referring back to the deadly wound mentioned in chapter 13. This verse talks about that beast being also the eight, indicating that just as Jesus resurrected from the dead, the beast also resurrects after the mortal wound was inflicted and becomes the eighth kingdom, like if it were a new power.

In times of John, people used to triangulate the numbers. Taking the number eight, they added all the numbers from one thru eight and they got 36 (1+2+3+4+5+6+7+8=36). The triangular number of 36 (all its numbers added up) is 666, the identifying number of the beast in chapter 13.

12And the ten horns which thou sawest are ten kings, which have received no kingdom as yet; but receive power as kings one hour with the beast.

One hour in prophetic time is 15 days. This is an indication that this power that pretends to decide who is king will grant temporary power to ten kings or kingdoms. This same period of time is mentioned in chapter 18 three times to indicated how fast the punishment of Babylon will be inflicted. This emphasized period of time is one good reason to interpret chapter 17 in the context of chapter 18.

13These have one mind, and shall give their power and strength unto the beast.

This verse seems to indicate that the world powers will be at peace with one another. This is the fulfillment of what Paul wrote: *"For when they shall say, Peace and safety; then sudden destruction cometh upon them, as travail upon a woman with child; and they shall not escape"* (1 Thessalonians 5:3). "'These have one mind.' There will be a universal bond of union, one great harmony, a confederacy of Satan's forces. 'And shall give their power and strength unto the beast.' Thus is manifested the same arbitrary, oppressive power against religious liberty, freedom to worship God according to the dictates of conscience, as was manifested by the papacy, when in the past it persecuted those who dared to refuse to conform with the religious rites and ceremonies of Romanism." *S.D.A. Bible Commentary Vol. 7*, page 983. We are practicing for that union right now as several nations in the world fight the bloody terrorist group ISIS or ISIL. President Obama called for an alliance even with Muslim nations to combat the common enemy.

[14]*These shall make war with the Lamb, and the Lamb shall overcome them: for he is Lord of lords, and King of kings: and they that are with him are called, and chosen, and faithful.*

Whoever wars against the saints, fights Jesus. When Saul was persecuting the saints, he had a vision and was asked "...Saul, why persecutest thou me?" (Acts 9:4). No evil look, no merciless act and no cruel word is pronounced against one of Jesus' followers that He does not take it as done to Himself: *"...for he that toucheth you toucheth the apple of his eye"* (Zechariah 2:8). The Lord is going to fight on our behalf (2 Chronicles 20:17). As Israel of old was told to stay still, so we will stay in our hiding places (Isaiah 33:16) while Jesus fights our enemies. Just before the Israelites crossed the Red Sea, *"Moses said unto the people, Fear ye not, <u>stand still</u>, and see the salvation of the LORD, which he will shew to you today: for the Egyptians whom ye have seen today, ye shall see them again no more for ever. <u>The LORD shall fight for you</u>, and ye shall hold your peace"* (Exodus 14:13, 14). This verse of Revelation contains one of the most encouraging promises: *"the Lamb shall overcome them."* In His victory, we will have our victory. He obtained a great victory at Calvary on our behalf and soon He will obtain another one over the beast and its associates also on our behalf. However, the most important victory that He can obtain is the one in the battle inside our hearts. He will obtain that one only if we allow Him.

[15]*And he saith unto me, <u>The waters</u> which thou sawest, where the whore sitteth, <u>are peoples</u>, and <u>multitudes</u>, and <u>nations</u>, and tongues.*

This verse helps to clarify the meaning of similar others from Daniel 7 and Revelation 13. God provided in the Scriptures enough light to explain most of the difficult passages. If we pray and use a concordance, He will show us where to look so we can understand the prophetic symbols. God did not leave anything to chance or to guessing. Being a God of order, He made provision for us to obtain the correct interpretation and not be left in the dark.

16And the ten horns which thou sawest upon the beast, these shall hate the whore, and shall make her desolate and naked, and shall eat her flesh, and burn her with fire.

The kings of the earth will finally open their eyes and realize- though too late- who the beast really is and will abandon her. Human support will be denied to the beast. She will no longer exert tyrannical influence over the human race. No longer will the kings of the earth be her puppets. This is the time when they discover that the beast had played the nations into believing that the small groups of Sabbath keepers around the world are the cause of the earthquakes, tornadoes, hurricanes, tsunamis, droughts, famines, plagues and other forms of suffering. They were lead to believe that those sincere worshippers needed to be exterminated. Now with the plagues falling on them, they realize that God never approved the change on the day of rest into Sunday, a papal child.

desolate – This passage parallels the writings of Isaiah: *"And Babylon, the glory of kingdoms, the beauty of the Chaldees' excellency, shall be as when God overthrew Sodom and Gomorrah. It shall never be inhabited, neither shall it be dwelt in from generation to generation...."* (Isaiah 13:19,20).

17For God hath put in their hearts to fulfill his will, and to agree, and give their kingdom unto the beast, until the words of God shall be fulfilled.

According to Daniel 2:21, God *"removeth kings, and setteth up kings,"* so he will allow the power transfer mentioned in this verse. After all, it will only be temporary until His divine purpose is fulfilled.

18And the woman which thou sawest is that great city, which reigneth over the kings of the earth.

What city exerts influence over the kings of the earth? If we also consider the facts that it sits over many waters, which represents the human population, that it sits on the seven hills of Rome and persecutes the saints of God, then we can safely conclude that this passage refers to the city of Rome from where the popes reign supreme and very soon, like in the middle ages, unopposed.

REVELATION 18

Power and Riches Vs. Obedience to God

[1]And after these things I saw another angel come down from heaven, having great power; and ***the earth was lightened with his glory****.*
[2]And he cried mightily with a strong voice, saying, Babylon the great is fallen, is fallen, and is become the habitation of devils, and the hold of every foul spirit, and a cage of every ***unclean*** *and hateful bird.*

Who is this angel? Ezekiel comes to help our understanding. *"And, behold, the glory of the God of Israel came from the way of the east: and his voice was like a noise of many waters: and* ***the earth shined with his glory****"* (Ezekiel 43:2). There is only one whose glory can lighten the earth. This "angel" is Jesus. Remember that the meaning of the word angel is messenger.

After being shown the condemnation of the great harlot in chapter 17, John is shown more of why that church is disapproved by God. This heavenly messenger is claiming with a loud voice that the system that oppressed the children of God is now fallen. The calls to repent went unheeded. The blood of Jesus was trampled on and a pagan system based on works took the place of the free plan of salvation provided at such a high cost. The nations of the world were made drunk with the false teachings as we saw in the previous chapter. The door of salvation was shut to millions of souls by keeping them in the darkness of ignorance. Ministers preached fables instead of the truth, keeping the souls in a state of stupor, impeding the reforming work of the Holy Spirit. Now is retribution time. The Holy Spirit is no longer pleading for them to repent because all the opportunities were rejected and wasted and now their consciences are seared. The time of grace is gone. In the previous chapters of Revelation, we saw His true church despised, persecuted, tortured and killed by the crusaders, the inquisition and through other means. The time of reckoning has arrived at last. It is midnight for Babylon. The power that usurped God's authority pretending to represent Him will cease to exist. Just as when the strong hand of God set His people free from the Egyptian bondage at midnight, He will intervene to bring justice to His oppressed children in their darkest hour. When it seems that all is lost, when there is no hope in sight, when the hordes of demons and evil men surround the elect ready to execute them, God's almighty hand once again set the oppressed free.

The Catholic leadership had plenty of time to repent but the bling blinded them. *"We wanted to heal Babylon, but it couldn't be healed. Let us abandon it and go to our own land. God has judged Babylon. Its judgment is complete"* (Jeremiah 51:9 *God's Word*). Now Satan has complete dominion of Babylon and will go full force for the great final battle of Armageddon.

the great – Why is Babylon here called the great but in the previous mention in chapter 14 is just Babylon? The reason is that now it is a triple alliance with the false prophet and the dragon. That is why this passage mentions that it is full of spirits of demons, referring to the triple coalition mentioned in chapter 16.

habitation of devils – Since they rejected the truth, the Holy Spirit departed from the members of the apostate churches and now they become <u>fully demon possessed</u>. For over one hundred years, the Pentecostals and evangelicals have claimed to be full of the Holy Spirit. If they only knew where that spirit came from and where it was leading them! The Bible describes what happens when a demon comes out of a man and he neglects to let the Lord in: *"When the unclean spirit is gone out of a man, he walketh through dry places, seeking rest, and findeth none. Then he saith, I will return into my house from whence I came out; and when he is come, he findeth it empty, swept, and garnished. Then goeth he, and taketh with himself seven other spirits more wicked than himself, and they enter in and dwell there: and the last state of that man is worse than the first. Even so shall it be also unto this wicked generation"* (Matthew 12:43-45). If that happens when a bad spirit comes out of a man, it is even a lot worse when the Holy Spirit is the one who departs after the truth is stubbornly rejected. The nation of Israel received many blessings from God for centuries, but His mercy was abused. Finally, Jesus had to pronounce some of the most terrible words that He ever uttered: *"Behold, your house is left unto you desolate" (Matthew 23:38).* If you are reading this, it is because you are still curious about knowing the truth and Jesus is still knocking at the door of your heart. Please let Him in your life and take His side or you will also become habitation of demons and forever lost. Nothing in this world is worth losing eternal life over.

and a cage of every ***unclean*** *and hateful bird.*

Many people – even committed Christians-misunderstand some Bible passages to justify consuming anything they wish. In doing this, they work against God's original design. They teach that the prohibition to eat certain animals was a ritual law for the Jewish people only and that, as Christians, we are completely exempt from following it. One of those animals considered unclean by God the Creator is the pig (see Leviticus 11:2-23 and Deuteronomy 14:3-20). The distinction between clean and unclean animals was established centuries before the founding of the Jewish nation and was not eliminated at the cross as we will see soon. It was one of those things that God wanted for the whole human race to follow for their own good. When Noah was told to build the ark, he was instructed to get just one pair of each unclean animal but seven pairs of clean animals (Genesis 7:2). As everybody familiar with the Bible knows, Noah was not a Jew. When Noah came out of the ark, he was granted permission to eat meat- only of clean animals. This was only transitory because the trees were not mature to produce the food they needed. It usually takes about four years for trees to start producing fruit. We must remember that man's original diet was completely vegan- See Genesis 1:29; 3:18. Over a thousand years later, God chose manna for the Israelites' diet in the desert. When they asked God for meat, He was displeased because that is not the natural diet for man. I remember that when my father had a heart attack the doctor told him to never again eat pig. I was about 14 years old and understood from the doctor's instructions that eating pig shortens the life. He did not want to follow the doctor's advice and the following year death deprived me of my father. Of all the meats that we eat in the so-called civilized world, pork is the most acid forming and predisposes the body to cancer, arthritis and other inflammatory diseases. Millions of people every year die premature deaths due to the way they eat and their lifestyle in general. There are so many diseases transmitted by the consumption of unclean animals, including leprosy and trichinosis that will require a separate book to discuss them.

Some Christians claim that when Christ died on the cross He cleaned the animals that He had designated as unclean. However, this verse of Revelation teaches otherwise. Everything in this creation has a purpose. In the same way that God determined to have the sun to shine in the day and the moon to reflect its light by night, and plants to produce oxygen while benefiting from our carbon dioxide, He placed some animals to keep the environment clean for other creatures and for us. This passage in Revelation 18:2 indicates that even at the time of the end there would be some of those animals still categorized as <u>unclean</u>. *"Who can bring a clean thing out of an unclean? not one"* (Job 14:4). If God designed a good plan to keep the environment safer for us, why would He change it for the only reason of allowing people to eat anything that moves? If we check the health of individuals whose diet consist mostly of scavengers (God's housekeepers), we will realize that they live shorter lives and are vastly affected by diseases that they should not be afflicted with. As a loving parent, He is concerned about our well-being and tells us to stay away from eating those creatures.

Many quote the passage from Acts 10 where Peter is shown a *"vessel descending upon him, as it had been a great sheet knit at the four corners, and let down to the earth: Wherein were all manner of four footed beasts of the earth, and wild beasts, and creeping things, and fowls of the air. And there came a voice to him, Rise, Peter; kill, and eat"* (Acts 10:11-13). As the passage indicates, Peter knew that this vision was symbolic and he was pondering what it meant (verse 17). Later on in the chapter, he declared that God <u>has shown him</u> *"that I should <u>not call any man</u> impure or <u>unclean</u>"* (verse 28 NIV). <u>Those unclean animals represented the gentiles</u>, whom the Jewish considered unclean. If the vision was literal, then the book of Acts would have presented Peter not only going to Red Lobster to order a big plate of scavengers, but also eating them. We cannot find Peter eating the unclean animals in Acts 10 or in any other passage of the Bible.

Since God does not change, what He told about unclean animals once still stands. As our Designer, he is the one that knows which type of fuel our bodies need. Would you fill the tank of your car with sewer water (forgive me for that comparison) when it was designed to run on gasoline? Unclean animals are to be considered disgusting and the idea of eating them is to be repulsive. The Creator determined that if an animal dies, others (like vultures) would eat the flesh and thus help the others to survive from a possible epidemic. Pigs are trash collectors and their duty is to clean the environment on the land. The role of catfish, crabs, lobsters and shrimps is to act as walking sewers to clean the waters. The task of these animals is to contain the spread of diseases. Many maladies are transmitted by the consumption of animal flesh and God wants us to live a long, healthy life and protect us from unnecessary suffering. *"Be not over much wicked, neither be thou foolish: why shouldest thou die before thy time?"* (Ecclesiastes 7:17). The Contemporary English Version translates that verse this way: *"Don't die before your time by being too evil or acting like a fool."* You can chose to follow the owner's manual and have your machine last and work great for the maximum length of time. *"Beloved, I wish above all things that thou mayest prosper and be in health, even as thy soul prospereth"* (3 John 2). Even on the issue of the correct diet, Babylon is conspiring against humanity. Why? Because whatever weakens the body affects also the brain. A feeble mind has a harder time to understand the truth. That is why Satan is using Monsanto and other companies to produce GMO crops that will make people sick. That is why our water and air are contaminated. By making us sick, he can manage to take our minds away from the spiritual and eternal. We have a body to take care of. *"What? know ye not that your body is the temple of the Holy Ghost which is in you, which ye have of God, and ye are not your own? For ye are bought with a price: therefore glorify God in your body, and in your spirit, which are God's"* (1 Corinthians 6:19,20). Rich foods are also a cause of alarm because its effects over the whole body are detrimental. Overuse of sugar, spices, artificial ingredients-many of them derived from petroleum and understudied (so we do not really know the long-term effects on the human body until decades later), too much fat, refined foods, together with eating at all hours without giving the stomach proper rest, improper food combinations, etc. are causing too many of the diseases that we see today. Not only that, studies done among violent prisoners show a relationship with their behavior and the diet they consumed before they committed their crimes. "Indulgence of appetite is the cause of dissention, strife, discord, and many other evils. Impatient words are spoken, and unkind things done, dishonest practices are followed and passion is manifested, and all because the nerves of the brain are diseased by the abuse heaped upon the stomach." *Counsels on Diet and Foods*, page 53.

Many feel that they are free to eat anything they want as they want to eat it. To them, Paul wrote: *"Whether therefore ye eat, or drink, or whatsoever ye do, do all to the glory of God"* (1 Corinthians 10:31). "And yet you would say, 'It is none of your business what I eat, or what course I pursue?' Does anybody around dyspeptics suffer? Just take a course that will irritate them in any way. How natural to be fretful! They feel bad, and it appears to them that their children are very bad. They cannot speak calmly to them, nor, without special grace, act calmly in their families. All around them are affected by the disease upon them, all have to suffer the consequences of their infirmity." *Counsels on Diet and Foods*, pages 135-136. One thing that comes to mind is that man was created, he was placed in a garden but there is no mention of a supermarket or the need for a stove to cook his meals, which indicates that Adam and Eve were consuming their meals as raw and natural as possible.

How sad is to see people dying premature deaths just because their church leaders taught them that it is OK to eat anything as long as they pray before they consume it. I prefer to live 90 healthy years with a clear mind in a healthy body and not just live 70 with all kinds of maladies and having to take treatments and pills for high cholesterol, heart disease, diabetes, arthritis, Alzheimer's, cancer and so many other health challengers. God's way is always the best way, the one that ultimately will bring the best results. We must understand that, as a loving Parent, when God removes something from us, it is because He has something that is better.

[3]For all nations have drunk of the wine of the wrath of her fornication, and the kings of the earth have committed fornication with her, and the merchants of the earth are waxed rich through the abundance of her delicacies.

As explained earlier, fornication refers to the mix of truth with false doctrines. Here the passage repeats the words of chapter 17 regarding the wine of Babylon. It was given to every nation to drink but it came through the government leaders to be enforced on the masses. Ezekiel 27 presents a similar message regarding Tyrus. There, it mentions how the merchants of the earth became rich by dealing with the power that had rejected God's mercy. Tyrus had been an ally of Israel in times of Solomon and even provided the wood used to build the temple and the royal palace. They had been exposed to the truth and the knowledge of God, but ultimately rejected His love and followed their own ways. In like manner, the early church flirted with paganism and soon corrupted the truth, adopting practices and beliefs that were contrary to Jesus' teachings.

"the inhabitants of the earth have been made drunk"- I have, since childhood, dealt with several drunken people (not in my family). They are very difficult to reason with because their brains are numbed. Alcohol specifically affects the frontal lobes, were the seat of the conscience and moral judgment resides. Likewise, spiritual drunkenness inhibits the reasoning powers of the mind and rejection of the truth follows.

Revelation 18 is like a compilation of Old Testament passages. The following table shows some of the parallels between this chapter and Old Testament prophecies:

Old Testament	Revelation 18
"And, behold, the glory of the God of Israel came from the way of the east: and his <u>voice *was* like a noise of many waters</u>: and <u>the earth shined with his glory</u>" (Ezekiel 43:2).	"And after these things I saw another angel come down from heaven, having great power; and <u>the earth was lightened with his glory</u>. And he cried mightily with a <u>strong voice</u>..." (Revelation 18:1,2a).
"Babylon is fallen, is fallen; and all the graven images of her gods he hath broken unto the ground" (Isaiah 21:9b).	"...Babylon the great is fallen, is fallen..." (Revelation 18:2).
"Flee from the midst of Babylon, and go out of the land of the Chaldeans..." (Jeremiah 50:8; 51:6; 51:45 *ESV*)	"I heard another voice from heaven saying, "Come out of Babylon, my people..." (Revelation 18:4 *GW*)
"We would have healed Babylon, but she is not healed: forsake her, and let us go every one into his own country: for her judgment reacheth unto heaven, and is lifted up *even* to the skies." (Jeremiah 51:9)	"For her sins have reached unto heaven, and God hath remembered her iniquities." (Revelation 18:5)

"Give a loud cry against her on every side; she has given herself up, her supports are overturned, her walls are broken down: for it is the payment taken by the Lord; give her payment; as she has done, so do to her" (Jeremiah 50:15 *Bible in Basic English)*	"Reward her even as she rewarded you, and double unto her double according to her works: in the cup which she hath filled fill to her double." (Revelation 18:6)
"And thou saidst, I shall be a lady for ever: *so* that thou didst not lay these *things* to thy heart, neither didst remember the latter end of it. Therefore hear now this, *thou that art* given to pleasures, that dwellest carelessly, that sayest in thine heart, I *am,* and none else beside me; I shall not sit *as* a widow, neither shall I know the loss of children." (Isaiah 47:7,8)	"How much she hath glorified herself, and lived deliciously, so much torment and sorrow give her: for she saith in her heart, I sit a queen, and am no widow, and shall see no sorrow." (Revelation 18:7)
"I beheld then because of the voice of the great words which the horn spake: I beheld *even* till the beast was slain, and his body destroyed, and given to the burning flame." (Daniel 7:11)	"Therefore shall her plagues come in one day, death, and mourning, and famine; and she shall be utterly burned with fire: for strong *is* the Lord God who judgeth her." (Revelation 18:8)
"At the noise of the taking of Babylon the earth is moved, and the cry is heard among the nations." (Jeremiah 50:46)	"And the kings of the earth, who have committed fornication and lived deliciously with her, shall bewail her, and lament for her, when they shall see the smoke of her burning." (Revelation 18:9)
"Because of the wrath of the Lord no one will be living in it, and it will be quite unpeopled: everyone who goes by Babylon will be overcome with wonder, and make sounds of fear at all her punishments." (Jeremiah 50:13 *Bible in Basic English*, 1965)	"The merchants of these things, which were made rich by her, shall stand afar off for the fear of her torment, weeping and wailing" (Revelation 18:15)
"And it shall be, when thou hast made an end of reading this book, *that* thou shalt bind a stone to it, and cast it into the midst of Euphrates: And thou shalt say, Thus shall Babylon sink, and shall not rise from the evil that I will bring upon her: and they shall be weary." (Jeremiah 51:63,64)	"And a mighty angel took up a stone like a great millstone, and cast *it* into the sea, saying, Thus with violence shall that great city Babylon be thrown down, and shall be found no more at all." (Revelation 18:21)

Although I concentrated on passages referring directly to Babylon in the Old Testament, there are several passages in Revelation 18 that had their origin on the prophecies pronounced against Tyre and Nineveh. (See for example Ezekiel 27:32-36; Ezekiel

27:13 "Javan, Tubal, and Meshech, they were thy merchants: they traded the persons of men and vessels of brass in thy market. ***Nah 3:4*** *"Because of the multitude of the whoredoms of the well-favored harlot, the mistress of witchcrafts, that selleth nations through her whoredoms, and families through her witchcrafts.")*

[4]And I heard another voice from heaven, saying, Come out of her, my people, that ye be not partakers of her sins, and that ye receive not of her plagues.

What a tender call offering mercy to those that will listen to the Great Shepherd! God always warns His people about the imminent destruction so they can escape unharmed:

- He told Noah to build an ark so he and his family could escape the flood
- He told Lot to leave the city before Sodom and Gomorrah were destroyed by fire
- He told the disciples how to recognize when Jerusalem was going to be destroyed so they would not perish (Luke 21:20)

In the last two examples, God asked His children to abandon the cities. Surely, living in the cities has its advantages, but the time will soon come that if we want to save our families, we need to move to the country. Just consider the case of Lot. The corrupt influence of the city dwellers swayed his wife's lifestyle to such degree that she could not bear the thought of leaving her friends and possessions behind, which cost her life and salvation. As a socialite, if there was a famous designer, she was next to the runway, if there was an opera or play, she was in the first row, if there was a new line of expensive perfumes or an auction of jewels or artwork, there she was. His daughters were also morally corrupt. Instead of waiting to find husbands, they made their father drunk and had children from him, bringing two wicked races to the world. By being in such proximity with evil, their characters got stained and their consciences became numbed. Lot's wife was lost because she valued the temporary over the eternal. She was offered real gold and exchanged it for sand. That is why Jesus advised us to make treasure in heaven (Luke 12:33).

God is in the saving business and does not want anyone to perish. Now He is calling people to leave Babylon before the seven last plagues are poured on the inhabitants of the earth. If you are still there, leave before it is too late. What is holding you up? Family? Friends? A church membership? If you love anyone or anything more than Jesus, He cannot save you from what is coming. Please leave at once. If you leave, there is a good chance that your loved ones will come out of Babylon too and be saved. Show them that it is well worth it to follow Jesus. If you stay, regardless of God's most tender invitations to get out, then all- you and those that you profess to love- will perish together. Others will follow your example. Please come out and follow the truth as it is in Jesus. The reward will be incredible. *"But as it is written, Eye hath not seen, nor ear heard, neither have entered into the heart of man, the things which God hath prepared for them that love him"* (1 Corinthians 2:9).

The books of Isaiah and Jeremiah show several passages that are similar to this chapter. As an example of this, let us see how Jeremiah 51:9 (Contemporary English Version) reads: *"We have already tried to treat Babylon's wounds, but they would not heal. Come on, Let us all go home to our own countries. Nothing is left in Babylonia; everything is destroyed."* God gave Babylon generous time and opportunities to repent but she refused (Revelation 2:21). The same opportunities that He gave to Israel, gave also to Babylon. Of Israel, it was written: *"...Repent! Turn away from all your offenses; then sin will not be your downfall. Rid yourselves of all the offenses you have committed, and get a new heart and a new spirit. Why will you die, O house of Israel? For I take no pleasure in the death of anyone, declares the Sovereign LORD. Repent and live!"* Ezekiel 18:30-32 NIV).

What would entail to heed the counsel to come out of spiritual Babylon? It will require a complete separation. God cannot accept half a heart. He wants it all. *"My son, give me thine heart, and let thine eyes observe my ways"* (Proverbs 23:26). We cannot have divided affections. *"No man can serve two masters: for either he will hate the one, and love the other; or else he will hold to the one, and despise the other. Ye cannot serve God and mammon"* (Matthew 6:24). Could a woman be happy if she finds out that her future husband still loves his previous girlfriend and still visits her?

Wouldn't she consider their relationship shaky? The call to come out of Babylon stresses in itself a complete abandonment of the traditions and false teachings as well as any worldliness acquired from our environment throughout our lives. Only a complete separation will enable God to prepare our hearts for the kingdom of heaven. *"Remember Lot's wife"* (Luke 17:32). As mentioned above, Lot's wife died because her heart was divided. She was told to leave the city, just as we are called to leave Babylon the great city. Unfortunately for her and her family, she had her treasure in the wrong place. God has promised us life eternal in a better city with streets of gold and a river of life. Why would we want to stay in the city of destruction?

In order to be ready to deliver the last call of mercy to those that are still in Babylon, the real church of God has to revive the primitive seal. Such revival will be surely met with a counterfeit in the false churches in order to entice people to stay. Strong delusions will convince them that they are in the true church. It is said that Satan will even make fire come down from heaven in the presence of men and this chapter mentions the use of sorceries (verse 23). Many miracles will be performed by both sides and only a careful study of the Scriptures will aid in identifying the true manifestation of the Spirit and power of God. Those that have neglected the careful and deep study of their Bibles will fall for the spurious and false and will unite with the enemies of the children of God to persecute the saints, even their own relatives and friends. *"And a man's foes shall be they of his own household"* (Mat. 10:36). *"The father shall be divided against the son, and the son against the father; the mother against the daughter, and the daughter against the mother; the mother in law against her daughter in law, and the daughter in law against her mother in law"* (Luke 12:53).

5 For her sins have reached unto heaven, and God hath remembered her iniquities.

The sins of Babylon listed in this chapter as the reason for her fall are:

- She hath glorified herself
- Lived deliciously
- Committed fornication with the kings of the earth

- By her sorceries were all nations deceived
- In her was found the blood of prophets, and of saints, and of all that were slain upon the earth

We serve a merciful and patient God who gives us many opportunities to reconcile with Him. Regardless, His patience is like a cup; if there is one drop too many, it will be overfilled. Abram was told: *"In the fourth generation your descendants will come back here, for the sin of the Amorites has not yet reached its full measure"* (Genesis 15:16 NIV). The Amorites were known among other things, for sacrificing their own children to demons. However, there were a few that still could be saved from among them, as it was the case of Rahab. In His dealings with individuals and nations, He always works for the salvation of His creatures with fairness. No one will ever be lost without having ample opportunity to accept the offer of salvation.

This passage also teaches us that there is nothing done in the darkness that would not be brought to light (see Matthew 10:26). God keeps records of all our deeds, words and thoughts, and one day, unless we repent, those sins will come back to hunt us. For the person that has accepted Jesus and confessed his sins, he has nothing to fear because Jesus' life will take the place of his in the judgment and God will see the repented sinner as if he has never committed a sin in his life. Halleluiah!!!

[6]*Reward her even as she rewarded you, and double unto her double* ***according to her works****: in the cup which she hath filled fill to her double.*

Revelation chapter 13:10 says that *"If anyone is to be killed with the sword, with the sword he will be killed"* (NIV). We are told that *"A man* ***reaps*** *what he* ***sows****"* (Galatians 6:7). The sin of Babylon is the sin of rebellion. Her punishment will be fair because she is going to receive a reward "according to her works." Those that defend the heresy of an eternal hell, portray God as a vengeful lunatic. Let us suppose that when sinners die, they go directly to hell. For that purpose, we can compare two well-known sinners:

Sinner	How many people killed	How many years spent in hell:
Cain	Only 1	Almost 6,000 years already
Adolf Hitler	Over 6,000,000	Less than 70 years so far

Therefore, if sinners go straight to hell when they die, those who died first are receiving more punishment than those that died more recently regardless of their degree of sinfulness or how terrible their actions were. So if the sin of Cain is being punished thousands of years more than the sins of Hitler, where is the justice on this? If you have twin sons and one dies at age 20 and just did not believe in Jesus and the other son lived to be 40 and became a serial killer, bank robber, rapist and alcoholic, your first son is going to be tortured 20 more years than the one that caused so much pain and suffering to his fellow human beings. What kind of God is being portrayed in that hideous doctrine? Obviously it is not Christ, for He will return *"to give every man* ***<u>according as his work</u>*** *shall be"* (Revelation 22:12). I am so glad that God is fair.

7How much she hath glorified herself, and lived deliciously, so much torment and sorrow give her: for she saith in her heart, <u>I sit a queen, and am no widow, and shall see no sorrow</u>.

The arrogance of spiritual Babylon parallels the way ancient Babylon saw herself. *"And thou saidst, I shall be a lady for ever: so that thou didst not lay these things to thy heart, neither didst remember the latter end of it. Therefore hear now this, thou that art given to pleasures, that dwellest carelessly, that sayest in thine heart, I am, and none else beside me; <u>I shall not sit as a widow, neither shall I know the loss of children</u>"* (Isaiah 47:7,8). Nebuchadnezzar wanted his kingdom to last forever but as his vision had revealed, it would give way to another kingdom until the kingdom of the Most High would be established. That time is fast approaching and God will bring His judgments against the proud religious system.

8Therefore shall her plagues come ***<u>in one day</u>****, death, and mourning, and famine; and she shall be utterly burned with fire: for strong is the Lord God who judgeth her.*

This chapter emphasizes that the plagues will be of short duration. This verse reads "one day" and three other verses read "one hour." The opulent power will be ruined and end up in misery by the fire of God that no man can quench. Why fire? Because Rome killed "heretics"- the saints of God- at the stake and because she contaminated that which was supposed to be kept pure- the gospel of salvation by faith through Christ alone.

9And the kings of the earth, who have committed fornication and lived deliciously with her, shall bewail her, and lament for her, when they shall see the smoke of her burning,

A rich person has many friends but many despise the poor. Babylon has gone to the rich and powerful to increment its influence and grip on the masses. The care that the false church has for the poor is just a screen to get more money from the rich and powerful. How come "caring for the poor" finds her more and more opulent in her riches every year that goes by?

10Standing afar off for the fear of her torment, saying, Alas, alas that great city Babylon, that mighty city! for in one hour is thy judgment come.

The kings of the earth know that Babylon is a sinister power and still they do business with her. Why would a church need to have an intelligence department that is more efficient than any other on earth, including the KGB and the CIA? Why her leaders live in palaces like royalty when Jesus and His disciples lived so simple lives?

11And the merchants of the earth shall weep and mourn over her;
for no man buyeth their merchandise any more: 12The merchandise
of gold, and silver, and precious stones, and of pearls, and fine linen,
and purple, and silk, and scarlet, and all thyine wood, and all manner
vessels of ivory, and all manner vessels of most precious wood, and
of brass, and iron, and marble, 13And cinnamon, and odours, and
ointments, and frankincense, and wine, and oil, and fine flour, and
wheat, and beasts, and sheep, and horses, and chariots, and slaves,
and souls of men. 14And the fruits that thy soul lusted after are
departed from thee, and all things which were dainty and goodly are
departed from thee, and thou shalt find them no more at all.

As mentioned above, the Catholic Church leaders have been living in luxury. The pope lives in palaces. In summer, he lives at Castel Gandolfo, a palace and villa. The palace walls are decked with marble and all kinds of beautiful decorations. The rest of the year, he lives in the papal palace in Vatican City, the place that not only has enormous monetary riches but also the most astounding works of art. Works by Michael Angelo, Rafael, Da Vinci, Giotto, Caravaggio and many other famous artists decorate the chapels and every room of that place (estimated at 11,000 rooms- you read right: 11,000!). Their worth is estimated beyond market value (it cannot be estimated). What a contrast with Jesus! *"And Jesus said unto him, Foxes have holes, and birds of the air have nests; but the Son of man hath not where to lay his head"* (Luke 9:58). Visiting any one of their cathedrals, especially in rich countries, is an impressing experience. The statues are decked with gold and jewels. It is said that the church has more money than the United States and Russia combined.

cinnamon, and odours, and ointments, and frankincense – Like the harlot of Proverbs seven that used myrrh, aloes, and cinnamon to seduce her victim, Rome uses articles of perfumery to captivate the senses of the worshippers.

slaves, and souls of men – My understanding is that this refers to the members of religious orders with vows of blind obedience to the pope. Their submission must be absolute without consideration to family, friends or loyalty to any power on earth.

the fruits that thy soul lusted after – It was the lust for a fruit that introduced sin into this world and it was the prevailing sin in Babylon. The lust for power and possessions and above all, the same desire that motivated Eve to extend her hand and grab the fruit: to be like God (2 Thessalonians 2:4). All the riches of Babylon would not be enough to save her from the imminent wrath. *"Neither their silver nor their gold shall be able to deliver them in the day of the LORD'S wrath; but the whole land shall be devoured by the fire of his jealousy: for he shall make even a speedy riddance of all them that dwell in the land"* (Zephaniah 1:18).

15The merchants of these things, which were made rich by her, shall stand afar off for the fear of her torment, weeping and wailing,

Merchants- mentioned frequently in this chapter, the term refers to the preachers of Babylonian wine (doctrines). These are the preachers whose churches are full for fear of going to hell, instead of being full of people responding to the incomparable love of Jesus. This is quite a contrast with what the apostle Paul wrote: *"Unlike so many, we do not peddle the word of God for profit. On the contrary, in Christ we speak before God with sincerity, like men sent from God"* (2 Corinthians 2:17 -NIV). *"But have renounced the hidden things of dishonesty, not walking in craftiness, nor handling the word of God deceitfully; but by manifestation of the truth commending ourselves to every man's conscience in the sight of God"* (2 Corinthians 4:2). Paul admonishes the end time believers about the false preachers that maintain the Babylonian approach to the truth and counsels to stay away from them. *"For the time will come when they will not endure sound doctrine; but after their own lusts shall they heap to themselves teachers, having itching ears; and they shall turn away their ears from the truth, and shall be turned unto fables"* (2 Timothy 4:3,4). *"If any man teach otherwise, and consent not to wholesome words, even the words of our Lord Jesus Christ, and to the doctrine which is according to godliness; he is proud, knowing nothing, but doting about questions and strifes of words, whereof cometh envy, strife, railings, evil surmisings, perverse disputings of men of corrupt minds, and destitute of the truth, supposing that gain is godliness:* ***from such withdraw thyself****"* (1 Timothy 6:3-5). *"This know also, that in the last days perilous times shall come. For men shall be lovers of their own selves, covetous, boasters, proud, blasphemers, disobedient to parents, unthankful, unholy, without natural affection* [gay and lesbian], *trucebreakers, false accusers, incontinent, fierce, despisers of those that are good, traitors, heady, highminded, lovers of pleasures more than lovers of God; having a form of godliness, but denying the power thereof:* ***from such turn away****"* (2 Timothy 3:1-5). If your preacher is an entertainer, preaches only feel-good-sermons, if your church leader has turned the pulpit into a political forum, if he promotes the union of church and state, if truth is considered relative, them it is time to run and find the church that keeps the *"commandments of God, and have the testimony of Jesus Christ"* (Revelation 12:17). *"Come out of her, my people."*

stand afar off for the fear of her torment If a child sees that one of his siblings is being punished for something they did together, he knows that he better stay as far as possible. The knowledge of their common guilt (for teaching falsehood and keeping the truth from their members) will keep at that time the false pastors away, just as witnesses, wondering when they will get their share because of their complicity in preaching falsehood and hiding the truth from the people.

16And saying, Alas, alas that great city, that was clothed in fine linen, and purple, and scarlet, and decked with gold, and precious stones, and pearls!

Purple and scarlet are the colors worn by the church leaders. The word "alas" (means unfortunately, sadly) indicates that their sorrow is not for the things that the false church and they themselves did, but because they could not continue their business of deception to obtain more riches. See next verse:

17For in one hour so great riches is come to nought. And every shipmaster, and all the company in ships, and sailors, and as many as trade by sea, stood afar off,

Noah's ark, the instrument to save him and his family from the flood, became the symbol of the true church where sinners could seek refuge. The ships here are a symbol of the fallen churches (a.k.a. the false prophet). The sea represents the multitude of people that support the false churches, just as a literal sea supports the ships by allowing them to navigate for commerce.

18And cried when they saw the smoke of her burning, saying, What city is like unto this great city!

That cry is similar to the one found in chapter 13: "*who is like the beast*..."

19And they cast dust on their heads, and cried, weeping and wailing, saying, Alas, alas that great city, wherein were made rich all that had ships in the sea by reason of her costliness! for in one hour is she made desolate.

The lament seems to go on and on over the loss of the great city. Sin brings a bitter harvest of pain and in this case, no repentance. The pain is for what they lost. It is the same pain expressed by Achan when, instead of an open confession, he tried to justify why he had taken that which was forbidden in the war against Jericho: "goodly Babylonish garment." He was trying to get Joshua to agree with him! These pastors defend the gospel of prosperity that they learned from the Catholic Church popes and cardinals, while so many millions starve. Very soon, that will happen no more. Justice will be done:

20Rejoice over her, thou heaven, and ye holy apostles and prophets; for God hath avenged you on her.

In chapter 6, John was shown the souls under the altar. *"And they cried with a loud voice, saying, How long, O Lord, holy and true, dost thou not judge and avenge our blood on them that dwell on the earth"* Now that time of retribution has come at last.

21And a mighty angel took up a stone like a great millstone, and cast it into the sea, saying, Thus with violence shall that great city Babylon be thrown down, and shall be found no more at all.

Matthew 18:6 tells us that it is better to tie a millstone to the neck and sink in the sea, than to become a stumbling block for one of the children of God. Babylon became the greatest stumbling block because of its rebellion against God, by its teaching of heresies and her crimes committed against those that dared to believe on the pure Scriptures. They even killed those that dare to try to reform her, like pope John Paul the first in 1978. Even the previous liberal pope (although not completely liberal) who bled for days, an indication of poisoning.

22And the voice of harpers, and musicians, and of pipers, and trumpeters, shall be heard no more at all in thee; and no craftsman, of whatsoever craft he be, shall be found any more in thee; and the sound of a millstone shall be heard no more at all in thee;

The church cultivated all kinds of arts promoting the formations of choirs like the singing choir of children from Vienna. It is said that the boys were castrated to keep their soprano voices. The craftsmen must refer to the statue makers. The art collections of the Vatican are priceless. While they cultivate the arts, they could care less for the salvation of the human race- so valuable in the eyes of God, whom they pretend to serve. Power and intrigue was Rome's only interest.

musicians – Satan, the choir and orchestra director in heaven, has used music to drive people away from God- or should I say, to drive God away from some churches whose "contemporary" style of worship appeals to the sensual part of human nature. Since when it is OK to bring the world into the church? Wasn't this what Israel kept doing until full apostasy caused their fall? Rock music has no place in worship. It has been used to glorify Satan, drugs and promiscuity. I have been in some of those contemporary style worship services and the dance movements are the same as those that I observed when I was in the world. The musicians sport long hair, body piercings and dress and behave like their worldly counterparts. The reason given is that this kind of music attracts young people to the church. However, it drives away the mature people with experience and wisdom to discern the danger of this strategy.

It is good to remember too that the early Christian church also relaxed the rules in order to attract pagans into the church and it became Babylon. Instead of the world being converted to the church, the church has turned to the world and now it is difficult to distinguish a Christian in a crowd, for they smoke, look, dress, act, dance and sing alike. Christians even drink alcohol, of which the Bible says not to even look at it (Proverbs 23:31). Rock music makes all this possible because it makes people drop their guard.

Does a Christian have to be sinless? Even though He is aware of our shortfalls, God does want us to be different. *"Ye adulterers and adulteresses, know ye not that <u>the friendship of the world is enmity with God</u>? whosoever therefore will be a friend of the world is the enemy of God"* (James 4:4). *"Love not the world, neither the things that are in the world. <u>If any man love the world, the love of the Father is not in him</u>"* (1John 2:15). While we are in this world we are tempted daily- constantly- and some times, we do sin. However, when we fall, we should strive to get up, lick our wounds and keep trying in the power of God to overcome temptation and be different from the world. *"Rejoice not against me, O mine enemy: <u>when I fall, I shall arise</u>; when I sit in darkness, the LORD shall be a* *light unto me"* (Micah 7:8). God has provided all the resources from heaven to give us victory and keep us separated from the world. But, what if we have fallen for such a long time and we think we have gone too far? Fortunately, God has, in His infinite love, made ample provision: *"My little children, these things write I unto you, that ye sin not. And if any man sin, we have an advocate with the Father, Jesus Christ the righteous"* (1 John 2:1). *"If we confess our sins, he is faithful and just to forgive us our sins, and to cleanse us from all unrighteousness"* (1John 1:9). If you return to Him, He will restore you to the position of His son or daughter. Regardless of how far you think you have gone, come back home while there is still time.

With open arms and a fixed gaze,

He scans the way where you strayed.

He longs to hug you

and welcome you home.

To your Father return

for the feast will not start without you (Luke 15).

23*And the light of a candle shall shine no more at all in thee; and the voice of the bridegroom and of the bride shall be heard no more at all in thee: for thy merchants were the great men of the earth; for by thy sorceries were all nations deceived.*

Candles have been used as offerings to the saints and the Virgin, while the sorceries resulted in miracles that enticed the believers.

by thy sorceries were all nations deceived – Sorceries are the instrument used by Babylon to produce the miracles needed to make everyone believe that she is the real thing and unite the world in rebellion against God and His people. *"Even him, whose coming is after the working of Satan with all power and signs and lying wonders, and with all deceivableness of unrighteousness in them that perish; because they received not the love of the truth, that they might be saved. And for this cause God shall send them strong delusion, that they should believe a lie: that they all might be damned who believed not the truth, but had pleasure in unrighteousness"* (2 Thessalonians 2:9-12). Remember the meaning of Vatican? It means "mount of divination." They deal with the power of the darkness to stay in power. During the last part of the middle ages, God sent a scourge against Rome to get her away from her evil practices, including the sorceries, but to no avail. *"Neither repented they of their murders, nor of their sorceries, nor of their fornication, nor of their thefts"* (Revelation 9:21). It is those apparitions of the Virgin that keep the faithful tied to the church. The real historic Virgin Mary was a wonderful human being, but she is resting in her grave waiting for Jesus her son to return in glory to bring her back to life. No place in the Bible shows her ascending to heaven. Neither can it be found one single verse that calls her co-redemptor or that we must go through her to find salvation.

At the beginning of this chapter, it was mentioned that the attitude of spiritual Babylon was similar to that of the historical nation and Isaiah 47 was quoted. That same chapter also parallels the punishment and for the same reason of the sorceries, although with slight difference, since modern Babylon does not openly promotes astrology. *"But these two things shall come to thee in a moment in one day, the loss of children* [the harlot daughters], *and widowhood* [the church separated from the state]*: they shall come upon thee in their perfection for the multitude of thy sorceries, and for the great abundance of thine enchantments. For thou hast trusted in thy wickedness: thou hast said, None seeth me. Thy wisdom and thy knowledge, it hath perverted thee; and thou hast said in thine heart, I am, and none else beside me. Therefore shall evil come upon thee; thou shalt not know from whence it riseth: and mischief shall fall upon thee; thou shalt not be able to put it off: and desolation shall come upon thee suddenly, which thou shalt not know. Stand now with thine enchantments, and with the multitude of thy sorceries, wherein thou hast laboured from thy youth; if so be thou shalt be able to profit, if so be thou mayest prevail. Thou art wearied in the multitude of thy counsels. Let now the astrologers, the stargazers, the monthly prognosticators, stand up, and save thee from these things that shall come upon thee. Behold, they shall be as stubble; the fire shall burn them; they shall not deliver themselves from the power of the flame: there shall not be a coal to warm at, nor fire to sit before it. Thus shall they be unto thee with whom thou hast laboured, even* *thy merchants, from thy youth: they shall wander every one to his quarter; none shall save thee"* (Isaiah 47:9-15).

[24]*And in her was found the blood of prophets, and of saints, and of all that were slain upon the earth.*

Now it is the time for God to avenge the blood of the millions of His faithful followers, shed by the false system of worship. Just like those helpless victims of the middle ages, now the beast will have no one to help her at the time of divine retribution. Just remember God's call to your soul: *"Come out of her, my people."*

Revelation 19

The wedding Invitation

"And when he had spoken these things, while they beheld, he was taken up; and a cloud received him out of their sight. And while they looked stedfastly toward heaven as he went up, behold, two men stood by them in white apparel; Which also said, Ye men of Galilee, why stand ye gazing up into heaven? this same Jesus, which is taken up from you into heaven, shall so come in like manner as ye have seen him go into heaven" (Acts 1:9-11). When Jesus went to heaven, He was visible to his disciples. He went to heaven in one stage. If the angels told the disciples that He would return in like manner, why should we believe men that twist the Scriptures to make us believe on a fallacy of a two-stage (one of them invisible) return?

This chapter deals with the second coming of Christ as a conqueror. Since the River Euphrates water has been dried up (chapter 16:12), the way is clear now for the kings of the east (Christ and His angels) to come and set the captives from Babylon free. The second coming of Christ in glory and majesty marks the beginning of the millennium.

1 *And after these things I heard a great voice of much people in heaven, saying, Alleluia; Salvation, and glory, and honour, and power, unto the Lord our God:* 2 For true and righteous are his judgments: for he hath judged the great whore, which did corrupt the earth with her fornication, and hath avenged the blood of his servants at her hand.

Remember those "souls" under the altar asking for revenge? Now is the time to even the score for their shed blood. *"When he maketh inquisition for blood, he remembereth them: he forgetteth not the cry of the humble"* (Psalm 9:12). *"And shall not God avenge his own elect, which cry day and night unto him, though he bear long with them?"* (Luke 18:7). The Roman church killed over 60 million innocent people in the dark ages and has continued to the present day. Soon that blood will be demanded from their hands. *"Then the heaven and the earth, and all that is therein, shall sing for Babylon:*

for the spoilers shall come unto her from the north, saith the LORD" (Jeremiah 1:48).

In three consecutive chapters (17,18 & 19), the reason is given why Babylon is being judged. In addition to her persecuting of the saints, she is guilty of spiritual fornication, or teaching falsehoods, and of honoring the commandments of men more than the Commandments of God.

3 And again they said, Alleluia. And her smoke rose up for ever and ever.

This passage is similar to the description of the conquest of Ai in Canaan. *"And when the men of Ai looked behind them, they saw, and, behold, the smoke of the city ascended up to heaven, and they had no power to flee this way or that way ..."* (Joshua 8:20). *"As smoke is driven away, so drive them away: as wax melteth before the fire, so let the wicked perish at the presence of God"* (Psalm 68:2). Both passages clearly imply that where there is smoke, there is death, not eternal punishment. So the smoke indicates their inability to escape the punishment and their ultimate destruction. Even logic tells me that if I take an object, let us say a paper, and set it on fire, two things will happen:

1. That paper will be burn completely until no longer it can be called a paper
2. The smoke will ascend until the paper is consumed. Then, after the paper is burned up and the flame extinguished, not even smoke will be left.

The wicked will be utterly consumed and disappear to the point that they will be forgotten. Then, there will be no wicked, no fire, no smoke and no memories of them left. We will see the evidence in chapter 20. This thorough destruction might sound sad but, on the other hand, the blasphemous idea of the doctrine of hell is even more cruel since it presents the wicked suffering for ages without end and the saved seeing them burning and screaming in pain and anguish. Luke 19:41 describes the reaction of Jesus when He approached Jerusalem: *"...when he was come near, he beheld the city, and wept over it."* If He wept because they were going to be massacred by the Romans in a few decades (70 AD), do you think that He has a heart to torture people forever? We satanize God with the concept of hell. Again, chapter 20 contains more information about the final punishment of the wicked after the 1,000 years.

[4] And the four and twenty elders and the four beasts fell down and worshipped God that sat on the throne, saying, Amen; Alleluia.[5] And a voice came out of the throne, saying, Praise our God, all ye his servants, and ye that fear him, both small and great.

Very soon, there are going to be multiple reasons to celebrate. This chapter mentions five great reasons for the rejoicing:

- For true and righteous *are* his judgments
- he hath judged the great whore
- hath avenged the blood of his servants at her hand
- the Lord God omnipotent reigneth
- the marriage of the Lamb is come, and his wife hath made herself ready

[6] And I heard as it were the voice of a great multitude, and as the voice of many waters, and as the voice of mighty thunderings, saying, Alleluia: for the Lord God omnipotent reigneth.

This chapter inspired Georg Friedrich Händel to write the most famous of all oratorios: the *Messiah*.

Although Satan rebelled and got many adepts, the throne of God has never been threatened. However, Satan had usurped the principality of this world from Adam. That is why he was present at two universe representatives meetings in the book of Job and is called the prince of this world and has been behind the political moves in the nations (John 14:30; 16:11; Daniel 10:13,20). Now his time is up. He will no longer be in charge and will lose what he took by deception. Now this planet will be purified and renewed; returned to the heavenly standard of perfection and beauty that had been marred by sin. Now the whole universe will be saved to never again know the tragedy of sin.

Reigneth- More accurately: "began to reign". Christ will receive His kingdom as "King of kings" at the end of the investigative judgment, but before He leaves the heavenly sanctuary to return to earth.

[7] Let us be glad and rejoice, and give honour to him: for the marriage of the Lamb is come, and his wife hath made herself ready.

Unfortunately, we human beings in general are too superficial in our appreciation of other human beings. Sometimes we place too much attention on the external. Such is the case with some women that we consider not attractive enough. However, when a man takes his time to get to know her and appreciate her for her qualities of character, she seems more physically attractive. However, the wedding day is when that woman will be so radiant and look so beautiful that will take the groom's breath away. I heard someone say that there are no ugly brides. Other times we pay too much attention to the social background of the bride. We all know that it is not looked on with "good eyes" when a king chooses a commoner as his future queen. The church of God is compared to a woman that was not of noble origin. Ezekiel wrote: *"And say, Thus saith the Lord GOD unto Jerusalem; Thy birth and thy nativity is of the land of Canaan; thy father was an Amorite, and thy mother an Hittite. And as for thy nativity, in the day thou wast born thy navel was not cut, neither wast thou washed in water to supple thee; thou wast not salted at all, nor swaddled at all. None eye pitied thee, to do any of these unto thee, to have compassion upon thee; but thou wast cast out in the open field, to the lothing of thy person, in the day that thou wast born"* (Ezekiel 16:3-5). No, the church of Christ did not have a dignified origin. It was compared to a non-legitimate child abandoned at birth, that later grew up to become a woman of questionable reputation according to Ezekiel. However, God saw potential in her and kept loving her regardless of her deliberate actions until she responded and became the dream bride. Now she is His bride covered with His glory and cannot look more beautiful.

There might be many things in your life that you are not proud of and rob your peace (and who does not have skeletons in his closet- I myself have many!). You might not like what you see in your mirror. You might be too ashamed about your sinfulness, your pride and selfishness, but Jesus came to assure you of God's love. If you respond to His call to the door of your heart, He will come in, forgive you and give you <u>a new start</u>. You will become more valuable than the most precious jewel for Him. He is the God of second chances (and thirds, fourths, etc.).

his wife- According to chapter 21, the bride is the New Jerusalem: *"And one of the seven angels who had the seven vials full of the seven last plagues came to me and talked with me, saying, Come here, I will show you the bride, the Lamb's wife. And he carried me away in the Spirit to a great and high mountain and showed me that great city, the holy Jerusalem, descending out of Heaven from God, having the glory of God. And its light was like a stone most precious, even like a jasper stone, clear as crystal"* Revelation 21:9-11.

[8] *And to her was granted that she should be arrayed in fine linen, clean and white: for the fine linen is the righteousness of saints.*

In the parable of the wedding, a man refused to wear the garment provided to him, which caused his expulsion to the darkness. That robe represented the righteousness of Jesus (His perfect life of obedience) applied to the sinner. Without it, we cannot have access to the kingdom of God. The church has been granted to wear the robe. Notice that the word used is "granted" for we do not deserve it. It is only acquired by the grace of our loving God. *"I will greatly rejoice in the LORD, my soul shall be joyful in my God; for he hath clothed me with the garments of salvation, he hath covered me with the robe of righteousness, as a bridegroom decketh himself with ornaments, and as a bride adorneth herself with her jewels"* (Isaiah 61:10). Notice also that we do not clothe ourselves. God does that. Every attempt that we make to improve how we look before a holy God is futile and contaminate by sin. All the work of salvation belongs to God and only He can provide every element necessary for our salvation.

[9] *And he saith unto me, Write, Blessed are they which are called unto the marriage supper of the Lamb. And he saith unto me, These are the true sayings of God.*

That supper is by invitation only and all are invited. However, just a few will accept the special clothing provided by the groom as mentioned above. Only those that accept it will be allowed to participate.

In comparing this passage of Revelation with some parables of Jesus, we can learn more about the wedding, especially because in times of Jesus there were different customs. Understanding these can give us a greater insight on the descriptions from Matthew and Revelation and how the plan of God will unfold. "The wedding started with a procession of the groom and his companions to the bride's home. The company would then escort the bride and her companions back to the groom's home where there would be a special supper prepared." http://www.families.com/blog/betrothal-and-wedding-customs-at-the-time-of-christ. "Although the bride was expecting her groom to come for her, she did not know the exact time of his coming. As a result, the groom's arrival would be preceded by a shout. This shout would forewarn the bride to be prepared for the coming of the groom." http://www.biblestudymanuals.net/jewish_marriage_customs.htm This is the shout that Paul mentions with respect to the returning of the Groom to claim His bride: *"For the Lord himself shall descend from heaven with a shout, with the voice of the archangel, and with the trump of God: and the dead in Christ shall rise first"* (Thessalonians 4:16).

In the following table, we can compare the weddings mentioned in Matthew and Revelation and the points in common between both books.

The wedding garment and the oil

Matthew 22:1-14	Matthew 25:1-13	Revelation 19:7-9
And Jesus answered and spake unto them again by parables, and said, **The kingdom of heaven** is like unto a certain king, which made a marriage for his son, And sent forth his servants to call them that were bidden to the wedding: and they would not come. Again, he sent forth other servants, saying, Tell them which are bidden, Behold, I have prepared my dinner: my oxen and my fatlings are killed, and all things are ready: come unto the marriage. But they made light of it, and went their ways, one to his farm, another to his merchandise: And the remnant took his servants, and entreated them spitefully, and slew them. But when the king heard thereof, he was wroth: and he sent forth his armies, and destroyed those murderers, and burned up their city. Then saith he to his servants, The wedding is ready, but they which were bidden were not worthy. Go ye therefore into the highways, and as many as ye shall find, bid to the marriage. So those servants went out into the highways, and gathered together all as many as they found, both bad and good: and the wedding was furnished with guests.	Then shall **the kingdom of heaven** be likened unto ten virgins, which took their lamps, and went forth to meet the bridegroom. And five of them were wise, and five were foolish. They that were foolish took their lamps, and took no oil with them But the wise took oil in their vessels with their lamps. While the bridegroom tarried, they all slumbered and slept. And at midnight there was a cry made, Behold, the bridegroom cometh; go ye out to meet him. Then all those virgins arose, and trimmed their lamps. And the foolish said unto the wise, Give us of your oil; for our lamps are gone out. But the wise answered, saying, Not so; lest there be not enough for us and you: but go ye rather to them that sell, and buy for yourselves.	Let us be glad and rejoice, and give honour to him: for the marriage of the Lamb is come, and his wife hath made herself ready. And to her was granted that she should be arrayed in fine linen, clean and white: for the fine linen is the righteousness of saints. And he saith unto me, Write, Blessed *are* they which are called unto the marriage supper of the Lamb. And he saith unto me, These are the true sayings of God.

And when the king came in to see the guests, he saw there a man which had not on a wedding garment: And he saith unto him, Friend, how camest thou in hither not having a wedding garment? And he was speechless. Then said the king to the servants, Bind him hand and foot, and take him away, and cast him into outer darkness; there shall be weeping and gnashing of teeth. For many are called, but few are chosen.	And while they went to buy, the bridegroom came; and they that were ready went in with him to the marriage: and the door was shut. Afterward came also the other virgins, saying, Lord, Lord, open to us. But he answered and said, Verily I say unto you, I know you not. Watch therefore, for ye know neither the day nor the hour wherein the Son of man cometh.	
This parable deals with a wedding in which the original guests were invited but they scorned the invitation and went about their business. Some others were invited to take their place and the requisite was that they had to wear the garment provided by the host. One person refused to wear the robe provided and was cast out into the outer darkness.	This parable shows ten virgins going to a wedding. Five of them made preparations and the other five did not bother. Since the unprepared ones left the site of the wedding to do a last minute effort to be ready, the doors were closed and they were left outside.	Here it is shown also that the important element is the robe, which is identified with righteousness. We in ourselves lack righteousness but God can impute the righteousness of Jesus and that will give us the invitation to the heavenly wedding.
The missing element was the robe.	The missing element was the oil.	The important element was the robe of righteousness

The two parables and the passage of Revelation above deal with the establishment of the kingdom of God and the final reward. In the times of Jesus, it was customary for the father of the groom to provide robes for those invited to the wedding of the heir. Not wearing the robe chosen was considered an insult to the generosity of the host and caused the expulsion from the wedding celebration. The lack of oil in the lamps is equivalent to not having the robe from Matthew 22 and Revelation 19, so the oil is equivalent to, and represents the robe, not the Holy Spirit in this case.

Another element of notice in apostolic times is that when the parties agreed on the wedding, the groom went away to built the house where he would take his bride, after which, he would return with his wedding party to claim his bride and take her home. We find this illustrated in John 14:1-3: *"Let not your heart be troubled: ye believe in God, believe also in me. In my Father's house are many mansions: if it were not so, I would have told you. I go to prepare a place for you. And if I go and prepare a place for you, I will come again, and receive you unto myself; that where I am, there ye may be also."* Our beloved went to prepare a place and soon He will return to celebrate the wedding. "Before leaving, the young man would announce, 'I am going to prepare a place for you', and 'I will return for you when it is ready'. The usual practice was for the young man to return to his father's house and build a honeymoon room there. This is what is symbolized by the *chuppah* or canopy, which is characteristic of Jewish weddings. He was not allowed to skimp on the work and had to get his father's approval before he could consider it ready for his bride. If asked the date of his wedding he would have to reply, 'Only my father knows.'

"Meanwhile the bride would be making herself ready so that she would be pure and beautiful for her bridegroom. During this time she would wear a veil when she went out to show she was spoken for (she has been bought with a price)."

"When the wedding chamber was ready the bridegroom could collect his bride. He could do this at any time so the bride would make special arrangements. It was the custom for a bride to keep a lamp, her veil and her other things beside her bed. Her bridesmaids were also waiting and had to have oil ready for their lamps.

"When the groom and his friends got close to the bride's house they would give a shout and blow a *shofar* to let her know to be ready." http://www.wildolive.co.uk/weddings.htm

This following table will summarize this beautiful illustration. However, we must remember that since the bride is the New Jerusalem, the passages apply to those invited to the wedding as part of the wedding party. The bride is the city; the church is the wedding party, like the virgins in the parable:

Type in Jewish weddings	Antitype in the work of Christ
Bridegroom comes to the bride's house to obtain her through a marriage covenant	Jesus came as an incarnated human being to our house. John 1:14
The bridegroom drinks wine with the bride to seal the covenant	On the last night with His disciples (the church), He instituted communion with wine as a symbol of a covenant. 1 Corinthians 11:25
The bridegroom pays a price for the bride	Jesus died on the cross to pay the price of redemption- John 3:16; 1 Corinthians 6:20; 1 Peter 1:18,19
The bride is considered to be sanctified or set apart exclusively for her groom	"We have been <u>set apart as holy</u> because Jesus Christ did what God wanted him to do by sacrificing his body once and for all." Hebrews 10:10 *God's Word*
The bridegroom goes back to his father's house to prepare a place where to live	Jesus went to prepare a place for the bride. John 14:1-3
The bride does not know when the bridegroom will return for her so she must be ready at all times	This corresponds with the parable of the ten virgins (bridesmaids) from Matthew 25. "Therefore be ye also ready: for in such an hour as ye think not the Son of man cometh." Matthew 24:44
The father is the one who decides when the home is ready and is time to for the bridegroom to go back to take his bride	Only the Father knows when He will send Jesus. Mark 13:32

The bridegroom's friends accompany him and blow a trumpet to announce that he is on his way to take her as his bride	Jesus will come back with all His angels to take His wedding guests home. "The great trumpet will sound, and he will send out his angels to the four corners of the earth, and they will gather his chosen people from one end of the world to the other." Matthew 24:31 *GNB* "In a moment, in the twinkling of an eye, at the last trump: for the trumpet shall sound, and the dead shall be raised incorruptible, and we shall be changed." 1 Corinthians 15:52
The bridal procession goes to the father's house where there is a celebration. All guests receive a robe or garment provided by the father. Not wearing it is considered an insult	This is illustrated in the parable of the wedding guests. The robe represents the righteousness of Jesus. Matthew 22:2, 11-14
After the wedding, the bride and groom drink wine again	"I tell you, I will never again drink this wine until the day I drink the new wine with you in my Father's Kingdom." Matthew 26:29 *Good News Bible*
And the bride and the groom will always be together	"Then, together with them, we who are still alive will be taken in the clouds to meet the Lord in the air. In this way we will always be with the Lord" in the New Jerusalem. 1 Thessalonians 4:17 *GW*; Revelation 22:14

"So then, comfort each other with these words!" 1 Thessalonians 4:18 *GW*

Jewish weddings were never held on the Sabbath, so it is very likely that the second coming of our beloved Lord is not going to happen on the holy day of rest. When He announced the impending crisis over Jerusalem, He said: *"But pray ye that your flight be not in the winter, neither on the Sabbath day"* (Matthew 24:20). Another thing is that after the wedding ceremony was held, the celebration lasted seven days, after which the groom presented the bride to those invited. Our trip to heaven will also last seven days (Revelation 8:1- silence in heaven for ½ hour), during which we will keep a Sabbath for the benefit of those who lived faithful lives without the knowledge of the Sabbath (Romans 2:11-16). That trip also will introduce Jesus to those that never heard of Him but whose lives reflected the light of heaven. *"And one shall say unto him, What are these wounds in thine hands? Then he shall answer, Those with which I was wounded in the house of my friends"* (Zechariah 13:6). My idea is that since Jesus started creation on a Sunday, He will return on the first day also so the last day on the trip to heaven will be on the Sabbath when He will introduce His wedding guests to the Father and the universe.

10 And I fell at his feet to worship him. And he said unto me, See thou do it not: I am thy fellow servant, and of thy brethren that have the testimony of Jesus: worship God: for the testimony of Jesus is the spirit of prophecy.

John was so impressed with what was been shown him that he felt compelled to worship the majestic angel dressed in light that happened to be right there in front of him. The angel immediately stopped John in his foolish attempt and told him to worship God, not the creature (this angel refused the homage that Satan was craving since his fall from heaven). There is a lesson for us here since we often praise the instrument, be it the preacher, a writer or a teacher for the gems that the Holy Spirit inspires. The glory should be given to God. Talking about glory, why are religious men called Reverend? That word was originally used exclusively for God, but men thirsty of humans' approval and admiration started to apply it to themselves. With time, nobody objected and today people insist that their leaders should be called Reverends. This title, when applied to men, is blasphemous.

The angel also mentions the spirit of prophecy, which was to be a sign of the last day church (Revelation 12:17). The Bible never says that the gift of prophecy would end with the last disciple, as some teach. Are these people scared of the prophets? Today's preachers emphasize the gift of tongues, disregarding the advice of Paul in 1 Corinthians 14:5: *"...greater is he that prophesieth than he that speaketh with tongues...."* Nowhere does the Bible say that there would never be any more prophets. Rather, we find in Ephesians that there would be prophets until the church would be ready for encountering the Savior. *"And he gave some, apostles; and some, prophets; and some, evangelists; and some, pastors and teachers; For the perfecting of the saints, for the work of the ministry, for the edifying of the body of Christ: Till we all come in the unity of the faith, and of the knowledge of the Son of God, unto a perfect man, unto the measure of the stature of the fullness of Christ"* (Ephesians 4:11-13). Have we reached the "stature of the fullness of Christ" yet? No. Notice also that there is no mention of the gift of tongues in this passage. The church will need the gift of prophecy until it reflects the character of Christ and is ready for translation into heaven. Again, could we say that the church has attained that goal? Absolutely not! We are still experiencing growing pains with internal strife, worldliness, divorce, pride, lust, envy and so many spiritually childish behaviors that we are in reality far from reflecting Christ's character before the world. If Christ were to return today, maybe not even one in ten of His professed followers would be ready. Even after the ascension of Christ to heaven, God found it necessary to raise prophets who helped guide the church- and this included giving messages to the apostles themselves! (see Acts 21:9-11).

One of the crucial roles of the prophet is to protect against heresy: *"That we henceforth be no more children, tossed to and fro, and carried about with every wind of doctrine, by the sleight of men, and cunning craftiness, whereby they lie in wait to deceive"* (Ephesians 4:14). This was precisely Paul's intent when he announced the apostasy in his farewell discourse at Miletus: *"For I know this, that after my departing shall grievous wolves enter in among you, not sparing the flock. Also of your own selves shall men arise, speaking perverse things, to draw away disciples after them"* (Acts 20:29,30). Peter also concurred with this statement from Paul in his second letter: *"But there were false prophets also among the people, even as there shall be false teachers among you, who privily shall bring in damnable heresies, even denying the Lord that bought them, and bring upon themselves swift destruction. And many shall follow their pernicious ways; by reason of whom the way of truth shall be evil spoken of"* (2 Peter 2:1,2).

Given that this passage and the one found in Revelation 16:13 both indicate that false prophets will be active at the time of the end (see also Matthew 24:24), it is logical to infer that there are going to be true prophets too. This was indicated in the prophecy of Joel, which had a partial fulfillment in the outpouring of the Holy Spirit in Pentecost. *"And it shall come to pass afterward, that I will pour out my spirit upon all flesh; and your sons and your daughters shall prophesy, your old men shall dream dreams, your young men shall see visions: And also upon the servants and upon the handmaids in those days will I pour out my spirit. And I will shew wonders in the heavens and in the earth, blood, and fire, and pillars of smoke. The sun shall be turned into darkness, and the moon into blood, before the great and the terrible day of the LORD come. And it shall come to pass, that whosoever shall call on the name of the LORD shall be delivered: for in mount Zion and in Jerusalem shall be deliverance, as the LORD hath said, and in the remnant whom the LORD shall call"* (Joel 2:28-32).

Since the Holy Spirit gives the gift of prophecy, He also inspires them in such way that whatever the prophets say or write is in harmony with the sayings or writings of previous prophets: *"And the spirits of the prophets are subject to the prophets"* (1 Corinthians 14:32).

A prophet is an instrument of communication between God and fallen humanity. God reveals Himself in dreams or visions. Seldom had He spoken directly to anyone, although we find Him speaking to Moses (face to face – Deuteronomy 34:10), Elijah and Job, undoubtedly three of the holiest men that ever lived. The prophet bridges the gap that separates us from God: *"But your iniquities have separated between you and your God, and your sins have hid his face from you, that he will not hear"* (Isaiah 59:2). The role of the prophet is not only to announce what is going to happen in the future but to admonish for bad behavior and also to encourage people to be faithful.

Just before each of the greatest events or critical stages in the history of the church, God has sent a prophet to pave the way. Before the exodus, He sent Moses; when Israel needed a great revival, He sent Elijah and Elisha. During the exile, he sent Daniel and Ezekiel. Before Jesus' birth, He sent John the Baptist. Would it be any different now that we are fast approaching the end of our earth history, when Jesus is returning for His people? After His crucifixion, His return is the second most important event in history.

Has there been a manifestation of this gift of the Spirit in recent times? Why would we need guidance in our times?

1. First, Christians are lax in regards to Bible study. Church members do not feel the need to study the Scriptures deeply to draw treasures on their own and their only exposure to them is from church leaders that have embraced error.
2. Second, there are so many different Christian denominations that just cause confusion.
3. Third, the Catholic Church has been gaining ground with the Protestant churches and the world had to be admonished regarding the wolf getting ready to devour the sheep.
4. Fourth, the church needed to be alerted about upcoming world conditions, such as wars, economic woes and social degradation.
5. Fifth, health in these last days has declined significantly and a health reform was necessary.
6. Sixth, it was necessary to help organize a people free of the prevalent heresies to fulfill the great commission.
7. Seventh, the Laodicean church would need to be awaken from its slumber or otherwise would not be ready to meet Jesus. I have no doubt that the ministry of Ellen G. White is the authentic work of a prophet. Her writings on many different subjects such as family, medicine, education and accurate predictions reveal a degree of knowledge far beyond her third grade of elementary school education.

One of her articles prophesied the American civil war. There is a vivid passage in her writings that described a supernatural intervention in one of the battles (Manassas, Virginia), whose eyewitness description agrees with her conclusion that an angel intervened to save many lives on both sides. In Testimonies, volume 1 she wrote: "In positions of trust in the Northern army there are men who are rebels at heart, who value the life of a soldier no more than they would the life of a dog. They can see them torn, and mangled, and dying, by thousands, unmoved. The officers of the Southern army are constantly receiving information in regard to the plans of the Northern army. Correct information has been given to Northern officers in regard to the movements and approach of rebels, which has been disregarded and despised because the informer was black. And by neglecting to prepare for an attack, the Union forces have been surprised and nearly cut to pieces, or what is as bad, many of the poor soldiers have been taken prisoners to suffer worse than death.

"If there were union in the Northern army, this Rebellion would soon cease. Rebels know they have sympathizers all through the Northern army. The pages of history are growing darker and still darker. Loyal men, who have had no sympathy with the Rebellion, or with slavery which has caused it, have been imposed upon. Their influence has helped place in authority men to whose principles they were opposed." Thankfully, the tide was turned and the slaves eventually became free.

On one occasion she sent a letter to a man who was skeptical of her gift from God. He took her unopened letter and put in a trunk. Years of accumulated items covered the letter. Eighteen years later, he decided to clear the trunk. In it, he found the letter and decided to open it. The letter detailed every tragedy that would touch his family during that period of time, including the premature death of his wife. Nothing was missing and nothing failed to happen as described. All of those heartaches could have been prevented had he read it when it was sent to him. Only God knows the future.

Her knowledge of medicine is astounding, since in her days, microbes, which she mentions in her writings, were generally unknown and she wrote about hygiene in times when chirurgical and examination instruments were not even washed between patients. Due to this, the mortality rate was unjustifiably high. She was the first person to indicate that tobacco in all its forms causes cancer, a surprising declaration in times when doctors prescribed tobacco for bronchitis! She also wrote against the use of certain common prescription drugs in her times that were poisons (such as mercury, strychnine, arsenic, nux vomica and opium) and her eight natural remedies were at that time revolutionary (*Counsels on Health* p. 90), proving to be more efficient than regular medicines. Today they have been listed as an acronym:

N utrition
E xercise
W ater

S unshine
T emperance
A ir
R est
T rust in God

Many times, she had been accused of borrowing ideas from other authors to which a nutrition expert argued: "How would Mrs. White know which ideas to borrow and which to reject out of the bewildering array of theories and health teachings current in the nineteenth century?" (As quoted in *Prophet of the End*, page 61).

It is not my intent to reply to her critics, whose opinions were formed with prejudice and misunderstanding of her writings and prophecies. Many of those have never read her writings and base their opinion on what others said or wrote. Jeremiah was thought to be a false prophet to his contemporaries. Ahab also pleasantly listened to the many false prophets in his court but disliked Micah, the real messenger of the Lord. All throughout Israel's history men of the stature of Moses and Elijah found challengers to their inspired message, so I am not surprised if a person with such an unstained life as Ellen G. White is vilified and called a false prophet. I myself was skeptical at first, being cautious, until I studied what she wrote and compared it to the Bible and history. Some point to a few of her prophecies that never came to pass. If that is the proof that they submit, the jury cannot reach a fair verdict because the promises and threats of God are both conditional in the Bible. Take for example the astounding news that Jonah brought to Nineveh: *"Forty days from now, Nineveh* ***will*** *be destroyed!"* (Jonah 3:4 CEV). We all know that the message preached with such urgency and certainty was not fulfilled. Did that make the prophet a false one? No. God looked at the reform produced in the hearts of those that heard Jonah's message and He changed His mind, showing them mercy instead of bringing destruction. What about the promise from Isaiah 52:1b? *"...O Jerusalem, the holy city: for henceforth there shall no more come into thee the uncircumcised and the unclean."* We all know that their territory has been invaded ceaselessly by many nations from Romans to Muslims. It is the reaction of the people listening to the prophecy, what they do with the message received, what makes the difference in the outcome.

If the words of our Lord Jesus Himself were twisted and taken out of context, how much more would be those written by a woman- specially one with little education? Read her writings and see how they harmonize with the Bible. I must also indicate here that her writings are never to occupy the place of the Bible or even to be placed at the same level. If the children of God would have dedicated their time to dig deep in the fountains of Bible truth, the Lord would not have seen necessary to raise her to wake up His people. I just want to encourage my readers to read her books. My favorites are:

- Steps to Christ
- The Desire of Ages
- The Great Controversy

These can be read free on line at: http://www.whiteestate.org/books/books.asp. For more information about her life and significance to today's church: http://www.ellengwhitetruth.com/. *"Believe in the Lord your God, so shall ye be established; believe his prophets, so shall ye prosper"* (*2 Chronicles* 20:20).

11 And I saw heaven opened, and behold a white horse; and he that sat upon him was called Faithful and True, and in righteousness he doth judge and make war.

Heaven opened-as if the doors were now swinging on their hinges to allow the rider of this white horse to go out and conquer. This white horse is similar to the one presented in chapter 6:1,2. John wants to reassure us of the character of this rider and calls Him "Faithful and True," knowing how hurtful is to be betrayed by those that we follow. This leader we can trust.

12 His eyes were as a flame of fire, and on his head were many crowns; and he had a name written, that no man knew, but he himself.

Two other verses in Revelation describe the eyes as a flame of fire:

"His head and his hairs were white like wool, as white as snow; and his eyes were as a flame of fire" (Revelation 1:14).

"And unto the angel of the church in Thyatira write; These things saith the Son of God, who hath his eyes like unto a flame of fire, and his feet are like fine brass" (Revelation 2:18).

Both passages refer to Jesus, the Son of God, so there is no doubt that the rider in this passage is also Jesus. Verse 15 of chapter 2 helps us to understand the meaning of the symbol: *"**I know** thy works, and charity, and service, and faith, and thy patience, and thy works; and the last to be more than the first"* (Revelation 2:19). Verse 11 above indicates that He is coming to judge and in such capacity He must be able to know the facts in order to make a fair decision regarding the future of those judged. The fire generates light that will penetrate even the darkest secrets of those judged.

Crowns- Greek διάδημα – diadema. Always used by royalty. Notice that Christ is wearing many crowns, not just one.

13 And he was clothed with a vesture dipped in blood: and his name is called The Word of God.

This passage has been taken from Isaiah 63:1-5: *"Who is this that cometh from Edom, with dyed garments from Bozrah? this that is glorious in his apparel, travelling in the greatness of his strength? I that speak in righteousness, mighty to save. Wherefore art thou red in thine apparel, and thy garments like him that treadeth in the winefat? I have trodden the winepress alone; and of the people there was none with me: for I will tread them in mine anger, and trample them in my fury; and their blood shall be sprinkled upon my garments, and I will stain all my raiment. For the day of vengeance is in mine heart, and the year of my redeemed is come. And I looked, and there was none to help; and I wondered that there was none to uphold: therefore mine own arm brought salvation unto me; and my fury, it upheld me."*

The "Word of God" refers to John 1:14 where Jesus is called the verb or word by the same author: *"And the Word was made flesh, and dwelt among us, (and we beheld his glory, the glory as of the only begotten of the Father,) full of grace and truth."*

Parallels between Revelation 19:11-18,21 and the Old Testament:

Revelation	Old Testament
The rider of the white horse in heaven- 11	"There's no one like your God, Jeshurun! He rides through the heavens to help you. In majesty he rides through the clouds." Deut. 33:26 *GW*
He fights with righteousness- 11	"But with righteousness shall he judge the poor, and reprove with equity for the meek of the earth: and he shall smite the earth with the rod of his mouth...." Isaiah 11:4
he *was* clothed with a vesture dipped in blood-13	"I have trodden the winepress alone; and of the people *there was* none with me: for I will tread them in mine anger, and trample them in my fury; and their blood shall be sprinkled upon my garments, and I will stain all my raiment." Isaiah 63:3. See also Psalm 68:23
"And the armies *which were* in heaven followed him upon white horses, clothed in fine linen, white and clean." -14	"Your soldiers are willing volunteers on your day of battle; in majestic holiness, from the womb, from the dawn, the dew of your youth belongs to you." Psalm 110:3

"And I saw an angel standing in the sun; and he cried with a loud voice, saying to all the fowls that fly in the midst of heaven, Come and gather yourselves together unto the supper of the great God"- 17	"And, thou son of man, thus saith the Lord GOD; Speak unto every feathered fowl, and to every beast of the field, Assemble yourselves, and come; gather yourselves on every side to my sacrifice that I do sacrifice for you, *even* a great sacrifice upon the mountains of Israel, that ye may eat flesh, and drink blood. Ye shall eat the flesh of the mighty, and drink the blood of the princes of the earth, of rams, of lambs, and of goats, of bullocks, all of them fatlings of Bashan. And ye shall eat fat till ye be full, and drink blood till ye be drunken, of my sacrifice which I have sacrificed for you. Thus, ye shall be filled at my table with horses and chariots, with mighty men, and with all men of war, saith the Lord GOD. And I will set my glory among the heathen, and <u>all the heathen shall see my judgment that I have executed</u>, and my hand that I have laid upon them." Ezekiel 39:17-21
"And the remnant were slain with the sword of him that sat upon the horse, which *sword* proceeded out of his mouth..."- 21	"With the breath of his lips shall he slay the wicked." Isaiah 11:4

[14] And the armies which were in heaven followed him upon white horses, clothed in fine linen, white and clean.

The armies are His angels: *"For the Son of man shall come in the glory of his Father with his angels; and then he shall reward every man according to his works"* (Matthew 16:27).

[15] And out of his mouth goeth a sharp <u>sword</u>, that with it he should <u>smite</u> the nations: and he shall rule them with a rod of iron: and he treadeth the winepress of the fierceness and wrath of Almighty God.

Sword- Greek ῥομφαία (rhomphaia)- a large sword used to attack, in contrast with the little sword (Greek μάχαιρα- machaira) used for defense. The first time Christ came as a meek lamb. Now the Lamb is a lion on His way as a conqueror to avenge His people.

rod of iron- During the dark history of this planet, the rod was used to correct, guide and bring God's strayed people back to the fold. Now the Good Shepherd's rod is to be used to fight and destroy the enemies of His flock.

This continues the line of thought mentioned in the passage of Isaiah 63 above. The day of retribution is coming over the wicked, who in many ways oppressed the saints for 6,000 years.

[16] *And he hath on his vesture and on his thigh a name written, KING OF KINGS, AND LORD OF LORDS.*

This verse parallels the words found in chapter 17:14, although it reverses the titles order: *"These shall make war with the Lamb, and the Lamb shall overcome them: for he is Lord of lords, and King of kings: and they that are with him are called, and chosen, and faithful."*

[17] *And I saw an angel standing in the sun; and he cried with a loud voice, saying to all the fowls that fly in the midst of heaven, Come and gather yourselves together unto the supper of the great God;*

Old testament prophets had similar warnings as a curse for the impenitent: *"They shall die of grievous deaths; they shall not be lamented; neither shall they be buried; but they shall be as dung upon the face of the earth: and they shall be consumed by the sword, and by famine; and their carcasses shall be meat for the fowls of heaven, and for the beasts of the earth"* (Jeremiah 16:4). *"Thus saith the LORD of hosts, Behold, evil shall go forth from nation to nation, and a great whirlwind shall be raised up from the coasts of the earth. And the slain of the LORD shall be at that day from one end of the earth even unto the other end of the earth: they shall not be lamented, neither gathered, nor buried; they shall be dung upon the ground"* (Jeremiah 25:32,33). *"Hold thy peace at the presence of the Lord GOD: for the day of the LORD is at hand: for the LORD hath prepared a sacrifice, he hath bid his guests"* (Zephaniah 1:7). *"When you die, birds and wild animals will come and eat your bodies, and there will be no one to scare them off"* (Deuteronomy 28:26).

We either accept the invitation to the supper of the Lamb or become food for the birds in the supper of the Great God. There is no middle ground. We either cast our lot with Jesus or suffer the wrath of the vengeance of God. Either we eat or we will be eaten. We have a choice to make. Thank God for offering always His mercy. We are all invited to the Lamb's supper. Let us shun the second one.

[18] *That ye may eat the flesh of kings, and the flesh of captains, and the flesh of mighty men, and the flesh of horses, and of them that sit on them, and the flesh of all men, both free and bond, both small and great.*

The rich, powerful and influent are mentioned first because their leadership talents and skills were used to seduce the souls into rebellion against God.

[19] *And I saw the beast, and the kings of the earth, and their armies, gathered together to make war against him that sat on the horse, and against his army.*

No amount of punishment can reform those rebels at this time. They have suffered the seven last plagues and they are more opposed to God than they had in their whole lives. They have reached the point of no return and their hate for God makes them join forces in a desperate attempt to rid themselves of the heavenly Ruler. This is the first part of the battle of Armageddon.

gathered together- This union will have a very short duration because Revelation 16:19 indicates that they will end up warring among themselves (*"the great city was divided into three parts"*), turning against each other just like when God intervened three times on behalf of His people in the Old Testament. We already mentioned that the trumpet will sound when Jesus returns. In the book of Judges, it reads that when Gideon (means *warrior*) ordered to sound the trumpets, that was when the enemy soldiers turned one against the other: *"While Gideon's men were blowing their trumpets, the LORD made the enemy troops attack each other with their swords...."* Judges 7:22. In like manner, when the loud trumpet sounds announcing the presence of Jesus, the enemies will break their allegiance and turn against each other instead of killing the children of God. Also, just like the Passover before the exodus, Gideon's attack occurred around midnight. It would be in the darkest time for the people of God that their liberation would come.

[20] *And the beast was taken, and with him the false prophet that wrought miracles before him, with which he deceived them that had received the mark of the beast, and them that worshipped his image. These both were cast alive into a lake of fire burning with brimstone.*

false prophet- apostate Protestantism, mainly influenced by those in the USA. We must remember that a prophet is a speaker on behalf of another person or entity. In this case, the false prophet promoted the cause of the first beast of Revelation 13 by enforcing its mark upon the whole earth.

Every effort to fight against God proves futile. Now Catholicism and apostate Protestantism are both condemned. Those that filled their churches on Sunday but never allowed the Holy Spirit to guide them into the acceptance of the whole truth will harvest the seed of rebellion that they chose.

lake of fire- there will be two lakes of fire- one at each end of the millennium. The first one will kill the enemies at the second coming of Jesus. The second one will destroy the wicked of all ages for good. This is the lake of fire mentioned in chapter 20.

[21] *And the remnant were slain with the sword of him that sat upon the horse, which sword proceeded out of his mouth: and all the fowls were filled with their flesh.*

Those that survive the plagues will witness Jesus returning in glory to rescue His children and will perish with the splendor of His glory. *"And then shall that Wicked be revealed, whom the Lord shall consume with the spirit of his mouth, and shall destroy with the brightness of his coming: Even him, whose coming is after the working of Satan with all power and signs and lying wonders, And with all deceivableness of unrighteousness in them that perish;*

because they received not the love of the truth, that they might be saved. And for this cause God shall send them strong delusion, that they should believe a lie: That they all might be damned who believed not the truth, but had pleasure in unrighteousness" (2 Thessalonians 2:8-12). Notice that the lost will be punished for rejecting the truth. *"He shall judge among the heathen, he shall fill the places with the dead bodies; he shall wound the heads over many countries"* (Psalm 110:6). *"Our God shall come, and shall not keep silence: a fire shall devour before him, and it shall be very tempestuous round about him"* (Psalm 50:3). *"A fire goeth before him, and burneth up his enemies round about"* (Psalm 97:3). Notice that the Bible is consistent regarding the fate of the wicked by using words such as consume, destroy, devour and burned up. All of those words carry a common message: complete obliteration of the wicked, which indicate elimination, annihilation and reduction to nothing. Chapter 20 contains more information on this subject. The books of Zephaniah and Hosea go beyond the annihilation of the wicked as we will see next.

There is also a mercy work to be done: *"I will consume man and beast; I will consume the fowls of the heaven, and the fishes of the sea, and the stumbling blocks with the wicked; and I will cut off man from off the land, saith the LORD"* (Zephaniah 1:3). *"And so the land will dry up, and everything that lives on it will die. All the animals and birds, and even the fish, will die"* (Hosea 4:3 *Good News Bible*). Why the animals too? First, there is not going to be enough food left after the plagues. Second, no one will be around to care for them. Third, Paul wrote that all creation is groaning. The animals will be put to sleep out of compassion because they are sick and suffering with man-caused diseases but the good news are that the new earth will be full of animals- now healthy of course, so we will enjoy their company again- not to eat or abuse them in any way.

Jeremiah, a man who really cared for the people of his nation, a man that begged all his co-citizens to repent from their evil and violent ways and turn to God, whose testimony was rejected and landed him in prison, wrote: *"The dead bodies of those killed by the LORD will reach from one end of the earth to the other. No one will cry for them. No one will gather up their bodies and bury them. They will be left lying on the ground like dung"* (Jeremiah 25:33 *Easy-to-Read- Version*). There is no doubt in my mind that Jeremiah cried when he wrote those words, just like Jesus Himself must have cried when He inspired them because He came to save even the worst sinner that repents. He wept next to the city of Jerusalem, the city that was about to reject and crucify Him. Do not harden your heart and see by yourself how good Jesus is. I cannot describe the peace that came to my heart when I let Him come to my life and He forgave my sins.

Revelation 20

Satan Goes on Vacation

[1]*And I saw an angel come down from heaven, having the key of the bottomless pit and a great chain in his hand.* [2]*And he laid hold on the dragon, that old serpent, which is the Devil, and Satan, and bound him a thousand years,*

"It is very probable that this angel is no other than the Lord Jesus Christ; the description of him will hardly agree with any other...He laid hold on the dragon, that old serpent, which is the devil, and Satan. Neither the strength of the dragon, nor the subtlety of the serpent, was sufficient to rescue him out of the hands of Christ; he caught hold, and kept his hold." (*Matthew Henry's Commentary on The Whole Bible*).

The bottomless pit or abyss refers to the earth in chaos, empty, uninhabited. See Gen 1:2; Jer. 4:23-27; 2 Peter 3:10. The chain represents the circumstances under which Satan will find himself since he will not have anyone to tempt due to all the wicked being dead (Revelation 19:21) and he will be forbidden to deceive (verse 3).

"a thousand years"- Mentioned six times in this chapter (and twice in 2 Peter 3:8). This period is commonly called the millennium. The number six is associated with man. He was created in the sixth day of the week. Now mankind is at the end of six thousand years of earth history and then will come the millennium of rest. That will be a sabbatical millennium in which the planet will rest from the abuse of the previous six millenniums. "The Jewish Rabbis thought, as the world was created in six days and on the *seventh* God rested, so there would be six millenary periods, followed by a sabbatical millennium. Out of seven years every seventh is the year of remission, so out of the seven thousand years of the world the seventh millenary shall be the millenary of remission. A tradition in the house of Elias, a.d. 200, states that the world is to endure six thousand years; two thousand before the law, two thousand under the law, and two thousand under Messiah" (*Jamieson, Fausset and*

Brown Commentary). This period of time will be the start of the jubilee, when the land worldwide should rest for a thousand years.

Chapter 12:9 presents the same sequence used here to identify the enemy: dragon, serpent, Devil and Satan. However, in chapter 12 he was a persecutor; here in chapter 20 he is a prisoner.

[3]*And cast him into the bottomless pit, and shut him up, and set a seal upon him, that he should deceive the nations no more, till the thousand years should be fulfilled: and after that <u>he must be loosed a little season</u>.*

Verse five shows that the wicked will not come to life again until the thousand years are over. At the end of the thousand years, Satan will be allowed to tempt the wicked, but only for a short time. *"For yet a little while, and <u>the wicked shall not be</u>: yea, thou shalt diligently consider his place, and it <u>shall not be</u>"* (Psalm 37:10).

What does it mean that Satan will be shut up for one thousand years? The same verse gives a clue in indicating that he will not be able to deceive the nations for that period of time. But where would everybody be that he could not tempt him or her? Let us see what happen to the wicked at the end time. First, many millions will be killed by the plagues. Second, those that survive the plagues will try to kill the saints. However, when they attempt to do so, they will kill each other instead. And finally, third, the remaining *"were slain with the sword of him that sat upon the horse, which sword proceeded out of his mouth: and all the fowls were filled with their flesh"* (Revelation 19:21). When the Lord Jesus returns to take home all that have remain faithful to the end, all that will be left behind will be corpses and demons. That is why Satan will not have anyone to tempt. Jeremiah foresaw this condition and wrote: *"I beheld the earth, and, lo, it was without form, and <u>void</u>; and the heavens, and they had no light. I beheld the mountains, and, lo, they trembled, and all the hills moved lightly. I beheld, and, lo, <u>there was no man</u>, and all the birds of the heavens were fled. I beheld, and, lo, the fruitful place was a wilderness, and all the cities thereof were broken down at the presence of the LORD, and by his fierce anger. For thus hath the LORD said, The whole land shall be desolate; yet will I not make a full end"* (Jeremiah 4:23-27). The birds will flee after their banquet on the wicked (see Revelation 19: 17,18). Even the fish will die (Hosea 4:3). *"For we know that the whole creation groaneth and travaileth in pain together until now"* (Romans 8:22). Right now, the animal kingdom is suffering the consequences of us humans contaminating the environment in which all live. Chickens, cows and fish are developing cancer and other diseases. The whole creation is suffering. In His infinite wisdom and mercy, he puts all His creatures to rest until He creates everything new. According to Peter everything will be destroyed: *"But the day of the Lord will come as a thief in the night; in the which the heavens shall pass away with a great noise, and the elements shall melt with fervent heat, the earth also and the works that are therein shall be burned up"* (2 Peter 3:10).

The thousand years were prefigured in the sanctuary services, specifically in the Day of Atonement. That day the high priest was to take two goats; one for God- to be sacrificed for the sins of the people, and the other for Azazel. *"Then he shall take the two goats to the entrance of the Tent of the LORD's presence. There he shall draw lots, using two stones, one marked 'for the LORD' and the other 'for Azazel.' Aaron shall sacrifice the goat chosen by lot for the LORD and offer it as a sin offering. The goat chosen for Azazel shall be presented alive to the LORD and sent off into the desert to Azazel, in order to take away the sins of the people"* (Leviticus 16:7-10 *GNB*). It is interesting that among some Arab tribes, the world Azazel means "the powerful angel that rebelled." Some believe that it comes from two words: *azaz*, meaning cruel and *el*, meaning god. The first goat represented Jesus who carried our sins on Himself and paid the penalty for our sins. Before I discuss the other goat, it will be helpful to explain what was going on in the sanctuary for the previous year. Whenever a person sinned, he had to bring a lamb to the sanctuary. That lamb represented Jesus- *"the Lamb of God, which taketh away the sin of the world"* (John 1:29). Then, placing his hands on the head of the animal, he confessed his sins (thus transferring his sins to the innocent lamb) and cut its throat. Then the priest collected some the blood, which he later sprinkled on the curtain of the sanctuary. In this manner, the sin passed from the sinner to the lamb and then to the sanctuary. Once a year, on the seventh month, the high priest entered the sanctuary and cleansed it from the sins of the previous 12 months (Leviticus 16:16). After the ceremonial cleansing of the sanctuary, the high priest laid *"both his hands upon the head of the live goat, and confess over him all the iniquities of the children of Israel, and all their transgressions in all their sins, putting them upon the head of the goat, and shall send him away by the hand of a fit man into the wilderness"* (Leviticus 16:21,22). Of the two goats, only one represented Jesus, thus it was sacrificed. The second represented Satan and that is why it was sent to the desert alive, representing the one thousand years that he will spend in the desert of this empty planet. The fact that the priest confessed the sins of the people over Azazel did not make him a sin-bearer in the sense of a redeemer, but as an <u>instigator</u> of those sins. Jesus will not be a sin bearer forever. He carried our sins on the cross. Then those sins were transferred to the heavenly sanctuary where they remained in the books until the time of the judgment, which started in 1844. When Jesus our High Priest comes, those sins will be placed on the head of Satan because he was the ultimate responsible for those sins being committed as the tempter. The following illustration shows how God deals with the sin of His people, first with the type and then with the antitype:

Sinner ⟶ Innocent Victim ⟶ Earthly Sanctuary ⟶ Azazel

In the same way, the antitype:

Sinner ⟶ Jesus ⟶ Heavenly Sanctuary ⟶ Satan

The wicked will carry their own sins. At the end of the thousand years, Satan will be *"loosed a little season"* and then God will deal with him according to His justice.

[4]*And I saw thrones, and they sat upon them, and judgment was given unto them: and I saw the souls of them that were beheaded for the witness of Jesus, and for the word of God, and which had not worshipped the beast, neither his image, neither had received his mark upon their foreheads, or in their hands; and they lived and reigned with Christ a thousand years.*

them that were beheaded – Satan's followers thought that they had the upper hand when they decapitated the saints in the past. What they did not know was that decapitation is only temporary. If Jesus created us from the dust of the ground, he can reconnect those lose heads to their bodies. The Devil will be defeated once more.

He decided to become a loser and will remain one for the rest of his soon to be short life.

During the thousand years that Satan will be bound on earth, the saved will be given the assignment of judging the lost. This judgment will be fairly based on the facts written on the books in heaven. Every frivolous conversation, every evil act, every selfish though will be examined, together with every opportunity to repent wasted and every invitation to receive Christ as Savior rejected.

The martyrs mentioned in this verse are still in the future since the mark of the beast has not being imposed by legislation yet. Once the time of grace is finished, there will be no more martyrs ("*witness of Jesus*") because the need for witnessing will be over. The purpose of witnessing is to win more followers for the kingdom. Once the door of grace closes, witnessing would prove fruitless because no one will ever accept Jesus as Savior from that time on. At that time, the plagues (see Revelation 16) will fall on the impenitent while the righteous will be protected.

"That ye may eat and drink at my table in my kingdom, and <u>sit on thrones judging</u> the twelve tribes of Israel" (Luke 22:30).

"The queen of the south shall <u>rise up in the judgment</u> with the men of this generation, <u>and condemn them</u>..." (Luke 11:31).

"Do ye not know that <u>the saints shall judge the world</u>?..." (1 Corinthians 6:2).

This is known as the vindicative judgment because God's character in His dealings with sinners will be cleared. It follows the investigative phase done by Christ which started in 1844 *("...we shall all stand before the judgment seat of Christ"*- Romans 14:10). At that time, all the secrets of the hearts will be uncovered. We will know why Brother X, who looked so faithful, is not among the redeemed, or why the town's drunkard made it to heaven when no one thought he stood a chance. God knows the hearts and will uncover which materials we chose to build with. *"Now if any man build upon this foundation gold, silver, precious stones, wood, hay, stubble; Every man's work shall be made manifest: for the day shall declare it, because it shall be revealed by fire; and the fire shall try every man's work of what sort it is. If any man's work abide which he hath built thereupon, he shall receive a reward. If any man's work shall be burned, he shall suffer loss: but he himself shall be saved; yet so as by fire"* (1 Corinthians 3:12-15). That judgment will reveal to the flock of the saved that those lost are so because they willed to be lost. God gave them many daily opportunities to repent and be saved but they trampled the heavenly grace and chose their own way via either open rebellion or simple neglect.

[5]*But the rest of the dead lived not again until the thousand years were finished.*

The wicked will be dead for a thousand years while the saved will be revising their records in heaven. Satan will be limited to this planet with ample time to meditate on the fruits of his rebellion. For sure, he will be trembling at the prospect of his future. Peter wrote regarding Satan that he knows he has little time. He will be like a death row convict who he is told the date of his execution, a date that he cannot appeal.

This is the first resurrection. [6]Blessed and holy is he that hath part in the first resurrection: on such the second death hath no power, but they shall be priests of God and of Christ, and shall reign with him a thousand years.

The division of verse five is not correct (remember that the Scriptures were not originally written in chapters and verses). "*This is the first resurrection*" should be read as part of verse six and that is why I included them together. This verse presents one of the seven blessings in the book of Revelation. Literally "supremely blest."

Here it is clear that the redeemed will live with Christ for 1,000 years. That will happen in heaven after Jesus' second coming.

[7]*And when the thousand years are expired, Satan shall be loosed out of his prison, [8]And shall go out to deceive the nations which are in the four quarters of the earth, Gog, and Magog, to gather them together to battle: the number of whom is as the sand of the sea.*

Now Satan will be free because he will have the wicked humans to tempt. The following two words have a simple explanation:

Gog= king

Magog= kingdom

The speculation that these two words refer to Russia and China is not Biblically sound. It is based on suppositions by misguided theologians, not in facts. There is no place in the Bible where it mentions those two eastern nations. "*Gog and Magog*. We need not be too inquisitive as to what particular powers are meant by these names, since the army was gathered <u>from all parts of the world</u>" (*Matthew Henry's Commentary on The Whole Bible*). The only important nations ever mentioned in the Bible were those that one way or the other attacked or were allies of Israel in the past. By referring to king and kingdom, the words simply indicate that both great and small, leaders and followers, kings and commoners will be united in their rebellion against God under the personal leadership of Satan.

The purpose of Satan will be to deceive the nations into battle against the saints in a final attempt to defeat God's people.

to gather them together to battle- This will be the second part of the battle of Armageddon.

9*And they went up on the breadth of the earth, and compassed the camp of the saints about, and the beloved city: and <u>fire came down</u> from God out of heaven, <u>and devoured them</u>.*

The city referred to in this passage is not the earthly Jerusalem, but the New one that descends from God. See chapter 21. The wicked, lead by Satan, will try to conquer the city with its immense bounty of gold and precious jewels, but as always, God will intervene to save His people. When the prophet Elijah offered sacrifice before the priests of Baal, God sent fire that completely burned up everything. *"Then the fire of the LORD fell, and consumed the burnt sacrifice, and the wood, and the stones, and the dust, and licked up the water that was in the trench"* (1 Kings 18:38). So it will be with the wicked and the satanic hosts, which will be completely obliterated. *"The LORD is my light and my salvation; whom shall I fear? the LORD is the strength of my life; of whom shall I be afraid? When the wicked, even mine enemies and my foes, came upon me to eat up my flesh, they stumbled and fell. Though an host should encamp against me, my heart shall not fear: though war should rise against me, in this will I be confident"* (Psalm 27:1-3).

Many picture a place away from earth where the wicked will be punished, but the Bible teaches different: *"Behold, the righteous shall be recompensed in the earth: much more the wicked and the sinner"* (Proverbs 11:31). See comment on chapter sixteen.

Millions of sermons have been preached regarding hell (why not preached about heaven?). It is common to hear preachers talking about the terrible torments that await the wicked as soon as they die. But what does the Bible have to say on this subject? When would the wicked be punished by fire, at the moment of death or at a time still in the future? Let us allow the Lord Jesus Himself to answer this question:

"Again, the kingdom of heaven is like unto a net, that was cast into the sea, and gathered of every kind: Which, when it was full, they drew to shore, and sat down, and gathered the good into vessels, but cast the bad away. So shall it be at the end of the world: the angels shall come forth, and sever the wicked from among the just, And shall cast them into the furnace of fire: there shall be wailing and gnashing of teeth" (Matthew 13:47-50).

"And they went up on the breadth of the earth, and compassed [surrounded] the camp of the saints about" The intent of the wicked is to conquer the city to which entrance has been denied to them. They were not found worthy of the heavenly dwellings and they now want to take it by force. The book *The Great Controversy,* in chapter 42 describes the attempted attack on the New Jerusalem:

"As soon as the books of record are opened [verse 12], and the eye of Jesus looks upon the wicked, they are conscious of every sin which they have ever committed. They see just where their feet diverged from the path of purity and holiness, just how far pride and rebellion have carried them in the violation of the law of God. The seductive temptations which they encouraged by indulgence in sin, the blessings perverted, the messengers of God despised, the warnings rejected, the waves of mercy beaten back by the stubborn, unrepentant heart--all appear as if written in letters of fire.

"Above the throne is revealed the cross; and like a panoramic view appear the scenes of Adam's temptation and fall, and the successive steps in the great plan of redemption. The Saviour's lowly birth; His early life of simplicity and obedience; His baptism in Jordan; the fast and temptation in the wilderness; His public ministry, unfolding to men heaven's most precious blessings; the days crowded with deeds of love and mercy, the nights of prayer and watching in the solitude of the mountains; the plottings of envy, hate, and malice which repaid His benefits; the awful, mysterious agony in Gethsemane beneath the crushing weight of the sins of the whole world; His betrayal into the hands of the murderous mob; the fearful events of that night of horror--the unresisting prisoner, forsaken by His best-loved disciples, rudely hurried through the streets of Jerusalem; the Son of God exultingly displayed before Annas, arraigned in the high priest's palace, in the judgment hall of Pilate, before the cowardly and cruel Herod, mocked, insulted, tortured, and condemned to die--all are vividly portrayed.

"And now before the swaying multitude are revealed the final scenes--the patient Sufferer treading the path to Calvary; the Prince of heaven hanging upon the cross; the haughty priests and the jeering rabble deriding His expiring agony; the supernatural darkness; the heaving earth, the rent rocks, the open graves, marking the moment when the world's Redeemer yielded up His life.

"The awful spectacle appears just as it was. Satan, his angels, and his subjects have no power to turn from the picture of their own work. Each actor recalls the part which he performed. Herod, who slew the innocent children of Bethlehem that he might destroy the King of Israel; the base Herodias, upon whose guilty soul rests the blood of John the Baptist; the weak, time serving Pilate; the mocking soldiers; the priests and rulers and the maddened throng who cried, 'His blood be on us, and on our children!'--all behold the enormity of their guilt. They vainly seek to hide from the divine majesty of His countenance, outshining the glory of the sun, while the redeemed cast their crowns at the Saviour's feet, exclaiming: 'He died for me!'

"Amid the ransomed throng are the apostles of Christ, the heroic Paul, the ardent Peter, the loved and loving John, and their true hearted brethren, and with them the vast host of martyrs; while outside the walls, with every vile and abominable thing, are those by whom they were persecuted, imprisoned, and slain. There is Nero, that monster of cruelty and vice, beholding the joy and exaltation of those whom he once tortured, and in whose extremest anguish he found satanic delight. His mother is there to witness the result of her own work; to see how the evil stamp of character transmitted to her son, the passions encouraged and developed by her influence and example, have borne fruit in crimes that caused the world to shudder.

"There are papist priests and prelates, who claimed to be Christ's ambassadors, yet employed the rack, the dungeon, and the stake to control the consciences of His people. There are the proud pontiffs who exalted themselves above God and presumed to change the law of the Most High. Those pretended fathers of the church have an account to render to God from which they would fain be excused. Too late they are made to see that the Omniscient One is jealous of His law and that He will in no wise clear the guilty. They learn now that Christ identifies His interest with that of His suffering people; and they feel the force of His own words: 'Inasmuch as ye have done it unto one of the least of these My brethren, ye have done it unto Me.' Matthew 25:40.

"The whole wicked world stand arraigned at the bar of God on the charge of high treason against the government of heaven. They have none to plead their cause; they are without excuse; and the sentence of eternal death is pronounced against them.

"It is now evident to all that the wages of sin is not noble independence and eternal life, but slavery, ruin, and death. The wicked see what they have forfeited by their life of rebellion. The far more exceeding and eternal weight of glory was despised when offered them; but how desirable it now appears. 'All this,' cries the lost soul, 'I might have had; but I chose to put these things far from me. Oh, strange infatuation! I have exchanged peace, happiness, and honor for wretchedness, infamy, and despair.' All see that their exclusion from heaven is just. By their lives, they have declared: 'We will not have this Man [Jesus] to reign over us.'"

"devoured them." There is no place in the Scriptures where we can find a solid passage to sustain that the wicked will be burning forever. The word "devoured" indicates that they will disappear. When we sit down to eat and we say that we devoured our dinner, we certainly say it after our plate is empty. The food is gone. So it will be with the wicked. Fire will devour them and they will be no more. The following often-ignored passages teach complete obliteration:

Psalm 21:9-11 *"Thou shalt make them as a fiery oven in the time of thine anger: the LORD shall swallow them up in his wrath, and the fire shall devour them. Their fruit shalt thou destroy from the earth, and their seed from among the children of men. For they intended evil against thee: they imagined a mischievous device, which they are not able to perform"* This last sentence refers to their failed attempt to conquer the city of the redeemed. Likewise, we can apply this following verse to that time too: *"Praise the LORD! How wonderfully he showed his love for me when I was surrounded and attacked!"* (Psalm 31:21 Good News Bible). The phrases *"swallow them up"* and *"fire shall devour them"* imply complete obliteration. The Hebrew word used by David for "devour" is אכל (aw-kal'), which means "to eat, burn up, consume, devour." Interestingly, it is the same word used in 1 Kings 18 to describe what the fire from heaven accomplished at Mount Carmel. That vivid passage reads: *"Then the fire of the LORD fell, and consumed the burnt sacrifice, and the wood, and the stones, and the dust, and licked up the water that was in the trench"* (1Kings 18:38). If the sample of fire from heaven in times of Elijah was so destructive, how could we expect less in the executive judgment over the unrepentant wicked? In Revelation, the word used is Κατεσθίω (*kat-es-thee'-o*), which according to Strong means "to eat down, devour" and Thayer adds "to utterly consume." It is thus very clear, that the wicked will not survive for endless ages the devastation of any place called hell. Very clearly the Scripture says that even hell will be *"cast into the lake of fire"* (Revelation 20:14). Preachers need to tell the truth and follow Christ method of preaching grace, not fear, because even in the punishment of the wicked God shows mercy.

Psalm 11:6 *"Upon the wicked he shall* ***rain*** *snares, fire and brimstone, and an horrible tempest: this shall be the portion of their cup."* Notice that it says "rain" just like in the times of Elijah. The result at that time and after the millennium will be the same: complete consumption, as mentioned above.

Psalm 37:20 *"But the wicked shall perish, and the enemies of the LORD shall be as the fat of lambs:* ***they shall consume****; into smoke shall they consume away."* We all know that whatever is consumed disappears.

Psalm 37:22 *"For such as be blessed of him shall inherit the earth; and they that be cursed of him shall be* ***cut off****."* The following verse helps to define the meaning of "cut off:"

Psalm 37:38 *"But the transgressors shall be* ***destroyed*** *together: the end of the wicked shall be* ***cut off****."* It is equivalent to "destroyed" and no part of that word needs to be defined.

Psalm 68:2 *"As smoke is driven away, so drive them away: as wax melteth before the fire, so let* ***the wicked perish*** *at the presence of God."* God, although sovereign, is not a tyrant. He is not pleased with the death of the wicked. They receive many opportunities to repent daily. Being lost is their choice, but God does not torture them forever and ever as it is taught from the pulpits and in the series *Left Behind*, maligning the character of God. The doctrine of hell is the main reason why there are so many atheists in this world.

Psalm 92:6,7 *"The stupid man cannot know; the fool cannot understand this: that though the wicked sprout like grass and all evildoers flourish, they are doomed to destruction forever"* (*English Standard Version*). Not torture forever.

Isaiah 26;11 *"O LORD, your hand is lifted up, but they do not see it. Let them see your zeal for your people, and be ashamed. Let the fire for your adversaries consume them"* (*English Standard Version*).

Malachi 4:1 *"For, behold, the day cometh, that shall burn as an oven; and all the proud, yea, and all that do wickedly,* ***shall be stubble****: and the day that cometh shall* ***burn them up****, saith the LORD of hosts, that it* ***shall leave them neither root nor branch****."* Three times the verse indicates a total destruction. Since those without Christ are not really happy in this life, they will not be happy in heaven either. Besides, they will be a hindrance to the happiness of the saved. Here we see a Jesus/ Satan contrast: Satan is the root, his followers the branches, just as Christ is the true vine and his followers are the branches. Each one of us bares fruit for his chosen master and will reap the elected results. *"Know ye not, that to whom ye yield yourselves servants to obey, his servants ye are to whom ye obey; whether of sin unto death, or of obedience unto righteousness?"* (Romans 6:16). Please choose Jesus as your Master so you can be free indeed. Real freedom and joy can be found only in Christ.

A few verses later in the same chapter six of Romans, Paul wrote one of the most misunderstood verses of the Bible: *"For the wages of sin is* ***death****; but the gift of God is eternal life through Jesus Christ our Lord"* (Romans 6:23). Notice that the wages of sin is death, not eternal punishment burning in hell. The emphasis here is on the eternal life that God offers freely. I like, during public speaking engagements, to pull paper money from my pocket and, after asking the audience to recognize what is in my hand, I ask: "who wants it?" Just about every hand goes up. After repeating the same question eight to ten times, someone stands up- usually a child, and takes it from my hand. The sounds of grieve and disappointment are heard soon after the audience realizes that I was seriously parting with my money. There were so many hands expressing the desire to have it, but only one grabbed it. So it is with salvation. Accustomed to work for material goods ("nothing in life is free"), humans do not believe that salvation is a gift from God. There is nothing we can do to earn it but every one has the same right to have it. The penalty for our sins is death (not hell) but we DO NOT have to die because God has made ample provision to save us. God will take you as you are now, just as He accepted the woman caught in adultery (John 8:3-11). In the same way that He instantly cleansed a leper (Matthew 8:1-3), He will cleanse you from your sins. When the leper approached Jesus, he asked Him: "Lord, if you want to, you can make me clean" (my translation). Jesus' answer was: "I want to, be clean." The passage continues saying that "instantly" he was healed. If God spoke things into existence (Psalm 33:9) and they instantly appeared, why do we doubt that He can forgive us the instance that repented we ask Him for forgiveness? He will also give *"...power to become the sons of God, even to them that believe on his name"* (John 1:12). That is, power which will enable us to overcome temptation. That was the power given to the above woman: *"Go and sin no more."* There was a promise implied in the command.

Malachi 4:3 *"And ye shall tread down the wicked; for **they shall be ashes** under the soles of your feet in the day that I shall do this, saith the LORD of hosts."* Ashes are all that will remain, not people burning for eternity. Peter wrote: *"The Lord knoweth how to deliver the godly out of temptations, and to reserve the unjust unto the day of judgment to be punished"* (2 Peter 2:9). That verse clearly tells us that no one is being punished now because the wicked are being reserved for the day of judgment. In the eyes of today's popular preachers, Hitler was more compassionate than God was because the former tortured his victims for a few months (nevertheless, it was torture), but God will torture the wicked forever and ever and ever and eeeever...(well, you get the point, right?). How sadistic these preachers are, and many of them knowing the truth still continue preaching the lie. They love to see dozens of people responding to an altar call after a sermon in the style of the classic Jonathan Edwards' *"Sinners in the Hands of an Angry God."* Jesus favorite call was: *"...The time has come, and the kingdom of God is near. Change the way you think and act, and believe the Good News."* (Mark 1:15 *God's Word Bible*). In other words, repent because I have come to offer you salvation, to show you that I care about you, that I came to die for you, that the Father Himself loves you dearly. His invitation was not "repent or go to hell" but "repent because the kingdom of God is near." In other words, "repent because the hand of God is extended to save you." Isn't it great that the reason why Jesus asked His audience to repent was not hell but grace? A real preacher's title for a sermon would be: *"Sinners in the Hands of a Loving God."*

This final punishment of the wicked will be the executive judgment and, as it was indicated before, it will be according to each one's deeds (Revelation 22:12). This on itself proves how wrong is the doctrine of hell because if it were true (as mentioned previously), Cain is being punished 6,000 years for killing one man but Hitler has being receiving his punishment for a lot less years for killing 6,000,000 people and the death of 50 million soldiers and civilians from the countries involved or affected by the conflict.

That fire will not burn for a long time. When the wicked are destroyed, not even a flame will remain of the fire: *"Behold, they shall be as stubble; the fire shall burn them; they shall not deliver themselves from the power of the flame:* ***there shall not be a coal to warm at, nor fire to sit before it****"* (Isaiah 47:14). God will even erase all memories of them, thus fulfilling His promise to wipe away all tears (Revelation 21:4): *"They are dead, they shall not live; they are deceased, they shall not rise: therefore hast thou visited and destroyed them, and* ***made all their memory to perish****"* (Isaiah 26:14).

"On the day when the LORD shows his fury, not even all their silver and gold will save them. The whole earth will be destroyed by the fire of his anger. He will put an end---a sudden end---to everyone who lives on earth." (Zephaniah 1:18 *Good News Bible*).

"Therefore wait ye upon me, saith the LORD, until the day that I rise up to the prey: for my determination is to gather the nations, that I may assemble the kingdoms, to pour upon them mine indignation, even all my fierce anger: for all the earth shall be devoured with the fire of my jealousy" (Zephaniah 3:8). That fire will purify the earth to give way to the new creation.

*"****At evening they cause terror, but by morning they are gone****. That is the fate of everyone who plunders our land."* (Isaiah 17:14 *Good News Bible).*

"For as ye have drunk upon my holy mountain, so shall all the heathen drink continually, yea, they shall drink, and they shall swallow down, and they shall be as though they had not been" (Obadiah 1:16).

"Wait on the LORD, and keep his way, and he shall exalt thee to inherit the land: when the wicked are cut off, thou shalt see it" (Psalm 37:34). We will witness the executive judgment when the wicked

surround the holy city, trying to conquer it. After that, we will not even remember them (see chapter 21).

"But the ***transgressors shall be destroyed together****: the end of the wicked shall be cut off"* (Psalm 37: 38).

"Let the sinners be consumed out of the earth, and let the wicked be no more. Bless thou the LORD, O my soul. Praise ye the LORD" (Psalm 104:35). No more means no existence at all- gone for good.

"The LORD preserveth all them that love him: but all the wicked will he destroy" (Psalm 145:20).

"Upon the wicked He shall ***rain*** *quick burning coals, fire and brimstone and a horrible tempest: this shall be the portion of their cup"* (Isaiah 34:2). The wicked will not be in a place of torment through fire, but rather will be burned from above.

"And this shall be the plague wherewith the LORD will smite all the people that have fought against Jerusalem; Their flesh shall consume away while they stand upon their feet, and their eyes shall consume away in their holes, and their tongue shall consume away in their mouth" (Zechariah 14:12).

"Thou hast rebuked the heathen, thou hast destroyed the wicked, thou hast put out their name for ever and ever. O thou enemy, destructions are come to a perpetual end: and thou hast destroyed cities; their memorial is perished with them" (Psalm 9:5,6). Just like the ancient city of Babylon of which Nebuchadnezzar was so boastful of (Daniel 4:30) was destroyed, all the cities of which man is so proud are condemned to disappear to give way to the New Jerusalem and the new creation. The memory of the wicked will perish with them. Very soon no more Paris, New York, London, Hong Kong or any other city, be it big or small, will stand as monuments of men achievements.

10 And the devil that deceived them was cast into the lake of fire and brimstone, where the beast and the false prophet are, and shall be tormented day and night for ever and ever.

Are the demons in hell right now? That is a very common misconception that proves my point that the doctrine of hell does not come from the Bible. From hell itself probably. *"For if God spared not the angels that sinned, but cast them down to hell, and delivered them into chains of darkness, to be reserved unto judgment"* (2 Peter 2:4). According to the preceding verse, the punishment of the demons is still in the future. Can there be fire with darkness? Hell, thus, as people conceive it, is empty. There is no one, fallen angel or wicked human, roasting or broiling in there. Is Satan going to be punished by fire? Yes, according to Malachi 4:1,3 and Revelation 20:9. Would Satan burn forever? Ezekiel 28 has the answer. After describing the previous heavenly home of Satan and his downfall, verse 19 clearly states that he will cease to exist: *"All the nations who knew you are horrified because of you. You have come to a terrible end, and you will never exist again"* (*God's Word*). As we saw in Malachi 4:1 above, the fire from God *"**shall leave them neither root nor branch**-"* Satan the root, his followers the branches.

Now let us see the Biblical definition of terms such as eternal fire and forever in regards to human beings:

Referring to slaves that did not want their freedom after the jubilee, Moses wrote: *"Then his master shall bring him unto the judges; he shall also bring him to the door, or unto the door post; and his master shall bore his ear through with an awl; and he shall serve him for ever"* (Exodus 21:6). The thought that there are going to be people who will be slaves forever is anti-Christian. By the way, slaves in the Hebrew culture had rights and could not be abused. They even had the right to redeem themselves. They were more like servants.

"Even as Sodom and Gomorrah, and the cities about them in like manner, giving themselves over to fornication, and going after strange flesh, are set forth for an example, suffering the vengeance of eternal fire" (Jude 7). Sodom was located where the Dead Sea is now. Everybody knows that it is not burning because it is immersed. Once the fire fulfilled its purpose, it quenches itself.

"But if ye will not hearken unto me to hallow the Sabbath day, and not to bear a burden, even entering in at the gates of Jerusalem

on the Sabbath day; then will I kindle a fire in the gates thereof, and it shall devour the palaces of Jerusalem, and it shall not be quenched" (Jeremiah 17:27). The following verse shows the fulfillment of that prophecy:

"And they said unto me, the remnant that are left of the captivity there in the province are in great affliction and reproach: the wall of Jerusalem also is broken down, and the gates thereof are burned with fire" (Nehemiah 1:3). This verse refers to the prophecy of Jeremiah 17:27. The doors are no longer burning.

These previous two verses teach that the fire burns until it fulfills its purpose. Let us see what Amos has to say on this subject: *"Seek the LORD, and ye shall live; lest he break out like fire in the house of Joseph, and devour it, and there be none to quench it in Bethel."* (Amos 5:6). When God starts a fire, no man can quench it because it is divine fire like the one that consumed the sacrifice at Mount Carmel. Strange fire is man's fire and can be quenched. It is not so with the Lord's fire. Once the punishment of the last wicked is over (they will be punished according to their works- Revelation 22:12, so Hitler will be punished longer than Cain will), the fire disappears as we can read in Isaiah 47:14. Before I wrote this sentence, I set a paper on fire. I stood to watch it burn. Once there were only ashes left, the fire disappeared. I could not make that fire last forever. So it will be with the wicked; once they are punished, the fire goes out. Just as the Bible says. Now you know that your preacher has been lying to you all along.

Since we have seen that the fire does not last forever, now is the best time to explain the parable of the rich and Lazarus found in Luke 16:19-31. What is a parable? It is something like a fable: a story with a lesson. Parables are not always to be understood literally. The following two examples will illustrate this point:

Judges 9:8-15- this passage presents trees in the forest talking to each other trying to select a king.

Ezekiel 17:3-9- this parable portrays an eagle practicing arboriculture.

We all know that trees do not vote and eagles could care less about transplanting trees. The parable of the rich and Lazarus had a teaching purpose that is explained in verses 14 & 15 (the only parable explained in advance): *"No servant can serve two masters: for either he will hate the one, and love the other; or else he will hold to the one, and despise the other. Ye cannot serve God and mammon* [riches or material wealth]. *And the Pharisees also, who were covetous, heard all these things: and they derided him. And he said unto them, Ye are they which justify yourselves before men; but God knoweth your hearts: for that which is highly esteemed among men is abomination in the sight of God."* So the intent was to wake up the Pharisees, who were prosperity preachers, and try to save them because they were covetous, selfish and believed themselves to be superior to all other men. In regards to this, Jesus also told the audience about the Pharisee and the Publican (Luke 18:10-14). Here is the parable of the rich and Lazarus:

"There was a certain rich man, which was clothed in purple and fine linen, and fared sumptuously every day: And there was a certain beggar named Lazarus, which was laid at his gate, full of sores, And desiring to be fed with the crumbs which fell from the rich man's table: moreover the dogs came and licked his sores. And it came to pass, that the beggar died, and was carried by the angels into Abraham's bosom: the rich man also died, and was buried And in hell he lift up his eyes, being in torments, and seeth Abraham afar off, and Lazarus in his bosom And he cried and said, Father Abraham, have mercy on me, and send Lazarus, that he may dip the tip of his finger in water, and cool my tongue; for I am tormented in this flame. But Abraham said, Son, remember that thou in thy lifetime receivedst thy good things, and likewise Lazarus evil things: but now he is comforted, and thou art tormented. And beside all this, between us and you there is a great gulf fixed: so that they which would pass from hence to you cannot; neither can they pass to us, that would come from thence. Then he said, I pray thee therefore, father, that thou wouldest send him to my father's house For I have five brethren; that he may testify unto them, lest they also come into this place of torment. Abraham saith unto him, They have Moses and the prophets; let them hear them. And he said, Nay, father Abraham: but if one went unto them from the dead, they will repent. And he said unto him, If they hear not Moses and the prophets, neither will they be persuaded, though one rose from the dead" (Luke 16:19-31).

There are a few points that I would like to discuss:

- The beggar went to Abraham's bosom. If the saved go to his bosom, it really has to be a huge one. If the parable is literal, then being saved in heaven is boooooring and can be construed as captivity, since there is no indication that Lazarus ever left Abraham's bosom to go anywhere. That is worst than the belief that we will spend eternity playing a harp sitting on a cloud.
- Abraham could not give what he himself did not have. The Bible says that David was a man after God's own heart. Yet, in Acts 2:29, 34 says that he did not ascend to heaven, but rather he is in the tomb, where he is certainly waiting for the resurrection. So it is with Abraham. Hebrews 11:13 clearly indicates that he did not receive the reward. "These all died in faith, not having received the promises, but having seen them afar off, and were persuaded of *them,* and embraced *them,* and confessed that they were strangers and pilgrims on the earth." Abraham is not enjoying heavenly bliss right now because he is in his grave waiting for reunion day when Jesus will return and resurrect him and all the saints.
- The prayer of the rich man was addressed to Abraham, not to God. No mortal can listen to so many prayers that can be elevated by millions of people at once. If the parable were true, then Abraham has been elevated to a divine status. Praying to him would be no different than praying to Mary or the saints.
- The parable presents the righteous and the wicked within sight of each other. If someone you love is lost, would you enjoy heaven if every time you look out your window you see him or her burning and screaming because of pain and the horrors of hell, not to mention, asking you to wet your finger to relieve their suffering? What kind of heavenly bliss would it be if we can see our children, siblings, parents and friends being roasted for ages without end? And what about listening to their simultaneous deafening screams all day long? With so many more lost than saved people, the praises of the saints would be muffled.
- If the soul is what goes to hell, how come the rich had a tongue? Well, with so much money he was probably able to afford it. Genesis 2:7 teaches clearly that <u>we do not</u>

have a soul, but rather we **are** a soul. When both essential elements are present (body and the breath of God), we become a soul. *"And the LORD God formed man of the dust of the ground, and breathed into his nostrils the breath of life; and man became a living soul."* Job equals the spirit with breath: *"All the while my breath is in me, and the spirit of God is in my nostrils"* (Job 37:3), so we cannot find Biblical evidence of the spirit or soul existing as a separate and independent entity (after death). When Ecclesiastes speaks about the spirit going up, it uses the same word (רוּח - rûach) for the animals as for humans. We cannot say that Fido went to heaven when he died. That spirit is the hot air leaving the lungs for the last time. *"After all, the same fate awaits human beings and animals alike. One dies just like the other. They are the same kind of creature. A human being is no better off than an animal, because life has no meaning for either. They are both going to the same place---the dust. They both came from it; they will both go back to it. How can anyone be sure that the human spirit goes upward while an animal's spirit goes down into the ground?"* (Ecclesiastes 3:19-21 *Good News Bible*).

- The parable contradicts the Bible because it presents the rich worrying about his five brothers. Both David and Solomon wrote that there is no memory after death (Psalm 6:5 & Ecclesiastes 9:5,6). The doctrine of hell can be substantiated only by tradition, not by the Scriptures. It is imperative that we believe God and not man-made doctrines of devils, regardless of who is teaching them.

It is scriptural that both wicked and saved go to the same place until Jesus calls each group back to life. Job mentions a case in which there was a rich and a poor man, just like in the parable, and both went to the same place after death: *"One dieth in his full strength, being wholly at ease and quiet. His breasts are full of milk, and his bones are moistened with marrow. And another dieth in the bitterness of his soul, and never eateth with pleasure. They shall lie down alike in the dust, and the worms shall cover them"* (Job 21:23-26). That place is the grave from where all will hear Jesus' voice (John 5:28,29). He will not call anyone from heaven or hell to give the reward because that would be ludicrous. As mentioned a couple of times previously, the reward will be given at Jesus' second coming (Revelation 22:11,12). The punishment through fire will be at the end (Matthew 13:38-42). Jesus Himself emphasized this truth in Matthew 16:27: *"For the Son of man shall come in the glory of his Father with his angels; and* ***then*** *he shall reward every man* ***according*** *to his works."* It is believed that the parable was a common story in the times of Jesus that being so well known, He took it to illustrate His point, in the same way that Paul used common sayings to make a point with the hearers and readers of his sermons (Acts 17:28) and letters (Philippians 3:19).

[11]*And I saw a great white throne, and him that sat on it, from whose face the earth and the heaven fled away; and there was found no place for them.* [12]*And I saw the dead, small and great, stand before God; and the books were opened: and another book was opened, which is the book of life: and the dead were judged out of those things which were written in the books, according to their works.* We are saved by faith alone but judge by works, because these show to men and angels what is in our hearts.

The believers will be judging all the lost: *"...we shall all stand before the judgment seat of Christ"* (Romans 14:10). The judgment will start with the house of God (1 Peter 4:17) and then deal with those that never professed faith in Jesus.

[13]*And the sea gave up the dead which were in it; and death and hell delivered up the dead which were in them: and they were judged every man according to their works.*

No man will escape being judged, regardless of where his body lays. All will be judged and there will be no place to hide, because the ultimate reward of everyone depends on the results of that judgment. The word "hell" is translated from hades, which simply means "the grave."

[14]*And death and hell were cast into the lake of fire. This is the second death.* [15]*And whosoever was not found written in the book of life was cast into the lake of fire.*

"Hell" is going to be destroyed. The second death is eternal separation from God, the source of life. We must strive to have our names written in the book of life and keep it there. For that, we must remain faithful to the end by daily surrendering our wills to God. He is the only one *"able to keep you from falling, and to present you faultless before the presence of his glory with exceeding joy"* (Jude 1:24).

the second death- eternal separation from God, the source of life. This was the death that Jesus suffered on the cross. "He will take revenge on those who refuse to acknowledge God and on those who refuse to respond to the Good News about our Lord Jesus. 2Th 1:9 They will pay the penalty by being destroyed forever, by being separated from the Lord's presence and from his glorious power" (2 Thessalonians 1:8).

It is evident that those that believe in hell have not paid attention to this verse for it reads: *"death and hell were cast into the lake of fire,"* indicating that hell will not last forever; only until the last wicked and Satan himself are utterly destroyed.

REVELATION 21

The Flying City

Signs of His return: In December 2004, a deadly tsunami, triggered by an 8.9-magnitude earthquake in the Indian Ocean, killed more than 150,000 people in Southeast and South Asia. Every year we hear about tragedies that seem to be worse than the previous ones- and they are. When Jesus spoke of earthquakes in His days (Matthew 24; Luke 21), there were just a few of them of big magnitude per year. Now they have increased to the hundreds and regular ones to the thousands. He also spoke of false prophets and people claiming to be Him. I have seen a few of those in my lifetime and, as the prophecy reads, they drag multitudes to follow them. The epidemics are getting out of control. We suffer from diseases that our grandparents never heard of when they were young, such as AIDS. The political turmoil and economical collapses are making people nervous and causing depression and sleepless nights. Jesus also mentioned the wars and rumors of wars. This world has never seen wars like World War I and Word War II with the carnage and destruction. Over 70 million people were killed in those wars. However, with the bad news, Jesus also included a ray of hope that promises to pierce through the darkness to announce the soon arrival of a better world: the preaching of the gospel to all nations and then the end will come. At the time of this writing, the gospel is being preached in over 200 countries spanning the whole globe. Yes, Jesus is indeed coming again for His people, for those that accept Him as their personal Lord and Savior. Have you opened your heart to Him yet?

1 *And I saw a new heaven and a new earth: for the first heaven and the first earth were passed away; and there was no more sea.*

It is not that we are not going to have a sea, but that it will be very different to whatever sea we have ever seen. *"And before the throne <u>there was a sea of glass</u> like unto crystal: and in the midst of the throne, and round about the throne, were four beasts full of eyes before and behind"* (Revelation 4:6). *"And <u>I saw as it were a sea of glass mingled with fire</u>: and them that had gotten the victory over the* *beast, and over his image, and over his mark, and over the number of his name, stand on the sea of glass, having the harps of God"* (Revelation 15:2). In the same manner that both the earth and the first heaven (atmosphere) are going to be new, so it will be with the sea. This new sea will be transparent, refulgent, calmed and we will be able to stand on it like when Jesus walked on the water. Right now, the seas separate the continents and islands but when God restores everything to its original pre-sin glory, there is going to be again a mass of land in the middle of the water. This is what Peter described: *"in the old days there was a heaven, and an earth lifted out of the water and circled by water, by the word of God"* (2 Peter 3:5 Bible in Basic English).

2 *And I John saw the holy city, new Jerusalem, coming down from God out of heaven, prepared as a bride adorned for her husband.*

"For he looked for a city which hath foundations, whose builder and maker is God" (Hebrews 11:10). Ever since Abraham walked on this world, believers are aware of a better place. Many saints died with that blessed anticipation of dwelling with God in a better world: *"These all died in faith, not having received the promises, but having seen them afar off, and were persuaded of them, and embraced them, and confessed that they were strangers and pilgrims on the earth. For they that say such things declare plainly that they seek a country. And truly, if they had been mindful of that country from whence they came out, they might have had opportunity to have returned. But now they desire a better country, that is, an heavenly: wherefore God is not ashamed to be called their God: for he hath prepared for them a city"* (Hebrews 11:13-16). Isaiah even describes the proclamation to allow the believers in the new city: *"Open ye the gates, that the righteous nation which keepeth the truth may enter in"* (Isaiah 26:2). Jesus Himself made a promise to His disciples, which has resonated through the centuries, giving encouragement to those oppressed by their own governments. *"Let not your heart be troubled: ye believe in God, believe also in me. In my Father's house are many mansions: if it were not so, I would have told you. I go to prepare a place for you. And if I go and prepare a place for you, I will come again, and receive you unto myself; that where I am, there ye may be also"* (John 14:1-3). This passage teaches that there is not going to be homelessness in heaven. Everybody will have a great place to live made by Jesus

for His beloved. There are not going to be punch lists needed to claim manufacturing shortcomings in those mansions because everything that Jesus makes is "good" (Genesis 1). Furthermore, "If he has prepared the place for us, he will prepare us for it, and in due time put us in possession of it." *Matthew Henry's Commentary on the Whole Bible.*

[3] *And I heard a great voice out of heaven saying, Behold, the tabernacle of God is with men, and he will dwell with them, and they shall be his people, and God himself shall be with them, and be their God.*

Sin is no longer going to be a wedge causing separation between God and us. Now He is moving in with us! After spending a thousand years with Him in heaven, God will make His dwelling with us. There is nothing greater than the divine grace that saw man swimming in a puddle of iniquity and reached down to offer reconciliation. That salvation was so great and complete that enabled God to see us as if we have never sinned against Him and to move His throne with us.

[4] *And God shall wipe away all tears from their eyes; and there shall be no more death, neither sorrow, nor crying, neither shall there be any more pain: for the former things are passed away.*

"And <u>the inhabitant shall not say, I am sick</u>: the people that dwell therein shall be forgiven their iniquity" (Isaiah 33:24). How sad is to watch the news and see all the devastation that human selfishness through wars and crime on one hand, and natural disasters on the other, produce daily on humanity worldwide. I read about a 10-year-old Washington state boy who was sentenced to up to 5-½ years in a juvenile detention facility for his role in a foiled plot to rape and kill a girl at his school and harm other 6 children. As we can see in the book of Job chapters 1 and 2, it is not God who causes hurricanes and other natural tragedies; it is Satan and his demons. However, we have precious promises to cling on to, such as this one from Isaiah: *"The Sovereign LORD will destroy death forever! He will wipe away the tears from everyone's eyes and take away the disgrace his people have suffered throughout the world. The LORD himself has spoken"* (Isaiah 25:8 *Good News Bible*).

God shall wipe away all tears from their eyes- Ever since the tragedy of sin hit this world, tears have been mostly a sign of distress, suffering, pain and despair. We shed tears when we ache, when we fear, when we lose a dear relative or friend to death, when we lose our job or when our spouse files for divorce. There are also tears when we feel lonely and abandoned. It can also bring tears to our eyes seeing a friend moving away with the possibility of never on this earth be together again. These feelings can produce depression. It is estimated that ten percent of the population suffers from it, many without knowing it or without seeking any help. The following are some depression symptoms:

- Sadness, anxiety, or "empty" feelings
- Decreased energy, fatigue, being "slowed down"
- Loss of interest or pleasure in activities that were once enjoyed, including sex
- Insomnia, oversleeping, or waking much earlier than usual
- Loss of weight or appetite, or overeating and weight gain
- Feelings of hopelessness and pessimism
- Feelings of helplessness, guilt, and worthlessness
- Thoughts of death or suicide, or suicide attempts
- Difficulty concentrating, making decisions, or remembering
- Restlessness, irritability or excessive crying
- Chronic aches and pains or physical problems that do not respond to treatment

Source: http://www.allaboutdepression.com/gen_01.html

"Clinical depression affects all aspects of a person's life. It impairs our ability to sleep, eat, work, and get along with others. It damages our self-esteem, self-confidence, and our ability to accomplish everyday tasks. People who are depressed find daily tasks to be a significant struggle. They tire easily, yet cannot get a good night's sleep. They have no motivation and lose interest in activities that were once enjoyable. Depression puts a dark, gloomy cloud over how we see ourselves, the world, and our future. This cloud cannot be willed away, nor can we ignore it and have it magically disappear." *Ibid.*

The world that Jesus has promised us will not be like anything that we know here. Nothing in this planet is perfect; we get sick, we die, everything deteriorates. Flowers wither, grass dries up, trees die, and even the Dead Sea is dying. We know that sadly we all die. Many people see in death the end of all because they do not have the hope of eternal life but we have precious promises from God and He is faithful to keep His word. He has prepared something so incredible that Paul, one of the most eloquent persons who ever lived, could not find words to describe it: *"But as it is written, Eye hath not seen, nor ear heard, neither have entered into the heart of man, the things which God hath prepared for them that love him"* (1 Corinthians 2:9). Just think with delight about a world where flowers are always fresh, where leaves never fall off the trees, the grass is always green, where there are no floods, tornadoes, hurricanes, earthquakes, tsunamis, hunger, divorce, drug addiction, plagues or any of the causes of suffering that we embattled us here. Imagine a place with great neighbors- without crime- with a perfect weather, with a sky always blue, with perfect peace and harmony, where the words envy, strife, hate, fear and death will not be known. It is going to be a place where we will be able to constantly grow in the knowledge of God and His creation. We always will have a whole eternity ahead of us to plan and carry out those plans without worries of our lives being cut short before those plants can bear fruit. We have a God that will make everything that we have dreamed and then a lot more a reality.

5 *And he that sat upon the throne said, Behold, I make all things new. And he said unto me, Write: for these words are true and faithful.*

Very soon, we will move to a renovated planet earth. Every mark left by sin will be erased. The words are true and faithful are a reinforcement of the promise of making everything new. *"For all God's promises are 'Yes' in him. And so through him we can say 'Amen,' to the glory of God"* (2 Corinthians 1:20). God, in contrast with the politicians that promise impossibilities to get elected, has always kept His word and all His promises still in the future are certainly going to be kept.

6 *And he said unto me, It is done. I am Alpha and Omega, the beginning and the end. I will give unto him that is athirst of the fountain of the water of life freely.*

Again we see the phrase alpha and omega from chapter one, reminding us of His eternity. As eternal, He can watch over us and we can be ascertain of His promises. Talking to the Samaritan woman, Jesus said: *"But whosoever drinketh of the water that I shall give him shall never thirst; but the water that I shall give him shall be in him a well of water springing up into everlasting life"* (John 4:14). The world will never quench your thirst and it will only leave you empty. As you can see in the verse, that satisfying water is free.

[7] He that overcometh shall inherit all things; and I will be his God, and he shall be my son.

God never said that life on this earth would be easy, stress-free and devoid of challenges. There is, however, a rich reward for those that are found faithful. *"And if children, then heirs; heirs of God, and joint-heirs with Christ; if so be that we suffer with him, that we may be also glorified together"* (Romans 8:17). The title "son" indicates that God sees us at the same level of His Son Jesus.

[8] But the fearful, and unbelieving, and the abominable, and murderers, and whoremongers, and sorcerers, and idolaters, and all liars, shall have their part in the lake which burneth with fire and brimstone: which is the second death.

No unrepentant evildoer will be allowed to enter the Holy City. We must make peace with God without delay. He is willing to forgive us and grant us salvation.

[9] And there came unto me one of the seven angels which had the seven vials full of the seven last plagues, and talked with me, saying, Come hither, I will shew thee the bride, the Lamb's wife.[10] And he carried me away in the spirit to a great and high mountain, and shewed me that great city, the holy Jerusalem, descending out of heaven from God,

The church is not the bride. It is clear hear that it is the New Jerusalem. Let us see the description of that eternal city:

[11] Having the glory of God: and her light was like unto a stone most precious, even like a jasper stone, clear as crystal;

12 And had a wall great and high, and had twelve gates, and at the gates twelve angels, and names written thereon, which are the names of the twelve tribes of the children of Israel:

13 On the east three gates; on the north three gates; on the south three gates; and on the west three gates.

14 And the wall of the city had twelve foundations, and in them the names of the twelve apostles of the Lamb.

15 And he that talked with me had a golden reed to measure the city, and the gates thereof, and the wall thereof.

16 And the city lieth foursquare, and the length is as large as the breadth: and he measured the city with the reed, twelve thousand furlongs. The length and the breadth and the height of it are equal.

17 And he measured the wall thereof, an hundred and forty and four cubits, according to the measure of a man, that is, of the angel.

18 And the building of the wall of it was of jasper: and the city was pure gold, like unto clear glass.

19 And the foundations of the wall of the city were garnished with all manner of precious stones. The first foundation was jasper; the second, sapphire; the third, a chalcedony; the fourth, an emerald;

20 The fifth, sardonyx; the sixth, sardius; the seventh, chrysolite; the eighth, beryl; the ninth, a topaz; the tenth, a chrysoprasus; the eleventh, a jacinth; the twelfth, an amethyst.

21 And the twelve gates were twelve pearls; every several gate was of one pearl: and the street of the city was pure gold, as it were transparent glass.

22 And I saw no temple therein: for the Lord God Almighty and the Lamb are the temple of it.

23 And the city had no need of the sun, neither of the moon, to shine in it: for the glory of God did lighten it, and the Lamb is the light thereof.

24 *And the nations of them which are saved shall walk in the light of it: and the kings of the earth do bring their glory and honour into it.*

25 *And the gates of it shall not be shut at all by day: for there shall be no night there.*

26 *And they shall bring the glory and honour of the nations into it.*

27 *And there shall in no wise enter into it any thing that defileth, neither whatsoever worketh abomination, or maketh a lie: but they which are written in the Lamb's book of life.* It is great to know that God has prepared such an outstanding city free of all kinds of suffering, where no one will ever experience fear again and where all the inhabitants will live in harmony and peace.

REVELATION 22

A Better Neighborhood

[1] *And he shewed me a pure river of water of life, clear as crystal, proceeding out of the throne of God and of the Lamb.*

All the contamination in this world is going to be removed and the earth purified with fire (2 Peter 3:10). On the new earth, the rivers and other bodies of water are going to be clear. The river of life is going to be like crystal without any kind of impurity, which would be a symbol of sin.

[2] *In the midst of the street of it, and on either side of the river, was there the tree of life, which bare twelve manner of fruits, and yielded her fruit every month: and the leaves of the tree were for the healing of the nations.*

The tree of life from Eden makes a comeback for the benefit of all the saved. It is not that we are going to be sick, since disease came to this world as a result of sin. *"And the inhabitant shall not say, I am sick: the people that dwell therein shall be forgiven their iniquity"* (Isa 33:24). Once sin is removed, no one will ever be sick or weak. *"But they that wait upon the LORD shall renew their strength; they shall mount up with wings as eagles; they shall run, and not be weary; and they shall walk, and not faint"* (Isaiah 40:31). According to this promise, those that are saved, will be like the angels, capable of flying.

[3] *And there shall be no more curse: but the throne of God and of the Lamb shall be in it; and his servants shall serve him:*

"Nevertheless we, according to his promise, look for new heavens and a new earth, wherein dwelleth righteousness" (2 Peter 3:13). This earth was cursed when Adam and Eve betrayed God's trust in the Garden of Eden but soon that curse is going to be removed and we will live free. Is God expecting anything from us? He certainly does: *"Wherefore, beloved, seeing that ye look for such things, be diligent that ye may be found of him in peace, without spot, and blameless"*

(2 Peter 3:14). In the same way that a parent looks forward to observe a positive behavior from his children, our heavenly Father expects that our conduct reflect the principles of His kingdom as presented in the Ten Commandments. Paul wrote: *"I beseech you therefore, brethren, by the mercies of God, that ye <u>present your bodies a living sacrifice</u>, holy, acceptable unto God, which is your reasonable service. And <u>be not conformed to this world</u>: but <u>be ye transformed</u> by <u>the renewing of your mind</u>, that ye may prove what is that good, and acceptable, and perfect, will of God"* (Romans 12:1,2). Both Peter and Paul put an emphasis on <u>the process of sanctification</u>, through which we become *"partakers of the divine nature"* (2 Peter 1:4). *"Therefore if any man be in Christ, he is a new creature: old things are passed away; behold, all things are become new"* (2 Corinthians 5:17). In other words, we become like Jesus. Our thoughts, words, attitudes, actions and reactions, all will reflect the way Jesus would act if He were in our place in our present situation. *"I am crucified with Christ: nevertheless I live; yet not I, but Christ liveth in me: and the life which I now live in the flesh I live by the faith of the Son of God, who loved me, and gave himself for me"* (Galatians 2:20).

Holiness, or likeness to God, is possible for those that surrender their lives to the guidance of the Holy Spirit. *"Follow peace with all men, and <u>holiness</u>, without which no man shall see the Lord"* (Hebrews 12:14). If we are going to wait to experience holiness when Jesus comes, we are in for a great disappointment. God gave the Ten Commandments and told us to keep them. <u>There are called "commandments" for a good reason. Otherwise, they would be called "suggestions</u>." Time and over again, God tells His children to obey. As we resist evil in the power of God (just as Jesus did on earth), we become more and more like Jesus in our characters until the time will come that we are like Enoch or Elijah and we are ready either to rest in the grave until we are raised for immortality, or we are alive ready for our beloved Savior's return.

<u>there shall be no more curse</u>- No more abrupt cliffs, precipices, dead trees, wilted flowers, erupting volcanoes, earthquakes, tsunamis, tornadoes, hurricanes, floods, wild fires, soil erosion, or any other sign of the curse of sin.

"the throne of God and of the Lamb shall be in it"- What an honor! We are going to have God and Jesus as our neighbors in the new

city! Can you imagine that? God loves us so much that He will establish the center of the universe divine worship here among us, the former rebellious race. Our situation will be a lot better than if we have never sinned because God Himself will be with us permanently, instead of just visiting.

[4] And they shall see his face; and his name shall be in their foreheads.

Paul wrote that we now see like in a mirror. Mirrors in his time were made of brass, which made the images blurry. But he also wrote that one day we would see clearly. *"What we see now is like a dim image in a mirror; then we shall see face-to-face. What I know now is only partial; then it will be complete---as complete as God's knowledge of me."* (1 Corinthians 13:12 *GW*). "when we all get to heaven, what a day of rejoicing that will be, when we all see Jesus...." That day is when we will see the sweet face of Jesus. Right now, we can only allow our imaginations to take us to the Palestine and imagine His life on earth and is ministry in heaven. Soon our imaginations will prove how short they have fallen when we are given the honor of contemplating the reality and see Jesus smile to us.

his name shall be in their foreheads- As explained previously in chapter 2:17 and in chapter 7, the name is a representation of the character. I once saw a news clip on TV where, according to a study, couples that have been married for decades, start to resemble one another. This is true in the spiritual realm too according to Paul, only that in our case, we only reflect His character and He is not affected by ours. *"But we all, with open face beholding as in a glass the glory of the Lord, are changed into the same image from glory to glory, even as by the Spirit of the Lord"* (2 Corinthians 3:18). We will reflect the character of our Creator.

[5] And there shall be no night there; and they need no candle, neither light of the sun; for the Lord God giveth them light: and they shall reign forever and ever.

I never liked the night, even if I was tired. I like to be busy working outside or just enjoying nature. Soon night would not be a hindrance to enjoy my favorite outdoors activities. God had spared no blessing to make us happy and enjoy life to the fullest in His new creation. What will happen to the sun and the moon? Regarding the sun, it is not written what will happen to it but the moon will still somehow be around because it is mentioned in Isaiah on the topic of the new earth. *"And it shall come to pass, that from one new moon to another, and from one Sabbath to another, shall all flesh come to worship before me, saith the LORD"* (Isaiah 66:23).

[6] *And he said unto me, these sayings are faithful and true: and the Lord God of the holy prophets sent his angel to shew unto his servants the things which must shortly be done.*

Paul wrote that *"... the promises of God in him are yea, and in him Amen, unto the glory of God by us"* (2 Corinthians 1:20). All His promises are trustworthy. He is the only one that we can trust and He will never fail any of us.

[7] *Behold, I come quickly: blessed is he that keepeth the sayings of the prophecy of this book.*

Behold, I come quickly -This is the promise that had kept the church going through 2,000 years. The only thing that had sustained the dying on their deathbed, the martyr on the fire post and the persecuted in the mountains. "Jesus is coming again" says the hymn. He is our blessed hope. *"Looking for that blessed hope, and the glorious appearing of the great God and our Saviour Jesus Christ"* (Titus 2:13). Amidst the suffering in this world, we can raise our heads up because we have something to look forward to and this is the return of our Savior. Multitudes reject or pay no importance to this great truth and turn their backs on their loving Savior with His offer of salvation. Just imagine yourself acquiring a very expensive present, you wrap it up, take a trip to your friend's house, knock on the door, only to have slammed on your face despising not only the gift but you as a friend. That is what mankind is doing with God's offer of salvation. We prefer to "enjoy the pleasures of sin for a season" (Hebrews 11:25). It is incredible that we prefer to neglect such a great salvation (Hebrews 2:3) in order to enjoy what later will bring pain, suffering, disease and loss of eternal life. For the heavenly intelligences, it is inconceivable that we reject so much for so little, just as Edom sold his rights for a plate of lentils that were probably not even condimented.

keepeth - Chapter one refers to the one that reads, hears and keeps the words of this book. However, here and in verse nine, the emphasis is in the act of keeping, preparing the way for verse 14, where the keeping of the commandments is stressed.

[8] And I John saw these things, and heard them. And when I had heard and seen, I fell down to worship before the feet of the angel which shewed me these things. [9] Then saith he unto me, See thou do it not: for I am thy fellow servant, and of thy brethren the prophets, and of them which keep the sayings of this book: worship God.

Just like in chapter 19, John was so impressed with the great news that he got from the angel that he felt compelled to worship him,

[10] And he saith unto me, Seal not the sayings of the prophecy of this book: for the time is at hand.

Contrary to what many preachers tell their congregations, the book of Revelation, as we discussed in chapter one, is an open book that we can understand with prayer and interpreting its symbols at the light of other Bible passages. The reason why they do it? The book identifies their errors. If they dedicate themselves to understand and properly interpret and explain the book to their congregations, many will leave to seek the true church and their bu$iness will suffer. Many are in for the money and not because they really care for the flock.

[11] He that is unjust, let him be unjust still: and he which is filthy, let him be filthy still: and he that is righteous, let him be righteous still: and he that is holy, let him be holy still.

[12] And, behold, I come quickly; and my reward is with me, to give every man according as his work shall be.

Would a just judge condemn a person to be punished without having the evidence examined in trial first? Over a billion people today have been fooled into believing that their loved ones are either in heaven or in hell already receiving their reward. This passage clearly teaches that Jesus will come with the reward for everybody- it does not teach that anyone is already being rewarded in heaven or hell. According to these verses (11 & 12), every case must have been decided previous to the second coming of Christ, who will give the appropriate reward to everyone.

[13] I am Alpha and Omega, the beginning and the end, the first and the last.

This implied declaration of eternity is our assurance that because He lives, we will also live. If He is eternal and sustains us, we will live too.

[14] Blessed are they that do his commandments, that they may have right to the tree of life, and may enter in through the gates into the city.

The commandments, including the Sabbath, are not out of style, or abolished, or for the Jewish nation. They exist for the benefit of all mankind. "The Sabbath was not for Israel merely, but for the world. It had been made known to man in Eden, and, like the other precepts of the Decalogue, it is of imperishable obligation. Of that law of which the fourth commandment forms a part, Christ declares, 'Till heaven and earth pass, one jot or one tittle shall in nowise pass from the law.' So long as the heavens and the earth endure, the Sabbath will continue as a sign of the Creator's power. And when Eden shall bloom on earth again, God's holy rest day will be honored by all beneath the sun. 'From one Sabbath to another' the inhabitants of the glorified new earth shall go up 'to worship before Me, saith the Lord.'" See Matthew 5:18; Isaiah 66:23. *Desire of Ages* P. 283.2

[15] For without are dogs, and sorcerers, and whoremongers, and murderers, and idolaters, and whosoever loveth and maketh a lie.

What are these dogs? Moses comes to our rescue in understanding this passage: *"Thou shalt not bring the hire of a whore, or the price of a dog, into the house of the LORD thy God for any vow: for even both these are abomination unto the LORD thy God"* (Deuteronomy 23:18). This refers to homosexuals.

[16] I Jesus have sent mine angel to testify unto you these things in the churches. I am the root and the offspring of David, and the bright and morning star.

Peter, writing about prophecy, wrote: *"We have also a more sure word of prophecy; whereunto ye do well that ye take heed, as unto a light that shineth in a dark place, until the day dawn, and the day star arise in your hearts"* (2 Peter 1:19). We must make every effort to allow the day bright star arise and shine in our hearts daily. Every single morning we must consecrate ourselves for that day and in His power fight every temptation that comes our way.

[17] And the Spirit and the bride say, Come. And let him that heareth say, Come. And let him that is athirst come. And whosoever will, let him take the water of life freely.

Ever since the fall, mankind has been experiencing a hunger and a thirst that only our Creator can satisfy. We look for entertainment, pleasures of the flesh, the acquisition of riches, possessions and fame in a futile attempt to be happy. However, the emptiness remains and it seems to become worst with the passing of time and with the many trials that we make. God, who provided for our salvation, has not neglected to provide a solution for this need of the soul. *"In the last day, that great day of the feast, Jesus stood and cried, saying,* If any man thirst, let him come unto me, and drink. He that believeth on me, as the scripture hath said, out of his belly shall flow rivers of living water" (John 7:37,38).

let him that heareth say, Come- All who come to Christ become His messengers of mercy to reconcile the world to Him. We cannot keep this glorious message of salvation to ourselves. We must share it with others so they to have this hope in Jesus and one day soon see it become a reality.

[18] For I testify unto every man that heareth the words of the prophecy of this book, If any man shall add unto these things, God shall add unto him the plagues that are written in this book: [19] And if any man shall take away from the words of the book of this prophecy, God shall take away his part out of the book of life, and out of the holy city, and from the things which are written in this book.

A quote from Moses' writings, this passage reminds us whose word this is. It is the divinely inspired Word of the Living God and we must respect His author's rights. His rights claims do not expire. Although we get the Bible message for free, we do not have any right to make any changes to it. Hiding or twisting the truth would be equivalents to taking away from the Word. Preachers take away from the Bible because it is about achieving and keeping control. Those are merchants, not true messengers. The majority of TV preachers and websites teach error, many times in full conscience of what they are teaching for the sole purpose of making money off people and grow their empires. We can see their true character through the lifestyle that they live with mansions, luxury cars, private jets, servants, etc. when the Jesus they claim to serve did not even have a place to rest His head.

[20] He which testifieth these things saith, Surely I come quickly. Amen. Even so, come, Lord Jesus.

John's greatest desire was to see Jesus again. He was the same juvenile disciple that used to lean his head on the chest of Jesus. He was also at His trial and at the foot of the cross. He took care of Mary like a son and kept daily communion with Christ through prayer. Now in his old age, after having living a life of full consecration to His Savior, he longed for nothing less than to see His face again and never experience the pain of separation that he surely felt the day of the crucifixion and on the day of the ascension. With a deep breath, he expressed the deepest desire that every true believer treasures in his heart. The return of Jesus will put an end to our misery and daily trials. Our day of freedom is fast approaching and we must prepare for it. Our hope must be kept alive regardless of the apparent delay. His return is near and we must keep the flame of our hope burning. Come, Lord Jesus!

[21] The grace of our Lord Jesus Christ be with you all. Amen.

Not by works, but by grace are we saved and that is what Jesus offers His followers. Our lives might not be trouble-free but they are definitely neither grace-free. His grace is sufficient to sustain us and His presence has been promised until the last day on this earth and then for the whole eternity.

INDEX

B

C

D

E

F

G

H

M

N

O

P

Q

R

S

T

U

V

W

Y

Z

Printed in the United States
By Bookmasters